THE
TERROR
DREAM

WHAT 9/11 REVEALED
ABOUT AMERICA

SUSAN FALUDI

Atlantic Books
LONDON

First published in hardback in the United States in 2007
by Metropolitan Books, Henry Holt and Company, LLC.

First published in trade paperback in Great Britain in 2008
by Atlantic Books, an imprint of Grove Atlantic Ltd.

Grateful acknowledgment is made to the following for permission to reprint previously
published material: Zieba Shorish-Shamley: Excerpts from *Look into my World*, 1998.
ABC News: Excerpts from 'Jessica Lynch: An American Story', *Primetime*, air date
11 November 2003. A full transcript is available from ABC News. *Palm Beach Post*:
Excerpts from 'Real Men Fight Fires, Win Wars, Push Pencils' by Dan Neal, *Palm
Beach Post*, 21 October 2001. International Creative Management: Excerpts from
'Four 9/11 Moms Battle Bush', *New York Observer*, 25 August 2003, by Gail Sheehy.
Reprinted by permission of International Creative Management, Inc., copyright 2003 by
Gail Sheehy. HarperCollins: Excerpts from *Because Each Life Is Precious: Why an
Iraqi Man Risked Everything for Private Jessica Lynch* by Mohammed Odeh al-Rehaief,
copyright 2003, HarperCollins Publishers.

1 2 3 4 5 6 7 8 9

A CIP catalogue record for this book is available from the British Library.

ISBN: 978 1 84354 779 2

Designed by Maryl Sussman Levavi

Printed in Great Britain
by MPG Books Ltd, Bodmin, Cornwall

Atlantic Books
An imprint of Grove Atlantic Ltd.
Ormond House
26–27 Boswell Street
London WC1N 3JZ
www.groveatlantic.co.uk

For Russ

A bitter chill crept along the whole length of his body. The frozen ground seemed to drain the heat from his blood, and the blood from his heart itself. Perhaps it was that, and knowing where he was, that accounted for what happened next. Or maybe scars, almost as old as he was, were still in existence, down at the bottom of his mind, long buried under everything that had happened in between. The sky seemed to darken, while a ringing, buzzing sound came into his ears, and when the sky was completely black it began to redden with a bloody glow. His stomach dropped from under his heart, and a horrible fear filled him—the fear of a small helpless child, abandoned and alone in the night. He tried to spring up and out of that, and he could not move; he lay there rigid, seemingly frozen to the ground. Behind the ringing in his ears began to rise the unearthly yammer of the terror-dream—not heard, not even remembered, but coming to him like an awareness of something happening in some unknown dimension not of the living world.

—Alan Le May, *The Searchers*

A people unaware of its myths is likely to continue living by them, though the world around that people may change and demand changes in their psychology, their world view, their ethics, and their institutions.

—Richard Slotkin, *Regeneration through Violence*

Contents

THE
TERROR
DREAM

The Terror Dream

I N *TRAUMA AT HOME: AFTER 9/11*, ONE OF SEVERAL HIGH-TONED anthologies published in the early aughts that strived to "make meaning" out of the twin towers' rubble, Judith Greenberg, a professor of comparative literature, offered "an example of how this tragedy has been played out upon the body and in the mind." Curiously, given that the tragedy's casualties were overwhelmingly adult and male, the bodies and minds in her anecdote all belonged to girls. In the weeks following the terrorist attacks on the World Trade Center, Greenberg recounted, five gaunt teenage girls had arrived separately at a Manhattan hospital complaining of identical symptoms. They were wasting away because they couldn't "swallow." And they were sure they knew the reason: "All five *believed* that some debris or body part from the destruction of the towers had lodged in their throats and *produced* the symptom." The ear, nose, and throat surgeon who examined the girls discovered that their throats were, indeed, constricted. But he could find no obstruction, no debris, and, needless to say, no body parts.[1]

Greenberg read the girls' ailment in metaphorical terms: "They expressed hysterically what many of us feel," she wrote, "that the information is too difficult to swallow." An inability to digest the catastrophe seemed evident throughout *Trauma at Home*, which, as Greenberg ruefully conceded in the book's introduction, amounted to little more than "attempts to construct a narrative." Another contributor to the collection, Dori Laub, a psychoanalyst and, as a Holocaust survivor, no stranger to atrocity, reached the same conclusion. September 11, she wrote, remained "a story in search of a voice."[2]

Which begged the question: were the choking girls a metaphor for our failure to "swallow" the experience of 9/11—or for our inability to express it? In the electronic square, the gruesome visuals of the calamity replayed day after day, anniversary after anniversary, as if footage could substitute for fathoming, repetition for revelation. "Everything has changed" was our insta-bite mantra, recited in lieu of insight. Our media chattered on about "the death of irony" and "the death of postmodernism," without ever getting close to the birth of comprehension. The cacophony of chanted verities induced a kind of cultural hypnosis; Americans seemed to slip into a somnambulistic state. As Laub wrote of other witnesses to massive violence, "What they felt, what they saw, what they experienced, what they remembered—it suddenly becomes unavailable to them. It's all a haze, like walking in a dream."[3]

By mid-2007, long after the nation had passed the five-year-anniversary mark of the attacks, we were still sleepwalking. Virtually no film, television drama, play, or novel on 9/11 had begun to plumb what the trauma meant for our national psyche. Slavishly literal reenactments of the physical attack—preapproved and presanitized by the new Production Code committee known as "The 9/11 Families"—or unrepresentative tales of triumphal rescue at ground zero seemed all the national imagination could handle. *United 93*, Paul Greengrass's almost real-time chronology of the events on the last hijacked plane, released in April 2006, seemed to have no purpose other than to repeat what we already knew. "What is Greengrass actually trying to *say* about 9/11?" wondered *Slate* critic Dana Stevens. "That it was a terrible day on which innocent people suffered and died?" Remarking on director

Oliver Stone's uncharacteristically timid treatment of 9/11 on the occasion of his film's premiere in August 2006, *New York Times* critic Alessandra Stanley wrote, "For all its awe-inspiring special effects and operatic touches, *World Trade Center* is as focused on the effort to rescue two Port Authority officers as a made-for-television movie; it could almost as easily have been about trapped West Virginia miners or mountain climbers buried under an avalanche." In other words, it did precisely what it was meant to do, and what other American cultural presentations of 9/11 have done before and since: replicate, not delve.[4]

We explained our failure to probe the same way that the Bush administration explained its failures to protect us: the attack was "unimaginable." Nothing like this had ever happened before, so we didn't know how to assimilate the experience. And yet, in the weeks and months to follow, we kept rummaging through the past to make sense of the disaster, as if the trauma of 9/11 had stirred some distant memory, reminded us of something disturbingly familiar. As if we had been here before, after all.

Throughout the fall of 2001, the media attempted to position the assault on the World Trade Center and the Pentagon as a reprise of Pearl Harbor, a new "day of infamy" that would reinvigorate our World War II ethic of national unity and sacrifice, a long-awaited crucible in which self-absorbed Americans would, at long last, be forged into the twenty-first century's stoic army of the latest Greatest Generation. But the summons to actual sacrifice never came. No draft ensued, no Rosie the Riveters were called to duty, no ration cards issued, no victory gardens planted. Most of all, no official moral leadership emerged to challenge Americans to think constructively about our place in the world, to redefine civic commitment and public responsibility. There was no man in a wheelchair in the White House urging on us a reassessment of American strength and weakness. What we had was a chest beater in a borrowed flight suit, instructing us to max out our credit cards for the cause.

Allusions to Pearl Harbor provided no traction, and we soon turned our attention to another chapter in U.S. history—the 1950s Cold War. This one seemed a better fit. In the aftermath of the attacks, the cultural troika of media, entertainment, and advertising declared the post-9/11 age an era of neofifties nuclear family "togetherness," redomesticated femininity, and reconstituted Cold Warrior manhood. "Security moms" were said to be salving their fears of terrorists by sticking close to the hearth and stocking their pantries with canned goods and anthrax antidotes, while suburban dads were stockpiling guns in their families' linen closets. Scared single women, the media held, were reassessing their independence and heading for the altar; working mothers were "opting out" for the protected suburbs. The nation's men, from the inhabitants of the White House on down, were reportedly assuming a hard-boiled comportment last seen in post–World War II cinema. They were anointed "the new hawks" of the new consensus, "fighting a new Cold War," as tough on terrorists as the old hawks had been on Communists. They were men prepared to mete out "torture" and "focused brutality," take "nasty and brutish means," and chuck the "niceties" of avoiding civilian casualties, as muscle-flexing columnists in *Newsweek, Time, Atlantic Monthly*, the *Washington Post*, and other publications intoned. "We will destroy innocent villages by accident, shrug our shoulders and continue fighting," columnist David Brooks wrote in the *Weekly Standard*, approvingly.[5] A new John Wayne masculinity was ascendant, the punditry insisted. "Welcome back, Duke!" Peggy Noonan wrote in a much-quoted October 12 *Wall Street Journal* op-ed piece. "From the ashes of September 11, arise the manly virtues." In tribute to those resurrected virtues, Turner Broadcasting System devoted all its programming on Christmas of 2001 to reruns of John Wayne films, while MPI Media reissued Wayne's *America, Why I Love Her*, with the Duke reciting the Pledge of Allegiance, patriotic speeches and poems, and lyrics sung to military taps.[6]

We reacted to our trauma, in other words, not by interrogating it but by cocooning ourselves in the celluloid chrysalis of the baby boom's childhood. In the male version of that reverie, some nameless reflex had returned us to that 1950s Hollywood badlands where conquest and triumph played and replayed in an infinite loop. (For some, that replay was literal: *High Noon, National Review* writer Rob Long told readers, was "a movie I've been watching every few days since September 11.") From deep within that dream world, our commander in chief issued remarks like "We'll smoke him out" and "Wanted: dead or alive," our political candidates proved their double-barreled worthiness for post-9/11 office by brandishing guns on the campaign trail, our journalists cast city firefighters as tall-in-the-saddle cowboys patrolling a Wild West stage set, and our pundits proclaimed our nation's ability to vanquish "barbarians" in a faraway land they dubbed "Indian Country." The retreat into a fantasized yesteryear was pervasive, from the morning of the televised attack (ABC news anchor Peter Jennings called the national electronic conclave "the equivalent to a campfire in the days as the wagon trains were making their way westward"), to the first post-9/11 supper at Camp David (the war cabinet was served a "Wild West menu" of buffalo meat), to our invasion of Iraq (which tank crews from the Sixty-fourth Armor Regiment inaugurated with a "Seminole Indian war dance"), to our ongoing prosecution of the war on terror (which *Wall Street Journal* editor Max Boot equated with the small-scale "savage wars" waged in the republic's earliest days and which *Atlantic Monthly* correspondent Robert Kaplan hailed as "back to the days of fighting the Indians" and "really about taming the frontier").[7]

In the post-9/11 reenactment of the fifties Western, women figured largely as vulnerable maidens. Never mind that the fatalities that day were three-to-one male-to-female and that most of the female office workers at the World Trade Center (like their male counterparts) rescued themselves by walking down the stairs on their own two feet. The most showcased victims bore female faces. "We will never forget the photos of them, the brawny young man in his helmet carrying the wounded young woman in his arms," conservative commentator Charlotte Allen wrote in early 2002, one of many to marvel over these putative rescue shots. There were, in fact, very few such photos to remember—as Allen's awkward shift from plural to singular betrayed. *Newsweek* did run one shot of a firefighter carrying a child in its post-9/11 coverage, captioned "Horror at Home." But it was actually a picture from the Oklahoma City bombing in 1995.[8]

In the absence of female victims at the site, the media substituted homemakers in the suburbs held hostage by fear and little children traumatized by television footage. The threat, according to this revised script, wasn't to our commercial and governmental hubs but to our domestic hearth. "We face an enemy determined to bring death and suffering into our homes," George W. Bush emphasized in his speech on the fifth anniversary of September 11, as if the hijackers had aimed their planes not at office towers and government buildings but at the white picket fences of the American domicile. In the president's October 7, 2001, speech announcing the invasion of Afghanistan, he singled out a little girl, the only individual cited in his remarks:

> I recently received a touching letter that says a lot about the state of America in these difficult times—a letter from a fourth-grade girl, with a father in the military: "As much as I don't want my dad to fight," she wrote, "I'm willing to give him to you." This is a precious gift, the greatest she could give. This young girl knows what America is all about.

On the fifth anniversary of the attacks, Bush again offered a lone anecdote to exemplify post-9/11 virtue: the story of RoseEllen Dowdell, who had lost her husband, a New York firefighter, but was "a proud mom" because her two sons, recent graduates of the New York Fire Academy and West Point, had stepped into the protective gap. When Bush ran for reelection in 2004, the most ubiquitous photo op featured the president wrapping his arms around a girl whose mother had died in the twin towers. The new designation of roles was nicely spelled out in the first two frames of a Daryl Cagle cartoon that ran in *Slate* called "How We Remember September 11th": in the first frame, titled "The Heroes," a square-jawed fireman in a helmet clutches an ax; in the second, titled "The Victims," a little girl in pigtails weeps.[9]

Several weeks after the attacks, the Bush administration called on Hollywood directly to help "communicate"—or rather, market—the new war on terror to the American people. Entertainment moguls were twice summoned to the White House and, on the two-month anniversary of 9/11, Bush's chief political adviser, Karl Rove, invited more than forty of the top movie and television executives to a five-star Beverly Hills hotel to lodge a personal appeal (complete with a PowerPoint presentation offering bullet items like "This is a war against evil"). In mid-December 2001, the entertainment industry unveiled its first response on more than ten thousand movie screens—a quarter of all American cinemas—and in classrooms across the country. *The Spirit of America*, a rapid-fire movie montage, celebrated American screen heroes whom the film's director, Chuck Workman, defined as "reluctant but defiant revenge takers," cowboy-code-of-honor types who never throw the first punch but are relentless and invincible once riled. Workman was an old hand at the greatest-moments genre (his previous credits included the annual Oscar entertainment pastiche; *Playboy: Story of X*, a high-speed romp through a century of porn; *Stoogemania*; and *Fifty Years of Bugs Bunny in 3½ Minutes*); he packed 110 scenes of valorous vengeance from *Birth of a Nation* to *Shane* to *Dirty Harry* to *The Patriot* into 180 seconds. Despite the space constraints, Workman felt compelled to include one of the films twice and grant it double pride of place: he bookended his homage with the opening and closing scenes of John Ford's 1956 Western classic, *The Searchers*. "I chose it," Workman told me, "because John Wayne is the quintessential American hero for what I was trying to say. He's a rescuer. When he rescues the girl, *that's* what the movie is all about. *Rescue* is a good word to describe what a lot of these movies are all about." The final image in *The Spirit of America* is of Ethan Edwards, John Wayne's character, framed by a Texan homestead door in the 1870s, a leather-faced outlaw returned from a five-year quest to snatch his niece Debbie from the clutches of Comanche savages. Edwards has succeeded: the girl returns limp, pietà-style, in his arms, the bloody scalp of her captor, Scar, firmly in his possession.[10] This was the Duke we were so desperate to "welcome back" in the aftermath of 9/11, a stone-cold killer and Indian hater who would stand guard over our virginal girls. But why did our cultural dream life conjure into being this man—and on that mission? Brokers, busboys, municipal workers, and military bureaucrats, not little girls, were the victims of the terrorist attacks. Why did we perceive an assault on the urban workplace as a threat to the domestic circle? Why were we willing ourselves back onto a frontier where pigtailed damsels clutched rag dolls and prayed for a male avenger to return them to the home?

IN ISLAMIC CULTURE, dreams are often received as omens or presentiments. The prophet Muhammad himself is said to have received his first revelation of the Koran from the angel Gabriel in a dream. In the lead-up to 9/11, dreams among the Muslim faithful of planes crashing into tall buildings or American pilots succumbing to supercharged Arab combatants were so descriptive of the plot being hatched that Osama bin Laden told his lieutenants, in a conversation caught on videotape and later commandeered by American troops, "I was worried that maybe the secret would be revealed." In the psychology of the West, dreams are invested with more ambiguous properties. "The ancient belief that dreams reveal the future is not indeed entirely devoid of truth," Freud wrote in *The Interpretation of Dreams*. "By representing a wish as fulfilled the dream certainly leads us into the future; but this future, which the dreamer accepts as his present, has been shaped in the likeness of the past by the indestructible wish." If the dreams that Al Qaeda supporters reported in the months before 9/11 were premonitions of history on the cusp, then the dreamscape in which Americans dwelled since the disaster was a historical journey in the other direction. We were endeavoring to wish into the present our chosen "likeness of the past." What's not clear is why we dreamed this particular likeness — John Wayne the avenger and rescuer — and not others. What were we struggling to overcome with our 1950s fantasies?[11]

Our post-9/11 "sleeper cell" fears also seemed to find their likeness in the Cold War anxieties about "the enemy among us": the Commies under every bed, the body-snatching invaders on every Main Street, the Red nuclear warheads aimed priapically at every American nuclear family, and (the flip side of that John Wayne steely-eyed ethos) the suspicion that the nation and its men had gone "soft." The post-9/11 commentaries were riddled with apprehensions that America was lacking in masculine fortitude, that the masses of weak-chinned BlackBerry clutchers had left the nation open to attack and wouldn't have the cojones for the confrontations ahead. We were in danger of giving in to a "self-doubting gloominess" and a "weakness unbecoming" to our station, writer David Brooks fretted three months after 9/11. "In our uncertainty about ourselves, we respond to disasters with an emotional sensitivity that would have been foreign to our countrymen 60 years ago." American "weakness" and "vacillation," Vice President Dick Cheney maintained, had "encouraged people like Osama bin Laden" to "launch repeated strikes against the

United States, and our people overseas and here at home, with the view that he could, in fact, do so with impunity." Even the stories supposedly celebrating "the return of the manly man" unintentionally exposed fears of just the opposite with their nervous hand-wringing over "sissy sex symbols," "dot-com geeks," "girlie boys," "Alan Alda clones," and "the pussification of the American man." A *Washington Post* article heralding a post-9/11 virile renaissance began with the author asking hopefully, "Is the alpha male making a comeback?"—before plunging into a petulant diatribe against "those shaved-and-waxed male bimbos," the "touchy-feely sensitive male," and the demoralization of he-men who had been "psychopathologized by howling fems."[12]

Delete a few modern references to metrosexuals and hair mousse, and these eruptions could easily have been lifted from the postwar classics of male panic. We were back in the overwrought landscape of *The Incredible Shrinking Man* and Philip Wylie's momism, plagued by visions of Dad in an apron and a male populace drained of its "purity of essence." The "international Communist conspiracy to sap and impurify all of our precious bodily fluids" that so unhinged *Dr. Strangelove*'s General Jack Ripper had its modern echo on a disconcerting number of post-9/11 Web sites that pondered the twin towers' collapse as a symbol of the nation's "emasculation." The blog ruminations of the director of mensaction.net, who was a former military officer himself, was particularly Ripperian. "The phallic symbol of America had been cut off," he wrote of the World Trade Center, "and at its base was a large smoldering vagina, the true symbol of the American culture, for it is the western culture that represents the feminine materialistic principle, and it is at its extreme in America."[13]

There is a mystery here: the last remaining superpower, a nation attacked precisely *because* of its imperial preeminence, responded by fixating on its weakness and ineffectuality. Even more peculiar was our displacement of that fixation into the domestic realm, into a sexualized struggle between depleted masculinity and overbearing womanhood. What well of insecurity did this mystery unearth?

American analysts have remarked on the "intense humiliation" that seems to drive our Islamic male antagonists. Indeed, the military interrogation policies that led to the abusive treatment of prisoners at Abu

Ghraib were based on the conviction, as one source explained it to the *New Yorker's* Seymour Hersh, that "the biggest weakness of Arabs is shame and humiliation."[14] But what of our own shame, our own humiliation? Even in the films designed to restore our virile confidence, fears about the hero's incapacity are so often on display—as if the story line were seeking, through improbable triumph, to blot out the memory of a deep and defining defeat. In Steven Spielberg's post-9/11 blockbuster, *The War of the Worlds*, the hero, a divorced dad played by Tom Cruise, navigates an Earth under siege by Martians and triumphs against all odds by saving his nine-year-old daughter and returning her to the arms of the family (in a scene that replays the finale of *The Searchers*). At the same time, the hero is plagued with evidence of his unmanly ineptitude: his ex-wife regards him with contempt and won't even let him carry the children's luggage, his son thinks he's a coward, and he can't keep control of his own car or, worse, his gun. Only after he hatchets to death a man who tries to molest his daughter while they are hiding in a farmhouse cellar can the hero reclaim his manhood. Wayne's Ethan Edwards in *The Searchers* prevails against all enemies, yet he never succeeds in exorcising the ghosts that stalk him in the film. Those ghosts were even more vivid in the 1954 novel on which the film was based. In Alan Le May's *The Searchers*, Edwards is a secondary character who is ultimately shot in the face by an Indian woman. The novel's main protagonist is a young man whose entire family was murdered in a Comanche raid when he was a boy—while he hid in the bushes. Though he retains no conscious recollection of the trauma, he cannot escape its grip. He is haunted by his fear and shame, by a flickering sense of failed protection that afflicts him like a recurring fever, "the unearthly yammer of the terror-dream—not heard, not even remembered, but coming to him like an awareness of something happening in some unknown dimension not of the living world."[15]

"HE WHO IS ashamed would like to force the world not to look at him, not to notice his exposure," Erik Erikson wrote in *Childhood and Society*. "He would like to destroy the eyes of the world."[16] After 9/11, our eyes were on ourselves, disordering our dreams, exposing us to our nightmares.

Collections of September 11–related dreams were amassed by psychologists, sleep researchers, and amateurs after the attacks.[17] Reading through them, I was struck by how often they revolved around the dreamers' shame. On the Electric Dreams Web site, a man described a nightmare he had three nights after 9/11, in which he finds himself back at his boyhood home, which is littered with dead bodies, trying in vain to fend off a knife-hurling terrorist with a broomstick, while "a girl I used to work with" stands beside him, taking note of his incompetence. On the September 11 Dream Project site, a Brooklyn man recounted a post-9/11 dream in which he observes a line of marching men, "decked out in any uniform they could dig out of their closets, mostly in old Boy Scout uniforms a few sizes too small. They look like overlarge children playing military dress-up. They are pathetic, and yet proud to be in official procession. At this point I realize that I may be wearing my own old Boy Scout uniform as well." Another man dreamed, six days after the attack, that he is sent on a combat mission to "a massive skyscraper" armed only with a pair of scissors. Then he finds himself transported to a gun range ("sitting next to a girl I haven't seen in years"), where he is expected to "take a test." Suddenly he is at the building where he works; when he hears invaders coming, he flees, jumps a fence, and falls to the ground. "As my face laid in the dirt, I awoke."[18]

The women's dreams were different. They concentrated on the flip side of failed male protection: the menace of masculine violence invading their lives. One woman reported that the night after 9/11, she had a dream where a mass of people are "being rounded up and being moved in a large ring." She added, "I think everyone in the dream was female." Another woman dreamed on the night after 9/11 that she was trapped in a "death factory" and forced to watch a man torture a huge fish with a giant iron hook. "He has jabbed this hook into the belly of the fish and jerks the hook with long strokes upward and then downward—again and again." The man seems intent on making the fish "so injured that it vomits out its guts through its mouth," but the fish "just suffers silently with huge wide eyes staring." In the dream, she asks the man: "Why all of this needless suffering?" And he "replies without stopping what he is doing. He says to me, matter of factly, 'This is how it is done.'" Still another woman, whose friend John died on the 101st floor of the World Trade Center, related this dream: She is holding her dead friend's hand and walking "silently" down a brownstone-lined street in New York City. Suddenly she realizes that her body is "completely covered in traditional Muslim women's clothing, the jilbab (dress) and hijab (veil)."[19]

The phenomenon of the nightmare is one that psychoanalysts since Freud have termed the "failed dream," the mayhem that ensues when a mental burglar picks the locks of our best defenses. The successful dream orders experience; the nightmare confounds order, alerts the sleeper that the wished-for narrative isn't holding.[20] The intrusions of September 11 broke the dead bolt on our protective myth, the illusion that we are masters of our security, that our might makes our homeland impregnable, that our families are safe in the bower of their communities and our women and children safe in the arms of their men. The events of that morning told us that we could not depend on our protectors: that the White House had not acted on warnings of an impending attack, that the Federal Aviation Administration had not made safe our airports and planes, that the military had not secured our skies, that the 911 dispatchers had not issued the necessary warnings, and that the city's rescue workers, through no fault of their own, could not pluck their fellow citizens from danger—in short, that the entire edifice of American security had failed to provide a shield. In all the disparate nightmares of men and women after 9/11, what accompanied the sundering of our faith in our own indomitability was not just rage but shock at that revelation, and, with the shock, fear, ignominy, and shame. Those disturbing emotions inundated our cultural dream life, belying the bluster of the "United We Stand" logos. They underlay the anxious commentaries about our "impotence" and "weakness" and the talk show and blogosphere rants about our susceptibilities as a "feminized society" unmanned by feminist dictates. If we couldn't figure out "whom to strike back at," Newsweek warned, we would be left "even more vulnerable, even more impotent—a helpless victim." "Do we now panic," Time asked, "or will we be brave?" We no longer knew the answer.[21]

IN THE YEARS since 2001, we've been on a circus ride of impractical policies and improbable "protective" politics predicated as much on the desire to reinstate a social fiction as on the need to respond to actual threats. The enemy that hit us on September 11 was real. But our citizenry wasn't just asked to confront a real enemy. The arrest and prosecution of our antagonists seemed to be only a part of our concern. We were also enlisted in a symbolic war at home, a war to repair and restore a national myth. Our retreat to the fifties reached beyond movie tropes and the era's odd mix of national insecurity and domestic containment. It reached back beyond the fifties themselves. For this particular reaction to 9/11 — our fixation on restoring an invincible manhood by saving little girls — was not so anomalous. It belonged to a long-standing American pattern of response to threat, a response that we've been perfecting since our original wilderness experience.

"Ontogeny recapitulates phylogeny," German zoologist Ernst Haeckel, a contemporary of Darwin's, famously held in 1866. That is, an embryo as it develops repeats in compressed form the evolutionary stages of its species: in the space of nine months, a human in utero passes from fish to reptile to mammal. Whatever the scientific value of recapitulation theory (modern biology no longer applies it literally), Haeckel's hypothesis retains a metaphorical power in the realm of cultural history. The ways that we act, say, in response to a crisis can recapitulate in quick time the centuries-long evolution of our character as a society and of the mythologies we live by. September 11 presented just such a crisis. Our cultural response to it had distinct developmental phases that seemed to have little bearing on the actual circumstances we faced; they seemed instead to retrace some hidden road map. We sped through our memory bank the way *The Spirit of America* whipped through a hundred years of Hollywood heroism in three minutes. Like the young man in *The Searchers* caught in "the terror-dream," we were involuntarily revisiting some buried experience and systematically reinterring it. But what experience? We *have* been here before, but when? The "unimaginable" assault on our home soil was, in fact, anything but unimaginable. The anxieties it awakened reside deep in our cultural memory. And the myth we deployed to keep those anxieties buried is one we've been constructing for more than three hundred years.

This is not a book about what September 11 "did" to women or men, no matter how absurd or insulting the mantras of post-9/11 "new tradition-alism" may have been to its targets. Nor does it purport to take the full measure of our national reaction to the attacks: the panoply of botched military and foreign policy stratagems, the self-righteous media fanfares to American virtue, the governmental whacks at civil liberties, the neo-conservative campaigns to pin the 9/11 tail on "liberal" and "cultural elite" donkeys, and the maneuverings of corporate and oil interests. Rather, this is a book about one facet of our response, a facet that runs deep in the American psyche, yet has gone largely unrecognized and undiagnosed. To perceive its form and force is essential to perceiving why we responded the way we did on 9/11, why we insisted on "walking in a dream," weeks, months, years after the events of that terrible morning. Our reaction to the terrorist attacks provoked reflexes barely concealed beneath our usual decorum. Concealed but not quiet. Taken individually, the various im-pulses that surfaced after 9/11—the denigration of capable women, the magnification of manly men, the heightened call for domesticity, the search for and sanctification of helpless girls—might seem random ex-pressions of some profound cultural derangement. But taken together, they form a coherent and inexorable whole, the cumulative elements of a national fantasy in which we are deeply invested, our elaborately con-structed myth of invincibility.

That myth and the reflexes attending it color our view of the sexes, the family, and our society in general, throughout the best and calmest of times. When these same reflexes provide the template for our reaction in a time of crisis, they can lead us into jeopardy. The adherence to the myth, post-9/11, came with penalties, and America as a whole paid them. Adolescent fictions about "homeland protection" substituted for actions that would have enhanced our security. Cartoon declarations about "evil-doers" masqueraded as foreign policy. Our self-confinement to our dream state helped lead us into a misbegotten war against people who had not attacked us, crippled our fight against those who had, and destroyed so many lives, soldier and civilian, American and Arab. Recovering from our wound and prevailing against our enemies required sagacity and hard re-alism; instead we dreamed ourselves into a penny-dreadful plot that had little to do with the actual world in which we must live.

To not understand the mythic underpinnings of our response to 9/11 is, in a fundamental way, to not understand ourselves, to be so unknowing about the way we inhabit our cultural roles that we are stunned, insensible, when confronted by a moment that requires our full awareness. To fail to comprehend the historical provenance of our reaction, the phylogeny behind our ontogeny, is to find ourselves thwarted in our ability to express what we have undergone—as constricted as those girls who came to a Manhattan hospital with a national catastrophe lodged in their throats.

In the end, this is not a book about what September 11 did to anyone. It is a book about what September 11 revealed about all of us and, to that degree, about the opportunities that this great tragedy provided to look at ourselves anew.

PART ONE

ONTOGENY

CHAPTER 1

We're at War, Sweetheart

EARLY ON THE MORNING OF SEPTEMBER 11, 2001, I HAD A NIGHTMARE. I don't know how to explain it—I lay no claim to oracular powers. Maybe it was just a coincidental convergence. I dreamed I was sitting in an aisle seat of a commercial airliner. Next to me was another passenger, a woman. A hand jostled my headrest, and I looked up to see two young men bearing down on us. They both held pistols. One put his gun to my neck and shot. Then he shot again. I watched, as if from outside my body, as the first bullet entered at an angle and lodged in my throat. Moments later, the second bullet grazed by me and disappeared into the neck of my seatmate. I noticed that I was still alive but unable to speak. Then I woke up. A glorious dawn was filtering through the window blinds of my bedroom in Los Angeles. I described the dream to my boyfriend, in hopes of releasing its grip on my mind. I feared falling asleep and returning to that plane. As we lay there talking, the phone rang.

"Are you watching television?" a friend asked.

"No," I said. "Why?"

"Go turn on your television."

What I saw on the screen only deepened my sensation of being caught in some insane realm beyond reality, unable to wake up. It was a feeling that would linger.

My induction into a more willful unreality came later that day, when the phone rang again. A reporter in the Los Angeles bureau of an East Coast newspaper was pursuing a "reaction story." I was perplexed—he had hardly reached an authority on terrorism. As it turns out, that wasn't his concern. After a couple of vague questions about what this tragedy would "mean to our social fabric," he answered his own question with, given the morning's events, a bizarrely gleeful tone: "Well, this sure pushes feminism off the map!" In the ensuing days, I would receive more calls from journalists on the 9/11 "social fabric" beat, bearing more proclamations of gender restructuring—among them a *New York Times* reporter researching an article on "the return of the manly man" and a *New York Observer* writer seeking comment on "the trend" of women "becoming more feminine after 9/11." By which, as she made clear, she meant *less feminist*. Women were going to regret their "independence," she said, and devote themselves to "baking cookies" and finding husbands "to take care of them."

The calls left me baffled. By what mental process had these journalists traveled from the inferno at ground zero to a repudiation of female independence? Why would they respond to terrorist attack by heralding feminism's demise—especially an attack hatched by avowed antagonists of Western women's liberation? That a cataclysmic event might eclipse other concerns would hardly seem to warrant special mention. Unremarkably, celebrity scandals, Hollywood marital crises, and the disappearance of government intern Chandra Levy all slipped from the front pages. But my gloating caller and his cohorts weren't talking about the normal displacement of small stories by the big one. Feminist perspectives, and those of independent women more generally, didn't just naturally fade from view after 9/11.

In the weeks that followed, I had occasion to see this phenomenon repeated in many different ways. Of all the peculiar responses our culture manifested to 9/11, perhaps none was more incongruous than the desire to rein in a liberated female population. In some murky fashion, women's independence had become implicated in our nation's failure to protect itself. And, conversely, the need to remedy that failure somehow required a distaff correction, a discounting of female opinions, a demeaning of the female voice, and a general shrinkage of the female profile. As it turned out, feminists weren't the only women to be "pushed off the map"; their expulsion was just the preview for the larger erasures to follow.

WITHIN DAYS OF the attack, a number of media venues sounded the death knell of feminism. In light of the national tragedy, the women's movement had proved itself, as we were variously informed, "parochial," "frivolous," and "an unaffordable luxury" that had now "met its Waterloo." The terrorist assault had levied "a blow to feminism," or, as a headline on the op-ed page of the *Houston Chronicle* pithily put it, "No Place for Feminist Victims in Post 9-11 America."[1]

"The feminist movement, already at low ebb, has slid further into irrelevancy," syndicated columnist Cathy Young asserted. "Now that the peaceful life can no longer be guaranteed," military historian Martin van Creveld declared in *Newsday*, "one of the principal losers is likely to be feminism, which is based partly on the false belief that the average woman is as able to defend herself as the average man." In a column titled "Hooray for Men," syndicated columnist Mona Charen anticipated the end of the old reign of feminism: "Perhaps the new climate of danger—danger from evil men—will quiet the anti-male agitation we've endured for so long." *New York Times* columnist John Tierney held out the same hope. "Since Sept. 11, the 'culture of the warrior' doesn't seem quite so bad to Americans worried about the culture of terrorism," he wrote, impugning the supposed feminist "determination to put boys in touch with their inner feelings." "American males' fascination with guns doesn't seem so misplaced now that they're attacking Al Qaeda's fortress," he sniffed. "No one is suggesting a Million Mom March on Tora Bora."[2]

These were, of course, familiar themes, the same old nostrums marching under a bright new banner. Long before the towers fell, conservative efforts to roll back women's rights had been making inroads, and the media had been issuing periodic pronouncements on "the death of feminism." In part, what the attack on the World Trade Center did was foreground and speed up a process already under way. "Any kind of conflict at a time of unrest in society typically accentuates the fault lines that already exist," Geeta Rao Gupta, president of the International Center for Research on Women, told the *Christian Science Monitor* in a story headlined "Are Women Being Relegated to Old Roles?," one of the few articles to acknowledge what was happening.[3] The seismic jolt of September 11 elevated to new legitimacy the ventings of longtime conservative antifeminists, who were accorded a far greater media presence after the attacks. It also invited closet antifeminists within the mainstream media to come out in force, as a "not now, honey, we're at war" mentality made more palatable the airing of buried resentments toward women's demands for equal status.

What was most striking, and passing strange, was the *way* feminism's detractors framed their assault. In the fall and winter of 2001, the women's movement wasn't just a domestic annoyance; it was a declared domestic enemy, a fifth column in the war on terror. To the old rap sheet of feminist crimes—man hating, dogmatism, humorlessness—was added a new "wartime" indictment: feminism was treason. That charge was made most famously, and most cartoonishly, by Rev. Jerry Falwell. "I point the finger in their face and say, 'You helped this happen,'" Falwell thundered on 9/12 on the Christian Broadcast Network, addressing his *j'accuse* to "the pagans, and the abortionists, and the feminists, and the gays and the lesbians who are actively trying to make that an alternative lifestyle." By altering traditional gender roles, feminists and their fellow travelers had "caused God to lift the veil of protection which has allowed no one to attack America on our soil since 1812."[4] Falwell's outburst struck even his compatriots as unfortunate, or at least unsubtle. But his allegations, sanitized and stripped of their Old Testament terms, would soon be taken up by conservative pundits and in mainstream outlets; old subpoenas would be reissued, upgraded with new counts of traitorous behavior.

Post-9/11, feminism's defense of legal abortion was accordingly deemed a Benedict Arnold act. "After September 11th the American people are valuing life more and realizing that we need policies to value the dignity and worth of every life," Bush's senior counselor Karen Hughes said on CNN, on the same day as a massive reproductive-rights march was in progress in the capital. In fact, American opposition to abortion was "really the fundamental difference between us and the terror network we fight," Hughes stressed. (A curious contention, considering that our assailants were hardly prochoice, but her CNN interviewers let it stand.) Others, like Focus on the Family founder James C. Dobson, stated the equation less decorously. "Has God withdrawn his protective hand from the US?" he asked on his organization's Web site—and answered that God is "displeased" with America for "killing 40 million unborn babies." A thirty-second television commercial likening abortion to terrorism was rushed on the air some weeks after the attack by an antiabortion organization—"to take advantage of the 9-11 events to press our case for sparing the lives of babies," as the executive director candidly put it.[5]

The October 15, 2001, edition of the *National Review* could have passed for a special issue on the subject of feminist treachery. In "Their Amerika," John O'Sullivan accused feminists of "taking the side of medieval Islamists against the common American enemy. They feel more comfortable in such superior company than alongside a hard-hat construction worker or a suburban golfer in plaid pants." Another article, "The Conflict at Home," blamed American feminism's "multiculturalist" tendencies for allowing Sharia extremism to thrive in the Arab world. And a third piece claimed that women's rights activists have so browbeaten the American military that our armed services have "simply surrendered to feminist demands" and allowed an insistence on equal opportunity to "trump combat effectiveness."[6]

As the denouncers made their media rounds, they homed in on two aspects of feminist sedition: women's liberation had "feminized" our men and, in so doing, left the nation vulnerable to attack. "Well, you see, there is a very serious problem in this country," Camille Paglia explained to CNN host Paula Zahn a few weeks after 9/11. Thanks to feminism, Paglia said, "men and women are virtually indistinguishable in the workplace." Indeed, especially among the American upper middle class, the man has "become like a woman." (Paglia was weirdly, albeit inadvertently, echoing the words of Taliban attorney general Maulvi Jalilullah Maulvizada, who had earlier told a journalist that when women are given freedom, "men become like women.") This gender confusion in the workplace would bode ill for our coming conflicts with the Arab world, Paglia warned. "There is a kind of a threat to national security here," she said. "I think that the nation is not going to be able to confront and to defeat other countries where the code of masculinity is more traditional."[7]

The editors and writers in the centrist media expressed such sentiments more euphemistically—as furrow-browed concern that a "soft" America might not be able to rise to the occasion, that a womanly "therapeutic culture" would cause the nation to value the feminine ritual of mourning over martial "action," that a "Band of Brothers" ethic, as one newsmagazine put it, could not take root in a female-centered "Sex and the City culture." "For once, let's have no 'grief counselors,'" Time editor Lance Morrow lectured. "For once, let's have no fatuous rhetoric about 'healing.'" Coddled Americans had let themselves go and needed to "toughen up." Our World War II elders say we have "become too soft," a story in the San Francisco Chronicle warned. Numerous press reports fixated on a report that bin Laden thought Americans were "soft and weak." Beneath the press's incessant fretting lurked anxious questions that all seemed to converge on a single point: would a feminized nation have the will to fight?[8]

The conservative commentariat had an answer and wasn't shy about stating it. The problem, according to the opinion makers from Fox News, the Weekly Standard, National Review, and the many right-wing-financed think tanks who seemed to be on endless rotation on the political talk shows after 9/11, was simple: the baleful feminist influence had turned us into a "nanny state." In the wake of 9/11, a battle needed to be waged between the forces of besieged masculinity and the nursemaids of overweening womanhood—or, rather, the "vultures" in the "Sisterhood of Grief," as American Spectator's January–February 2002 issue termed them. "When we go soft," Northwestern University psychology professor and American Enterprise scholar David Gutmann warned, "there are still plenty of 'hard' peoples—the Nazis and Japanese in World War II, the radical Islamists now—who will see us as decadent sybarites, and who will exploit, through war, our perceived weaknesses." And why had our spine turned to rubber? The conservative analysis proffered an answer: the femocracy.[9]

"Our culture has undergone a process that one observer has aptly termed 'debellicization,'" former drug czar William Bennett advised in *Why We Fight*, his 2002 call to arms against the domestic forces that were weakening our "resolve." The "debellicizers" that he identified were, over and over, women—a female army of schoolteachers, psychologists, professors, journalists, authors, and, especially, feminists who taught "that male aggression is a wild and malignant force that needs to be repressed or medicated lest it burst out, as it is always on the verge of doing, in murderous behavior." Since the sixties and seventies, Bennett wrote, this purse-lipped army had denounced American manhood as "a sort of deranged Wild West machismo"; it had derided the Boy Scouts "as irrelevant, 'patriarchal,' and bigoted"; it had infected "generations of American children" with "the principle that violence is always wrong." And with the terrorist attack on our nation, the chicken hawks had come home to roost. "Having been softened up, we might not be able to sustain collective momentum in what we were now being called upon to do," Bennett wrote. "We have been caught with our defenses down."[10]

"What's happening now is not pacifism but passivism," *National Review*'s Mark Steyn maintained soon after the attack in an article titled "Fight Now, Love Later: The Awfulness of an Oprahesque Response." "Passivism" was a pathogen that had invaded the body politic—and American women were its Typhoid Marys, American men its victims. The women who ruled our culture had induced "a terrible inertia filled with feel-good platitudes that absolve us from action," Steyn wrote. He found particularly telling Oprah Winfrey's call, at a post-9/11 prayer service in Yankee Stadium, to "love" one another. "Not right now, Oprah," he instructed. If we were to prevail in the coming war, the nation first needed to unseat this regiment of "grief counselors" and silence all their "drooling about 'healing' and 'closure.'" "You can't begin 'healing' until the guys have stopped firing."[11]

As if feminizing our domestic culture weren't bad enough, the women's movement was also jeopardizing our readiness on the battlefield. "Bands of brothers don't need girls," a *Rocky Mountain News* columnist held, denouncing feminists for depleting the military muscle we would need for the upcoming war on terror. "To them, the military is just another symbol of the male patriarchy that ought to be feminized, anyway, along with the rest of society." Our first lady of antifeminism, Ann Coulter, cast this argument in her usual vituperous fashion. "This is right where you want to be after Sept. 11—complaining about guns and patriarchy," she addressed feminists in a column titled "Women We'd Like to See . . . in Burkas." "If you didn't already realize how absurd it is to defang men, a surprise attack on U.S. soil is a good reminder. . . . Blather about male patriarchy and phallic guns suddenly sounds as brilliantly prescient as assurances that the Fuhrer would stop at Czechoslovakia."[12]

A few weeks after 9/11, the Independent Women's Forum (an all-female think tank supported by right-wing foundations) inaugurated its onslaught against martial emasculation at the National Press Club. Under the banner "IWF Women Facing War," one female panelist after another rose to face the enemy within. "Our freedoms and way of life depend on a strong national defense," Elaine Donnelly, president of the Center for Military Readiness and soon to be a ubiquitous media presence, told the assembled. "And yet, for far too long, a minority of feminist women have presumed to tell not just the commander-in-chief but the secretary of defense and the heads of all the armed forces what to do to advance the feminist agenda in the institution of the military." An "ungendered" armed services with "mandatory assignments" of women to "close combat units" was "the premiere item on the feminist agenda," Donnelly warned, and that agenda had seriously damaged the U.S. military's "morale, discipline, recruiting, retention, and overall readiness."[13]

The IWF, which had been lobbying for years against efforts to bring more women into the military and the police and fire services, celebrated what it saw as vindication. The group's spokeswomen fanned out on television and radio and in print. "It took an act of monstrous criminality to show us this," IWF member and commentator Charlotte Allen declared. "But sometimes, perhaps most of the time, those are jobs that only a guy can do, and if we lower our standards because some women may feel bad about not living up to them, it is going to cost lives." Kate O'Beirne, a *National Review* editor and regular presence on CNN's *Capital Gang*, accused feminists of ruining the military. "Kumbaya confidence courses have replaced ego-bruising obstacle challenges," she wrote a week and a half after 9/11. "Let's hope that stepstools will be provided for female soldiers in Afghanistan."

In late October 2001, Pentagon brass who shared such sentiments announced they would soon be reversing Clinton-era policies that had sought to expand women's roles in battle zones. "That's all changing," a senior defense official told *U.S. News & World Report*. Frontline "units won't involve women," another said. After women's rights groups protested, the effort was shelved for the time being. But the Bush administration quietly began dismembering the Defense Advisory Committee on Women in the Services, a long-standing internal institution that had promoted women's progress in the military for more than half a century: the committee's charter was allowed to lapse, women's rights advocates were replaced with GOP party loyalists, and the organization's purview was restricted to family and health issues.[14]

THE FEW FEMINIST—or even perceived-to-be feminist—pundits that managed to find a forum in this cacophony received a less than congenial reception. "I wanted to walk barefoot on broken glass across the Brooklyn Bridge, up to that despicable woman's apartment, grab her by the neck, drag her down to ground zero and force her to say that to the firefighters," *New York Post* columnist Rod Dreher ranted on September 20, 2001. The object of his venom was Susan Sontag and the less than five hundred words she had famously contributed to the *New Yorker* on the subject of 9/11. What was so "despicable"? Was it her suggestion that "a few shreds of historical awareness might help us to understand what has just happened, and what may continue to happen"? Or perhaps it was her weariness over the muscle-flexing mantras: "Who doubts that America is strong? But that's not all America has to be." Dreher was too busy seething to specify his objections. In any case, he was not alone in his overheated fury. The *New Republic* ranked Sontag with Osama bin Laden and Saddam Hussein. Former *New Republic* editor Andrew Sullivan called her an "ally of evil" and "deranged." Yet another *New York Post* columnist, John Podhoretz, said she suffered from "moral idiocy." *National Review*'s Jay Nordlinger accused her of having "always hated America and the West and freedom and democratic goodness." In an article titled "Blame America at Your Peril," *Newsweek*'s Jonathan Alter charged the "haughty" Sontag with dressing the nation in girl's clothes. It was "ironic," he wrote, that "the same people urging us to not blame the victim in rape cases are now saying Uncle Sam wore a short skirt and asked for it."[15]

Sontag was no more provocative than any number of male left-leaning intellectuals and pundits whose remarks sparked criticism but nowhere near the personal and moral evisceration that she was made to endure. No one called them, as Sontag was called in the *Chicago Tribune*, "stupefyingly dumb."[16] A few nights before Sontag's *New Yorker* article was published, ABC's *Politically Incorrect* host, Bill Maher, raised hackles when he remarked that flying an airplane into a building was hardly "cowardly." FedEx and Sears pulled ads and a dozen local affiliates suspended the show's broadcast. But in the media court of opinion, Maher received a comparatively gentle dressing down—and was then forgiven and even feted after he made the electronic rounds, seeking absolution. (Rush Limbaugh actually defended Maher, saying, "In a way, he was right.") ABC pulled the plug on *Politically Incorrect* the next year when the show's contract expired. The network contended that the show just wasn't making enough money; Maher maintained his remarks sealed his doom. He wasn't out in the cold for long: in a matter of months he was back on the air with his own HBO show.[17]*

---

*Maher was, in fact, echoing conservative writer Dinesh D'Souza, a guest on the show, who had just said of the terrorists, "These are warriors." Maher agreed and added, "We have been the cowards lobbing cruise missiles from two thousand miles away." After Maher made his apologies to, among other father confessors, Jay Leno, Bill O'Reilly, and Howard Stern, he received media support from some surprising corners. Even O'Reilly was sympathetic, choosing to construe Maher's remark about "lobbing cruise missiles" as criticism of the Clinton administration, not the troops. "I don't like a lot of the things that Bill Maher has said in the past," Fox's conservative host Sean Hannity said on *Hannity & Colmes*. "But I do think there is this mentality out there to jump on somebody, never give them an opportunity for clarification, never give them an opportunity to apologize." *National Review*'s Jay Nordlinger, who had heaped such scorn on Sontag, declared his support for Maher and his program: "I liked the show, approved of it, appeared on it." (Needless to say, no denunciations of their fellow conservative, Dinesh D'Souza, were tendered.) More mainstream venues and pundits went even further, paying tribute to Maher as a free-speech patriot. "*Politically Incorrect* is downright American," a *BusinessWeek* writer declared. "To see Maher—the always irrepressible, often irritating wiseacre—sitting rigid next to Leno as he explained himself was to watch McCarthyism-in-the-making."

But the stoning of Sontag went on and on. More than a year after the offending issue of the *New Yorker* had departed the newsstands, former New York mayor Ed Koch was inveighing against her. "Susan Sontag will occupy the Ninth Circle of Hell," he declared in a radio address in December 2002. "I will no longer read her works."[18]

Anyone who has followed the commentaries of feminist writer Katha Pollitt in the *Nation* knows she can stir the pot. But pot stirring hardly describes her subdued and almost mournful October 8, 2001, column, in which she related her discussion with her thirteen-year-old daughter about whether to fly an American flag from their apartment window. Pollitt pointed out the flag's historic use as a symbol of "jingoism and vengeance and war"; her daughter said she was wrong, that the flag "means standing together and honoring the dead and saying no to terrorism." Pollitt agreed that, sadly, "The Stars and Stripes is the only available symbol right now." She closed by lamenting the lack of "symbolic representations right now for the things the world really needs—equality and justice and humanity and solidarity and intelligence."[19]

These words unleashed a torrent of wrath. Pollitt noted with some amazement that she had received more hostile responses to that column "than on anything I've ever written." The harangue came from across the political media spectrum, from *Dissent* to the *Washington Post* to the *Washington Times*. She was called a bad mother, charged with, variously, "lunacy," "ignorance," "idiocy," "facile insipidities," and designated one of the "chattering asses." The *Chicago Sun-Times* excerpted a few lines of her piece under the headline "Oh, Shut Up." "We're at war, sweetheart,"

The few dissenting male journalists who were harshly punished, it's worth noting, had called Bush's manhood into question. At the Grant Pass, Oregon, *Daily Courier*, Dan Guthrie was fired after he wrote that Bush had "skedaddled" the day of the attacks. Tom Gutting at the *Texas City Sun* lost his job after he wrote that Bush flew across the United States "like a scared child" ("Bill Maher on the Defensive," *The O'Reilly Factor*, Fox News Network, September 20, 2001; "Interview with Dennis Prager, Ellen Ratner," *Hannity & Colmes*, Fox News Network, September 21, 2001; Jay Nordlinger, "Bush *Knew*? 'Dr. Win the War.' The Pearl Video. And More," *National Review Online*, May 20, 2002; Ciro Scotti, "Politically Incorrect Is Downright American," *BusinessWeek Online*, September 26, 2001; Linda Diebel, "Freedom of Speech Casualty of a New War," *Toronto Star*, October 3, 2001).

a column in the *New York Post* instructed her. "Pollitt, honey, it's time to take your brain to the dry cleaners." Both the *Weekly Standard* and the *New York Post* published her address so readers could inundate her daughter with flags. During a radio interview on an NPR talk show, Katha Pollitt was taken aback when Andrew Sullivan accused her of supporting the Taliban and then, in an almost verbatim repeat of the *Newsweek* commentator's attack on Sontag, likened her, she recalled, "to someone who refuses to help a rape victim and blames her for wearing a short skirt."[20]

In the midst of the fracas, Pollitt came home one day to a message on her answering machine. "You should just go back to Afghanistan, you bitch," a male voice said. Pollitt played the tape for her daughter. "And a little later," Pollitt recalled, "she came to me and said, 'You know, I think you might have been right about the flag.'"[21]

The novelist Barbara Kingsolver was similarly bewildered by the fierce response to two op-ed pieces she wrote for the *San Francisco Chronicle* and the *Los Angeles Times*—in which she appealed to "our capacity of mercy" and proposed that one of "a hundred ways to be a good citizen" was to learn "honest truths from wrongful deaths." Two weeks later she reported that "I've already been called every name in the Rush Limbaugh handbook: traitor, sinner, naïve, liberal, peacenik, whiner. . . . Some people are praying for my immortal soul, and some have offered to buy me a one-way ticket out of the country, to anywhere." The *Los Angeles Times* received a letter from a collection agency owner who called Kingsolver's essay "nothing less than another act of terror" and "pure sedition"; he promised to subject Kingsolver to "the most massive personal and business investigation ever conducted on an individual" and to send the results to the FBI, because "this little horror of a human being" needed to be "surveilled."

Things only got worse after the *Wall Street Journal* ran a piece by writer Gregg Easterbrook claiming Kingsolver had said the American flag stood for "bigotry, sexism, homophobia and shoving the Constitution through a paper shredder." (She had actually said the exact opposite, that the flag *shouldn't* stand for these things.) The story was accompanied by a cartoon of a wild-haired figure on a soapbox wearing an "I [Heart] Osama" T-shirt. The misquote was picked up in scores of publications, including

Stars and Stripes. "It became *the* most quoted thing I ever said," King-solver told me, "and I didn't say it." The *New Republic* put her on "Idiocy Watch"; the *Chicago-Sun Times* denounced her "vicious and unpatriotic drivel" and "hatred of America"; the *National Review* called her "hysteri-cal," "moronic," and, more obscurely, "Miss Metternich," and even the al-ternative paper, the *Tucson Weekly,* in the town where Kingsolver had lived for a quarter century, sneered with the headline "The Bean Trees Must've Fallen on Her Head." Kingsolver's family received threatening mail; a trustee at Kingsolver's alma mater sought to revoke her honorary degree; invitations, both social and professional, were retracted; and read-ers shipped back copies of her books "with notes saying, 'I don't want this trash in my house,'" Kingsolver recalled. Her efforts to correct the record were spurned. After Kingsolver's attorney wrote the *Wall Street Journal* to protest the mangling of her words, a dismissive letter arrived from the news-paper's associate general counsel, Stuart D. Karle, who deemed the article "a perfectly reasonable interpretation of Ms. Kingsolver's text." He added strangely that Kingsolver seemed to believe the flag's stars should now symbolize not the fifty states but "entertainers of the moment" like Julia Roberts and Britney Spears. No retraction was forthcoming.[22]

The scenario repeated whenever a feminist-minded writer dared chal-lenge the party line. Epithets were hurled at novelist Arundhati Roy ("re-pulsive," "foaming-at-the-mouth," "ungracious operator")—for pointing out pertinent historical facts about America's role in the mujaheddin's rise and for suggesting that "it will be a pity if, instead of using this as an oppor-tunity to try to understand why September 11 happened, Americans use it as an opportunity to usurp the whole world's sorrow to mourn and avenge only their own." Columnist Naomi Klein was deemed traitorous—for sug-gesting that an international response to terrorism might be more effec-tive than a unilateral one. (William Bennett claimed she was "taking from us" our "right to self-defense.") Humorist Fran Lebowitz was de-nounced as "disloyal" on an MSNBC talk show—for finding humor in Bush's shoot-'em-up rhetoric. Female journalists who so much as re-ported on the treatment of these women were roughed up, too. While re-searching a story on the post-9/11 attacks on dissenters, *Vanity Fair* columnist Leslie Bennetts made the mistake of phoning the *New York*

Post's John Podhoretz. She asked him if he had any regrets about accusing Sontag of "moral idiocy." He didn't. After a few brief questions, she rang off. Two days later, Bennetts opened the *Post* to find Podhoretz had devoted his latest column to an attack on *her*. "I was getting this for simply *raising* these issues," Bennetts marveled.[23]

Even feminists across the border weren't safe. "Never before—or at least not since the War Measures Act—have I watched such a calculated, hot and hateful propaganda campaign," *Toronto Star*'s columnist Michele Landsberg observed. She was referring to the response, in the United States and Canada, to some remarks at an Ottawa women's rights conference on October 1, 2001. One conference panelist, Sunera Thobani, a University of British Columbia women's studies professor, had said that Third World women might be dubious about the U.S. government's vow to "save" them, considering that American foreign policy in the past had spurred "prolific levels of violence all over the world." Overnight, Thobani became the favorite media and blogosphere whipping girl, dubbed "sick," "hateful and destructive," "Communist-linked," guilty of "sucking on the front teat of society," and "shockingly similar to Osama bin Laden." She was inundated with so much hate mail and violent pornography and so many death threats that the university assigned her security guards. Even so, when the Ottawa police received a formal hate-crimes complaint, the anonymously filed grievance was submitted not on Thobani's behalf but against her. The accuser charged her with "publicly inciting hatred against Americans."[24]

Some weeks into these media drubbings, Barbara Kingsolver picked up *Newsweek* and came across Jonathan Alter's article "Blame America at Your Peril," which singled out her, Susan Sontag, and Arundhati Roy for yet another round of reprimand and ridicule. "And I understood when I read that piece that Arundhati and Susan and I were the bad girls who had been mounted on poles for public whipping," she told me. "They whipped us with words like *bitch* and *airhead* and *moron* and *silly*." At first, the patronizing tone made Kingsolver think that the detractors regarded her and the other women as children. "But if we were so silly and moronic, why was it so important to bring us up and attack us again and again and again? The response was not the response you would expect toward a child. It was more like we were witches."[25]

• • •

Wᴛ sᴏ ᴍᴀɴʏ feminist-minded writers disenfranchised by the post-9/11 press, such calumny stood unchallenged. There was no counterpoint perspective to blunt its force. In fact, a feminist perspective on *any* topic was increasingly AWOL. This reality was reinforced to me on a morning three years after 9/11, as I sat in a dim back room of the public library in Portland, Oregon, scrolling through reels of faded microfilm. I had been invited to speak at the thirtieth anniversary of a graduate fellowship program for women. Perhaps it was the gilt-framed oil portraits of the city's founding fathers, all of them whiskered, staring down at me as I ascended the library's marble staircase, that led me to indulge in some Pollyanna thoughts about how far my sex had come in the last three decades. In any event, I decided it might hearten the female "fellows" to hear some evidence of progress from the antediluvian days of their fellowship's first year. My search, however, unearthed an opposite trend.

In the yellowing pages of the 1973–74 *Readers' Guide to Periodical Literature*, I found a category titled "Women's Liberation Movement"— with a list of stories that reported in overwhelmingly favorable terms on women's clamor for change. Under "Women," another long string of stories reported on efforts to expose sex discrimination and advance women's rights in virtually every occupation—from architecture to construction, fine arts to sports, publishing to plumbing. These weren't just stories in *Ms.* magazine. Publications like *Christianity Today* and *New Catholic World* boasted the headlines "First at the Cradle, Last at the Cross," "Liberation of Mother Church," "Bless Me, Mother," and "All We're Meant to Be: A Biblical Approach to Women's Liberation." Even *Motor Boat and Sailing* magazine was offering "Skipper Is a Ms.," "Sailors Lib," and "No Men Aboard." Prominent feminist bylines included Gloria Steinem, Betty Friedan, Germaine Greer, Kate Millett, Vivian Gornick, Juliet Mitchell, Phyllis Chesler, Mary Daly, Ellen Willis, Barbara Deming, Jo Freeman, Nora Ephron, and Helen Reddy, and magazines featured interviews with feminists from Simone de Beauvoir to Rita Mae Brown.[26]

Then I pulled the 2004 *Readers' Guide* off the shelf to see what was listed under "Women's Liberation Movement." The category had been discontinued; readers were advised to see "Feminism." But judging by its contents, "Feminism" had become little more than a repository for the paltry remains of the women's liberation movement and, especially, for obituaries celebrating the movement's demise. The category featured antifeminist articles from the *Weekly Standard, Reason, Atlantic Monthly, Commentary* (which hailed "the end of the era of feminism"), and *Society* (which declared "the looming failure of the feminist project" and equated feminist efforts to challenge sex differences with "the effort by the German Nazis to craft The New Aryan Man"). Other stories listed under "Feminism" could most charitably be characterized as "postfeminist"—like "Beautiful Girl," a feature on the life of a supermodel, or the article in *Men's Health* called "Babes in Boyland." Only a few stories actually expressed a feminist point of view—nearly all of them by Katha Pollitt.[27]

I flipped to the "Women" section and scanned the subheadings for more authentically feminist entries. While there were a few (particularly when the subject was women's oppression in Islamic countries), they were vastly outnumbered by articles of the "Beautiful Girl" variety. The categories "Women in Motion Pictures" and "Women in the Motion Picture Industry" offered such headlines as "Killer Chicks" and "Six Crazy Men and a Blonde," along with articles on the remakes of *Charlie's Angels* and *The Stepford Wives*. "Women in TV" offered "Invasion of the Dumb Blonds" and stories about mean girls on reality TV shows and catfights on *Desperate Housewives*. "Women in Literature" and "Women Authors" offered "The Chick-Lit Challenge" and "Breaking Out Bombshells." The category "Women Disc Jockeys" listed only one article, called "Barenaked Ladies." I leafed back some pages to see if there might be something more elevating under "Female"—and came on the subcategory "Female Friendships," where a lengthy list gave me hope for a refreshing alternative. Then I read the headlines: "All She Does Is Complain," "She Thinks Her Life Matters More than Mine," "She Never Has Time for Me Anymore," "Can You Truly Trust an Office Friend?," and "I Can't Stand Her New Husband." Two articles on the list promised sisterhood of a sort: one was called "Shopping Buddies," the other "Two Women Joined by Murder."[28]

This depressing selection didn't emerge overnight. Perusing the *Readers' Guide* from the late nineties, I could see what Geeta Rao Gupta called "the fault lines that already exist." But those lines were clearly accentuated in the years after 9/11. By 2004, the difference between where we once were and where we now seemed to be was an untraversable chasm.

IN THE AFTERMATH of September 11, you didn't have to be a feminist to feel the purge. Soon after the World Trade Center vaporized into two biblical plumes of smoke, another vanishing act occurred on television sets and newspaper pages across the country. Women began disappearing.

The morning after the attack, Geneva Overholser opened the *Washington Post* and turned to the opinion section, where she had formerly written the ombudsman column. She saw that the editors had responded to the disaster by doubling the section's size. The expansion, however, only magnified a certain contraction. "Instead of the typical five opinion columns, there were ten," Overholser noted. "And every one was written by a man." Nor would that morning's paper prove anomalous. "A few days into that awful time," Overholser later wrote, "I started to notice a haunting silence amid the views I was finding in America's newspapers: it was the absence of women's voices." As one of the few women to have run a major American newspaper, the *Des Moines Register*, Overholser had long been aware of the gender imbalances in her profession. During her tenure as editor in chief in the late eighties and early nineties, the *Des Moines Register* increased coverage of so-called women's issues and won a Pulitzer Prize for its reporting on the media's treatment of rape victims. But this latest setback for women seemed to come with a new and insulting twist. "Here we have the editors at the *Washington Post* expanding their opinion-column inches dramatically because they understood how important it was to give voice to more people at this crucial time," Overholser told me. "And yet it still didn't occur to them to expand those voices to women."[29]

Nor would it occur to their brethren at the nation's other leading newspapers. At the end of the first week after 9/11, Overholser reviewed the eighty-eight opinion pieces in the *New York Times,* the *Washington*

Post, and the *Los Angeles Times*. Only five, she found, had female bylines. Three weeks after 9/11, the media watchdog group Fairness & Accuracy in Reporting (FAIR) counted the op-ed bylines in the nation's major newspapers and reported similar results: the *New York Times* had now run seventy-nine opinion pieces—eight by women. (In the same three weeks a month earlier, by my count, the *Times* had run seventy-three opinion pieces, sixteen by women; in other words, the female bylines on the *Times*'s op-ed page had dropped from 22 percent to 9 percent). The *Washington Post* was even worse: it had published 107 commentaries in the three weeks after 9/11—and only seven were by women. The phenomenon wasn't restricted to centrist publications, either. On October 8, 2001, the *Nation*'s cover announced "A Just Response," a set of commentaries on the terrorist attack. All of them were by men. In fact, with the exception of Katha Pollitt's regular column (which that week was the much-decried flag story), the entire issue—including articles unrelated to 9/11, the books and arts section, and even the illustrations—was a male production.[30]

Marie Wilson was watching the same attrition in another medium. The president of the feminist White House Project flipped from CBS's *Face the Nation* to NBC's *Meet the Press* to ABC's *This Week* to CNN's *Late Edition with Wolf Blitzer* to *Fox News Sunday* and wondered: where are the women? As it happened, the White House Project was in the midst of a study of women's representation on the Sunday talk shows—and in the seven weeks following the attacks, that census recorded a plunge: the number of appearances by American women shrank by nearly 40 percent; all told, less than 10 percent of the total number of guests in that period were women. On *This Week*, thirty-two people were invited to speak; only one was a woman.[31]

The disappearances continued as the next year wore on. "Since Sept. 11, pictures of Afghan women in burkas have been seen more often on American television than female talking heads," Boston University journalism professor Caryl Rivers observed on the online *Women's eNews*, one of the rare media outlets registering the decline.[32] At the end of 2002, Rivers leafed through the last twelve issues of a venerable national magazine published in her backyard. What she saw—or didn't see—troubled her:

If you're a regular reader of [the *Atlantic*], which I am, you'd think that some sort of plague had decimated the female population. Between December 2001 and December 2002, for example, I found 38 major articles by men and seven by women. Two of these women were writing with their more famous husbands; another was doing an anecdotal piece on cross-dressing. So for serious pieces, the total is 38 to 4. The essays were even worse. During this period, I found 41 essays by men and two by women. Or to be precise, two essays by the same woman. For the *Atlantic*, Margaret Talbot represented all of womanhood.[33]

The situation wasn't much different in the other publications she reviewed. "It hasn't been this bad for women scholars and journalists wanting to influence the national public agenda since the pre–women's movement days when women were completely invisible," Rivers concluded. "We're being systematically overlooked."[34]

The shunning in the media proceeded for the next several years. For the first six months of 2002, more than 75 percent of the Sunday talk shows on CBS, Fox, and NBC featured *no* female guests (Fox was female-free 83 percent of the time). There were other signs of slippage. By the end of 2002, the share of female newspaper executives had dropped to 26 percent (from 29 percent in 2000), the proportion of female top newspaper editors had slid to 20 percent (from 25 percent in 2000), and the number of women in the "heir apparent" second-in-command editor slots had declined to zero. By 2003, the percentage of women in daily newsrooms had fallen for two years running and, by 2004, the percentage of female news directors at TV and radio stations was also showing signs of erosion.[35]

In 2005, FAIR once again counted the male and female bylines on the op-ed pages of the major dailies and once again found whopping gender imbalances. (At the *Washington Post*, women had only 10.4 percent of the bylines. At the *New York Times*, the women had 16.9 percent, still worse than the proportion a month before 9/11, when it stood at 22 percent.) Female commentators on the TV talk shows similarly remained in short supply, and left-of-center female commentators, the FAIR study noted, were "virtually absent." "During the six months studied," FAIR reported, "only one progressive woman made an appearance on a Sunday panel: Katrina vanden Heuvel of the *Nation* (*Chris Matthews Show*, 2/6/05)." The few slots that did remain for women were overwhelmingly occupied by conservatives.

By the mid-2000s, and despite Katie Couric's much-touted elevation to *CBS Evening News* anchor, women's media profile remained depressed. In 2006, Ruth Davis Konigsberg, an editor at *Glamour* who was struck by the recent masculinizing of bylines in general-interest magazines, crunched the numbers and found dismayingly lopsided ratios of male-to-female writers: 3:1 on average, 4:1 in the *New Yorker*, and 7:1 in *Harper's*. That November, television news coverage of the national election reflected the new realities. How had we wound up in this "throwback to the days of Brylcreem and cigarette smoke," *New York Times* critic Alessandra Stanley asked two days later. "Tuesday night's tableau of men talking to men all across prime time was oddly atavistic, a stag party circa 1962."[36]

Jennifer L. Pozner, the executive director of Women in Media & News, was among the few to go looking for an explanation for the disappearance of women from the media in the months after 9/11. The answers she got were less than satisfying. "Listen, this is a war situation," the executive producer of CBS's *Face the Nation* said when asked about the show's sudden paucity of female guests; gender was no longer pertinent. "We're a half-hour show; we can't have on everyone." The executive producer of NBC's *Meet the Press* told Pozner that the show's largely female audience would be "insulted" if the network were to "try to manipulate" the news to invite women instead of just "delivering newsmakers." "So, there are 'newsmakers,' and then there are women?" Pozner wondered. Significantly, the talk shows failed to invite some obvious 9/11 newsmakers who *were* women: neither Senator Barbara Boxer nor Senator Dianne Feinstein, both chairs of subcommittees on terrorism, was asked to make an appearance. Anyway, women were missing from the *non*-war-situation segments, too. The White House Project found that women on the Sunday talk shows were "underrepresented on every topic and in every category of experience."[37]

In December 2001, the White House Project unveiled what would be the first of three detailed studies documenting women's media erasure. The media coverage of the project's findings, as a Nexis database search of American newspapers, magazines, and television programs indicated, was sparse: one freelance article in the "Woman News" section of the *Chicago Tribune*, one short comment piece in the *Chicago Sun-Times*, and a cursory mention in a TV column in the *Boston Herald*. Over the next several years, various other studies of women's shrinking profile would be similarly disregarded. The silencing of women took place largely in silence.[38]

WHAT MADE THE post-9/11 disappearances of feminist and liberal female voices all the more strange was that, at first, it looked like the terrorist attacks might give the cause of women's equality a new lease on life. One feminist issue, at least, was deemed useful to the Bush White House: the repression of Afghan women. After months of being snubbed, the Feminist Majority Foundation, which had been trying to call attention to the Taliban's abuse of women since 1996, found itself in the astonishing position of playing belle of the capital ball. As did many other feminist groups. At the White House (which had just recently abolished the Office for Women's Initiatives), director of public liaison Lezlee Westine began contacting women's rights organizations and asking them to seek "common ground" with the administration that had iced them since its inception. "Let's really analyze where we can come together," she urged. Martha Burk of the National Council of Women's Organizations received three or four summonses to the White House and, for a while, was fielding calls from administration officials almost once a week.[39]

Feminist leaders were invited to brief, among others, Karen Hughes, national security adviser Condoleezza Rice, Secretary of State Colin Powell, and a bevy of top State Department officials. "They were *anxious* to meet with us," Eleanor Smeal, president of the Feminist Majority, told me. "In fact, they apologized" for not having met sooner—and even for not having more women on staff. Both houses of Congress held hearings on women's status in Afghanistan—in which they enthusiastically applauded Smeal's appeal to "make sure that women are at the table" and "not treated as a side issue." And the White House held a "women's-only" conference call with members of Congress on the situation of Afghan women.

The feminist message seemed to be adopted. "The central goal of the terrorists is the brutal oppression of women," Bush pronounced before an audience of women's rights activists as he signed the Afghan Women and Children Relief Act on December 12, 2001. Laura Bush gave the first First Lady presidential radio address "to kick off a world-wide effort," as she put it, "to focus on the brutality against women and children by the al-Qaida terrorist network and the regime it supports in Afghanistan, the Taliban." Colin Powell announced that "the rights of the women of Afghanistan will not be negotiable," and his State Department issued with much fanfare a "Report on the Taliban's War against Women," adorned with quotes from Afghan women detailing their oppression and even a poem from anthropologist and activist Zieba Shorish-Shamley's *Look into My World*. "They made me invisible, shrouded and non-being / A shadow, no existence, made silent and unseeing / Denied of freedom, confined to my cage / Tell me how to handle my anger and my rage?"[40]

The governmental glasnost had a counterpart in the media, where images of burka-clad women became a staple of television news and newsweekly features. Journalist Saira Shah's documentary about women under the Taliban, *Beneath the Veil*, made for British television and formerly overlooked and underexposed in America, enjoyed multiple airings on CNN and was excerpted on two of the networks. American press correspondents hastened to Afghanistan to write about "a world of ghost women": "blue ghosts," "walking ghosts," "shrouded ghosts," "downtrodden ghosts," and "silent ghosts." The media seemed riveted by that feminine silence and made some effort, albeit generally unsuccessful, to get these women to speak. "Over the last week I've been rebuffed by dozens of Afghan women," *New York Times* columnist Nicholas Kristof regretfully reported. Back home, press inquiries about the Taliban's oppression of women poured into the Feminist Majority, which had previously had so much trouble drawing media interest to the subject that it had been reduced to sending a letter about Afghan women's plight to "Dear Abby."[41]

And then it stopped. As soon as the bombs began dropping over Afghanistan in early October 2001, the White House claims of concern for women's rights came to a halt. The "betrayal by the Bush administration," as the national coordinator of the Feminist Majority cast it, came swiftly. One moment the Bush administration was declaring that "the restoration of women's rights" was the centerpiece of its mission in Afghanistan, the next it was busy bartering those rights away. "Right now we have other priorities," a senior administration official told the *New York Times* when asked, only two and a half weeks into the invasion of Afghanistan, what role women's rights would have in a future government. "We have to be careful not to look like we are imposing our values on them." The Bush administration–sanctioned final government draft of the Afghan constitution did not include an equal rights guarantee. After much protest from women's groups and women delegates to the Loya Jirga council on the constitution in January 2004, a guarantee was inserted, though hardly enforced. In the months and years to come, as Afghan women's lives once again became perilous, there would be no more calls to "kick off a worldwide effort" on behalf of women and no more claims purveyed that women's issues were nonnegotiable.[42]

In the media, too, women's rights in Afghanistan were abandoned as a cause, surviving only in sporadic regurgitations by mostly male voices. The most heralded of the American "feminist" contributions to the women of Afghanistan were beauty tips. "One of the first dramatic signs of liberation," *Afghan Communicator*, an English-language magazine, reported, "was the return of Afghan women to beauty salons." Backed by more than a million dollars from Revlon, Clairol, L'Oréal, Mac, and America's leading fashion magazines, "beauticians without borders" made repeated pilgrimages to Kabul to train a new generation of hair and makeup stylists. An American-backed beauty school even operated out of the new Afghani Women's Ministry, until government officials soured on its presence. *Vogue* contributed $25,000 to the effort and bestowed the "Anna Wintour Award" (a $500 pair of scissors) on one of the beauty school's graduates, Trina Ahmedi, for her way with a mascara wand. The feature film *The Beauty Academy of Kabul* was soon playing in American cineplexes. The endeavor was not without a certain utility: in Afghanistan, a beautician could earn more than a doctor and could ply her trade from home, an advantage in a nation where, despite the supposed defeat of the burka, many women were still housebound. But the target audience for this campaign was always here in the United States. The beauty industry was celebrating, as its representatives put it repeatedly, American women's "freedom of choice."[43]

Very quickly, women's rights went from being a reason to invade Afghanistan to an irrelevancy. The conservative media, which had never really supported a feminist campaign on behalf of Afghan women, saluted this turn of events. "Liberals should not support the war because the Taliban is hostile to feminism," the *National Review* instructed on November 5, 2001, in an article titled "What We're Not Fighting For." The magazine's list of "nots," which included "short skirts, dancing, and secularism" and the right to an abortion, was illustrated with a photograph of Britney Spears with a bared midriff. "They should support it because they are patriots." In the *Washington Times*, Cliff Kincaid, president of America's Survival, railed against U.S. feminist involvement in Afghanistan's reconstruction. "The Afghan people need food, water and shelter, not social experimentation directed by the National Organization for Women," he said. "This feminist interference in Afghanistan's future could give the term 'Ugly American' new meaning."[44]

Giving new meaning to "damned if you do, damned if you don't," conservative writers simultaneously harangued feminists for *abandoning* women's concerns in Afghanistan. "At the very moment feminists should be finishing the battle that they began, they are nowhere to be found," Sarah Wildman claimed in the *New Republic*. "As news of the appalling miseries of women in the Islamic world has piled up, where are the feminists?" Manhattan Institute's Kay Hymowitz demanded to know. "Where's the outrage?" After a dismissive one-sentence nod to the Feminist Majority's long-standing campaign for Afghan women's rights, she went on to insist: "You haven't heard a peep from feminists. . . . They have averted their eyes from the harsh, blatant oppression of millions of women, even while they have continued to stare into the Western patriarchal abyss, indignant over female executives who cannot join an exclusive golf club and college women who do not have their own lacrosse teams."[45]

Nicholas Kristof of the *New York Times* echoed that same bizarre claim in a somewhat different context. One of many journalists to become fixated on the scourge of "sex-slave trafficking" in the post-9/11 period (to the neglect of *work*-slave trafficking, a far more common problem), Kristof famously launched a one-man crusade to buy two Cambodian prostitute girls from their keepers. (His effort boomeranged when one of the girls fled her liberation and returned to the brothel.) In the midst of that campaign, the columnist rounded on the very feminist groups that had been fighting for women's rights in the Third World for years. Organizations like the Feminist Majority were "complacent on trafficking" and "shamefully lackadaisical about an issue that should be near the top of any feminist agenda," he wrote.[46]

Why would some pundits who were themselves sympathetic to the plight of Afghan women be so hostile to the American women combating that selfsame evil? That conundrum revealed a subtle yet profound distinction: the pundits were caught up in a separate drama that didn't have much to do with the feminist cause. If anything, feminists were seen as rivals who threatened to hijack the drama's starring roles. Behind the media fascination with Taliban oppression lay a desire to promote not women's rights but American chivalry. Which may explain why so much of the post-9/11 media coverage revolved around rescue fantasies instead of female liberation. Story after story seemed to confirm that America was "saving" women, if only from their burkas.

Dozens of dispatches reported with smug self-congratulation on the morning the U.S. troops took Kabul and a handful of women on the street celebrated by casting aside their floor-length veils. A condescending *Newsweek* article described a "giggling and babbling" circle of women who were so grateful they sprinkled a reporter with confetti and offered to wash her hair. The media made much, too, of the U.S. military's supposed "rescue" of two American women who were among eight aid workers jailed by the Taliban for three months for preaching Christianity. "I want to thank our military for rescuing these girls," Bush said of Heather Mercer and Dayna Curry, who were, in fact, adult women and who had been freed by Northern Alliance soldiers, not American troops. *Newsweek*'s headline announced that these two women had been "Delivered from

Evil," and the accompanying story took pains to note that Curry (who was thirty years old) was known as a "real girl" who "likes to wear cute clothes and fix her hair." CNN correspondent Tom Mintier enthused that the "girls'" story "sounded like the script from a Hollywood movie, but this was real life." That same week, CNN rushed to air *Unholy War*, the sequel to the documentary *Beneath the Veil*, which narrowed its focus to the attempted media rescue of three motherless little girls who had appeared in the first film. In an interview with Larry King, *Beneath the Veil* director Cassian Harrison said the concentration on the girls was warranted because their "image" was "a metaphor for the entire situation inside Afghanistan."[47]

Or maybe Afghanistan was a metaphor for the girl, the nation as female captive abducted by molesting desperadoes and waiting passively for virile America to save her from degradation. The captivity-and-rescue metaphor underlay Bush's declaration on the first anniversary of 9/11 that we had "raised this lamp of liberty to every captive land."[48] It was evident, too, in the words of Defense Secretary Donald Rumsfeld, who crowed in an interview with National Public Radio, in February 2002, that the United States had saved Afghan women: "Women have stopped being repressed. They can actually walk out in the street and not have their entire faces and bodies covered by burkas. They can laugh on the street." Whether they could actually wield power, he didn't say. The persistence of the rescue language was a sign of an insidious differentiation that had prevailed from the start. Coming to the rescue of women was a cause to be celebrated, as long as the rescuers were men and as long as the women acted as if they needed rescuing.[49] Interestingly, the initiative for Afghani women that the Bush administration most adamantly opposed was financing for women-run NGOs in Afghanistan. For all the talk about women being pivotal to democracy, the only proposal by feminist leaders that the White House seriously pursued was an office to monitor sex trafficking. If women proved capable of fending for themselves, if they laid claim to agency instead of violation and dependency, the rescue drama fell to pieces.[50]

A couple of years later, the administration was again claiming to come to the defense of women's rights—this time in Iraq. The State Department unveiled the Iraqi Women's Democracy Initiative, a grant program "to help women become full and vibrant partners in Iraq's developing democ-racy." That this pledge was less than heartfelt might be deduced from the announcement made that same day, identifying one of the first grant re-cipients: the antifeminist Independent Women's Forum. Once more, the narrative of female captives and male saviors prevailed over the lip service to female independence. Once more, a nation became the metaphor for the girl. As the December 17, 2001, cover of *National Review* cast it early on, Iraq was a violated country "in need of rescue from its regime." Bush spoke incessantly of avenging Hussein's "rape rooms" but rarely of safe-guarding Iraqi women's status as one of the most emancipated female populations in the Muslim world (a status they would soon lose, follow-ing the American invasion). In the years to come, the same sex-coded res-cue language would be invoked to justify the quagmire. America would never abandon Iraq or any nation, President Bush vowed, that wasn't "ca-pable of defending herself."[51]

CHAPTER 2

The Return of Superman

AMERICA WILL NEED MORE "HEROES," DEFENSE SECRETARY DONALD Rumsfeld told the Armed Forces one day after 9/11, and however reliable his intelligence on matters of actual defense, on this point he proved prescient.[1] The press, for its part, heeded Rumsfeld's pronouncement by nominating him to the role, in the process dressing him up in some curious costumes. *National Review*'s December 31, 2001, cover story featured a drawing of Rumsfeld in Betty Grable pose, beside the headline "The Stud: Don Rumsfeld, America's New Pin-Up." "Reports have it that people gather round to watch Rumsfeld press conferences the way they do Oprah," the story claimed. "Women confide that they have . . . well, un-defense-policy-like thoughts about the secretary of defense." Fox called Rumsfeld a "babe magnet," and *People* named him one of the "sexiest men alive." Conservative doyenne Midge Decter penned a book-length valentine, *Rumsfeld: A Personal Portrait*, which included beefcake shots of the young "Rumstud" as a bicep-bulging wrestler and a socialite's breathy confession that she kept his photo tacked to her dressing-room wall. "He works standing up at a tall writing table," Decter wrote, "as if energy, or perhaps determination, might begin to leak away from too much sitting down." His secret, she said, was "manliness."[2]

However odd the idolatry, Rumsfeld wasn't alone in receiving the award for best actor in an unconvincing role. His boss also got the treatment. Passing tactfully over the president's initial missing-in-action performance after 9/11, *Newsweek* assured readers that George Bush was exercising heroic control: "Behind the scenes, aides say, Bush never exhibited anything but serenity, focus and determination," and he was presiding over war-room sessions with "a commander's grip." In the *Weekly Standard*, Fred Barnes declared Bush "a man with a mission," driven by "a calling like that of a fireman who feels called to his work to save people." Barnes's evidence: "He could have taken a less dangerous, better paying job, but he didn't." David Brooks marveled at Bush's "strenuous tone" and likened his speaking style to Teddy Roosevelt's.[3]

The media seemed eager to turn our designated guardians of national security into action toys and superheroes. Long before Bush's own dress-up moment on the USS *Abraham Lincoln*, the press was draping him in metaphoric cape and tights and marveling at his "overnight transformation," as if Bush had stepped into a phone booth instead of a plane on 9/11. The president's vows to get the "evildoers" won him media praise *because* it sounded cartoonish. *Wall Street Journal* columnist and former Republican speechwriter Peggy Noonan exulted that she half expected Bush to "tear open his shirt and reveal the big 'S' on his chest." UPI's national political analyst, Peter Roff, said Bush's post-9/11 rhetoric reminded him of the " 'Whams,' 'Pows,' 'Biffs,' and 'Whaps' " of Batman, Bulletman, and the Shadow—a resemblance he applauded. "This is just the kind of hero America needs right now," Roff wrote, because comic book language "rallies the nation to even greater accomplishments and sacrifice, bringing forth great leaders to rescue the country." *Time* dubbed Bush, approvingly, our "Lone Ranger." *Newsweek* called him America's "dragon slayer" and "a boyish knight in a helmet of graying hair." Saint George hadn't slain any cave dwellers yet, but he was primed, *Newsweek* said, pointing, for lack of better evidence, to the president's exercise regimen. Bush was "in the best shape of his life," Howard Fineman wrote, "a fighting machine who has dropped 15 pounds and cut his time in the mile to seven minutes. . . . Drumming a pen on the conference table, he hummed with focused energy. There's a term for it in horse racing. When a thoroughbred is at peak condition, and twitching with eagerness to run, he is 'on the muscle.' That was Bush last week."[4]

A *Vanity Fair* cover-story photo essay featured Bush as a flinty cowboy in chief, sporting a Texas-sized presidential belt buckle—and assigned all the president's men superhero monikers: Dick Cheney was "The Rock," John Ashcroft "The Heat" ("Tough times demand a tough man"), and Tom Ridge "The Protector" ("At six feet three, with a prominent Buzz Lightyear jaw, he certainly has the right appearance for a director of homeland security"). Rumsfeld had "gone to the mat with al-Qaeda, displaying the same matter-of-fact, oddly reassuring ruthlessness." And national security officials Richard Armitage, Paul Wolfowitz, and Stephen Hadley were "almost as battle-scarred." At least at the gym, where Armitage "can bench-press 440 pounds."[5]

Not all readers were impressed. In the subsequent letters column—which reran the group shot of the White House's manliest in the Oval Office, this time with the caption "Magnificent Seven" affixed to it—a reader from Dallas said: "Please, I have never seen so much self-indulgent melodrama. Is our society so desperate for stimulation and drama that we can no longer see reality? This is not a war and G.W.B. sure as hell isn't Winston Churchill or FDR."[6] An explanation of a sort had been provided in advance by *Vanity Fair* editor in chief Graydon Carter, who asked himself in an "editor's letter" that accompanied the photo essay: "Why, during one of the most trying periods in U.S. history over the past half century, would the mandarins of the West Wing interrupt their normal course of business to allow our team to roam the halls, rig lights, and set up makeshift studios?" His answer: "Because it's not just strength but images of strength that matter in the 21st century war. And because, I like to think, the pages of *Vanity Fair* more than any other two-dimensional space in our culture, have taken on a status equivalent to the High Sierra of the Public Image."[7]

Whatever the realities, appearance was the thing. Thus the Rumsfeld *National Review* pinup or *Newsweek*'s gush over the macho glamour of

Rudy Giuliani. The mayor displayed a "gritty command presence," *Newsweek*'s Jonathan Alter informed us in "Grit, Guts, and Rudy Giuliani." Hizzoner had proven himself our savior—according to Alter's evidentiary list—by the way he told a "distraught" woman "It's going to be OK," by the way he gave a "young rowdy" the shushing "he deserved," and by the way he ate his first post-9/11 meal, "wolfing down" a sandwich made of "meats that sweat." *Time* named the mayor its 2001 "Person of the Year" in a cover story that likewise fixed on the accoutrements of "presence" more than actions. When the mayor retired for the evening, the magazine confided, he "parked his muddy boots next to the bed in case he needed to head out fast." Then he settled back and "pulled out a book—*Churchill*, the new biography."[8]

That particular comparison was not always implicit. "He's our Winston Churchill," Alter wrote in another *Newsweek* column devoted to the mayor in the very next issue. By "walking the rubble, calming and inspiring his heartbroken but defiant people," the mayor was "setting a new global standard for crisis leadership." But lest allusions to great statesmen prove insufficient, the *Time* cover presented the mayor as mighty superhero: the cover story, headlined "Rudy Giuliani: Tower of Strength," portrayed him at the edge of the observation deck of a Manhattan skyscraper, as if poised to make a Superman swoop on Metropolis.[9]

Not to be outdone on the action-hero front, Bush's handlers enlisted conservative screenwriter Lionel Chetwynd (*Hanoi Hilton* and *The Heroes of Desert Storm*) to make a docudrama championing Bush's post-9/11 valor. Like the *Vanity Fair* hagiographers before him, Chetwynd received full access to Bush, Rumsfeld, Rove, and the rest of the White House champions. The resulting fiction, *DC 9/11: Time of Crisis* (which was peer-reviewed for political correctness by fellow conservative writers Fred Barnes, Charles Krauthammer, and Morton Kondracke), aired on Showtime in the fall of 2003. The film features a Kryptonite-proof commander in chief (played by Timothy Bottoms) who, when he is not hefting barbells, pumping iron at the butterfly press, and running "three hard miles," is barking out lines like "Rummy, high-alert status! Delta. Military. CIA. FBI. Everything! And if you haven't gone to Def Con 3, you oughta." Rummy: "Done!" The Showtime Bush was part Hulk Hogan ("We're gonna kick the hell outta whoever did this! No slap-on-the-wrist game this time!"), part Rambo ("This will decidedly not be Vietnam!"), and part Dirty Harry ("If some tinhorn terrorist wants me, tell him to come over and get me! I'll be at home waiting for the bastard!") Like all good super-heroes, he saves the girls, comforting an adoring and weepy Condi, order-ing "full security" on Laura and his daughters, and guiding his nearsighted wife to safety in the White House basement (Laura's lack of contact lenses is presented as a Helen Keller situation. Laura: "I can't see!" Bush, consol-ing as he leads her down the steps: "You OK?"). Later, Bush visits a hospi-tal and soothes a woman injured in the World Trade Center collapse. "Take care of us," she whispers. Bush: "You count on it!"[10]

On October 17, 2001, the *Today* show interviewed a man who could be billed as an expert in heroic stature, Joe Quesada, editor in chief of Mar-vel. The company had hurried into production an oversized comic book lauding the "extraordinary heroes" of 9/11. "I was getting e-mails from fans almost instantly saying, you know, Marvel needs to step up," Quesada told *Today*. "And the idea just clicked in my brain and the name 'Heroes' came to mind, and—and right away, the—the slogan, the world's greatest comic creators honoring the world's greatest superh—or—or heroes, actually." He advised viewers to phone 1-888-COMICBO[OK] to locate their nearest comics store. *Heroes*, a sixty-four-page all-color poster book—featuring such images as a fireman carrying a limp woman away from the smoldering ruins—sold out its hundred thousand print run in one day.[11] In the months to follow, the comics industry churned out sim-ilar fare. "We needed to lift our pens, measure them against the swords of vengeance and the crumpled steel of anger," Paul Levitz of DC Comics declared in the introduction to *9-11*, volume 2, which was illustrated with a man and a boy donning, respectively, a fire helmet and a police cap, while a distressed young woman stood behind them, clutching a folded American flag to her breast. Each of these efforts attempted to demon-strate, as Quesada put it on a second *Today* appearance to hawk yet an-other 9/11 comic book, "that the heroic ideal was living amongst us."[12]

Comic book writers stretched the limits of that ideal, expanding the definition of hero to fit any and all acts, even putative ones. "Some of these tales we know are factual," a cartoon in 9-11, volume 2, titled "Silver Linings in a Big Dust Cloud," began, "and some we're pretty sure are accurate, and some others, well, they're just some rumors we heard, but we'd like to think they're all true!" The tales of derring-do and rumored derring-do included massage therapists who "lugged their equipment downtown" to offer "de-stressing" treatments to rescue workers, volunteers who "handed out peanut butter and jelly sandwiches, individually wrapped in baggies," and a Minnesota shoe company that made safety booties for the search dogs. At the same time, the actual superheroes— Superman, Spider-Man—were universally depicted as powerless. In the 9/11 comics, the superheroes stand in front of the smoldering mound with their arms dangling at their sides, a pose that inadvertently echoed the posture of the ground-zero searchers. In the 1940s, Superman whacked Nazi spies, while Captain America downed a "Super Soldier" serum to boost his killing powers and went to war on the front lines. Now, Spider-Man wandered ineffectually through the ruins. "Where were you?" two New Yorkers fleeing from the wreckage stop to ask him. "How could you let this happen?" Superman agonizes that "the one thing I can NOT do is break free from the fictional pages where I live and breathe, become real during times of crisis, and right the wrongs of an unjust world." But, Superman hastens to assure, America is "fortunately protected by heroes of its own." On the book's cover, he stands gazing up at a sea of men in fire helmets, hard hats, and police caps (and two female medical workers, who stand, literally, at the margins) and says, "Wow."[13]

The reversal of hero worship in the comic books underscored a troubling question in real life: why were our serious media insisting on portraying us and our leaders with such comic hyperbole? The implications of that heightening were a bit unnerving. Superheroes are fantasies for a particular type of reader: someone, typically a prepubescent boy, who feels weak in the world and insufficient to the demands of the day and who needs a Walter Mitty bellows to pump up his sense of self-worth. Was the same now true for the national audience, the American people, whose elected and appointed officials were being inflated with imaginary grit and guts into the Heat and the Protector and the Tower of Strength? Wasn't it enough that so many people had flocked to Lower Manhattan to offer their help? What about our national experience had us frantically searching for more?

IN MID-SEPTEMBER 2001, as soon as air traffic resumed, a neighbor of mine, a psychiatric social worker, flew to New York from the West Coast with no plan other than to be of service. We all knew the impulse; she was an American in an hour when, as the media kept repeating, Americans were "coming together." Then she returned, and what she brought back was silence, the silence of someone with nothing to report. And that, too, was coming to seem familiar.

It would certainly be familiar to the battalions of city firefighters, police officers, and paramedics who raced to ground zero on 9/11 from emergency services across the region, across the state, across the country; the medical and quasi-medical volunteers—internists, nurses, burn specialists, orthopedic surgeons, pediatricians, anesthesiologists, psychiatrists, even lifeguards—who staffed the dozens of MASH-style hospitals that materialized in marbled bank lobbies and shopping mall atriums and the courtyards of insurance firms; the doctors who jogged over the bridges from Brooklyn and the hundred surgeons attending a review course at Montefiore Hospital who sped to the scene in two packed buses. In front of the Salomon Smith Barney building, a mobile hospital boasted teams of twenty different specialties. At Chelsea Piers, a massive triage center filled a television studio lot with fifty operating suites and a sea of gurneys. Thousands of citizens stood in five-hour lines to offer their blood, and hundreds more showed up at the smoldering mound with garden trowels and beach buckets to dig for survivors. One man drove from Nebraska with a bulldozer in his flatbed truck.[14]

What met them was idleness. By early afternoon in front of the Salomon Smith Barney building, the mobile hospital had treated only two businessmen, both for minor breathing problems; by late afternoon at the courthouse on Foley Square, medics had tended to only one firefighter, for smoke inhalation; by dusk at Chelsea Piers, surgeons had received no visitors except a messenger with a delivery of ham-and-cheese sandwiches. The physicians and nurses who lined up beside a brigade of stretchers and wheelchairs outside New York Downtown Hospital and St. Vincent's and Bellevue and Mount Sinai and Beth Israel, waiting to greet the wounded, waited for hours, braced for a deluge that never came.[15]

Consider the tasks that followed: the turning away of the blood donors, the rolling back of the empty wheelchairs and stretchers, the folding of winding sheets meant for bodies that never arrived. Consider the fire and police and K-9 rescue teams that found no one to rescue, the volunteer excavators who excavated only a confetti of office memos and the occasional cell phone, and the medical examiners who examined only fragments of human flesh. And then consider the question: what was a rescuer without someone to rescue?

"Is there anything I can do?" one volunteer demanded of a firefighter. The firefighter replied: "There's nothing anybody can do. There's nothing anybody can do." NYPD pilot Patrick Walsh recalled what he had seen as his helicopter hovered above the World Trade Center: a man leaning from an upper window pleading for help. "He was waving a white towel," Walsh said. "And there was nothing we could do." A paramedic at a volunteer staging area surveyed the mob of idle Good Samaritans with dismay. "There's no rescue," he tried to explain. "It's just body parts. You're just going there to recover body parts."[16]

The despondency and humiliation induced by this lack of purpose eventually settled on everyone at ground zero, even on those search dogs fitted out with heroic booties. *People* magazine reported a few weeks into the recovery effort that the dogs were so demoralized their handlers had to fake "live finds," hiding for one another's animals "so that the dogs experience some success." There were no such consolation prizes for the human searchers. A *Washington Post* reporter tried to interview a physician's assistant in green scrubs, only to be treated to "a thousand-yard stare." It was "not the horror" generating the stare, the reporter wrote. "It was the impotence." An impotence that afflicted the nation at large. "It was strange that a day of war was a day we stood still," *Time* noted uneasily in its first post-9/11 issue. "We couldn't move—that must have been the whole idea—so we had no choice but to watch." We had become a nation of Chauncey Gardners.[17]

The search for survivors quickly gave way to a search for heroes, a "hero hunt," as an October 6 *New York Times* op-ed essay called it, and the hunt had a desperate quality to it. Within hours of the attack, the word was on every media lip. "There are going to be a lot of stories of heroes and miracles coming out of the mess down there," Fox News reporter Shepard Smith was saying by the evening of 9/11. "Miles, there are going to be no shortage of heroes here as we keep our eye on One Liberty Plaza," CNN correspondent Aaron Brown told fellow reporter Miles O'Brien. "We want to take a few moments and think about some of the heroes," CNN correspondent Garrick Utley said. Those few moments proved hard to fill. All Utley could offer was: "Of course, we don't know how many there were, or what was happening on that airplane that crashed in Pennsylvania, or in the Pentagon offices, or even here in Lower Manhattan." ABC correspondent Bob Brown was having similar difficulties. But he promised that exemplars were sure to surface soon. "'There is an electric fire in human nature,' John Keats said, that continually results in the birth of heroism," Brown told viewers. "Last night and today and through the long days that will follow, a lot of ordinary people will make those words come true many times."[18]

And no doubt many ordinary people did. A few of their stories would survive the World Trade Center's demise. There was John Demczur, the window washer who sawed through Sheetrock and tile with his squeegee to free himself and four other men trapped in an elevator. There was Brian Clark, an executive vice president at Euro Brokers who saved the life of Stanley Praimnath, a Fuji Bank loan officer, by digging him out from behind a wall of collapsed ceilings and office furniture. There were Michael Benfante and John Cerqueira, two telecommunications workers at Network Plus, who carried Tina Hansen, a forty-one-year-old woman in a wheelchair, down sixty-eight flights. But most of the stories of who saved whom were lost in the flames. With so few surviving Ishmaels to bear witness from the upper floors of the towers—and none in the four hijacked planes—the valor of people in the buildings and in the air so often had to be imagined.[19]

Another question, though, pressed upon Americans, a question that, as subsequent media coverage made clear, went beyond the actions of the people inside the towers and planes: what about the actions of the rest of us? The widespread feelings of helplessness led to other emotions—doubts about our own abilities to perform valorously prominent among them. A September 13 *New York Times* editorial called "The Necessary Courage" began, "Sooner or later, we all wonder if we have it in us to be brave when bravery is needed," as if confronting personal fainthearted-ness were the critical issue before the nation. "Ever since New York City was struck by a terrorist attack, the answer has been coming in, and it is just what we hoped for and expected." That same morning, the *Washington Post's* editorial, "The Horror and the Heroes," declared that the attack had "summoned heroes whose examples lift the spirits and make it easier to live on." The following day, the *Wall Street Journal* editorial, "Common Valor," proclaimed: "America has witnessed heroism on a Homeric scale."

But getting to Homeric required a sort of grade inflation. The *New York Times* asserted:

> It may simply be the strength to damp down the anxiety people natu-rally feel in the aftermath of this attack. It may be the ability to look neighbors who have lost someone directly in the eye and to accept the pain that comes with making connection. For most of us, who cannot perform medical triage or help shift debris from smoldering building sites, what needs doing most may not be obvious. But sooner or later it will make itself known, and doing it will be more than enough.[20]

Newsweek's Jonathan Alter devoted three columns to his own fruitless search for displays of Greatest Generation–style patriotism and heroism. "There is little concrete to do," he conceded. "No regiments to volunteer for or bandages to wrap or victory gardens to grow." Nonetheless, he maintained, "a more subtle collective task is, in fact, at hand, one that can be fulfilled in millions of conversations and small acts across the country." Very small, in fact, like "avoid depressive and sour thinking." Or maybe the task was to do nothing new at all. "After the early helpless-ness," *Time* writer Nancy Gibbs counseled in the magazine's lead story af-ter 9/11, "people started to realize that what they could do was exactly, as precisely as possible, whatever they would have done if all this hadn't happened."[21]

One of the day's darkest incidents offered the brightest hope. Flight 93 was more perfect for mythmaking for being so scant in its facts. "Did they do what we think they did?" *Time* asked in its September 24 issue. "Did three strangers on a flight in distress band together to fight their captors and ditch the Boeing 757 before it could harm untold thousands?" The magazine's answer: "We'd like to think they did it." This speculation wasn't far advanced from that of a week and a half earlier. "If, in fact, the passengers intervened and somehow thwarted the hijacking attempt," CBS reporter Bob Orr hypothesized on air to Dan Rather before noon of Septermber 12, "and the cockpit tape and the flight data recorder, when they're recovered, might make this case, then they should be observed in this case, Dan, as heroes." On CNN that day, correspondent Miles O'Brien was indulging in the same wistful speculations. He had no real information about what transpired aboard the hijacked United plane that crashed in a field in Shanksville, Pennsylvania. "We can only surmise," he said. Nonetheless he concluded, "If you're looking for heroes, the passengers on board that plane, obviously now perished, would be them." By September 13, the *Washington Post* was running the story of Flight 93 on page 1, with this declaration: "Some are already describing as heroes the passengers who may have tried to thwart the hijackers' plans."[22]

The recovered flight recordings yielded sounds of muffled shouts and screams just before the crash, but no great clarity. Flight 93 heroism rested on a few brief cell phone calls—most notably, medical-device executive Thomas Burnett's remark to his wife that they were going to "have to do something"—and the last enigmatic words of software salesman Todd Beamer, after reciting the Lord's Prayer, overheard by an Airfone operator: "You ready? OK. Let's roll." Beyond that, the media based their case on the assertions of family members that their loved one was "a take-charge guy" (Jeremy Glick), "a go-to guy" who "didn't take no for an answer" (Todd Beamer), and a man who would "never go down without a fight" (Thomas Burnett)—remarks treated by the network correspondents like hard news leads. In a September 18 interview on *Good Morning America*, Diane Sawyer peppered the men's widows with leading statements: "You really believe in your hearts you know what happened," she told Lyz Glick. "And, Lisa, you feel that way, too," she told Lisa Beamer. "So you feel maybe they got control, got into the cockpit but they weren't pilots, they didn't know how to fly the plane?"[23]

"There is something about the similarities of these three passengers that makes the portrait of them as confederates perfectly imaginable," Time said of passengers Thomas Burnett, Jeremy Glick, and another traveling businessman, Mark Bingham, who had been added to the list of heroes (based largely on the belief of Bingham's family and friends that "he would have jumped into action"). "All three were large, athletic, decisive types," Time said, ranking them by height: Mark Bingham: "6 ft. 5 in.," "played rugby when at the University of California, Berkeley"; Jeremy Glick: "6 ft. 4 in.," "a national collegiate judo champion"; and Thomas Burnett: "6 ft. 1 in.," "a former high school football player." Todd Beamer's basketball and baseball exploits in high school and college were much noted, as was the fact that he had hung a painting of Michael Jordan in his home office. "As a teenage basketball player," Time said typically, "Todd Beamer was the kind of guy you wanted on the free-throw line in a tied game." On CNBC, host Brian Williams tried to glean macho significance out of the flight's early hour. "At a very basic level," he said, this was "the overachievers' express. You've got to want to fly to San Francisco at 8 a.m. In the Jersey suburbs, that means waking up at 4 or 5 to get there; there are later flights later in the day."[24]

Such versions left out a somewhat shorter, lighter cohort. On Flight 93, flight attendant Sandra Bradshaw called home, too, to report her part in the cabin revolt: she and another flight attendant were boiling coffee pots of water to scald the terrorists. "We're going to throw water on them and try to take the airplane over," she told her husband. Then she said she had to hang up because she was "running to first class" with her chosen weapons. Other phone calls record female flight attendants and female passengers displaying courage. But these stories never garnered the same media adulation. The myth taking shape demanded male rescuers and female captives. In that story, Sandra Bradshaw's coffeepot could not become a symbol of American gumption. The flight attendants were assigned another role, as frightened damsels whose distress turned them into inadvertent sirens. As Newsweek put it, "The screams of the attendants may have lured the copilots out of their cockpits." There was no place for live-action superheroines—not even in the superheroic world of the comics. Dark Horse Comics' 9-11: *Artists Respond* was typical in its portrayal of the uprising as an all-male action show: its story about Flight 93 described how "the male passengers had voted" to assault the hijackers and how the wives and mothers at home on their cell phones begged the men to stay in their seats. (In fact, Lyz Glick had encouraged her husband to go on the attack, and Mark Bingham's mother had left two voice mails instructing her son to take command: "Mark, this is your mom. . . . I would say go ahead and do everything you can to overpower them because they're hell-bent" and, soon after, "So if you can, try to take over the aircraft.") The closest the Dark Horse narrative came to countenancing a female role was its concession that flight attendant CeeCee Lyles (a former police officer trained in hand-to-hand combat) may have "helped" the men.[25]

Meanwhile, the athletic pursuits and vital statistics of Flight 93's virile contingent, repeated over and over in media reports, assumed mythic dimensions. Here is the opening sequence from NBC's October 2 *Dateline* special on the flight:

HOST JANE PAULEY: With only 37 ticketed passengers, there'd be plenty of room to stretch out on a long trip. And some of the passengers were pretty big guys. Mark Bingham was a rugby player.

(Newark Airport sign; terminal sign; inside of plane; photo of Mark Bingham)

ALICE HOGLAN [Bingham's mother]: He is powerful. He's six foot five, a big, physically fit guy.

PAULEY: (Voiceover) So was Jeremy Glick, a six-footer.

(Photo of Jeremy Glick)

UNIDENTIFIED WOMAN NO. 1: He was like a giant teddy bear. You just fell into his arms and wanted to stay there forever.

PAULEY: (Voiceover) And Lou Nacke, only 5'9," but 200 pounds of muscle. He was a weight lifter with a Superman tattoo on his shoulder.

(Photo of Lou Nacke)

UNIDENTIFIED WOMAN NO. 2: When he was a little boy, he loved Superman. And he'd actually had a cape on and went through a glass window pretending to be Superman.[26]

The superhero preoccupations of the men on Flight 93 seemed pertinent to *New York Times* reporter Jere Longman, too, who cited them in his subsequent book, *Among the Heroes: United Flight 93 and the Passengers and Crew Who Fought Back*. Not only did Lou Nacke sport the "red-and-yellow Superman logo" on his arm, Longman reported, Jeremy Glick "had a great affection for superheroes," calling his mother Wonder Woman and once accidentally wearing "his Superman pajama top to elementary school." Just a few weeks before his fateful flight, Glick "had gone wakeboarding on costume day at his house on Greenwood Lake in northern New Jersey, and he had dressed as the Green Lantern." Moreover, Longman continued, Glick "favored movies like *Braveheart*, which featured a central hero, and, as a child, he and his older brother Jonah created extravagant rescue-and-adventure games based on the television series *Emergency*."[27]

Piecing together all the scraps of evidence, the 9/11 Commission ultimately concluded that the passengers of Flight 93 likely did attempt to confront the hijackers but did not succeed in entering the cockpit. "The hijackers remained at the controls but must have judged that the passengers were only seconds from overcoming them," the commission's report stated. But this version of events—valorous in its own right—was insufficient to support the grand opera the media was determined to stage. In a "ferocious assault," *Newsweek* said, a "band of patriots came together to defy death and save a symbol of freedom." The men of Flight 93 were a "group of citizen soldiers who rose up, like their forefathers, to defy tyranny. And when they came storming down the aisle, it wasn't the Americans who were afraid. It was the terrorists." The same theme was struck in article after article, book after book. "You see, as much as the terrorists had meticulously planned their suicide missions," *Heroes: 50 Stories of the American Spirit* held, "they could never have foreseen the problems they'd encounter trying to maintain control on a flight carrying what you have to concede was God's All-Star Team."[28]

"Courage and optimism led the passengers on Flight 93 to rush their murderers to save lives on the ground, led by a young man whose last known words were the Lord's Prayer and 'Let's roll,' " Bush declared in his national address on November 8, 2001. "We will, no doubt, face new challenges. But we have our marching orders: my fellow Americans, let's roll!" In a matter of weeks, polls were reporting that the most admired people in the country were President Bush, Mayor Rudy Giuliani, and . . . Todd Beamer. Post offices were named in his honor, and "Let's Roll!" was emblazoned on everything from a jet in the New Jersey Air National Guard's 177th Fighter Squadron to kids' backpacks to computer mouse pads to firecrackers. It became the title of a Neil Young song and the rallying cry (delivered, again, by Bush) to open the Olympics. The Florida State Seminoles adopted it as the team motto. The U.S. Patent and Trademark Office was besieged with applications from businesses wanting to use the phrase as part of their trademark. The rush to cash in on the credo proved so intense that the Todd M. Beamer Foundation, a 9/11 children's charity fund set up by Beamer's widow (now known as Heroic Choices), applied to trademark the phrase.[29]

By the time *Vanity Fair* ran its December 2001 account, "Manifest Courage: The Story of Flight 93," the male passengers had entered Valhalla. Theirs was perhaps "one of the greatest tales of heroism ever told," *Vanity Fair*'s Bryan Burrough wrote. The men "had not merely proved themselves heroes, but also created an authentic American legend and quite probably changed the course of American history as well." Their story "is swiftly passing into the realm of American mythology, a tale we will tell our children and grandchildren just as previous generations told tales of heroism during other wars; the names of the passengers may soon be known as other generations knew the names of Audie Murphy and the Sullivan brothers and John F. Kennedy."[30]

Congress drew up the True American Heroes Act to award gold medals to the heroes of Flight 93. At first, proposed legislation singled out the same four men the media had elevated: Burnett, Glick, Bingham, and Beamer. But then relatives of other male passengers began complaining that their loved ones also deserved hero status. Lori Guadagno, sister of Richard Guadagno, told the press that she felt sure her brother took on the terrorists, because he had been trained in law enforcement and was "a man of action." For him to be overlooked was "a very hurtful, painful thing for my family and I think for others," she said. Hamilton Peterson, son of passenger Donald Peterson, told the *Pittsburgh Tribune-Review*: "I think everyone involved was a hero. I think all the victims deserve recognition."[31] Ultimately, all thirty-seven passengers and seven crew members received medals—along with every officer, firefighter, emergency worker, and government employee who responded to the World Trade Center and Pentagon attacks, Mayor Giuliani, governor George Pataki, the Port Authority commissioners, and every city fire precinct.

The line between "hero" and "victim" was evidently thin. The "seeming passivity" of the passengers on the other hijacked planes, Charles Krauthammer worried in *Time*, "is reminiscent of the Holocaust." But with Flight 93, that was behind us. We should feel safe now, *Time*'s Nancy Gibbs assured in an October 22 article whose title, "Shadow of Fear," belied her assertion of resurging American confidence. "If anyone tries anything now, the guy in 9A will go low, 11C will hit high and the hijacker will end up stuffed in an overhead bin," she wrote, supporting her supposition with the examples of an unnamed St. Louis banker who was "spending extra time on the firing range these days" and an unnamed New York bartender who "packed a pair of heavy construction gloves for his flight to Los Angeles—just in case he has to confront someone with a box cutter."[32]

It was as though the medals handed out for Flight 93 were only secondarily about honoring a fight against foreign antagonists. The primary contest was a war against the wasting disease suspected to have overtaken the male professional class. Tribute was being paid to men who were corporate functionaries, who represented all those coffee-clutching, wrinkle-suited middle managers who sat in airport lounges, wielding their cell phones and speaking louder than was strictly necessary about quarterly sales composites. By taking on the terrorists, the white-collar men of Flight 93 were assuring their brethren that the "feminized society" wasn't irreversible, after all.

"Who are Beamer, Glick, Burnett, and the rest?" William Bennett asked in the finale of his book *Why We Fight*. "They were guys in jackets and ties, guys in white shirts, businessmen, family men, representatives of the great American middle class, the most maligned class in history." By which, he soon made clear, he meant the most maligned class of *men*. "Only a couple of years ago, the movie *American Beauty* had set out to capture the spirit of American suburbia today," he wrote, "the land of middle-class businessmen like Beamer and Glick and Burnett: married, white, comfortable . . . and utterly lost." But the actions on board United's hijacked plane showed that the American middle-class male was no longer "squashed down," as Bennett phrased it. The men of Flight 93 had prevailed in the culture wars, defeated their PC humiliators, and, Bennett concluded, proved that "*American Beauty* is a lie."[33]

Fighting the gender war seemed to be a preoccupying concern, too, of Mark Steyn's November 19 article, "Local Heroes," in the *National Review*, in which he denounced the proponents of nanny-state big government—"Hillary & Co." prominent among them—for having de-balled American men in the air just as they had on the ground. The airline cabin was "the perfect symbol" of "the modern social-democratic state," he wrote, with a female FAA director who stripped pilots of their handguns and an oligarchy of flight attendants on every plane whose dictates had to be obeyed or "there'll be officers waiting to arrest you when the plane lands." Sexual combat even roiled the heart of the 9/11 comics, such as cartoonist Mike Carey's "Hellblazer: Exposed," in which Paul, a stoop-shouldered and graying insurance agent, is inspired by the collapse of the towers to stick it to his bitchy and avaricious female boss. She wants to limit the company's exposure to claims filed by the families of World Trade Center victims; he shames her into doing the right thing. "Like I said, this is where it turns around," the insurance agent turned tough guy tells a buddy over a man-sized stein of beer. "We're all exposed, John, or we all need to be."[34]

In real life, the oppressive boss was more likely to be a man or a faceless corporate structure—as was evident in *Let's Roll!*, the memoir of Todd Beamer's widow, Lisa Beamer. She described the demoralizing strains of her husband's job as a sales manager at Oracle: the relentless "pressure to perform" that never seemed to lead anywhere but to more pressure to perform "in a 'what have you done lately' world," the closing of "the huge deal" that yielded nothing but a few back pats that quickly "faded to stilted silence," the deluge of office e-mails, the round-the-clock demands, and the incessant business trips to mollify ungrateful clients, all of which induced a constant background hum of anxiety and self-doubt. Lisa Beamer recalled the long list of "goals" her husband had drawn up back when he was in business school. Among them: "Strive to be like my father—to be respected even when I'm not around"; "Have a meaningful job and career"; "Be a leader in society"; and "Have a comfortable home, nice cars, and a 'mahogany room'" (in other words, Lisa Beamer wrote, an old-fashioned study "where he could retreat from the world and recharge his batteries").

A few weeks after her husband's death, Lisa recalled, she was sorting through his office documents when she came across a yellowing piece of paper at the bottom of his in-box. On it was a quote from Teddy Roosevelt:

> The credit belongs to the man who is actually in the arena . . . who strives valiantly, who knows the great enthusiasms, the great devotions, and spends himself in worthy causes. Who, at best, knows the triumph of his achievement and who, at worst, if he fails, fails while daring greatly so that his place shall never be with those cold and timid souls who know neither victory nor defeat.

Lisa Beamer tried to comfort herself with the thought that her husband "did not die with the 'cold and timid souls who know neither victory nor defeat.'" Yet, he had had to live with them. And what had all those years of corporate service granted him, besides the comfortable home, the nice cars, and the mahogany room?[35]

IDENTIFYING ACTS OF courage and acknowledging people whose heroism gives solace to others is an essential part of any war effort. In the persons of its first responders, its volunteers, and even its commuters turned combatants on a hijacked airplane, America had ample paragons of courage. But the national frenzy to apotheosize those people suggested a deep cultural unease beneath the hero worship; the culture lofted them into some ridiculously gilded firmament while, at the same time, dissatisfied with their example, it kept searching for more available chests to decorate with war medals. The suddenness of the attacks and the finality of the towers' collapse and the planes' obliteration left us with little in the way of ongoing chronicle or ennobling narrative. So a narrative was created and populated with pasteboard protagonists whose exploits would exist almost entirely in the realm of American archetype and American fantasy. There was a danger in being honored with such manufactured laurels, particularly for the tragedy's survivors: for the fantasy to hold, citizens would have to stay in character, never mind that their roles were constrained and deforming, never mind that the command performance prevented them from expressing what they really had witnessed and suffered that day.

CHAPTER 3

The Cowboys of Yesterday

I N THE END, THE CHARACTER ACTORS WHO WON THE 9/11 HERO SWEEP-
stakes, hands down, were the New York City firemen. They had arrived
to save others. Their uniforms and the direction they were heading in
provided a clear demarcation between them, the heroes, and the World
Trade Center office workers, the victims. The secretaries and financial
brokers ran down the stairs; the firemen ran up—343 of them to their
deaths. And conveniently for the mythmakers, the Fire Department of
New York, more than any other urban fire agency in the nation, was
male. Less than 0.3 percent of its firefighters were women. It seemed
there would be no need to rewrite the gender roles in this drama. The
adulation began at once—and with it, the Fire Department of New York
would be exposed to the disfiguring influence of the myth machine.[1]

"If one hero has come to stand for all, it is the New York City firefighter," a *New York Times* op-ed piece declared. They were our most glorious combatants. Under the headline "The Firefighter: An American
Hero," *People* began its homage this way: "Along with the roughly 3,000

civilians killed in the World Trade Center attacks, 60 police officers also died, as did 2 fire department paramedics and 3 court officers. Yet it is the firefighters, valiant warriors on a flame-filled vertical battlefield, who have taken on the mantle of legend, like the Spitfire pilots in the Battle of Britain or Leonidas's 300 Spartans holding the line at Thermopylae—the few, to paraphrase Churchill, giving so much for so many."[2]

In our "different kind of war," these uniformed men were assigned the role of our new supersoldiers, Green Berets in red hats. "These are the men who will fight our wars," President Bush intoned, after posing with the firefighters at the smoldering ruins, bullhorn in hand, as if he were their commanding officer. "These men are fighting the first battle," Mayor Giuliani declared. In fact, he maintained, they had already won it. "Our firefighters helped save more than twenty-five thousand lives that day—the greatest single rescue mission in America's history." That was a claim the surviving firefighters themselves would regard as preposterous. Of the sixteen to eighteen thousand occupants of the World Trade Center that day, 95 percent of those who died were on the upper floors, beyond reach of rescue, and most of those on the lower floors rescued themselves without uniformed help. The grim truth is that the human toll would have been significantly lower had the firefighters never entered the buildings (about three times more firefighters than office workers died on the floors below the impact of the planes).[3]

"We were just as much victims as everybody that was in the building," Derek Brogan of Engine 5 said in his personal account, one of more than five hundred oral histories the fire department amassed of firefighters who were at the scene on 9/11: "We didn't have a chance to do anything." James Murphy put it this way in his report: "We were just victims too. Basically the only difference between us and the victims is we had flashlights."[4]

Flashlights and nonworking radios. The firefighters entered the World Trade Center armed with fifteen-year-old radios that were well known to malfunction in high-rise buildings; in particular, they had failed when the fire department last responded to a crisis at the twin towers, after the 1993 bombing. (Nor did the radios communicate with the police department. If they had, the firefighters would have heard the warning from the police helicopter pilot that the second tower was about to fall—more than twenty minutes before its collapse.) When the South Tower fell, the firefighters in the North Tower had no idea what had happened. And when the fire chief radioed a Mayday order to evacuate the North Tower, almost none of the firefighters heard it. In the bureaucratic words of a 2005 National Institute of Standards and Technology study of the World Trade Center disaster, "A preponderence of the evidence indicates that emergency responder lives were likely lost at the World Trade Center resulting from the lack of timely information-sharing and inadequate communications capabilities." Firefighters made the same point more vividly in their oral history accounts; they said they were "clueless" and knew "absolutely nothing" about what was going on outside:

> Lieutenant Brian Becker: "We had very poor handy-talkie communications. We didn't hear much of anything. There must have been maydays galore out in the street. We didn't hear any of them."
>
> Firefighter Nicholas Borrillo: "We really didn't know what was going on. We didn't know the whole building fell down. We just didn't know that."
>
> Lieutenant Neil Brosnan: "We never knew 2 World Trade Center collapsed [from listening to the radios] on channel 3. My men didn't know it, I didn't know it. In fact, I didn't know for a week later the sequence of events."
>
> Lieutenant Robert Bohack: "There was no command structure. There was nothing. Nobody can get on the radio. The fucking radio was useless."[5]

These reports were repressed for three and a half years; the mayor's office refused to make the oral histories public and relented only after an order from the state's highest court. A year before their release, former mayor Rudy Giuliani testified at a 9/11 Commission hearing that plenty of firefighters heard the Mayday order but chose to stay and help civilians. "And the fact that so many of them interpreted it that way, kept a much calmer situation and a much better evacuation," he started to say, before being cut off by outraged firefighter families in the audience, who vehemently disagreed:

UNIDENTIFIED FEMALE: No!

UNIDENTIFIED FEMALE: No!

UNIDENTIFIED MALE: Radios!

GIULIANI: And these people—

UNIDENTIFIED MALE: Talk about the radios!

GIULIANI: These people—

UNIDENTIFIED MALE: Radios!

UNIDENTIFIED FEMALE: Radios!

UNIDENTIFIED FEMALE: Radios!

UNIDENTIFIED MALE: Talk about the radio!

9/11 COMMISSION CHAIRMAN THOMAS KEAN: Would you please ask—

UNIDENTIFIED FEMALE: My son was murdered! Murdered because of incompetence, and the radios didn't work.

KEAN: You are simply wasting time at this point that could be used for questions.

UNIDENTIFIED FEMALE: You're wasting time.[6]

The firefighter families' efforts to get at the truth were shunted aside. And the myth of effective rescue soon became an unassailable and sacred truth. When Terry Golway, city editor of the *New York Observer*, published his 368-page homage to the FDNY in 2002, *So Others Might Live*, he began the prologue with this sentence: "Three hundred and forty-three members of the Fire Department of New York died on September 11, 2001, while taking part in one of the most successful rescue efforts in history."[7] We'd been saved by "knights in shining fire helmets," as both the *New York Times* and *USA Today* called them, two of the many media outlets to envision the firefighters as medieval warriors. Or maybe even demigods. The *Wall Street Journal* editorial page maintained that New York's firemen "possess a gene lacking in the rest of us." *Publishers Weekly* went further: "If ever there were heroes possessing godlike prowess, beneficence and divinity, it is the firefighters of the FDNY."[8]

The publishing industry rushed out coffee-table-book encomiums—with rapturous adulations that often read more like outtakes from *Beowulf*. "They man a hose that could be a wild animal," novelist Frank McCourt wrote in the introduction to the 2001 tribute *Brotherhood*. "They hack and smash and isolate and drown that other wild animal, the old god fire."[9] On the talk shows, hosts one-upped each other with displays of idolatry. "You guys are amazing and real heroes, in every sense of the word," Sean Hannity of Fox's *Hannity & Colmes* gushed to Chris Ingvordsen, an out-of-town volunteer firefighter who had driven to Manhattan to offer his help at ground zero. "It's an honor to meet you," Hannity said. Cohost Alan Colmes was in awe, too:

COLMES: On your own, you decided this was the place to go?

INGVORDSEN: Yeah.

COLMES: . . . That you did that on your own I think speaks volumes about who we are as Americans."[10]

"I never in my career would have anticipated the amount of accolades and attention I've been subjected to," a perplexed Captain Harold Schapelhouman, division chief for the Menlo Park Fire District in northern California, told the *San Francisco Chronicle*. Schapelhouman, like many others around the country, had come to New York to join the search for survivors. "I've had dinner with former President Clinton and Barry Bonds and Ronnie Lott, and was a guest of Willie Mays," he said. "That's just a small picture. . . . Harrison Ford served me dinner, 'Hot Lips' Houlihan served me breakfast. We had Playboy bunnies. It was surreal. . . . We walk a fine line between reality and the fiction that can be created from these events."[11]

The Playboy bunnies, or any adoring female claque, were essential to the fiction. A couple of weeks into the post-9/11 era, the media declared

the "trend" of women lusting after firefighters and the phenomenon became international news, hailed under headlines like "Firefighters Are
a Hot Commodity in the Dating Game" and "Firefighters Are Hot, Hot,
Hot; Unprecedented Female Admiration." "Suddenly they're more desirable than Brad Pitt," *New York* announced. "Women are willing to go
to great lengths to land one." The article's evidence: "one 25-year-old
magazine editor," unnamed, who "told herself that she was doing it for
America when she made out with several firemen at the event" and "her
friend," also unnamed, who "donated socks to the cause and then slept
with a fireman from Miami." "Down at New York's ground zero, the yellow 'Do Not Cross' sign has become a veritable velvet rope as stories cir-
culate of scantily clad women vamping it up for the rescue workers,"
USA Today asserted. "Lately it seems like every single woman in New
York is trying to date a fireman," said an American correspondent for the
British *Observer*, quoting a Manhattan psychotherapist who claimed,
"Firemen today are like the cowboys of yesterday." Dating one of these
"Real Men" is "now as *de rigueur* as toting the latest Louis Vuitton bag
or waxing away stray eyebrow hairs," the *Orange County Register* in-
sisted, citing—in circular logic—"culture watchers at *The New York
Times, USA Today* and *The New Yorker*."[12]

The idea that hordes of women were drooling over the men in boots
was promoted by the purveyors of firefighter calendars (sales of the "2002
Hotlanta Firemen" are "going through the roof," its merchandiser claimed),
matchmakers eager to expand their date pool ("They certainly have a lot
more glamour and a lot more of that hero mystique," the proprietor of
Misty River Introductions said), and impresarios at celebrity benefits (De-
nis Leary, the creator and star of the TV firefighter drama *Rescue Me*,
auctioned off two dates with firemen at a Manhattan fund-raiser with this
come-on to grown women: "If you're a girl, kiss a fireman!"). The prom-
ulgators of the lust-for-firemen trend were hardly feminists, but their declarations were seized upon as evidence that women were shedding their
feminist principles. "In three decades, feminism has done a backflip," *New
York Times* columnist Maureen Dowd wrote. "Once men in uniform were
the oppressors. Now they're trophy mates. Once cops were pigs. Now
they're foxes."[13]

Few of the stories offered an actual woman in a romantic relationship with an actual fireman. Or even a one-night stand. On CBS, the *Early Show*'s Lisa Birnbach quizzed Mara Brandon, a massage therapist who had volunteered her services at the local fire station:

BIRNBACH: The firemen are cute. I would—I would massage one.

BRANDON: Oh, yeah. Oh, definitely.

BIRNBACH: Did you do any single firemen?

BRANDON: No. No.[14]

At the *Orange County Register*, reporter Emily Bittner got around the no-examples problem by paying a fireman to take her on a date. (The newspaper picked up the tab.) After a detour to the nail salon ("When my pedicurist asked what color to paint my toenails, I knew to answer, Fire-engine red"), she hurried over to the Santa Ana fire station armed with "a wad of $20s" to meet "my Real Man." Firefighter Jorge Vargas, whom she described as "5-foot-9, weighs 185 and is pure muscle," took Bittner out "in his 2001 Ford Ranger—fire-engine red." If his habits weren't as macho as she had envisioned—her first sight of him was "washing breakfast dishes" and his restaurant choice was a sushi bar— she assured her readers he fulfilled all the requirements of a dream date. "All day I'd wondered whether the Real Man could kiss. All I can say is wow, can he ever."[15]

After a while, the hero worshippers began to grate on their objects of veneration; to the firefighters, the adulation, the applause in bars, the celebrity tributes on TV, and the fund-raiser fests where they were raffled off for a date or a kiss seemed patronizing. A *Toronto Sun* reporter trolling a firefighters' benefit in search of a specimen on "the current female 'must-have' dating list" was taken aback when "none of the firemen felt they were the New Millennium Men at all. In fact, some were not at all impressed with the concept and chided me on the fact that making them objects of lust or whatever was 'demeaning' to their often-dangerous, dedicated profession." A firefighter with Engine 7 in downtown Manhattan, who had grown tired of tourists banging on the station door in the middle of the night to have their picture taken with a real live fireman, complained to *New York* magazine, "You're like a pet."[16]

Or a cartoon figure. On CNN's November 1 show, "Firefighters: America's Real-Life Superheroes," guest David Blankenhorn, president of the Institute for American Values, described New York's firefighters as if they had just popped out of a comic strip. "They just go in and get the innocent people!" he said. "They go in and save them—it's like Superman." Better than Superman, actually. In the months after 9/11, the media ran numerous stories expressing the opinion that the superhero-ism of New York's firefighters might eclipse that of their fictional counterparts. ("Will Superheroes Meet Their Doom?" a *Time* headline worried.) Comic book publishers rushed to issue new serials retailing the exploits of firemen. Marvel's "real-life" contribution, *The Call of Duty: The Brotherhood*, a multivolume set, featured a wholly fictional New York City firefighter named Lieutenant James MacDonald, a heartthrob with Ken doll good looks, who battles increasingly out-landish and even paranormal threats. Marvel's Quesada assured the press that "we consulted with firefighters" and "people will sense the au-thenticity in this book." As he told the *San Francisco Chronicle*, "Right now, the difference between Peter Parker putting on a costume to be-come Spider-Man and a man off the street putting on a uniform to be-come a fireman is really wafer-thin. Fantasy is almost matching up with reality."[17]

Newspaper cartoons were making similar declarations. "Who is your favorite superhero?" one much-recirculated example asked, under a drawing of three choices: Superman, Batman, or a New York City fire-man. In another, Superman, Batman, and Spider-Man implore a New York City fireman in unison, "Can I have your autograph?" Others de-picted the New York fireman with the Superman logo emblazoned on his turnout coat, or as a Bunyanesque hatchet-wielding giant, or, most fre-quently, as one of two skyscraper-high "Towering Heroes" (the other be-ing a similarly enormous New York City police officer) looming in place of the twin towers. "It's worse than an international task force," a cartoon mullah peering over a Tora Bora cliff reports to a terror-stricken Osama bin Laden. "It's New York firefighters."[18]

Photo ops with the new superhero firefighters became almost as desirable to our evildoer-fighting president as military appearances. Four years after 9/11, when Atlanta's fire department dispatched its force to Louisiana in the wake of Hurricane Katrina, the crew's first duty was ornamental: standing beside Bush as he inspected the devastation. Bush's marketers, no doubt, had the same sales strategy in mind as fashion designer Ralph Lauren, who took out double-truck ads (featuring himself modeling a sweater adorned with an American flag) in which he held forth on his personal affinity for America's latest male icons: "I have always been inspired by America and its heroes—the cowboy, the soldier and now the firefighters, police officers and rescue workers. There is one common thread in every hero. They are ordinary Americans, they come from nowhere, make their mark, get knocked down and rise up again."[19]

For the fiction to work, the firemen had to conform to stereotype. When they didn't, their behavior would be recast to fit it. The media were soon busy airbrushing the emotions of helplessness and fear out of firefighters' eyes and praising their "courage" to cry as a sign of unshaken manhood. "Tears can reveal strength, not weakness," the *New York Times* asserted; "compassion, not fear; maturity, not loss of control." When the two-hour documentary 9/11, which focused on a rookie New York City firefighter, aired on CBS on the six-month anniversary of the attack, it was billed as the story of "a boy becoming a man." Never mind that, when pressed to endorse that theme, rookie Tony Benetatos stared back, disconsolate, at the interviewer and replied: "Has it made me a man? No. What's a man?"[20]

At "the pile"—the term the rescue and recovery workers preferred to the martial moniker ground zero—the media insistence on portraying firefighters as superheroes induced a distorted mirror effect, as a few FDNY men tried to live up to their billing, sometimes resorting to dangerous stunts. The construction workers and Port Authority and New York City police officers (who often wound up logging more hours in the reclamation effort at ground zero) began to respond with annoyance, then rancor, at times bad-mouthing firefighters to the press or even refusing to help them recover the body parts of their comrades. The feuding degenerated into an adolescent "gang mentality," William Langewiesche, the lone journalist permitted unrestricted access to the recovery work at the disaster site, wrote in his 2003 book, *American Ground*, with every man loyal only to his "wolf pack":

> The firemen in particular felt that they had a special relationship with the site, not only because they had lost 343 people there—out of a force of 14,000—but also because afterward their survivors, along with their dead, had been idolized as national heroes, and subjected to the full force of modern publicity. A few of them reacted embarrassingly, by grandstanding on television and at public events, striking tragic poses and playing themselves up. Even at the site, where people generally disliked such behavior, you could find firemen signing autographs at the perimeter gates or, after the public viewing stand was built, drifting over to work the crowds.[21]

Supersizing the image of the New York City firefighter was only half of the new cultural script. More often than not, the glorification was paired with a contemptuous double slap—to the "soft" male and the feminist who supposedly made him what he was, or rather, wasn't. The *Washington Post*'s September 20 tribute to firemen, "Company of Heroes," boiled the equation down to its essence: "Out: dot-com geeks. In: burly men with axes." "Since the September attacks, the firefighter coated with ash and soot has provided a striking contrast to the now prehistoric-seeming male archetype of such a short time ago: the casually dressed dot-commer in khakis and a BMW," the *New York Times* said. "In contrast to past eras of touchy-feeliness (Alan Alda) and the vaguely feminized, rakish man-child of the 1990's (Leonardo DiCaprio), the notion of physical prowess in the service of patriotic duty is firmly back on the pedestal." To make the case, the *Times* turned, like CNN, to Camille Paglia. "I can't help noticing how robustly, dreamily masculine the faces of the firefighters are," Paglia told the *Times*. "These are working-class men, stoical, patriotic. They're not on Prozac or questioning their gender."[22]

These firefighters, we were assured, weren't playing rent boy to America's liberated women. *Vanity Fair* critic James Wolcott coupled his own list of what was in—the "stoic, trained devotion to duty" exhibited by New

York's firemen—with these outs: Hillary Clinton (thanks to 9/11, she was now undergoing "shrinkage"); Eve Ensler's feminist play (*"The Vagina Monologues* may have to pull up its panties"); "shock art" of the feminist variety (his prime evidence were gallery exhibits critiquing Barbie as a symbol of "female objectification," which, he held, did not "suggest the keenest sense of priorities"); gender-neutral clothing styles ("the androgynous droop that prevails in the fashion pages"); and even conservative female commentators (the *"femme* Nikitas," he said, will be "booted into early retirement"). In the same issue of *Vanity Fair*, columnist Christopher Hitchens slid seamlessly from praise for "the burly, uncomplaining stoic proletarian defenders, busting their sinews in the intractable and nameless wreckage and carnage of downtown" to the pronouncement that he wouldn't be caught dead at a "gender-specific" ceremony on 9/11. Not that anyone had asked him to attend such an event: his outburst was occasioned by an invitation to a memorial honoring *British*, not female, victims of the World Trade Center collapse. In a *National Review* article about how 9/11 "vindicates perfectly the decentralized, federalist, conservative view of the world," Mark Steyn engaged in a similarly non sequitur snit about imaginary challenges to firehouse sexuality: "The debate over government is between folks who want a fire chief and those who want a fire chief plus a transgendered cultural-outreach officer," he declared.[23]

The commentators who made the link between firemen's rise and feminism's fall most forthrightly belonged to the distaff side of conservative flackery. "The Mayor and the President weren't inspired by the city's 'firefighters,'" *National Review*'s Kate O'Beirne asserted ten days after 9/11. "They were talking about the firemen." She lauded the Fire Department of New York for keeping its ranks overwhelmingly male, thus resisting "the feminist assault." Independent Women's Forum writer Charlotte Allen went even further—she declared that the actions of the New York City firemen disproved the famous feminist line "A woman needs a man like a fish needs a bicycle" and put the lie to "feminist theorists" who, according to her, "condemned marriage as female enslavement," "preached divorce as liberation," and "pronounced the presence of a father in the household as unnecessary at best and oppressive and abusively 'patriarchal' at worst." The opposing of firemen and feminism was still going on two years later at an American Enterprise Institute conference in which two sex-segregated panels pondered the "state of modern manhood." The discussion kept returning to one theme: 9/11 showed how much we need male "protectors" and how little we need feminists. As *Woman's Quarterly* editor Charlotte Hays put it, "The post-9/11 love affair with police, firemen, and soldiers is a return of normal relations between men and women."[24]

The conservative female columnist who got the most mileage out of flaying feminists with a fire hose was former Reagan speechwriter Peggy Noonan. "From the ashes of September 11, arise the manly virtues," Noonan wrote a few weeks after the attack in the *Wall Street Journal*. "I am speaking of masculine men, men who push things and pull things." She preferred this explanation for "how manliness and its brother, gentlemanliness, went out of style": the women's movement had killed them.

> I know, because I was there. In fact, I may have done it. I remember exactly when: It was in the mid-'70s, and I was in my mid-20s, and a big, nice, middle-aged man got up from his seat to help me haul a big piece of luggage into the overhead luggage space on a plane. I was a feminist, and knew our rules and rants. "I can do it myself," I snapped.

She now regarded her show of independence as a gender crime. "I embarrassed a nice man who was attempting to help a lady," she wrote. "I bet he never offered to help a lady again. I bet he became an intellectual, or a writer, and not a good man like a fireman or a businessman who says, 'Let's roll.'" Feminists—in cahoots with "peaceniks, leftists, intellectuals"—"killed John Wayne," she said, and "we were left with John Wayne's friendly-antagonist sidekick in the old John Ford movies, Barry Fitzgerald. The small, nervous, gossiping neighborhood commentator Barry Fitzgerald, who wanted to talk about everything and do nothing."[25]

Noonan and her conservative sisters provided the petticoats behind which male journalists and commentators could hide when they launched their own attacks. Articles and opinion pieces by male writers followed Noonan's, declaring that the "manly man" was "back"—and citing her column as evidence. "Has a shocked society rediscovered the value of traditional masculinity in the rubble of the World Trade Center?" UPI writer Lou Marano asked in "Manliness Makes a Comeback." "Peggy Noonan thinks so." He phoned her for additional affirmation, which she was glad to provide. "For instance," Noonan told him, "when you remember that God is the father, and you think of the young fathers in the NYFD who slapped on their 20-pound rubber coats and picked up that 30-pound hose and took the ax and ran 40 flights up the stairs to save lives, you cannot fail to remember—at least unconsciously—what men are." Marano also called upon—who else?—Camille Paglia to explain why firemen hadn't gotten their due before. "Male-bashing was a poisonous feature of American feminism for 30 years," Paglia said. Marano agreed, concluding that feminists had led the "extraordinary assault on traditional masculinity that occurred in the West during the last third of the 20th century." Thanks to the women's movement, he wrote, being "a strong, silent man was suddenly grounds for divorce."[26]

This story recurred with some frequency—and longevity. "As War Looms, It's OK to Let Boys Be Boys Again," a *Chicago Tribune* headline asserted in November 2002. "Since the terrorist attack of Sept. 11 last year," the article's author, John Kass, wrote, "you don't hear or read anymore how boys are too wild, and that for their own good should have the boy taken out of them, and how they can be rewired at school, reeducated, gently, firmly, relentlessly." The attack, he said, had thankfully spelled the defeat of all those women's studies "Harvard scholars" who believe that "boys became emotionally crippled, ruined by something called the 'cult of competition,'" and who try to strip young men of their "aggressive, stoic" qualities. For support, he turned to yet another member of the Independent Women's Forum stable, Christina Hoff Sommers, author of such antifeminist works as *The War against Boys* and *Who Stole Feminism?*, whom he presented as "an expert on boys" with "fascinating" insights. She assured Kass he was right. "We heard male bashing for two decades," she said. "And some of our gender scholars were so carried away, they wanted to teach little boys to be more like girls, so they had boys quilting and using looms and so forth to calm them down and high-spirited play was discouraged."[27]

"Is Dirty Harry alive and well?" staff writer Phil McCombs asked in the *Washington Post*, as the country invaded Iraq in March 2003. "Are we heading back into a time when Real Men bring home the bacon and their women cook it up?" He certainly hoped so. McCombs cited Noonan's now one-and-a-half-year-old column as proof and bolstered it with quotes from two anonymous "female acquaintances" who supposedly told him that "I don't want a wuss" who wears one of "those bikini swimsuits" and that, since 9/11, "I'm more attracted to the kind of man my father was—a World War II man." With these feminine testimonials in his quiver—along with the observation that two books had come out recently titled *No More Mr. Nice Guy* and one titled *No More Mr. Christian Nice Guy*—McCombs was emboldened to indulge in some chest thumping. "It's High Noon for America," he crowed. President Bush had "that Gary Cooper glint in his eye," and American men were shucking their sensitive-male chains. "Okay, so maybe we're not so nice anymore," he swaggered, Dirty Harry–style. "So what?"[28]

"Men are back" stories became so legion that the *Palm Beach Post*'s "Practical Man" columnist, Dan Neal, felt compelled to offer his own half tongue-in-cheek version:

> So long, sissy boys!
>
> Goodbye, Sensitive Man!
>
> See ya, Jerry Seinfeld!
>
> Adios, male models, wine geeks, gadget freaks, Chanel for Men, "whimsy," spindly arms, *GQ*, "irony" and—heaven help us all!—hair gel.
>
> After 30 years of wimpifying its men, turning us all into spit-shined, dough-balled, eggheaded girlie boys who can clip a cuticle and crack wise but can't really do jack, Americans have finally seen the light. . . .
>
> When the chips are down, when it really counts, when the hooey hits the Hampton Bay, practical men get the call. The world turns to the guys with the strong backs, the hands-on, silent folks who know how to fix stuff, who keep the wheels of society spinning. As it should be, these get-the-job-done dudes are now our heroes, and the practical man is proud to be on their side—if only in spirit and not in deed. He is, after all, just a dweeby newspaper columnist.[29]

The articles always seemed to gravitate toward the same argument: "maleness" was making a comeback because New York City's fire*men* were heroes on 9/11, and they were heroes because they had saved untold numbers of civilians—especially *female* civilians. One would never think from studying the photos the press chose to publish that the survivors (like the victims) of the twin towers attack were predominantly male. The media foregrounded the few pictures they had of men tending to injured or at least distressed women. In a "To Our Readers" note at the front of *Time's* first post-9/11 issue, illustrated with a picture of a brawny man holding the hand of a weeping woman, the magazine's managing editor explained that, after "I looked at hundreds of photographs for this issue," he settled on "the faces of my fellow New Yorkers who escaped death and the cops and firefighters who helped them do it." Those two categories of faces turned out to be remarkably sex-segregated. The photos featured under the banner "Heroes" were all of men, while the one photo under "Survivor" showed a distraught bloodied woman in a red dress sitting on the curb, a man with a badge hovering above her, his hands on her shoulders. *Newsweek* ran a photograph of the very same woman, under the heading "Pain and Suffering." All but one of the photos in the "Heroes" section of *Newsweek's* 9/11 "Commemorative Issue" were of men, although the heroism at times seemed a stretch—like the surgeon who treated only one 9/11 victim, for "a small cut," or the executive chef from Tribeca Grill who served gourmet meals to rescue workers aboard a cruise boat. The one example of female heroism offered was a cameo of two women in the line of traditional feminine duty: they were elementary school teachers who "did their best to appear calm and look after their kids."[30]

And what of the women who defied the media divide of male heroes and female survivors? There was little hint of them.

ON NOVEMBER 19, 2001, invited guests gathered in the Empire Ballroom of New York City's Grand Hyatt Hotel to honor six female rescue workers of 9/11. The recipients of the newly minted Liberty Award of Valor were each summoned to the podium and their stories told. Among them were a police lieutenant who dug people out of the rubble and led one hundred people out of an unstable apartment building, despite a chunk of cement embedded in her skull, a section of windowpane stuck in her back, and a broken ankle; an emergency medical technician who was one of the first to charge into the South Tower and who dragged out office workers, including a woman paralyzed by multiple sclerosis; and an off-duty firefighter who raced from her home in Brooklyn, borrowed someone's gear and a police van, and dug relentlessly for survivors.[31]

Maureen McFadden, vice president of communications for the National Organization for Women's Legal Defense and Education Fund (NOW LDEF), had come up with the idea of honoring female rescue workers. She'd spent September 11 a few blocks from the disaster, gathering stories and securing a rooftop filming spot for her previous employer, CBS News, where she had worked as a producer. In the scenes she witnessed that day, she discerned the outlines of a neglected drama. "I saw women *rushing* into ground zero," she recalled, women who were as desperate to help as the men. She phoned her contacts in the media, urging them to chronicle this story. No one would. "Even CBS said, 'Well, maybe if you can get 'em in their outfits,'" she told me. "They kept calling them 'outfits.' Like they were just dressed up in costumes." Some weeks later, after McFadden spoke to a group of NOW LDEF funders about the media's refusal to acknowledge women's presence at ground zero, a man in the audience approached her and offered to finance a documentary about female rescue workers.[32]

The Women of Ground Zero, a short documentary focused on the Liberty Award winners, was screened at a few embassies and before a small congressional delegation toward the end of 2001. The film won prizes and inspired two women—a volunteer firefighter and an investigative social worker in California—to collect and publish interviews with thirty female rescue workers who "stood shoulder to shoulder with their male counterparts and gave their all," as the dust jacket of their book, *Women at Ground Zero*, put it. While numerous and lavishly produced documentaries, docudramas, TV specials, oversized picture books, calendars, children's toys, and all manner of memorabilia had heaped praise on the "brothers" of the FDNY, as they were invariably called, these two modest appreciations of women's services were the only cultural honors their sisters received.[33]

The paucity of tributes to women reflected the thorough erasure of women from ground zero, other than as victims, an erasure both immediate and chronic. In the media, the New York City fire department was described repeatedly as a "band of brothers," a "brotherhood of guys," a community of "fathers and sons," and a World War II unit. The popular off-Broadway play about the New York firefighters was titled simply *The Guys*. The Museum of the City of New York titled its 2002 exhibit on the city's firefighters "Brotherhood," and the Discovery Channel called its homage "New York Firefighters: The Brotherhood of September 11." The popular cable television drama *Rescue Me*, about fictional New York City firefighters after 9/11, revolved around an all-male firehouse brimming with buff studs in which women figured as bitchy ex-girlfriends, harridan wives, or, most frequently, "booty call" nymphets in spandex whose character development generally followed an arc from brain-dead sex machine to *Fatal Attraction* psychotic. Toward the end of the show's first season, a lone firewoman was introduced to the house: "The bean counters lower their standards so they can make their bitch quotas," the chief gripes to his men. She isn't quite up to the job, can't win the acceptance of the "brothers," initiates an affair with one of the firemen in the house—and is eliminated from the script by the end of the second season.[34]

Mainstream newspapers and network news shows relapsed to vocabulary habits abandoned thirty years earlier. "One thing most fire and rescue service women have noticed in the media coverage of the September 11 attacks, and particularly of the World Trade Center collapse, is a heavy use of the words 'fireman' and 'firemen,'" firefighter Terese Floren wrote in *Firework*, the newsletter of Women in the Fire Service. The same reversion applied to police officers, who were now suddenly "policemen." "Reporters haven't simply forgotten the word 'firefighter' exists," Floren wrote. "'Firemen' is the perfect word to use when you want to say, 'All (real) firefighters are men.' It is a deliberate rejection of the gender-neutral in order to define heroes as male. And that's exactly why these words are all over the news."[35]

At Ladder 12 in Manhattan, firefighter Brenda Berkman was also troubled by women's erasure. A long-term veteran of the force, Berkman was the lead plaintiff in a sex-discrimination lawsuit filed in 1978 against the Fire Department of New York that finally forced the department in 1982 to start hiring women—for the first time in its 117-year history. She was also one of the city firefighters who rushed to the scene on the morning of September 11 (on her day off) and joined the grueling search for comrades afterward. "I've been a firefighter for 20 years," Berkman said two months after the attack, "and I've never seen the contribution of women firefighters, police officers and paramedics so completely ignored. Suddenly, we've become invisible. It's as though we were wearing the American equivalent of the veil."[36]

But neglect would have been merciful compared with the outrage that greeted efforts to correct the record. If the television and print tributes to the brotherhood received somber appreciation from the media, the NOW LDEF film *Women of Ground Zero* drew the opposite.

"A disgraceful display," the *Weekly Standard* said of the documentary. The twin towers tragedy was being "mined for aggrieved heroes who would carry a banner of division," Jonathan Turley wrote in the *Los Angeles Times*.[37] Though it was only thirteen minutes long and screened in a very few locations before tiny audiences, *Women of Ground Zero* ignited anger across the country. Threatening calls and letters began rolling into NOW LDEF at once and kept on coming. The reaction reached fever pitch in early January 2002, after the *Washington Post* ran a story about the documentary that mentioned that NOW LDEF was urging legislators to ensure that female contractors weren't excluded from the $11 billion rebuilding effort at ground zero. "We have a new opportunity to rethink how we do things," NOW LDEF president Kathy Rodgers was quoted as saying. "We don't want to do business as usual, because it left too many women out, too many people of color out. . . . What we want to do is to raise the issue and say, 'Here's your chance to do it right.' "[38]

The conservative punditry pounced at once, twisting Rodgers's words to suggest that she wanted to tap into the funds for families of 9/11 victims. "NOW is so desperate that, at a time of national crisis, it is willing to divert money from its intended recipients," wrote Wendy McElroy, ifeminist.com columnist and Fox News blogger, who was one of the first to sound the false alarm. Rodgers was so greedy that not even "widows, orphans and others devastated by tragedy impede her vision." NOW LDEF's performance was "beyond cynical," McElroy concluded. "It is obscene." Subsequent commentary denounced feminists for trying to "shove their hand in the pot" reserved for 9/11 sufferers and behaving like "vultures."[39]

The federal money that Rodgers was referring to was designated for construction contracts to rebuild ground zero and had nothing to do with aid for victims' families, a distinction that was ignored in the ensuing outcry. NOW LDEF was robbing 9/11 widows and children "to help women change careers to high-paying jobs," Sean Hannity insisted on *Hannity & Colmes*. "Is that an appropriate use of government funds that are earmarked towards the victims of this event on September 11th?" he demanded of his guest, Kim Gandy, the president of the National Organization for Women and a board member of NOW LDEF, who tried fruitlessly to counter the canard.[40]

The feminists-taking-food-out-of-the-mouths-of-babes fable circulated in the media for months. Vicious e-mail messages barraged NOW LDEF's in-box. A typical specimen:

> Those funds were given by hard-working Americans for THE VIC-TIM'S [*sic*] FAMILIES!! Not so you can line your organization's pockets off the devastation of others. Your organization is a disgrace to every living and breathing American woman. I donated to the 9/11 charities and don't want one dime of mine going to an [*sic*] predatory organization like yours. Predators prey off the weak for their own gain. Kind of like bin Laden.

Or more succinctly:

> I say our money must go to our victims, not to a bunch of partial-birth sadomaso lesbos.[41]

That feminists were somehow using 9/11 to advance their "abortion on demand" agenda was a popular suspicion among the religious right, and it gave rise to some of the wackier accusations afloat in the fall of 2001. Planned Parenthood of New York City, which was, like so many other organizations in the area, seeking a way to feel useful after the terrorist attacks, extended free counseling and health care for a week to distraught New Yorkers. The announcement incited instant apoplexy on the antiabortion circuit. "That's right, Planned Parenthood's idea of *helping* traumatized New Yorkers is to rip their precious babies apart and throw the body parts in the landfill," Pro-Life America said in a mass mailing that declared the situation an "Abortion State of Emergency." Father Frank Pavone, "national adviser" to Pro-Life America, elaborated in the group's fund-raising letter:

> Many pregnant girls may be out of a job because of the terrorist attack. Many may have lost their place to live. They may be deeply depressed because they lost loved ones, or even their baby's father, in the rubble. They may be so traumatized that they can't function normally. They may be thinking this world is just too evil to bring a child into. *These desperate girls, and their little preborn babies, are ideal targets for Planned Parenthood's abortionists.* You can bet that Planned Parenthood and 355 other abortion centers in the states of New York and New Jersey are working shamelessly to lure these high school and college students into aborting their innocent little ones.[42]

In late January 2002, Maureen McFadden of NOW LDEF made one last attempt to set the record straight. She booked the organization's president, Kathy Rodgers, on Fox News's *O'Reilly Factor*. Bill O'Reilly was only too happy to accept—and took the opportunity to repeat the lie. "In the 'Impact' segment tonight," he announced in the teaser for the show, "the NOW Legal Defense and Education Fund wants federal money appropriated for 9/11 disaster relief to be directed towards affirmative action for women." Nothing Rodgers said in the course of the show could deter him from this claim.[43]

As it happened, NOW LDEF's efforts to include female contractors in the rebuilding projects in Lower Manhattan came to nought. Several years later, women's representation in the New York City construction trades remained at less than 3 percent. Efforts to improve women's numbers at the Fire Department of New York also ran aground. After 9/11, the fire department was engaged in a massive hiring effort to replace the 343 firefighters who had died and the hundreds of traumatized firefighters who were taking early retirement. Yet, when the department swore in its first round of post-9/11 hires in October, 308 were men, zero women. By March of the following year, the department had inducted exactly one woman. The pressure was off. After 9/11, the city's Equal Employment Practices Commission suspended its efforts to compel the fire department to hire a more diverse force "for the indefinite future." By 2003, despite hundreds of additional female applicants, women's numbers on the force were lower than ten years earlier; they had gone from thirty-five to twenty-four.[44]

The pressure was off at the federal level, too. A few weeks after 9/11, the Justice Department suddenly pulled out of two major sex-discrimination lawsuits; one of them had challenged the Philadelphia transit police authority's use of an unduly onerous running test that screened out 90 percent of women. The Justice Department offered no explanation for its abrupt turnaround, but the Philadelphia defendants were happy to provide one. "The World Trade Center pointed out the need for realistic standards to protect the public," Philadelphia transit police lawyer Saul Krenzel told the press. The Bush administration continued to curtail sex-discrimination litigation in the months and years to follow; by 2005, it had reduced its discrimination prosecutions by 40 percent, allowed existing consent decrees that mandated the hiring and promotion of women and minorities to lapse (and, in particular, decrees imposed on police and fire departments), and purged its most dedicated civil rights lawyers from its ranks.[45]

The organization Women in Fire Service began hearing from its members around the country that many fire departments seemed to be viewing 9/11 as a green light to quit recruiting women. "Male firefighters in one fire department that has been very progressive in diversifying its workforce in recent years went to the fire chief following the World Trade Center collapse," *Firework* reported. "They asked him, 'Now can we stop all this hiring of women?'" The National Center for Women and Policing received reports that some fire departments were considering adopting extreme "physical agility" tests to keep women off their forces. Similar talk surfaced in law enforcement. Penny Harrington, the first female police chief of Portland, Oregon, heard a recurring refrain as she made the rounds as a consultant to regional police departments. "There was this attitude of, 'Oh, we don't need to hire women anymore,'" she told me. "It was almost like throwing a switch and we were back in the '50s. Across the country, I was seeing what I saw decades ago." Among those repeat emotions she witnessed was "rage at any woman who spoke out." Law enforcement agencies, she noted, were also increasingly shifting funds away from community policing—where many female police officers had distinguished themselves—to all-male "counterterrorist squads" stocked with absurd amounts of firepower, financed by Department of Homeland Security grants.[46]

In such a climate, the few New York City firewomen who raised questions about their own dwindling numbers were promptly denounced as unpatriotic and selfish—and greeted with derision in the blogosphere. "Fire the bitch!" was a garden-variety response that circulated in Web chat rooms—after Brenda Berkman briefly tried to draw attention to the gender imbalance—along with such retorts as "Whining little &*$@," "Waaaaaaa!!!!!! Waaaaaaaaaaah!!!! I'm a victim too!!!!!!!!," and "Let it go you whining shrew. Men are dead. You could do them the highest honor by shutting your fricking pie-hole."[47]

As the lead plaintiff in the 1978 sex-discrimination suit, Berkman was used to attacks—although in the past they had mainly been internal—from her firefighting "brothers." The first class of New York City female firefighters experienced a catalog of horrors: men on the force, they recalled, had urinated in their boots, disabled their safety equipment, vandalized their property, slashed their tires, and deserted them in blazing buildings. The women reported being sexually harassed, fondled, assaulted, and, in at least one case, raped. One New York fireman tried to run over a female recruit with his car, another cut a firewoman with a knife, and at one firehouse, firemen locked the station's lone female colleague in a kitchen that they had filled with tear gas. For a very brief while, it looked like the collapse of the towers might shear this wall of hostility between the sexes, at least among the fire department's rank and file. Berkman recalled the rapprochement with surprised appreciation. "For the women, it was initially a tremendous bonding experience with the men that a lot of us had not really felt before," she said. "There was a huge level of grief and loss we were all feeling, both the men and the women. . . . The women and the men were very tight. . . . I just wish it could have lasted forever." It lasted only a few weeks, before the old resentments flooded back in, along with the new assumption that, in light of the tragedy, women's concerns had been rendered moot.[48]

Simply by calling attention to women at ground zero, NOW LDEF violated the dictates of the post-9/11 culture's rulebook. Those dictates determined who could be called a "hero" or a "victim" and who could not. The tragedy had yielded no victorious heroes, so the culture wound up anointing a set of victimized men instead: the firemen who had died in the stairwells of the World Trade Center and their surviving coworkers, who had been traumatized by the loss of their "brothers." No female firefighter qualified under this rubric: none had died in the attacks and, being women, none could claim membership in the bereft brotherhood. Perversely, because the firewomen *weren't* victims, they couldn't be heroes. If a firewoman like Brenda Berkman wanted to be honored, a *Wall Street Journal* Web columnist snapped, "maybe she should bring a right-to-die suit." His readers agreed. "This has GOT to be the sorry apex of feminism," a typical post in response read, "—complaining because your opportunities to die are fewer than those of men in your profession. The feminist agenda, once nobly-intended, has become sheer, unmitigated insanity."[49]

The media gave short shrift to the three female rescue workers who *did* die in the line of duty that day. They included the first female commander of the Port Authority's training academy, who had helped carry an obese woman in a wheelchair from the twenty-ninth floor to the lobby and had freed hundreds of people trapped in the North Tower lobby when the revolving doors jammed by shooting out several huge plate-glass windows; a New York City patrol officer who had ascended to the eighty-fourth floor of the South Tower and led many office workers to safety; and an emergency medical technician, a twenty-four-year-old single mother, who was one of the first paramedics on the scene and who repeatedly ran into the towers to pull people out of harm's way before she was crushed in the collapse.[50]

If women were ineligible for hero status, for what would they be celebrated?

CHAPTER 4

Perfect Virgins of Grief

SUDDEN TRAGEDY: FIANCÉES AND WIVES LEFT BEHIND," THE TEASER for *The Montel Williams Show* promised for April 24, 2002. The teaser was well aimed. Williams and his compatriots in the talk show universe understood the guidelines of the American morality play and were filling its dramatis personae as adeptly as any Broadway casting director. By spring 2002, the script had been established: 9/11's victims *were* female, after all. The promo cut to "Lisa":

LISA: The phone rang, I got up, and I just heard static.

WILLIAMS: On the next *Montel*, one of the most tragic stories you will ever hear.

LISA: I think maybe that was my husband trying to call me.

ANNOUNCER: She was nine months pregnant when she lost Joe in the World Trade Center.

LISA: I named him after his father. He looks a lot like his daddy.[1]

According to the media formula, the 9/11 "left behind" were *all* women—preferably women left alone with babes in arms. *U.S. News & World Report*'s incantation of the attack's victims was typical of how the press narrowed its focus: "wives without husbands, mothers without sons, and children without parents." Surviving husbands and fathers had mysteriously dropped from view. Even factoring in the three-to-one ratio of male to female deaths on 9/11, that still left hundreds of widowers unaccounted for. More than a year after 9/11, a writer for the *Boston Globe* went looking for news accounts of bereaved 9/11 men—and found only a brief item in the *New York Post* and one feature-length story in the *Hamilton Spectator*, a Canadian newspaper.[2]

The "9/11 Widows," by contrast, were everywhere. Their temperatures were taken on Thanksgiving and Christmas (Gannett News Service: "No Holiday from Pain of 9-11"), at various milestone marks (NBC's Katie Couric: "On the six-month anniversary, as you think about your husbands and your son, what will you miss about them the most?"), and on their wedding anniversaries (*Hartford Courant*: "This Sunday, Oct. 7, Pam will buy her own dozen roses—11 red ones and one white one, as her husband would have—to mark their 12th wedding anniversary"). The widows were hounded to write memoirs and inspirational children's books. Their pregnancies were monitored and their maternity wards invaded (*Good Morning America*: "Tiny faces with their father's eyes, with daddy's chin, telling us that life goes on even on the days you're not sure why"). Even therapy sessions weren't off-limits (ABC News host Barbara Walters: "We took our cameras to a blazingly honest group counseling session, sessions, more than one, at the North Shore Child and Family Guidance Center on Long Island. And we taped sessions at different times with widows and with their children. . . . So now firsthand, you'll hear their anger, their humor, and, most of all, their love").[3]

Marian Fontana, whose husband, Dave Fontana, a firefighter, died at the World Trade Center, was barraged by calls from *Oprah* producers, who had booked her for an upcoming show. "It was right after Dave's funeral," she told me. "I was really exhausted, just spent in every way. And these producers were calling every ten minutes wanting something else: they wanted wedding videotapes and they wanted family photos and they wanted close-up shots." Then they heard she was holding a service for her husband on the beach where he had been a lifeguard for sixteen years. "They were very pushy about wanting to come to that and get a long shot of Aidan [her five-year-old son] and me, walking hand in hand on the beach. And that just didn't sit right in my stomach at all." When she declined, they got cranky. "They were annoyed that I wasn't being cooperative and giving them what they wanted. Finally, they ended up canceling—which was fine with me." The experience inspired her first post-9/11 media rule: "No more talk shows."[4]

Fontana inadvertently broke that rule some months later, when she accepted an invitation to appear on what she mistakenly understood (thanks to a garbled cell phone conversation) to be *E-Online*, presumably a Web news program. By then, Fontana had organized the 9/11 Families Association, an advocacy group for New York City firefighters and surviving family members. Told she could speak about the organization's efforts, she agreed to go on the show. But she knew something was wrong when the location for the interview turned out to be Fox's television studios. She and the other guests were each ushered into individual plush dressing rooms "with a fruit basket and makeup lights," she recalled. "Then we got led backstage, and there were all these people going 'Hoo! Hoo! Hoo!' in the audience. I asked this woman sitting next to me, 'What is this?' She said, 'Iyanla.' I said, 'What's that?' She said, 'You know, she's like a late-night Oprah.' And I thought, 'Uh-oh.' I asked her, 'Well, do you know what the topic is?' And she said, 'Something about hell.'"

Just then, Iyanla barreled onstage to announce, "Today, the show's about people who've been to hell and back!" Fontana watched, with mounting distress, as they "brought in this woman whose son had found a gun next door and shot himself. She was crying and they showed this emotional video about her life." The scene became increasingly surreal: "Next they brought in this young guy who drank and did drugs and almost lost his life and got arrested for drunk driving and began teaching kids how to be a triathlete. And then they brought in this poor woman named Yvette who had lost a son ten or fifteen years before, and she had gained a hundred pounds and had taken up smoking and drinking. She was a mess, sweating and crying the whole time." And then, as the show cut to a commercial, Fontana heard, "And next, we have a 9/11 widow who's going to help Yvette come back from hell!" She thought to herself, "Me? I'm the most screwed up one here." An excruciating several minutes followed—with "Yvette looking all pleadingly at me" while Iyanla became increasingly annoyed at Fontana's halting efforts to come up with some piece of advice. "I kinda flubbed my way through it, feeling incredibly hypocritical. What did I know about getting beyond grief?" She was still deep in mourning herself. Iyanla finally took the reins and, channeling the dead son, ordered Yvette to work on "healing" herself. Fontana remembered thinking, "I *am* in hell—right here."[5]

While the talk show doyennes competed for healing rights, male hosts one-upped one another for the role of widow protector. Geraldo Rivera presented a $50,000 check to a group of wealthy suburban women from Middletown, New Jersey, whose high-finance husbands had died in the twin towers. Bill O'Reilly cast himself as rescuing knight to Lynda Fiori, a widow who said that her husband's employer, Cantor Fitzgerald, had ignored her and been slow to provide financial aid. In show after show, O'Reilly depicted chief executive Howard Lutnick as a moustache-twirling tormentor of imperiled maidens, and himself as the man who would snatch them from the Cantor train tracks:

o'REILLY: Oh, [Lutnick's] a prince, all right. I'm getting the picture on this guy. Ms. Fiori, we're going to help you here. We're going to track this now every step of the way, not only at Cantor Fitzgerald with their duty, but also the other agencies. We're going to make sure that they get in touch with you. This pain that you're going through now with the loss of your husband—the sudden loss of your husband—and you guys, what, are 30—very young. How long were you married?

FIORI: Four years.

o'REILLY: Four years. Is it compounded by the worry you have that you don't have any money, that you have two babies at home?

FIORI: Exactly. My mortgage—I have a big mortgage. No savings. . . . I'm not looking for a handout from Mr. Lutnick. . . .

O'REILLY: Sure. I mean, you're just looking for—certainly, this company, Cantor Fitzgerald, should take care of you. There's no question. And they will. Or we'll provide you a lawyer pro bono to sue them and make sure they will. We will provide you that.[6]

The 9/11 widows who were most singled out and deemed worthy of being "taken care of" fit a particular profile. They weren't ambitious careerists trading commodities on the eighty-fourth floor. They were at home that day tending to the hearth, models of all-American housewifery. *New York* magazine's one-year anniversary feature on the families of the 9/11 dead chose four widows to showcase: Lori Kane, "a stay-at-home New Jersey mom"; Anna Mojica, "who worked at a bank after high school but gave up the job when Stephanie was born"; Emily Terry, an "Upper West Side mother of three" who "left a job at the International Center of Photography after her first child, Hannah, was born"; and LaChanze Sapp-Gooding, an "actress and mother of two" who was "taking a work break this fall"—at the suggestion of her male psychiatrist. "I was starting to snap at my babies," Sapp-Gooding confessed to *New York*.[7]

Rarely entertained was the possibility that employment might be a balm and an emotional lifesaver to the bereaved—not to mention a source of much-needed income. The women who went back to work after their catastrophic loss, a far more typical arc, rarely made the media cut. The widows the media liked best were the ones who accepted that their "job" now was to devote themselves to their families and the memory of their dead husbands.

The latter role was time-honored; since at least the Civil War, American widows have been expected to take the lead in memorializing and exalting the nation's fallen heroes, even (or especially) when certain claims of heroism did not bear inspection. LaSalle Corbell, widow of Confederate general George E. Pickett, devoted the last fifty years of her life to cleansing her husband's reputation of his bloody rout, contrasting his supposedly "dauntless courage and self-control" with her "child-bride" frailty. The virile confections she spun on the lecture circuit of her husband sacrificing all to save "a whole city full of helpless, defenceless women and children"—not to mention the letters she likely forged to serve that same purpose—transformed Pickett from a man nearly indicted for war crimes into the tragic hero of Pickett's Charge and guardian of the Old South.[8] Now, that feminine job was retooled to fit the modern media melodrama. With triumphal heroes so hard to find at ground zero, the widows became even more essential buttresses to the post-9/11 mythmaking process. The women who received the most airtime were the ones who contributed the most to their husbands' posthumous elevation, both by lauding the men's valor and displaying their own vulnerability. These young wives formed an amen corner on 20/20, *Good Morning America*, and all the other television chat programs. The September 18, 2001, interview on *Good Morning America* with two Flight 93 widows was a typical illustration of what was expected of them:

DIANE SAWYER: You never know when the moment comes what kind of courage you'll have. Well, there are two women who know what kind of courage their husbands had. They're going to take us inside the plane that crashed into Shanksville, Pennsylvania. . . . And I just want to tell everybody the two of you were holding hands and holding on to each other a few minutes ago. . . . When we say that these were athletic men, these were big and brave men. What, Jeremy was six one, 220 pounds?

LYZ GLICK [Identified on camera with the caption "Wife of Jeremy Glick Who Foiled Attack"]: Mm-hmm. He's a national judo champion, wrestled all throughout high school. Just an incredible athlete. . . .

SAWYER [to Lisa Beamer]: And I heard that you said to someone that it makes all the difference in the world to know that you can tell this child what his dad did or her dad did.

LISA BEAMER: Yeah, yeah. You know, throughout the first three days, I didn't know what Todd's role was. And everyone asked me, "Well, what do you think he did?" and I said, "I know Todd. I know he wouldn't sit back and let—let something happen like this to other people or to himself. He was a competitor and he would have fought it." And—and knowing that I have the concrete evidence of his character that I can pass on to all three of my children, you know, people are going to tell them how great their daddy was because he's not here anymore, but we're going to be able to show them how great he was. And that's a great legacy for them that—that they'll be able to hold on to. And—and I do. . . .

SAWYER: And as you pay tribute, so do we.[9]

For the most part, the widows had little more knowledge of their husbands' actions on the planes and inside the towers than the media. But their fragility and dependence went a long way to magnifying their heroic mates. The more fragile the wives seemed—the more they were seen "holding on to each other" like the Gish sisters in *Orphans of the Storm*— the more formidable and potent their husbands. And the more dependent, the better: a stay-at-home mom trumped a mere stay-at-home wife, and the most coveted "get" on the media circuit was the stay-at-home mom who was pregnant on the day of the attack.

In early 2002, *People* flew thirty-one of that last category of women, along with some of their now newborn infants, to New York City for a group photo. The magazine had put twenty-two of its correspondents on this demanding story and conducted an intensive search of databases, news clipping services, and television archives to locate the new moms. The photo shoot took place in the Chelsea Piers studio lot—the same place where, four months earlier, doctors had waited helplessly at a massive triage center for World Trade Center patients who never came. *People* assigned thirty-five members of its staff to attend to the mothers and their babies, a greeting committee that included news correspondents, art directors, photographer's assistants, and five makeup artists and hairstylists. It stocked the hall with changing tables and plush sofas "where the women could nurse and relax," as the magazine put it later in a self-congratulatory sidebar to the cover story. "Another part of the studio was equipped with a VCR and art supplies where the 16 older children could watch videos or draw."[10]

Not to be outdone, *Primetime Live* rented out the Palm House at the Brooklyn Botanical Garden a half year later for its own babyfest—with double the number of newborns. "Sixty-three babies!" Diane Sawyer effused at the opening of the show. "All children born this year to fathers who died on September 11." The effusions continued:

> We're bringing them together for one amazing moment in time. Sixty-three squirming, determined babies. Two hundred fifty-two flailing arms and legs. For the first time, we'll see hilarious and heartbreaking home videos. . . . Tonight, for the first time, the widows and their babies come together to share sweet laughter, and haunting facts about body parts, their husbands' remains. The riotous joy, the consolation. The affirmation of life and light after the darkness. . . . We hug, we coo, we chase, we dance, we laugh. And if you wandered into this room not knowing who was there, you would only see the radiant smiles of mothers. You'd never know, behind each smile is a universe of sadness.

Viewers, Sawyer promised, would get to see 9/11 mothers in action: "Rocking, soothing, comforting. Bonding mother and child, uniting mother with mother. Mother as a cradle, a perfect counterpoint to Dad." The last was the key point. "A dad like Craig Staub," Sawyer offered as an example, "a big, blond, handsome devil of a guy" with a "loud" voice, who "had his own financial Web show broadcasting from the 89th floor of Tower Two." The message was clear: those World Trade Center office workers seemed to stand a little taller when their wives bent to rock the cradle.[11]

On the one-year anniversary of the attacks, 102 widows and their post-9/11 infants were flown to New York City yet again, this time for a "baby shower" at Cipriani, a swank restaurant in Midtown Manhattan. The tablecloths were pink-and-white pastel; the décor was floral. A toy angel was placed on each chair, along with a check for $4,000. The checks were to go toward the babies' care and feeding. Governor George Pataki's wife, Libby, delivered remarks at the luncheon, and Laura Bush sent a congratulatory message. The luncheon was featured on *CBS Evening News*, MSNBC, and twenty-five local television affiliates, as well as in *American Baby*, *Parenting*, *BusinessWeek*, the *New York Times*, and more than 160 newspapers across the country. The event's sponsor? The same organization that had hailed 9/11 as the death knell of feminism: the Independent

Women's Forum. The IWF received ecstatic tributes from its sister commentators, including a salute on the op-ed page of the *Wall Street Journal*. A $4,000 stipend wouldn't go far in easing a single mother's child care needs. But maybe that was the point. As "pro-marriage" commentator Maggie Gallagher suggested in her admiring account of the pink-and-white luncheon, the plight of these widow-moms just went to show that the traditional familial arrangement was best: "A dad can never be replaced."[12]

No 9/11 widow seemed to fit the role better than the woman who became its archetype, the "Let's Roll" widow, Lisa Beamer. "A young mother recently widowed, with another child on the way," *People* said of her, "it's hard to imagine a more poignant description of vulnerability." Or a woman more devoted to making family and children "her first priority," as her media lionizers emphasized at every turn. She had, better yet, *chosen* traditional domesticity. She and her husband "were rising stars at the Oracle Corp., until Lisa decided to stay home when they had children," the *Dallas Morning News* made a point of noting. Beamer's interlocutors highlighted her lack of career aspirations. (Larry King: "What do you want to do with your life? Do you want to go to work?" Beamer: "Right now, I want to take care of my kids. That's what I wanted to do before September 11, and it is certainly a bigger job now than it ever was before.") And her lack of political opinions. (Q. "What do you make of all that's happened since: Al Qaeda, Afghanistan, war, airport security, people in Guantanamo?" A. "I need to really use all of my strength and energy on just my little world and my little family. And certainly I have confidence that the powers in our country that can effect change, the government and corporate America in the case of the airlines, are going to do the right things.") And her lack of spiritual doubts. (Q. "Did you not at all, Lisa, question your faith when this happened?" A. "I do just trust that God was in control that day and that he is, you know, taking care of me and loving me through this right now.") As required, she projected a persona defined by unassailably demure and virtuous composure. "Lisa has emerged as a symbol of national strength," *People* declared—"strength," that is, of the nonthreatening stripe, restricted to the nursery, the church pews, and the TV studios, where satisfying media fantasies became her seemingly full-time duty, her post-9/11 equivalent of employment. ABC News was one of the first to enlist her, as well as Lyz Glick, barely a week into their bereavement.[13]

LISA BEAMER: Todd was a winner. I showed Lyz [Glick] a picture of Todd this morning, and she said that looks like someone that Jeremy would have been friends with. . . .

DIANE SAWYER: And you're going to be able to tell your unborn baby that he was a hero.

BEAMER: Yeah. . . . You know, just to have something that's so factual and black and white to hold on to and pass on to those children someday is a unique blessing that I'm so thankful for.

SAWYER: If you learn that they didn't make it into the cockpit, if you learned from that voice recorder that they didn't get there. . . .

LYZ GLICK: They got there. They did what they had to do.

SAWYER: One way or the other.

BEAMER: Mm-hmm. And they took the action they needed to take, regardless of the results. And that's what character is.[14]

Beamer was expected to do more than vouch for her husband as a "winner"; she was asked to say that his valor made her feel *better* about losing him, that she took pride in his sacrifice. As commentator Mark Shields wrote in his September 17, 2001, column: " 'It is better,' a Spanish woman revolutionary once said, 'to be the widow of a hero than the wife of a coward.' "[15] When veterans of World War II and Vietnam began mailing Beamer their Purple Heart medals, she was supposed to be thrilled:

LARRY KING: Must make you feel terrific.

LISA BEAMER: It does.[16]

After President Bush singled out Todd Beamer for special mention in his State of the Union address—which Lisa observed from a House chamber balcony, seated next to the defense secretary's wife, Joyce Rumsfeld—*Good Morning America* rushed the widow back to the set for her reaction:

> CHARLES GIBSON: You talked to Diane [Sawyer] last half-hour, but, Lisa, as I watched you last night, I thought, you know, "I suspect when she sat down, she must have had a word to say to Todd."

> LISA BEAMER: I did. I said, I'm proud of Todd. I was proud of him before this, but seeing the Capitol Building standing and hearing the stories of so many people who feel like they owe their lives to Todd and his—his teammates on Flight 93 was something that I will be able to hold on to in those dark moments of emotion that come as waves now and will come as waves to me probably throughout the rest of my life.

> GIBSON: And did you say to him, "Todd, you're not going to believe where I am?"

> BEAMER: Yeah. . . . And he's, I know, just so thankful for what he was able to do for our country.

> GIBSON: All right, thank you very much, Lisa. It was a proud night for him, for you, for all the people involved with that flight.[17]

Beamer soon discovered the degree to which the media expected her to follow the teleprompter. "Some media with whom I did interviews had most of their story written before they ever talked with me," she wrote later in her memoir, *Let's Roll!* "Others took a grain of truth and twisted, planted or spun it any way they chose. For instance, one paper said that my learning about Todd's call 'made my life worth living again.'" Beamer had neither made such a statement nor, she noted, ever thought it for a moment.[18]

Had she voiced her misgivings, the treatment she received would no doubt have been different. As it was, a joint session of Congress gave her a standing ovation; she was the invited speaker at the National Prayer

Breakfast in Washington in 2002; politicians from Bush to Giuliani held forth on her virtues; *People* anointed her one of the "25 Most Intriguing People of 2001"; and Tyndale House signed her up for a ghostwritten "inspirational memoir," with a first print run of one million copies (greeted with headlines like "Lisa Beamer: Mom First, Author Second"). Beamer would remain in almost constant media rotation for a year, twelve months in which her process of "coping" was chronicled in obsessive detail and reduced to Hallmark moments: the decorating of the family Christmas tree, the opening of her Mother's Day gifts, the boarding of her first post-9/11 jetliner (on the same United Newark–San Francisco run as her husband's last flight), the address before a churchwomen's conference (theme: "What do you do if you are a beaten-down flower?"), and the delivery of her daughter in early January 2002, a media event rivaling little Ricky's arrival on *I Love Lucy*. ("We were there when Lisa Beamer gave birth," announced that perpetual monitor of post-9/11 nativity, *Primetime* host Diane Sawyer. "We even captured Morgan's first smile on videotape.") Both President Bush and First Lady Laura sent the newborn congratulatory letters, which Beamer dutifully read on the air. ("Dear Morgan, January 9th will always be a special day. . . . Your father was a hero on September 11, 2001. . . . God bless you and your family, George Bush.")[19]

Larry King featured Beamer on his show seven times in the first eight months after 9/11. King styled himself a kind of in loco patriarch to Beamer and her brood. He played the *Father Knows Best* version, TV daddy as mildly patronizing overseer, affecting fascination with any and all domestic developments in the Beamer household, no matter how trivial. "Are the children anxiously awaiting the arrival of their little brother or sister?" King wanted to know. "Did you send out Christmas cards this year? . . . I notice that pretty tree behind. Did Todd usually put the tree up? . . . So all the ornaments then or most of the ornaments have special meaning for you? . . . This Christmas, doesn't it make you sadder? . . . Are the kids going to get what they want for Christmas? . . . What do you want for Christmas? . . . Now, how do the boys like having a little sister? . . . And you're glad it was a girl? . . . Girls are different, are they not? . . . Does she sleep well at night? . . . What do you have, one boy in a bed and two in cribs now? . . . Oh, the little one is in a bed too?"[20]

Ultimately, the lavish attentions of the media left Beamer in an impossible bind. She was supposed to be just a "normal suburban mom," as she described herself, but all the celebrity treatment suggested otherwise. She soon found herself subjected to the rancor of rivals. Some of the other 9/11 widows were ready for her media reign to be over. Journalist Jere Longman described the fallout in *Among the Heroes*, his book on the Flight 93 passengers and their families:

> However misdirected, a backlash developed in occasional letters to the editor and in private remarks by some families of Flight 93 passengers. The letters and whispers suggested that Lisa received too much attention, that she was attempting to make her husband the preeminent hero. . . . Bitterness welled up in the perception that passengers aboard Flight 93 had attained unequal status in their deaths, that heroism had been divided into the ranks of generals and privates.[21]

Even Larry King began to pester his chosen widow with the question of her motives. "Why, Lisa, do you remain public like you do?" he asked. "Some people go quietly into the night with tragedy."

"Well, I have certainly said no to most opportunities that have come up as far as media and things like that," she replied, "because my primary role before all this and primary role after all this is to take care of my sons."

But King couldn't stop asking:

> KING: Do you have any at all discomfort, I guess is the right word, with all the attention you get? I mean, other mothers were in the same place and they had, you know, maybe their husbands weren't heroes. I guess they're all heroes of September 11. Do you feel kind of unusual?
>
> BEAMER: I'm very uncomfortable with that and I always try to as much as I can remind people that there's a lot of faces like mine that are left from September 11. There's a lot of faces like Morgan's

and Drew's and David's. And part of the reason we established the [Todd M. Beamer] Foundation in the beginning is because my family did receive a lot of publicity and many donations from around the country. And I wanted to make sure that those were put in a place that could benefit everyone who lost people that day.

KING: Because after all, you got to attend as a guest of the President and First Lady, the State of the Union.[22]

As the first anniversary of 9/11 neared, Beamer was beginning to rethink her spot on the public stage. She had done everything asked of her. She had delivered the approved lines or tactfully refrained from retracting the ones that had been placed in her mouth. And yet, the media Madonna was increasingly being painted as a media hound. She tried her best to defend herself. "In those mind-numbing days after the crash I had (and still have) no desire for publicity," she tried to explain in her 2002 memoir. She wanted nothing for herself, just "some small public record of who Todd was . . . for the sake of our children." But nothing Beamer said seemed to diminish the bitter snipes, and by the time she began her book tour in the late summer of 2002, she seemed ready to retreat. How did she feel about her "public persona," a Los Angeles Times reporter asked, as Beamer signed copies of Let's Roll! at a Los Angeles bookstore and a publicist yanked at her sleeve, reminding her that yet another appearance on Larry King Live awaited. "It's sort of another thing I have to deal with at this point," Beamer replied wearily. "I guess, for me, I'm sort of done reshaping Sept. 11, in a lot of ways."[23]

So were many of the other anointed widows. A. R. Torres, who was eight months pregnant when her husband died in the World Trade Center, recoiled from being typecast as "grieving widow with a post-9/11 baby, a newly minted American icon," as she put it in a first-person piece in Salon on January 25, 2002. "I feel so exposed. I cynically imagine a request from Playboy to pose on red, white and blue satin, patriotically baring myself to suckle my post-9/11 son. And then I seriously wonder who will be the first among the families to do it." Deanna Burnett, whose husband died on Flight 93, came to distrust the hosannas. "In the beginning, everyone asked, 'Aren't you proud of him? Aren't you happy that he's a hero?'" she said. "I thought, my goodness, the first thing you have to understand is, I'm just trying to put one foot in front of the other. For my husband to be anyone's hero, I'd much prefer him to be here with me. As selfish as that is, it's the truth. Use Thomas Jefferson as your hero, not my husband."[24]

Lyz Glick was having similar thoughts. She began to sicken at the packages of Purple Hearts and hero-worship memorabilia that kept arriving in her mailbox. In her memoir, *Your Father's Voice*, written as a series of letters to her newborn child, she wrote: "I wanted to say to them, this is not what Jeremy and I were about. Jeremy didn't sign up to fight terrorism. . . . He did what he did because he wanted so very badly to come home to his wife and baby daughter." Some of the gifts sent to the Glick home "really upset" her, she recalled:

> Someone sent a bumper sticker that said, "'Let's Roll': Todd Beamer's last words to Jeremy Glick." The last words of a young man blown out of the world in the prime of life don't belong on a bumper sticker. Or there was the local man who took to sending us a Beanie Baby at each holiday with a card saying, "Love, Daddy." Eventually, I started hurling them across the room. Couldn't you just sign them, "From a friend"?

After a while, Glick lost her willingness to stick to the script. "Although it had been flattering to hear President Bush express his personal gratitude for what Jeremy and the other passengers did to 'save' the White House," she recalled, "I knew when he said it that this simply wasn't true." If the plane hadn't crashed, the air force "was preparing to blast my husband and forty other civilians out of the sky," she pointed out. And anyway, she wondered, shouldn't the real question be why there were no efforts made to *save* her husband and the other passengers of Flight 93? Their plane was the last to be hijacked, yet "for almost an hour [from the time of the first hijacking], while all of this horror unfolded in the skies, nothing consequential was done." She began to say what she really thought. "In interviews, when someone lobbed what they thought was a soft question at me about whether or not I was proud that Jeremy saved the White House, they'd get a big surprise. I'd reply that I wasn't, because he didn't save it." A *Dateline* interviewer "just about fell out of her chair." The media inquisitors, Glick came to understand, weren't interested in her version of the truth; they were interested in their own fiction, "this wonderful story, a national myth to elevate our grief."[25]

Widows who didn't contribute to the "wonderful story" found themselves dropped from the media dance card. Widows who openly flouted its terms were treated far worse—they found themselves the objects of widespread censure. This was the lesson learned by one group of women in particular. As the wives of the most vaunted "heroes," the firefighters' widows were at first the most exalted—"perfect virgins of grief," *New York* magazine called them. That is, until the day the virgins began throwing off their habits, and—armed with an average $2 to $3 million in compensation and charity checks—began to exercise some economic and personal independence. Their private affairs—what they shopped for, where they chose to live, whom they dated—attracted public scrutiny and public reproach. It was as if by making their own choices the women had committed a kind of desecration, defaced the very statues erected to their virtuous victimhood. The widows were said to be spending "blood money" on what were invariably referred to as "lavish lifestyles."

Media censors took exception to "the many expensive Xboxes under one widow's Christmas tree." They seized on rumors about widows who supposedly had face-lifts, Botox injections, breast implants, and cosmetic surgery—one was even said to have gone under the knife "on her wedding anniversary." (These women were never named, except in one case—in which a widow who just had naturally large breasts was wrongly identified as having had implants.) They printed scuttlebutt about firefighters' widows who were supposedly going on "exotic vacations" or filling their garages with fleets of Mercedes-Benzes and Jaguars and Escalades. Some widows did trade in their old cars for new ones or move their families to better homes (and why not?), but by and large, the more egregious reports of "spending sprees" were unverified. The wagging tongue of an envious relative or neighbor was deemed sufficient confirmation.[26]

The same lack of hard data backed the media-declared trend of widows romancing their late husbands' firefighting buddies. Press reports variously set the number of women engaging in this "dirty little secret" at "many," "at least eight," "at least a dozen," and "10 or 11 such love triangles"—this last estimate, in the *New York Times Magazine*, attributed to "Fire Department sources." In the end, the press produced exactly two documented cases of a love affair between a firefighter and a firefighter's widow—and provided specific information on only one of them, thanks to nonstop bad-mouthing from the widow's resentful brother-in-law. According to him, Debbie Amato's sins included not only romance but the purchase of a "gold Acura SUV," a large home in an affluent suburb, and—God forbid—a condo for her son.[27]

That was evidence enough for the *New York Post*, which ran multiple stories on this domestic matter, under such headlines as "Boob Implants and Vacations? 'I'd Like to Knock in Her 40G Teeth.'" The quotation in the headline belonged to John Amato, the brother-in-law, who, despite such threatening outbursts, was cast as "heartsick John" and "heartbroken brother of fallen firefighter." His brother's widow, in Amato's opinion, wasn't fulfilling her maternal responsibilities: "I know I'm going to see my brother again one day, and I just don't know what I'm going to tell him," he told reporters. "The youngest is my main concern. She doesn't have a father—and now it seems, she doesn't have a mother, either." To hear the brother-in-law tell it, Debbie Amato was rushing off every other day to a five-star spa or a tropical island. She was guilty, as a *New York Post* caption under her photo put it, of "grieving in luxury."[28]

The story made the rounds nationally and, soon, internationally; the "merry widow" was denounced in the Melbourne *Sunday Herald Sun*, the Bristol *Western Daily Press*, and the London *Daily Mail*, which claimed she had "cut the grieving process to a minimum and found comfort instead in a new luxury lifestyle." The most deplored indulgences were those "boob implants," an investment that suggested the ultimate sacrilege: the perfect virgins of grief were starting to regard themselves as sexual beings who might not spend the rest of their lives in widow's weeds. A set of perky plastic breasts was the modern scarlet letter. Or, as the *New York Times* put it in a 2007 article about discord among 9/11 widows and their dead husbands' parents, "perhaps the most unmentionable issue" was "the desire of some surviving spouses to start over, to escape the veil of 9/11 widowhood, even if it means exiling the in-laws." As for

Debbie Amato, her sexual impropriety was compounded by the fact that the man in question was married. Firefigher John Zazulka had left his wife and family and moved in with Amato. His change of domicile, presumably, was voluntary. Nonetheless, the press labeled only Debbie Amato a "home-wrecker." "It made it seem like the women were the evil temptresses and it was the men who were seduced," firefighter widow Marian Fontana remarked to me later. "And that's just not reality. Everybody was just behaving like human beings."[29]

Amato had forfeited her victim tiara, and the media wasted no time transferring it to the head of Zazulka's ex-wife, Susan. "9/11, in a way, left her without a husband," journalist Susan Dominus wrote in her *New York Times Magazine* cover story on the affair. The ex-wife now "identifies" as a 9/11 widow, Dominus said. "In fact, she went ahead and applied to the Red Cross for assistance and received a case number." Susan Zazulka's afflictions were recounted in minute detail: the unpaid bills, the son who was acting out, the fourth mortgage payment she had missed on her home. Nothing eluded the *Times*'s pitying gaze, including a "malfunctioning sprinkler system" in her backyard that Zazulka didn't know how to fix; that was her ex-husband's job.[30]

At the same time the media were wringing their hankies over the abandoned firefighter wives, they were doing their best to keep the "hero" medal attached to the straying husbands of the FDNY. It wasn't really the men's fault, the media jurors ruled: they had been set up for temptation when the fire department had assigned them as "liaisons" to their buddies' widows. Media accounts noted with approval the efforts of the only other wife known to be abandoned, Mary Koenig, who had called on lawmakers to pass what she called the "John Bergin Act" (after the dead firefighter whose widow, Madeline Bergin, had gotten romantically involved with Koenig's husband, Gerry), which would have required the fire department's brass to supervise the liaisons more closely. In any event, the press reports maintained, the wandering husbands shouldn't be blamed; after the trauma of 9/11, maybe they felt they didn't deserve to enjoy a family life. Or maybe because they couldn't rescue their brothers that day, they were susceptible to conniving widows who played on their need to offer protection. Maybe "survivor's guilt" had rendered men like John

Zazulka *too* chivalrous. "People say that firefighters who marry widows have some kind of a rescue complex, that they left their own wives to swoop in and save someone else's," Dominus mused in the *New York Times Magazine*. John Zazulka didn't buy that. "No, that's not it," he told Dominus. "It's the other way around," he said. "She saved me."[31]

Even FDNY widows who didn't come in for quite the same drubbing as Debbie Amato understood the dangers of going off script. From the afternoon of 9/11 forward, "it was, get the widows into the church, get the widows out of the rain, get the widows to the front of the line," firefighter widow Charlene Fiore told *New York* magazine. Three years after 9/11, she was now engaged to another firefighter—in this case, an unwed one—and she feared the reaction. "The public wants you to live up to what they made you," she said. "They don't really want you to move on." Indeed, after *New York* ran its story—"The Dead Wives Club, or Char in Love"—the vitriol rolled in. One letter writer called the widows featured in the article "odious" and proposed, "Maybe they should consider doing a TV show—say *Checks and the City?*" Evidently, the independent wealth and the freedom that came with it offended public sensibilities. Beneath the popular crack that New York firefighters were "worth more to their wives dead than alive" lurked a greater fear: that the wives—no matter how many times they stood at the "front of the line" and wept—felt that way, too.[32]

The crimes of the firefighters' widows were fiscal and sexual—misdemeanors compared with the felonies of a final group of widows. The "Jersey Girls," as a group of women whose husbands died in the World Trade Center styled themselves, were "just four moms from New Jersey." They hadn't used their compensation checks to change their lifestyles: they were already leading comfortable lives, thanks to their husbands' careers as investment managers and securities traders. They weren't reported to be getting breast implants or buying time shares in Hawaii. They weren't said to be having affairs with married men. Yet, their violation of the script would be deemed the most egregious: the independence the Jersey Girls exercised after 9/11 was political.[33]

The Jersey Girls emerged from Middletown, New Jersey, a neofifties enclave for the families of nineties stock market strivers. In its prevailing hostility to working women, Middletown might have served as a scene set for *The Stepford Wives*. "The dream of these upwardly mobile Americans was to park the wife and children snug and safe in a virtually all-white suburb while the husband battled in the high-stakes, macho world of Wall Street," Gail Sheehy wrote in her 2003 book, *Middletown, America*. Middletown, Sheehy observed, was a place where not only women who worked but women who engaged in any public or civic pursuit were regarded as suspect. "At some point," she wrote, "most Middletowners ceased to function as citizens and became strictly taxpayers." They assumed their fiscal contribution would be sufficient and well spent without their involvement. Kristen Breitweiser, who would become the best known of the Jersey Girls, put it this way: "On the morning of 9/11 . . . I believed that my government was protecting me, was doing its job. I thought I was a stockholder in the country of America. I thought that my taxes were being spent wisely. I thought that things were being taken care of."[34]

Breitweiser, a 1996 graduate of Seton Hall Law School, had practiced law a grand total of three days before retiring. She met her husband, Ron, a money manager, that same year, and from then on, "things were being taken care of" as he scaled the ranks at Fiduciary Trust. She registered Republican because he did, quit reading the *New York Times* because he regarded it as a "liberal rag," and voted in 2000, as he did, for George Bush. Politics, however, held little interest for her. She spent her days tending to their preschooler, Caroline. The story was much the same for the other three Jersey Girls—Mindy Kleinberg, Patty Casazza, and Lorie van Auken—all women disconnected from public life and dedicated to the care and upbringing of their small children. There was, therefore, a certain irony in the image that provoked their political awakening after 9/11.[35]

"I think what really initially started it was I saw the picture of the president in, I think it was *Newsweek* or *Time* magazine," Breitweiser recalled in an interview in 2002. She was referring to a photograph of President Bush reading "The Pet Goat" to a classroom of schoolchildren on the morning of September 11. "And the caption said, you know, 'Andy Card telling the president about the second plane.' And then I read that he proceeded to read for twenty-five minutes to the second graders." His evident obliviousness to national calamity horrified her. Soon thereafter, Lorie van Auken found a video of Bush's classroom visit on the Internet, and the Jersey Girls played those twenty-five minutes of presidential passivity over and over. "I couldn't stop watching the president, sitting there listening to second graders, while my husband was burning in a building," van Auken said. What the four women saw was their commander in chief, in the midst of their nation's gravest modern crisis, behaving like a Middletown mom.[36]

Which raised two questions—one about their nation's leaders and one about themselves. Patty Casazza recalled that her eleven-year-old son had some "very profound" questions after 9/11, but none more striking than this: "Who is supposed to be protecting us?" The nation's protectors didn't seem to be taking their duties very seriously, whether it was Bush joking about how "that's some bad pilot" fifteen minutes after the first attack or Rumsfeld not bothering to leave a routine briefing session even after the second plane had hit the towers. The media portrayal of Bush as a "man of action," Breitweiser would eventually conclude in an article for *Salon*, was the product of "Karl Rove's art direction." Bush was "an action hero," she wrote. "Except, of course, when it really counts."[37]

The second question—why had American voters accepted such shoddy stewardship?—led the Jersey Girls to reflect on their own complicity, their failure to serve as anything other than taxpayers to their nation. "I felt responsible," Mindy Kleinberg said. "I really felt like, had I done what I should have done as a citizen . . . [and after] Lockerbie, had I called the senators and congressmen, had I rallied together with those people who are victims, then maybe we could have effected a change that could have stopped this. . . . Our role as citizens isn't just to sit and watch. If we really want to be a democracy we have to participate. That's what made me start to get involved." Getting involved meant refusing to play the part the culture had allotted them. As Patty Casazza put it, "You either remain a victim . . . or you say to yourself, 'No more.'"[38]

For months, the Jersey Girls scoured obscure databases, news archives, and government documents. They pieced together a sophisticated timeline of the missteps and mistakes leading to that terrible day. They began to frame questions and demand answers from law enforcement officers

and elected officials. They wanted to know: Why did so many government agencies dawdle on 9/11? Why didn't NORAD scramble planes in
time to intercept the two other hijacked planes heading for Washington,
D.C.? Why wasn't established protocol for dealing with renegade flights
followed? Why did the FBI fail to follow up on the many indications of a
plot in the works? How did the CIA fail to find the two hijackers who
were already on the CIA watch list—when one was listed in the San
Diego phone book and both rented a room from an undercover FBI in-
formant?[39]

By the time the Jersey Girls traveled to FBI headquarters in June
2002—on one of what would be scores of road trips to the nation's capital—
they had transformed themselves into knowledgeable sleuths, investiga-
tors who seemed to know more than their official counterparts. Sheehy
described Kristen Breitweiser's unrelenting interrogation of senior FBI
agents that day:

"I don't understand, with all the warnings about the possibilities of Al
Qaeda using planes as weapons, and the Phoenix Memo from one of
your own agents warning that Osama bin Laden was sending operatives
to this country for flight-school training, why didn't you check out flight
schools before Sept. 11?"

"Do you know how many flight schools there are in the U.S.? Thousands," a senior agent protested. "We couldn't have investigated them
all and found these few guys."

"Wait, you just told me there were too many flight schools and that
prohibited you from investigating them before 9/11," Kristen persisted.
"How is it that a few hours after the attacks, the nation is brought to its
knees, and miraculously F.B.I. agents showed up at Embry-Riddle flight
school in Florida where some of the terrorists trained?"

"We got lucky," was the reply.

Kristen then asked the agent how the F.B.I. had known exactly
which A.T.M. in Portland, Me., would yield a videotape of Mohammed
Atta, the leader of the attacks. The agent got some facts confused, then
changed his story. When Kristen wouldn't be pacified by evasive answers, the senior agent parried, "What are you getting at?"

"I think you had open investigations before Sept. 11 on some of the people responsible for the terrorist attacks," she said.

"We did not," the agent said unequivocally.

A month later, on the morning of July 24, before the scathing Congressional report on intelligence failures was released, Kristen and the three other moms from New Jersey with whom she'd been in league sat impassively at a briefing by staff director Eleanor Hill: In fact, they learned, the F.B.I. had open investigations on 14 individuals who had contact with the hijackers while they were in the United States.[40]

The families of 9/11 victims ultimately chose Breitweiser to represent them in the first televised public hearing of the congressional joint inquiry into the attacks. Congressional staffers advised Breitweiser that her job was to provide "a soft, emotional ploy," she recalled. They urged her to play up her personal angst and leave the nuts-and-bolts issues to others. "*Oprah* was what they were expecting," Breitweiser said. But she had other plans. "*60 Minutes* was what they were going to get." She delivered what was widely recognized as a powerful address, laying out, step by step, the failures of protection that had paved the way to national tragedy. "Our intelligence agencies," she testified, "suffered an utter collapse in their duties and responsibilities leading up to and on September 11." Holding up her hand with her husband's charred wedding ring—that and a piece of finger were all that remained of him—she reminded the members of the House and Senate intelligence committees that a "hallmark of democratic government is a willingness to admit to, analyze, and learn from mistakes."[41]

When it became clear that the congressional inquiry was hamstrung and compromised beyond repair, it was the Jersey Girls who played an essential role in forcing the creation of the independent 9/11 Commission. It was the Jersey Girls who continued to press for months to coerce a stonewalling Bush administration to produce the necessary documents. It was the Jersey Girls who strong-armed top White House officials into testifying before the commission. The women's force of persuasion took the authorities by surprise. "I'm enormously impressed that laypeople with no powers of subpoena, with no access to insider information of any sort, could put together a very powerful set of questions and set of facts that are a road map for this commission," Jamie Gorelick, former U.S. deputy attorney general, said at the first open hearing of the 9/11 Commission. "It is really quite striking. Now, what's your secret?"

"Eighteen months of doing nothing but grieving and connecting the dots," Mindy Kleinberg replied.[42]

Others were not so pleased. Mayor Giuliani and Representative Peter King, the chairman of the House Homeland Security Committee, told the Jersey Girls they needed to learn to "trust" their government. Before Breitweiser's second round of congressional testimony, she was summoned before two senators and a panel of committee staffers, who insisted on reviewing her remarks beforehand and warned her not to say anything that might be "embarrassing" to the president. The four widows were still calling themselves "girls," but they were regarded as furies by their targets, one of whom (Republican congressman and future CIA director Porter Goss) literally hid when they knocked on his door. These widows, a GOP staff member complained to UPI, "generally seem to get what they want." To the conservative establishment, they were loud-mouthed women who needed to be muzzled, especially after they raised a stink over Bush's reelection campaign commercials, which were using footage of 9/11 carnage to market the president as the nation's protective paterfamilias. In a matter of days, the conservative punditry launched its counteroffensive, calling Breitweiser a self-promoter who "never met a camera or mike or editorial writer she didn't like" and the Jersey Girls "quite insufferable" and "hysterical."[43]

"The 9/11 Widows: Americans Are Beginning to Tire of Them," read the headline over Dorothy Rabinowitz's *Wall Street Journal* column. There was a "darker side of this spectacle of the widows," Rabinowitz wrote. She never did say what that was. But "a fair number of Americans," she asserted, may be "experiencing Jersey Girls Fatigue" and "taking a hard look at the pronouncements of the widows." Rabinowitz offered only one such American to support that contention: Debra Burlingame, the sister of the pilot whose hijacked plane had hit the Pentagon. Burlingame was irritated by all the attention the Jersey Girls had received; in interviews, she called them "rock stars of grief" and avowed that "people are getting sick of them because they are being so demanding." She was soon invited to vent her grievances on the *Wall Street Journal*'s op-ed page, and her jabs at her sister widows, along with her willingness to shill for the Iraq invasion after it had gone south ("Right War, Right Place, Right Time" was the headline on her October 2, 2004, opinion piece in the *Wall Street Journal*), earned her fawning recognition on the right. She quickly became a fixture on Fox News and conservative opinion pages. In 2004, she ascended to the dais to deliver a keynote address at the Republican National Convention—a platitudinous speech that made much of her brother's military service, Cub Scout days, and summer job selling American flags.[44]

For their part, the Jersey Girls and one other 9/11 widow, Monica Gabrielle, stepped into the presidential campaign ring to announce their support for John Kerry. Two of the women had switched parties, after concluding that the Bush administration was derailing the search for answers to the September 11 disaster by its refusal to cooperate with official inquiries and its military adventurism in Iraq. The same conservatives who had applauded Burlingame for backing Bush called the Jersey Girls' endorsement of Kerry—as well as their objections to Bush campaign commercials that exploited 9/11 images—as the act of shameless "political operatives" and "Democrat hackettes" who were no longer "neutral innocents" and had relinquished their right to sympathy. Most famously, Ann Coulter denounced "the Democrat ratpack gals" as "self-obsessed women" who were "reveling in their status as celebrities"; they were "witches" and "harpies" who were "enjoying their husbands' deaths."[45]

The Jersey Girls were swiftly Swift-boated. They were accused of lining their pockets with money from liberal foundations. Rush Limbaugh ranted that the Jersey Girls "have literally been poisoned by their hate. They have been poisoned by their rage. It is unbelievable, the depths to which they will sink." They were "campaign consultants, not grieving family members," he said, engaged in an "incestuous" relationship with "a political organization that is funded in part by Teresa Heinz-Kerry."[46]

He was referring to an organization called Peaceful Tomorrows, which in fact wasn't receiving any money from Teresa Heinz or the Heinz family's foundation. But it was telling that Limbaugh, like so many other conservative media spokesmen, imagined a distaff plot, masterminded by a powerful woman whose independence made her suspect. The attacks on the Jersey Girls so often betrayed an underlying misogyny—most evident in the id-ruled realm of the Web. On the *Wall Street Journal's* online readers' page, Breitweiser was called "a prostitute for the radical left hate Bush and America groups." On other conservative Web sites, she was "the modern day Madame Defarge [*sic*]" and "a golddigging, attention addicted, useful idiot ghoul girl" who had "been taking speechmaking lessons from Hillary." When Monica Gabrielle was actually invited to be Hillary Clinton's guest at the 2005 State of the Union address, the denizens of the FreeRepublic.com chat room went berserk: "Sounds like this witch voted against GWB in 2000." "Is Gabrielle one of the 'Jersey Bitches'?" "What a waste of human flesh this dingbat is." "Sorry for your loss but you are a pathetic fool." "Monica Gabrielle. Porn star name." "OH . . . OH . . . OH . . . !!! I get it!!! Hillary 'Special Guest' . . . uh-hummmmm . . . Widows and Dykes, widows and dykes."[47]

DESPITE EVERYTHING THAT was thrown at them, the 9/11 widows would not return to their assigned seats. What could their tormentors do to them that could possibly be worse than what they'd already suffered? They *were* angry—as Limbaugh and others had charged—but women like the Jersey Girls had learned to channel their anger in a publicly productive direction. They weren't about to exchange that for figurehead status and condescending pity parties on the afternoon chat shows.

The "good widow" typecast, the women increasingly sensed, was a trap. Marian Fontana, the firefighter's widow who had organized the 9/11 Families Association, would come to chafe at playing "diplomat of grief," as she described her designated role. "We became symbols to the country in so many ways that were very unexpected," she told me. "We were being elevated to represent the event itself to some degree." The widows were the wounded site of attack, the violated motherland, expected to await decorously and passively the rescue by their masculine nation. But for Fontana at least, the trauma had the opposite effect.[48]

At one of the first rallies she organized—to protest cutbacks in the fire department that were levied only two weeks after the attack—a friend of hers teased, "I wouldn't fuck with ya." Without thinking, Fontana blurted out: "Don't. I'm an angry widow." In her 2005 memoir, *Widow's Walk*, Fontana considered the significance of that phrase:

> I *am* a widow. I picture myself standing on the roof of an elegant Victorian home, looking out at the vast expanse of ocean, a wrought-iron fence making a square around me. I stand on the widow's walk waiting in a long black dress, my shawl fluttering behind me like crows' wings. Then, suddenly angry, I imagine myself hiking up my dress and kicking the fence until it falls to the yard below.[49]

But even as Fontana and the other poster widows defected, the cultural smoke machine that had momentarily borrowed their image of immaculate grief churned on, undaunted. That machine operated in the service of myth, not reality. Its mission was to restore the image of an America invulnerable to attack, to conjure a dreamscape populated by John Wayne protectors guarding little captive Debbies, a reverie in which women were needed to play the helpless and dependent foil, whether in "a long black dress" or a white wedding veil. Fontana and her sister widows weren't so much the targets of that reconstruction effort as the designated proselytizers. The real intended audience was the female populace at large, which was soon to be saturated with a gauzy vision of resurrected American femininity, dedicated to home, family, domesticity. And dedicated to national security, insofar as "traditional" womanhood ("new traditional," as its advocates would have it) buttressed the masculine credentials on which our myth of imperviousness depended, a fantasy in which the homeland was never violated and our male leaders were always "action heroes," especially "when it really counts."

CHAPTER 5

Nesting Nation

IN THE WEEKS AFTER 9/11, MANY ILLUSTRATORS AND CARTOONISTS projected onto the burning towers two colossal apparitions—one of a New York City fireman and the other of a city policeman. Other observers, more eschatologically inclined, claimed to see the face of the devil shimmering through the smoke—an AP photo and CNN footage that supposedly captured Satan's visage enjoyed wide circulation on the Web. But *New York Times Magazine* writer Virginia Heffernan may have been one of the first to espy in the two vaporized edifices the outlines of conjugal togetherness. "The twin towers ruled over Lower Manhattan as more than just symbols of economic power," she wrote. "Standing side by side for almost 30 years, they could also seem romantic, the architecture of companionship. And when one fell, the other fell soon thereafter, in the manner of long-married couples." Now, if you weren't "long-married," Heffernan hastened to inform her readers—for this was the point of her strained analogy—then the attack on September 11 was sure to make you rue your unwedded state. "I started to hear stories of unmarried New

Yorkers," she wrote, "who out of nowhere began to exhibit near martial decisiveness." The turnaround was immediate, she claimed. "Even in my first phone conversations after the disaster, the change was evident. People who had once been afraid even to mention marriage were proposing. People who had long since parted were getting back together. People who'd been dating halfheartedly were breaking up."[1]

The "people" she had in mind were all women. There was "Casey," who hadn't spoken to her ex-boyfriend in six months, but when the towers fell "suddenly her wish to go home—and home to him—came into clear focus," and a few days later she was "suddenly planning their marriage." There was "Liza," for whom marriage used to seem "creepy and cultish, domesticating, anti-romantic, not for me," but after September 11, she found the marital state "enviable" and snagging the ring "immediately became a priority." To resist the wedding banns after the mutual immolation pact of Mr. and Mrs. Twin Towers was unseemly, selfish, *un-American*. "The old indecisiveness comes to seem out of sync with the country's renewed sense of purpose," Heffernan wrote. "It seems small-minded. It seems somehow unpatriotic."[2]

The media's lifestyle scribes were eager to guide women away from such treasonous thinking and toward a new veneration of the virtues of nesting. The terrorist attack had shocked us into "a new faith in our oldest values," *Time* pronounced in its October 1, 2001, feature, "Life on the Homefront," which presented those values as "a time of homecoming and housecleaning" and "couples renewing their vows." "And when each of us gets the chance to decide all over what matters most to us," *Time* concluded, "there is no telling what we may learn."[3]

Or rather, the lifestyle writers were going to *tell* us "what we may learn"—an instructional service that, more often than not, involved feminine correction. Whether women in the real world cooperated or not—whether they marched down the aisle or continued to regard marriage as "not for me"—was of little importance. *Time* and others were willing a transformation in another realm, the commercially mediated dream world in which "trends" attain an ersatz truth, fictional dramas command their own hyperreality, and the characters on *Sex and the City* stand in for real women. Americans didn't have to change their private behavior; they just had to subscribe to the sanctioned fantasy. And to judge themselves accordingly. They could adhere to its dictates and enjoy a pat of approval for their submission, or they could fail to meet its standards and suffer the shame of cultural and self-recrimination. Either way, they remained safely within the borders of the dream. If the myth's constructions ran afoul of the average American woman's reality, well, defying reality was the point. What mattered was restoring the illusion of a mythic America where women needed men's protection and men succeeded in providing it. What mattered was vanquishing the myth's dark twin, the humiliating "terror-dream" that 9/11 had forced to the surface of national consciousness.

Beginning with the demotion of independent-minded female commentators, the elevation of "manly men" at ground zero, and the adoration of widowed pregnant homemakers—that is, a cast of characters caught up in the September 11 trauma—the myth quickly rippled out to counsel—and chastise—the nation at large. Most particularly its women.

JUST TWO AND A HALF WEEKS after the towers fell, the *New York Times* style page ran a trend story on "lonely" Manhattan singles. It began:

> Claire Smithers is a woman considered to be good company, and she usually finds herself in good company. In her late 30's, she has her office friends and old-job friends, her boarding-school friends and church friends, friends made on the charity circuit during her 15 years in New York and those acquired over many more years at her family's summer home on the Connecticut shore. Ms. Smithers is unmarried, though no one who meets her would say her life is an island of one.

Those lines proved the stroke before the kick. The next paragraph delivered the boot:

> But in the aftermath of Sept. 11, like so many single men and women in New York, she has re-examined the meaning of being uncoupled. "It made me realize, really for the first time in my life, that I was alone,"

Ms. Smithers, the patient coordinator for a Park Avenue plastic surgeon, said. "I truly felt alone and questioned being alone. We've all had pangs of 'Oh no, what if I never get married? What's wrong with me?' But then you call your friends and you talk and go out and you forget about it."

"But this felt different—and deeper," she continued. "I've always loved being single, but during the crisis I pretty much hated it."

The newfound hatred of the single life was bound to outlive the crisis, the *Times* prognosticated: "Others seem to believe that changing values could lead single New Yorkers to reprioritize the rigid criteria they apply to selecting a mate." Though the story was ostensibly addressing both sexes— and quoted both—its instruction to "reprioritize" was aimed at women, as was evident in its one-sided references to evening purses, Diaper Genies, *Sex and the City, Fatal Attraction, That Girl*, and the long-disproved "man shortage." ("Media reports that women over 40 had a better chance of dying in a terrorist attack than of finding husbands," the story noted, were "now a chilling thought.") The article's real-world evidence boiled down to speculation from the single Claire Smithers—"Maybe it won't matter to women if [men] are five pounds overweight. Maybe we'll date men who are bald"—and hopeful declarations from the chief executive of It's Just Lunch, a matchmaking service: "This is a wake-up call," he said, "and people are asking themselves, 'Am I where I want to be?' "[4]

Real women "who have yet to commit" may or may not have regarded the terrorist attack as a "bucket of ice water," as the *Times* story put it. But the lifestyle writers were poised with their pails. "For those without a spouse or a network of relationships, the stress can be even worse," Joel Stein warned in his October 1, 2001, *Time* column, "Nation on the Couch." Life since the terrorist attacks "is more scary for everyone. But for many singles the absence of love feels like another layer of vulnerability," Lisa Birnbach advised on November 7, 2001, on CBS's *Early Show*. Birnbach prodded one thirty-six-year-old single woman to talk about "the void" she was feeling since 9/11. "When I speak with my friends who have serious relationships," the woman said, "it seems like so nice because they have someone who they can, you know, cuddle with, and who can, you know, they can be together because life is more scary." Psychologists said the aftermath of the attacks "can be especially hard on unattached people," Nancy Gibbs wrote in her *Time* cover story on November 19. Singles hear about those final calls home from the World Trade Center "and wonder whom they would call." The media fearmongers were particularly fond of pressing the you'll-have-no-one-to-call hot button. It was unclear which the press regarded as the greater grounds for panic: that a single person would have no spouse to speed dial or no mate to conduct the posthumous publicity campaign. "Who you gonna call?" the *Los Angeles Times* asked in its November 25 feature on the subject. "Two months into the scary world that terrorism has wrought, the question isn't just the goofy refrain of the 'Ghostbusters' anthem. It's the measure of isolation. Who would care if your plane crashed? Who would tell Katie Couric, with conviction, that you'd enriched their lives?"[5]

Single women who had placed "career ambition" ahead of matrimonial aspirations were said to be especially distraught, and desperate to remedy their "mistake." "I've spoken to real, strong executive women who thought they were fine on their own and happy," Paul Falzone, CEO of The Right One and Together Dating, the "world's largest dating service," told the press. Now they knew better: "They said, 'You know, I was making a living, but not a life.'" The *Los Angeles Times* served up two single women who were repenting their bad choices in the wake of the attacks. Anastasia Soare, who ran a Beverly Hills eyebrow grooming salon and cosmetics business, had put her work before her boyfriend's needs: "She told him her relationship rules: Don't call her at work, because she's too busy . . . to chat. Don't talk about marriage. Don't even think about more children." The collapse of the towers set her straight. A few weeks later, when her boyfriend "slyly dropped a diamond ring into Soare's glass of champagne and proposed," she promptly accepted. "The two will marry next summer." The *Times*'s other single penitent was thirty-three-year-old Desiree Gruber, who ran her own public relations firm in New York and had been planning a "commuter marriage" with her famous West Coast fiancé, Hollywood actor Kyle MacLachlan. After 9/11 she realized "we'd let romance become eclipsed by our careers." That had to be corrected, at least on her end. Gruber vowed to "no longer be seduced" by her work in Manhattan.[6]

Hollywood couples were leading the post-9/11 charge to the altar, according to media accounts, which seemed reconstituted from 1950s movie magazines. The tabloids, not surprisingly, were especially focused on connubial bliss. The *Star* published a special issue on the subject. "The terrorist attacks that stunned the world have changed Hollywood forever, too," the magazine's October 26, 2001, edition announced. "Now home and family are where the heart is for Tinseltown's movie and TV stars." September 11 made Tom Cruise and Nicole Kidman "realize what's really important and have convinced the pair to put an end to their bitter divorce bickering" (though not an end to their divorce). Meg Ryan and Dennis Quaid were considering getting back together (but didn't). And Lisa Marie Presley and Nicolas Cage "were brought so close together as they shared the horror . . . that they never want to be apart again" (but were divorced within the year). The stars weren't heeding the matrimonial casting call any more than their fifties counterparts (who likewise were held up as models of domestic bliss, while filing for divorce off camera). But the characters they played were more cooperative. "The family is looking awfully attractive in pop culture these days," *New York* reported in early 2002:

> In the fantasy New York of *Friends*, Monica and Rachel's fun-and-pigtails bachelorette pad has become Monica and Chandler's first home as man and wife. . . . On *Sex and the City*, once—recently—the televised manifesto of sharp-heeled sluts across the city, the focus has shifted from issues of dating and doing it to issues of marriage, cohabitation, and parenthood. There is a moment in one episode this season when Samantha—*Samantha!*—proclaims, "I think I have monogamy," looking at married Charlotte, engaged Carrie, and pregnant Miranda. "I must have got it from you people."[7]

Real women were encouraged to adjust their behavior to the Hollywood script. As a *Los Angeles Times* headline put it, "Like a Big-Screen Romance, Finding a Long-Term Relationship Has Taken on a New Urgency since Sept. 11." If the terrorist attack felt like a disaster film, the *Times* said, its emotional aftermath belonged to a different staple of cinematic experience: "Another Hollywood genre emerged from the rubble—the love story."[8]

If the actual Samanthas out there wanted to stay in the picture, they had better quit dating just for fun and "get serious" about finding a husband, no matter how dull. That cautionary tale was spun in *New York*, in Amy Sohn's November 12, 2001, column, "The Convert," which was subtitled "It took a tragedy to make her realize that dating a nice guy could be, well, nice." The tale's protagonist, an actress named Nina, used to date men in the theater world because she found them "charismatic, affectionate, and funny." The attacks changed everything: "Now I just want someone who's going to be good to me." Soon after the collapse of the World Trade Center, a friend set her up with an ordinary joe who worked in the unglamorous world of marketing. "I never would have given this guy a second chance before September 11," she said. After several dates, Nina "sent him an e-mail saying she didn't want to continue seeing him." Mr. Dullsville talked her out of it, by playing the terrorism card: did she really want to split up, he asked, "with everything that's going on in the world?" They resumed dating. In tribute to the national crisis that sealed their bond, he nicknamed her "Anthrax." She dubbed him "Little P" (after the short-lived smallpox scare), which she amended, after some hurt feelings on his part, to "Big P." When Nina's boyfriend went to Los Angeles on business, he offered her the now much-desired plum: "He told her that if there were hijackers on his plane, she would be the person he called on his cell phone."[9]

Beyond the anecdotal and pseudonymous, was there an actual sea change in conjugal relations? It was hard to tell from the media's statistic-free claims. "The matchmakers say they don't have enough staff to keep up with demand," *Time* magazine asserted. "Divorce lawyers report a drop in traffic." The *New York Times*, in one of its four stories on the subject in the space of two months—a September 23, 2001, article titled "What to Do in a Crisis? Wed"—had no documentation beyond the say-so of one New York psychoanalyst, Gail Saltz, who "has seen a number of couples who are separated or in the process of separating who decided to try to work things out," and the teary testimonial of Andrea Piazza, a twenty-seven-year-old Brooklyn resident who was vowing to wed her boyfriend: "I knew the moment the tower collapsed that we needed to get married as soon as possible." Two months after 9/11, an Associated Press article conceded that "there aren't any statistics to prove more people have been getting engaged since the attacks." Still, the story insisted, a "surge" in weddings was under way—a contention compelling enough to be heralded in media reports from coast to coast and as far away as Australia. (The headline in Australia's *Townsville Sun*: "Americans Not Terrified of Marriage.")[10]

New York mayor Rudolph Giuliani did his part for the post-9/11 wedding "surge" when, five days after the attack, he reported to St. James Lutheran Church in a tuxedo with a white rose pinned to his left lapel to give away Diane Gorumba, a bride whose firefighter brother had died, albeit in a blaze a month before 9/11. The media hailed the mayor's act as an augur of America's marital future (shelving for the moment Giuliani's less than inspiring marital past). Giuliani had "set an example," the *New York Times* declared. The *Chicago Tribune* applauded the mayor for playing "adopted papa." The mayor had delivered "a message many have taken to heart," *Dateline* said, pointing to the "hundreds" of couples lined up at the city clerk's office in Queens to purchase a marriage license in the weeks after 9/11 (an increase more reasonably explained by the fact that Queens was the only borough that kept its clerk's office open after the attacks).[11]

Getting married was "even more important these days," Eileen Monaghan, the vice president of the Association of Bridal Consultants, told the *New York Times*, because 9/11 made reluctant fiancés realize that their romantic relationships "are more important than jobs and money and titles." On the first installment of the *Today* show's four-part series titled "Love and War Today," Millie Martini Bratten, editor in chief of *Brides* magazine, informed viewers: "We are seeing more people getting married, rushing to get married, moving up their engagement dates, proposing right away, that type of thing. When you think of that—the phone calls that you heard from the trade center, you knew the priorities of those people were their spouses and their families and their friends. And we see people really looking closely at their priorities now."[12]

The December–January issue of *Brides*, the first issue produced after

9/11, featured a photo of Diane Gorumba on Giuliani's arm—"to help in-spire all Americans"—and an editorial exhorting readers not to make the mistake of delaying their nuptials out of some misplaced deference to the tragedy: "Even during this very sad period, don't be ashamed of your hap-piness. A wedding, with its inherent message of hope, sends a powerful and comforting signal to the world." Especially, the magazine went on to say, a wedding in a very expensive Watteau train, "an elegant treatment popularized in the late 19th century in which the train descends from high on the gown's back." Brides who wore Victorian garb were making an uplifting statement to a stricken nation, according to the wedding merchants. In the October 2, 2001, issue of *Women's Wear Daily*, design-ers predicted that the post-9/11 bridal fashions would feature "more romantic, princess-like elements, such as ballgown skirts, cap sleeves, form-fitting, embellished bodices and long veils" and "after several sea-sons of colorful wedding dresses walking down the aisle, white and ivory gowns will become more important again."[13]

Four months after the attacks, *New York* finally decided to ask actual singles about their post-9/11 marital plans. The poll the magazine com-missioned of more than six hundred single New Yorkers was released with great fanfare on the five-month anniversary of 9/11 in its special issue, "Single in the New City." The cover featured a staged photograph of a young woman in white aggressively smooching a fireman, who was prac-tically falling over from the force of her attentions. The magazine's con-tributing editor Ariel Levy explained the need for connubial connection. "The sky could fall—it already has once," she wrote. "Who will hold your hand?" The accompanying poll proclaimed the good news: New Yorkers were "changing their attitudes about dating, romance, and nightlife in surprisingly large numbers." About 36 percent of singles were "more in-terested in marriage" since 9/11, and about 32 percent were "more inter-ested in having a family." Like all statistics, there were various ways of reading them. For instance, a far larger percentage, 50 percent, said that their interest in marriage had *not* changed since 9/11, and 51 percent said their interest in family had not changed either. Responses to some of the other questions in the survey cast the results in a different light, too. "Do you think what you are looking for in an ideal partner has changed since the events of September 11?" the survey asked; 81 percent said no. "Have you dated someone since September 11th that you would not have dated before September 11th?"; 86 percent said no.[14]

There was, however, a notable gender distinction in these figures. "The women we polled were considerably more gunned up about fusing into a post–September 11 domestic cocoon than the men," Levy wrote. "Forty-two percent of women polled are more interested in marriage now, compared with 29 percent of the men, and 36 percent of women said 'more' to family versus 27 percent of men." Then again, by February 2002, single women—far more than single men—had been on the receiving end of a six-month matrimonial media campaign. What was the poll reflecting, women's private desires or the public expectations imposed on women—and was it even possible to separate the two?

In any event, the marketing effort had succeeded in darkening the image of the sexually liberated single woman. Levy, a longtime chronicler of the libidinous Manhattan gal and a single New Yorker herself, regarded the change with some ambivalence: "That exhilarating moment when women were supposed to be the new men—and all the ladies'-night-style sexual opportunism that implied—seems to be slipping away."[15]

As IF IN adherence to the old schoolyard chant "First comes love, then comes marriage . . . ," the media mythicizers soon moved on to the baby carriage. On the heels of the "wedding boom," prognostications turned to "baby boom."

New York, once again, was in the vanguard. Its October 29, 2001, story "Baby Talk," accompanied by a drawing of a war bride sending her husband off to the front, began: "For years, New York women managed to keep 'have kids' well below 'get promotion' or 'upgrade apartment' on their list of life's priorities. But the old priorities ain't what they used to be." The attacks had convinced New York career women that they better get pregnant before they made partner. "Since September 11, biological clocks all over town seem to be speeding up," New York asserted. "Are we on the verge of a baby boomlet?" There was no way of knowing; it was too early even for home pregnancy tests. But as Shari Lusskin, a "reproductive psychiatrist" from New York University, told the magazine, "people *were* home for a week." The story was substantiated by two testimonials. "I know three people who told me they wanted to conceive on the day of the attacks," said "a thirty-one-year-old editor," who claimed to share the urge. "I totally felt a deep, primal need." The other unidentified source, "a twenty-nine-year-old museum curator who lives on the Upper East Side," also was hearing the call of the womb. "After it happened, all these families were out walking around and it made me realize how much I wanted to reproduce," she said. "I told my fiancé, 'I'm having *major* baby pangs.'"[16]

Did a deep primal need—and a week at home in front of the TV—actually lead to a week of unprotected sex in the bedroom? The answer was moot. *New York* and its media brethren weren't investigating the possibility of a trend; they were trying to induce one. "Like getting married, deciding to have a baby is a testament of faith in the future," *Time*'s Nancy Gibbs instructed on November 19. After the attack on our homeland, American women were feeling "an even greater sense of urgency" to procreate. They owed it to their countrymen. "In the face of tremendous loss, the life-affirming aspect of childbirth has a powerful appeal," *New York* coached. "The mere sight of [pregnant] bellies is often a comfort to others." It was time for women to prove their loyalty by enlisting in Uncle Sam's reproductive services. As *New York* put it, "Now you can add baby-making to your list of patriotic duties."[17]

Bush underscored that message a few weeks after 9/11, when he singled out a 9/11 widow who was eight months pregnant for special honors. His encounter with Nancy Taylor just before a memorial service at the Pentagon—where her husband, an army major, had died—attracted network news coverage. The president "spent two minutes with me, consoling me," Taylor told a rapt Larry King. "He immediately became engaged in consoling me. He embraced me. Kissed me several times on the head. . . . And he said the most important thing for me to do was to bring a healthy baby into the world." The press presented Taylor as a double inspiration to the nation: not only was she pregnant, she had soldiered through "the agony of infertility," as *CBS Evening News* put it, to get there—and was now setting up a foundation in her husband's name that would help other military couples invest in infertility treatments:

> LARRY KING: You have had a tough time with that. Both your babies were in vitro, right?
>
> NANCY TAYLOR: That's correct . . . but I feel this is perhaps God's gift to me that we have these two children that will carry on Kip's legacy.[18]

The infertility industry was quick to climb aboard the post-9/11 baby-making wagon. Resolve, an infertility association, alerted the press to a "50% jump" in its Web site traffic after September 11. The press assisted in the effort, spotlighting infertile women who felt out of step in the new era. "Looking around at everyone touching and holding their kids made it all so much more raw for us not having them," Stephanie Greco told *Time*. After her attempt at in vitro fertilization on September 13 failed, she felt "really lost."[19]

As it happened, the American Society for Reproductive Medicine (ASRM) had issued its own marching orders to the maternity ward just before 9/11, a "public service" campaign with surgeon general–style warning posters that intoned, "Advancing Age Decreases Your Ability to Have Children." Consequently, women taking public transit in New York, Chicago, and Seattle (where the campaign made its initial rollout) received the pronatal message in visual stereo: if they looked down at their newspapers, they saw stories about the postattack "baby boom" trend; if they looked up in the bus or subway, they saw the ASRM's alarming placards, illustrated with an upside-down baby bottle in the shape of an hourglass, its milk running out.[20]

The post-9/11 media enthusiasm for patriotic pregnancy created a congenial environment for the marketing efforts of the infertility profession, whose publicists were much in evidence that fall. Infertility was at "epidemic" levels, Mike Soules, the president of the American Society of Reproductive Medicine, advised the press. "Infertility is a devastating disease." Fortunately, there was a cure: "Just like diseases like lung cancer or HIV/AIDS, infertility can often be prevented." That is, by setting down the briefcase and putting motherhood first. The press eagerly spread the word with a string of stories that largely regurgitated the ASRM's press release. The *Washington Post* published a "pop quiz" to "test your fertility IQ," and *Glamour* offered a "Be-Fertile Guide" (with such tips as "Live the clean life," "Watch the scale," and "Treat your body like a fertility temple").[21] A month after 9/11, the American Infertility Association (AIA) unleashed its attack on delayed childbirth, flooding physicians' offices with "educational pamphlets" about how older childless women risked the "disease" of infertility and plastering the press with the results of an Internet survey of more than twelve thousand women that proved how "unaware" modern women were of the dangers of postponing pregnancy. Organon, a fertility-drug manufacturer, underwrote the whole venture.[22]

The onslaught continued in the spring of 2002, when Sylvia Ann Hewlett published *Creating a Life: Professional Women and the Quest for Children*. The book was, in many respects, a reprise of her 1986 volume, *A Lesser Life: The Myth of Women's Liberation in America*, which had charged the women's movement with being "antimotherhood." Hewlett's new book—its cover illustrated with a baby in a briefcase—featured a study she had commissioned in 2001 that purportedly proved that "high-achieving women" were suffering "an epidemic of childlessness." In the terrorist attacks, Hewlett saw an opportunity to further her case, and she seized it. "Nothing drove this point home more powerfully than the terrible events of September 11," she wrote in her preface. "The awful carnage of that morning convinced many of us that our lives were filled with a great deal of noise and clamor, signifying . . . rather little. . . . In a post–September 11 world we may be able to better appreciate how much we need our children."[23]

Misled by the career-first tenets of modern liberation, Hewlett contended, the high-achieving woman had "delay[ed] commitment and marriage," "squandered her fertility"—and now faced "a mother lode of pain and yearning." According to her survey, 33 percent of "high-achieving" women were childless at age forty. "Among ultra-achieving women in corporate America (those earning more than $100,000 a year), the childlessness figure rises to 49 percent," she said. Moreover, "the vast majority of these women did not choose to be childless": only 14 percent intended never to have kids. Hewlett arrived at that last figure by asking older women to recall whether they thought they'd have children back when they graduated from college. The maternal aspirations of twenty-one-year-olds, much less the clouded recollections of those aspirations at a remove of several decades, are hardly the stuff of actuarial science. Moreover, she ignored the large database amassed by the National Center for Health Statistics— which showed women were increasingly having babies at a later age. By 1999, the number of women in their late thirties and early forties giving birth for the first time had skyrocketed; the birthrate for women forty to forty-four years old had risen 95 percent since 1981.[24]

These facts were shoved aside in the publicity frenzy that followed the release of Hewlett's book. *Creating a Life* achieved the media trifecta: *Oprah*, *60 Minutes*, and the cover of *Time*, each of which contributed its own lacerating judgments on the reproductive "mistakes" of "high-achieving" women. "Listen to a successful woman discuss her failure to bear a child, and the grief comes in layers of bitterness and regret," *Time* wrote with pity that barely concealed the underlying disapproval. "This was supposed to be the easy part, right? Not like getting into Harvard. Not like making partner. . . . What can be so hard, especially for a Mistress of the Universe?"[25]

In May 2002, *New York* magazine returned with its second natal bugle call to the city's post-9/11 single women in a cover story called "Baby Panic." Its prime source was Sylvia Ann Hewlett. A full-page ad for Americanbaby.com accompanied the article. Single women thought they "could do everything men could," the article's author, Vanessa Grigoriadis, wrote. "But while we were busy with business, bars, and Barneys, did we miss out on motherhood?" Grigoriadis rounded up the usual suspect sources. "I even have a couple of single female friends in their early thirties who talked openly about hitting the sperm bank," she wrote, naming none of them. "It's hard to find anyone who was alone during the World Trade Center attacks who didn't think seriously about making family a higher priority." Most of the evidence offered to support that contention was literally fictional: on *Friends*, the article noted, Rachel was having a baby, and on *Sex and the City*, Charlotte was suffering from infertility and Miranda was striding into single motherhood. For further illumination on the sitcom situation, *New York* turned to Hewlett, who homed in on Carrie in *Sex and the City*, whose failure to get with the program contained a "nefarious" message to America's women. "This is a woman who's portrayed as a 35-year-old," an indignant Hewlett said, yet "there's not one mention of the character's biological clock. Thirty-five is the age where your fertility drops off a cliff, and there she is breaking up a long relationship with this guy who loves her with no thought to what she's giving up—not only him but probably also a family. I was stunned. I felt like running up to the TV screen, knocking on it, and saying, 'Hey, what about your eggs?'" The whole problem, Hewlett concluded, boiled down to young women's "extraordinary sense of entitlement. Somehow they think they have the *right* to have kids whenever they want. . . . It's obnoxious. It's overweening. And I think it is now over."[26]

The media certainly hoped so. In early June, nine months after 9/11, they began their salutes to the new era. "Childbirth professionals around the country are expecting a nationwide baby boomlet this summer," *Newsweek* announced. "Now, exactly nine months later, delivery rooms are getting ready for a baby boom," CBS's *Early Show* declared. Across the country, newspaper headlines followed suit, from "Hospitals Bracing for 9-11 Baby Boom" (*Chattanooga Times Free Press*) to "Post–Sept. 11 Baby Boom Hits Due Date; Area Hospitals Are Preparing for a Radical Increase in Deliveries" (*San Antonio Express-News*).[27]

By late June, the baby boom had yet to materialize, but the media remained confident. "Baby Boom Is Just Beginning," the *Augusta Chronicle* asserted on June 25. "The boom is delayed because everyone didn't set out on the week of Sept. 11 to get pregnant." "Baby Boom May Come Months Later Here," the *Virginian-Pilot* reported on June 30. "Oh baby! Get ready for October. Instead of pumpkins and jack-o-lanterns outside homes, Outer Bankers may see a surge of pink and blue balloons and flags." As late as mid-August 2002, CNN was still talking about the big glut of infants due to be delivered any day now.[28]

But the boom never happened, not even in the region most traumatized by the 9/11 attacks. Reporters from New York's *Daily News* to Westchester County's *Journal News* to Bergen County, New Jersey's *Record* combed their local maternity wards in vain. In 2003, the National Center for Health Statistics released its official count of births for 2002: the birthrate had fallen to the lowest level since national data have been available. It had dropped 1 percent from 2001 and 17 percent from 1990. Among one group of women, there had been a rise, but it didn't fit the Hewlett thesis: birthrates for women in their thirties and forties had jumped again, the federal agency noted, and were now the highest they'd been in more than three decades.[29]

WHETHER ACTUAL WOMEN married and had babies or not didn't seem to faze the media, which pressed on inexorably to its grand domestic finale: the beatification of the ideal post-9/11 American woman—undemanding, uncompetitive, and, most of all, dependent. She didn't just want a man in her life, she *needed* one. The image of the homebound wife whose security depended on her spouse had never been extinguished; efforts to bring back the "new traditional" woman had been launched periodically since the rise of modern feminism. But 9/11 seemed to provide the best opportunity yet to bring her out of dormancy—and the media's first responders rushed to rouse Sleeping Beauty from her slumber.

Soon after 9/11, several polls indicated that Americans—male and female alike—were responding to the attacks by resolving to spend more time with family and friends. Eighty percent of adults told *American Demographics* that the attacks "have increased their appreciation for their families" and 69 percent said that family was now a "greater priority." These findings were soon recast as: women want to quit their jobs and go home.[30]

Thanks to the terrorist attacks, more women were "choosing to make a career out of raising their children," Newhouse News Service maintained. "Surveys have shown that many parents are focusing on family since September 11." The *Los Angeles Times*'s approach was typical: it identified "the psychological fallout from the World Trade Center disaster" as a key force "pushing some of the country's best-prepared career women toward stay-at-home motherhood." The *Times* singled out two women who were supposedly fleeing the workforce because of the attacks. One was Lisa Kells, a thirty-three-year-old interior designer with an infant son. "A longtime weekly airplane traveler for work, Kells recently discovered she feels less inclined to leave home," the *Times* reported. Kells told the paper, "I was like, 'Why am I feeling weird about going to the airport?' All of a sudden you have another set of values." Despite those new "values," she wasn't quitting work. "I feel I need this job to bring home the bacon," she said. The other woman was Belen Aranda-Alvarado, a member of the Harvard Business School class of 2002. After "the horror of watching so many working professionals perish in the terrorist attacks on the World Trade Center," the *Times* said, she was reexamining her "priorities." She now planned to "put her MBA to use from home, starting an entrepreneurial venture while staying close to her baby." But her decision, she revealed, was dictated not by terrorism fears but by recession jitters. If the economy were still booming, she said, "I would be feeling, 'Oh, I've got to get out there.' I would have considered a big media company career in New York, and we [she and her boyfriend] would have been in a long-distance relationship." Her decision received reinforcement from another quarter: "I was surprised at how many men said, 'Take a year off,'" she remarked.[31]

The headline on the New York *Daily News*'s story, "Analyst Makes Kids New Career; More Women 'Opting-Out,'" reflected the media's characteristic leap of logic—from one woman's post-9/11 anxieties to a national shift in female behavior. Carol Warner Wilke was "a top Wall Street analyst" who decided soon after the twin towers fell "to trade number crunching for nursery rhymes":

> First came Sept. 11 and the Orange Alert warnings that made her nervous about her daily commute to Grand Central from Rye Brook in Westchester. . . .
>
> Then Tucker [her son] knocked out his newly minted front teeth in a tumble off a rocking chair while Wilke was traveling on business in Switzerland.
>
> When the blackout last summer left Wilke stranded in midtown, unable to reach her husband or her nanny, she began weighing a lifestyle change.
>
> "I got choked up. It wasn't the clincher, but it helped me realize I didn't want to be in the city, far from my kids, when the next thing happens," she said.

Wilke's powerhouse career as managing director at Merrill Lynch, combined with her husband's high income at the branding firm Lippincott Mercer, allowed her "the financial stability to retire at age 38 with no promise of going back." Her financial circumstances were hardly representative, and Wilke herself was "loath to call herself part of any trend." Her reluctance hardly deterred the *Daily News*, which insisted that an "'opt-out' trend" was in the works and pointed to other media coverage to document its existence: "Talk of married, professional moms dropping out of the workforce to rear kids is all over magazines, talk shows and book store shelves."[32]

The November 21, 2001, *Oprah Winfrey Show* was one of many dedicated to this "talk." Winfrey invited Sarah Ban Breathnach, author of the self-help best seller *Simple Abundance,* and several of her acolytes to describe how September 11 had inspired them to stop "chasing the illusion of success," as Winfrey put it, and be "grateful" for the small comforts of domestic life. The post-9/11 gratitude "movement," as Breathnach called it, was "revolutionary." Carol, "a forty-five-year-old mother of three," was one of the grateful revolutionaries summoned to the studio's set:

> Now that my son's in first grade, I had planned to go back to work, and then disaster struck. That changed everything. This nightmare made me reexamine my priorities. Before September 11, I lived by a schedule. Everything was according to the plan. Now I'm relishing the fact that I'm just home with the children.

Carol was followed by Danielle, a twenty-six-year-old New Yorker who was "experiencing gratitude for the first time" since 9/11, because it inspired her to let go of her professional ambitions. "I was obsessed with my job and my career and how fast I could get promoted, and when I lost the job earlier this year, I felt like it was the end of my life," Danielle said. "I was completely devastated. And those events of September 11 really just put everything into perspective for me."[33]

Shape magazine conducted a poll to show how women had reembraced domesticity after the terrorist attacks. The results proved, its editor wrote, that 9/11 had "inspired [women] to reevaluate their attitudes toward family, love, and even food." Actually, judging by the responses featured in *Shape*, food seemed to be the main preoccupation, along with dieting, fitness, appearance, and shopping:

"I stopped feeling sorry for myself and took steps to change my life. I now run three miles a day, eat healthfully, and drink lots of water." —DANA DORNBURGH, 31, Schenectady, New York

"I've wanted a tattoo since I was a teenager, and after 9/11, I finally got one—a butterfly on my lower back. The events of that day made me realize, why be afraid or wait until the moment is 'right'?"—SANDRA FUMERO, 28, Miami

"I started using all the things I saved for special occasions—my Chanel perfume, the pen I received as an award, my crystal and china. 9/11 taught me that every day is a special occasion."—MAUREEN BECKETT, 35, Arlington, Texas

"Since the attacks, I have eased up on myself regarding food and weight issues. I used to beat myself up if I cheated and ate chocolate or cheese. Now I don't get so worked up about it. I'm still trying to eat healthfully, but if I indulge a little, I don't obsess about it, because life is too short to worry about eating cookies."—MILANN TAYLOR GWOSDZ, 35, Houston[34]

Media talk about the nesting trend was further fueled by merchandisers eager to relieve their own recessionary anxieties by turning post-9/11 jitters into a marketing juggernaut. They needed thrifty women to start using their Chanel perfume on any and all occasions. A Fragrance Foundation study nervously noted that the aftermath of the attacks had prolonged a downturn in the economy, which was making the American female shopper "uninspired." But perhaps retailers could capitalize on 9/11 fears to revive her enthusiasm.[35]

"If there is one word that we will start to see cross over all messaging for all product categories, it will be 'security,'" Ben Gervey, a director at Applied Research & Consulting, told *American Demographics* in the late fall of 2001. "People's fears of leaving the house for long periods of time," Unity Marketing president Pam Danziger advised, could "boost catalog and Internet sales." After conducting a "worldwide ethnographic survey"—of seventy people—Context-Based Research executive Chuck Donofrio urged his clients to take advantage of "the months following the attacks, when people's heightened attention to family may mean the most for marketers." The result of this "messaging" was to reinforce the appearance of a trend.[36]

The "people" targeted belonged primarily to one sex, as *Newsweek's* choice of pronoun clarified in its September 24, 2001, story on post-9/11 consumer spending: "The immediate future may hinge on the consumer: will she act shell-shocked and cautious, or will she choose to defy the terrorists with her pocketbook?" The term "family" was code, too—for a household where Mom tended to the nursery and Father knew best. Foote, Cone & Belding was advising Kraft and Sara Lee to "dust off their old commercials and jingles, and scoop up as much media time as possible." The ad agency was banking on the theory that post-9/11 Americans would want to retreat to fifties-era domesticity, at least in their consumer fantasies. Retailers from Banana Republic to Versace introduced mothers and babies in their new advertising campaigns. State Farm Insurance featured an ad with a mom tying her child's shoelaces, alongside a caption that read, "It's pretty simple, really. Your family depends on you to be there." (The ad ran, among other places, alongside a *Time* cover story warning career women of the perils of postponing motherhood.) In Kenneth Cole ads, which explicitly referred to 9/11 and the need for "protection," a wife rests her head on her husband's chest in one image and, in another, he holds his hand protectively to the side of her face, wedding ring in prominent view.[37]

The media, in turn, joined the marketing pitch, citing the sales of consumer goods as proof of the trend they had declared of a return to housewifery and homespun. In *Time*, Nancy Gibbs painted this picture: "Sales of sewing machines, the perfect apocalypse accessory, are way up: stay home, save money, sew your own drapes and dresses. Craft sales in general are up in a nesting nation, as are sales of roasting pans." That last purchase might have owed something to Gibbs's conducting her research a week before Thanksgiving. *Newsweek's* story on post-9/11 retailing, "Nesting Instincts," likewise fixed on the sales of Susie-homemaker kitchen utensils, pondered the significance of a new oversized chair on the market "with room enough for an adult and a child," and predicted that furnishings, like the newly domesticated women said to be nestling in them, were "likely to become less hard-edged and more traditional." Faith Popcorn, the trend forecaster who had already been trying to market her "cocooning chair" for women before 9/11, went into high gear with a new cocooning line of wallpaper and home furnishings. "Our cocoons are going to get deeper now," she told the press. "We're not going to come out of our cocoons for a long time." Sewing machines may not have flown off the shelves, but the summons to home improvement stuck. A Harvard University study later found that household remodeling expenditures were one of the bright spots of the 2001 recession and "helped to prevent the downturn from being even deeper and more prolonged."[38]

The post-9/11 fashions were also bent on returning women to a "less hard-edged" profile. In November 2001, the *International Herald Tribune,* which was then owned by the *Washington Post* and the *New York Times,* sponsored a fashion conference in Paris to grease the skids for "Crisis Couture," as the *Washington Post* dubbed the post-9/11 look in a subsequent article trumpeting the new dictates. "The fashion world of 2002 is likely to look softer, without the hard edges and S&M sexuality of recent years," the *Post* declared. "And stylish life is more likely to take place indoors, in the safe cocoon of your house." By the following spring, the racks were full of this "softer" postattack look—heavy on girlish peasant blouses, wispy baby-doll dresses, and lace Victorian garb conveying, in the words of one fashion scribe, "virginal innocence." "We're going back to romance, femininity, and sophisticated chic," designer Carolina Herrera pronounced. "What we're seeing is a return to romance with a lot of ruffles, flounces, lace, eyelet, and tulle," Nordstrom's fashion director said. The Color Association of the United States declared white the post-9/11 female fashion shade, because "white represents purity and serenity." Oscar de la Renta promptly issued white lace gowns, and Ralph Lauren produced an entirely white collection.

The fashion press hurried to pitch the new line. The new styles for women are "distinctively nonaggressive," a *Vogue* editor announced. "They're not about dominance, power . . . but instead gentle and private"—like the "diaphanous chiffon dress" that reflected "the internal landscape of a peaceful existence." *Allure's* fashion director asserted that, "as a result of the atrocities of Sept. 11," clothes should be white — it's "a very angelic, soothing, ethereal type of color" that makes us feel "like we're on some kind of road to recovery." The general media helped promote these new fashion priorities, too. "The toughness of last season has surrendered to a sweet, romantic, girlish sensibility," *Newsday* advised readers. "The clothes themselves are a lovely salve for our wounds." "The Gucci woman," a *New York Times* story on the spring fashions for 2002 noted, "has re-emerged after some life-altering decisions." Her pre-9/11 "quasi-thug posture" was gone, replaced by the demure carriage of a debutante. "Her loose curls are flowing, and she is wearing a virginal white dress laced up her tawny back." Even the *Times* fashion writer was a bit taken aback by the "unreconstructed" nature of the alteration: "It might as well have come with the tagline, 'Calgon take me away.'"[39]

Cosmetics, too, were said to be a new "priority" for post-9/11 female America. "In the lacerated light of September 2001, 'American Beauty' was no longer a term to be trifled with," the *New York Times Magazine* informed its readers, in a story titled "Jingo Belle." Makeup arbiters declared red lipstick to be "back," and even commentators outside the beauty beat agreed. "It's feminine and full of life," evidence that "a certain return to the essentials is going on," *Wall Street Journal* columnist Peggy Noonan proclaimed. In an ad for Revlon's Absolutely Fabulous lipstick, a model posed before what appeared to be the New York Stock Exchange trading floor, beside the slogan: "On a bad day, there's always lipstick." The photo shoot took place before 9/11, but Revlon saw no need to withdraw the image in light of recent events. Quite the contrary: with the advent of September 11, as one approving journalist put it, the ad "has found its moment." The pitch was effective, at least in the short term; by December 2001, lipstick sales were up 12 percent since the attacks.[40]

If the post-9/11 woman was dressed for domestication, her mate had to be adorned in protector gear. Soon after the attacks, men's fashions began tending toward hard-hat and "military chic," as the new style was invariably called. National Outdoors declared martial men's wear "definitely a hip trend." Armani peddled camo duds. Bloomingdale's opened "The Fire Zone" in its flagship Upper East Side store, where men could dude themselves up in firefighter's jackets and "FDNY job sweatshirts"; Kmart offered similar fare at more affordable prices. On the fashion runways, male couture had gone blue collar, supposedly to honor the working-class stiffs who had "saved" New York on September 11. "Think Jack Dawson on the Titanic, only about 30 pounds heavier," the *Daily News Record*, the rag trade magazine, said of the new men's clothes on display during Fashion Week. Designer William Garrett told the *Record* that he was "inspired by the working men who passed through Ellis Island and built this nation from the ground up, with their sweat and muscle." With the launch of the Iraq war, combat and he-man clothes enjoyed a second renaissance. A few hours before the first strike on March 19, 2003, the Guess online store announced that it had sold out of its cargo cadet pants. "Military surplus–style for your action-packed days!" was Old Navy's Web site sales pitch for its men's messenger bags, which came "with army-style numbers and letters and metallic dog tag on adjustable strap." *New York Times* columnist David Brooks mused in the fall of 2003 on the sudden sartorial need of affluent male shoppers to get "in touch with their inner longshoremen." These "manly upscale proles" seemed to "have taken their clues from *On the Waterfront*" and were buying "logger's boots, cargo pants, shoulder satchels with anchor chain straps and post-ironic John Deere and Peterbilt baseball caps," he wrote.[41]

On television, scriptwriters were trying to jump-start the same trends. "Prime time is family time," declared *Broadcasting & Cable*, noting that the 2002 television offerings seemed to be either Hallmark family dramas or all-male protection fantasies with firemen or cops. "This year's pilot topics are designed to resonate with viewers in a post-9/11 world," Stacey Lynn Koerner, the director of broadcast research at Initiative Media, announced. About half of the 110 fall network pilots "fall in that broader family/post-9/11-inspired category," and "our focus has changed from self-consumed single yuppies to shows more about families and what we think is important in our culture."

What was "important," according to the 2002 TV season, was programming that featured a return to nesting—with such unsubtle names as *Homeward Bound* (situation: a young woman abandons career aspirations and goes home)—or shows set in the fifties and early sixties, or shows that were literal remakes of Cold War fare, including *Family Affair*,

Dragnet, The Time Tunnel, and *The Twilight Zone.* NBC was offering an updated *My Three Sons,* this time with three *daughters* under Daddy's watchful eye. Warner Bros. offered *American Dreams,* set in Philadelphia in 1963, in which fifteen-year-old Meg Pryor achieves her fondest fantasy: dancing on *American Bandstand.* "In the shadow of 9/11, are people looking for comfort?" Jonathan Prince, creator of *American Dreams,* asked rhetorically. "Well, yes. Shouldn't they be? That's what [TV] is supposed to do." The "comfort" that television and the other pop culture manufacturers dispensed was of a particular variety—the consolations of a domestic idyll where men wore all the badges and women wielded all the roasting pans.[42]

The post-9/11 fixation on male protectors at work and mommies at home maintained in pop culture. By the end of 2005, there were so many tough-guy shows on television that the *New York Times* declared the triumph of "Neanderthal TV." The characters seemed to have answered the media's post-9/11 call for a more positive take on torture. On *The Shield,* the cop isn't afraid to mete out bloody justice with his bare hands; *24*'s Jack Bauer tortures terrorists; and the code of *Lost,* as one male fan aptly described it in the *New York Times,* was "Men gotta do what men gotta do, and if some people have to die in the process, so be it." A Human Rights First study found that acts of torture on prime-time television had gone from fewer than four a year before 9/11 to more than a hundred—and the torturers, who in the past were almost entirely villains, were now often the shows' heroes. Surveying the macho blitzkrieg—from *Prison Break* to *House,* from Miller Lite's "Man Law" commercials to Burger King's burly-male pitch ("Eat like a man, man!"), from Harvard professor Harvey Mansfield's much-touted book, *Manliness,* to Jim Belushi's *Real Men Don't Apologize*—the *Boston Globe* concluded in June 2006, "We're in the middle of a Menaissance." At the same time, television prime time was awash in suburban housewives, and the publishing industry was milking a thriving new genre, "mommy lit." By the end of 2006, the editor of *Momzillas* was cheering the "huge rise in the amount of books by stay-at-home moms writing fiction and nonfiction about that experience."[43]

In the real world, the post-9/11 media lavished praise on two high-profile women who fit the return-to-nesting fantasy. "The woman who helped her husband quit drinking and settle down so long ago," *Newsweek* wrote of Laura Bush in its October 8, 2001, issue, "will be indispensable in reminding Americans that the 'normal' things in life matter: children, family and church." In the "Leaders" section of its 9/11 commemorative issue—whose cover was illustrated with a little blond girl on her father's shoulders, waving an American flag—*Newsweek* repeated the theme. The leaders were all men, though the section did include a sidebar to leader Bush on his wife, Laura, "The Chief Caretaker," who "has emerged as a very public caretaker in chief—not only to her husband but to the whole nation." Her leadership was confined to maternal ministrations at home: "A touch to the back of [her husband's] neck and he visibly relaxes." On *60 Minutes*, correspondent Lesley Stahl praised the First Lady for her "very calming effect on the president." But the nation, too, was supposedly relaxing under Nurse Laura's "calming" touch as she made the talk show rounds, assuring viewers that her husband would keep them "safe" and dispensing tips on how to comfort kids. On *Oprah*, teamed with Dr. Phil, Laura Bush instructed women "to keep a very calm and relaxed atmosphere in the home," bring food to their kids' schools, and help their kids' teachers by thinking of "activities that would be distracting and reassuring for children."[44]

Laura Bush was a prominent woman without career ambition—the "anti-Hillary," as she was repeatedly called—but what the return-to-nesting trend required even more was the example of a prominent woman who had such ambition and was now renouncing it. By April 2002, the media had one: the president's trusted adviser Karen Hughes announced that she was returning to Texas to spend more time with her family. The media cheerleading commenced at once: "Count Karen Hughes among the brave leaders of that radical redirection," "More power to her," "Hats off to Hughes. . . . Karen, you're making a decision you will never regret. You go, girl!" Hughes's decision was "wise," "unselfish," and "so courageous and worthy of plaudits." The op-ed headlines exhorted women to follow her lead: "It's Sometimes Good to Take a Step Back," "There's No One Like Mom for the Home," and "Hughes Quits for Something Even Better." *New York Times* columnist Maureen Dowd wondered if Hughes's retirement was "the coup de grace for Have It All," and the networks ran segments using Hughes's decision as a cautionary tale to professional women.[45]

In the *Wall Street Journal*, the indefatigable Peggy Noonan declared Hughes's resignation a "public service." Like other American women, Hughes "got a case of Sept. 11, too," Noonan said. The terrorist attacks had made her "more urgently aware that life is not only what you're doing right this second at the desk." Hughes "wanted to return to life" and now she had her freedom—a liberation that would apparently involve using more beauty products and hitting the mall:

> When Karen Hughes worked in the White House she wore hard clothes. . . . She doesn't have to wear makeup now. She can have a soft face. She can wash her face in Dove foamy cleanser, pat it dry, put on a nice-smelling moisturizer and walk onward into the day.
>
> She can shop. Shopping is a wonderful thing. It's more wonderful if you have money to buy what catches your eye if you want to own it, but it's also fun if you don't have money. It's really wonderful to just sort of walk along the mall and see what your country is selling, buying, offering. You get to see the other people look at and judge your country's products. You can buy a big soft pretzel at a stand and sit on a bench and watch the mothers and daughters buy shoes together.[46]

Many male pundits, particularly those with stay-at-home wives, were eager to "congratulate" Hughes on her "good sense." "My wife deserves a medal," John Rolfe, a senior editor for *Sports Illustrated*, wrote in an opinion piece about the decision. "All I can say is, motherhood has to be the world's most demanding and important job." "Ladies, let me tell you," Fox News host John Kasich announced on his show about Hughes's departure. "I called my wife earlier. She had kids on both hips, our twin girls." Hughes herself remarked in an interview with CBS News, "It's been amazing to me how many men have come up to me" to offer their congratulations; even the White House guard told her, "I so admire what you're doing."[47]

The media soon seized on a U.S. Census Bureau report released in 2003 that stated that the percentage of married women with children younger than one year old who were working had slipped from 59 percent in 1998 to 55 percent in 2002. This was a group that represented a small portion of the female workforce, and there was no way to know if these women would *stay* home past their infants' first birthdays. Nonetheless, the report was greeted with headlines like the one in the *Chicago Sun-Times*: " 'Supermoms' Draw Line in Sandbox." Mothers "are quitting their jobs in droves and not looking back," the newspaper contended, and the percentage of working mothers is "expected to continue declining." For the next several years, the media trotted out the statistic on mothers with children younger than one year of age in scores of news features, television segments, and magazine cover stories that suggested mothers were leaving the workforce in dramatic numbers; their exit was presented as a "growing movement" involving—depending on what media outlet you consulted— "thousands," "hundreds of thousands," or "millions" of women. In its March 22, 2004, cover story, "The Case for Staying Home," *Time* asserted that, while a drop of a few percentage points "may sound modest," one government economist regarded it as "huge."[48]

This "movement" was heralded in one of the most discussed nesting stories of the period, the *New York Times Magazine*'s October 26, 2003, cover story, "The Opt-Out Revolution." The story's author, Lisa Belkin, offered up her life story as trendworthy (she had been writing her *Times* biweekly column and magazine stories from home since the birth of her second son)—along with the examples of a very few women, most of them culled from an Atlanta book club composed of ten women who had all graduated from Princeton, Belkin's alma mater. "Of the 10 members, half are not working at all; one is in business with her husband; one works part time; two freelance; and the only one with a full-time job has no children," Belkin said. She also cited "e-mail messages" she had received over the years from readers who believed "the relationship between work and life is different for women than for men." She conceded that her sample was not "scientific." Still, she maintained, it counted as part of "a continuing conversation."[49]

In late 2005, Heather Boushey, an economist at the Center for Economic and Policy Research, took a closer look at that statistical decline of married working women with very young children. Examining the results of a nationally representative survey conducted by the U.S. Bureau of Labor Statistics, she found that the recession, not motherhood, was responsible for the drop. In fact, the decline in labor participation was the same for women who had *no* children. But her report, *Are Women Opting Out? Debunking the Myth*, hardly inspired the same media frenzy.[50]*

Instead, the mythmaking machinery just moved on to another cohort. If older women couldn't be tailored to fit the fantasy, maybe their college-age sisters would prove more adaptable. They possessed the virtue of no life experience; there would be no pesky real choices about work and family to explain away. In a front-page story on September 20, 2005, the *New York Times* predicted that Ivy League female undergraduates were going to bail out of their jobs and become full-time mothers. Its author was Louise Story, who had graduated from Yale in 2003 and had worked on the article while a summer intern at the *Times*. Her piece, "Many Women at Elite Colleges Set Career Path to Motherhood," began with a case study of one:

> Cynthia Liu is precisely the kind of high achiever Yale wants: smart (1510 SAT), disciplined (4.0 grade point average), competitive (finalist in Texas oratory competition), musical (pianist), athletic (runner) and altruistic (hospital volunteer). And at the start of her sophomore year at Yale, Ms. Liu is full of ambition, planning to go to law school.
>
> So will she join the long tradition of famous Ivy League graduates? Not likely. By the time she is 30, this accomplished 19-year-old expects to be a stay-at-home mom.

"My mother's always told me you can't be the best career woman and the best mother at the same time," Ms. Liu told the *Times*. "You always have to choose one over the other."[51]

From there, it was the usual hop and a skip to the trend of "many": "Many" female undergraduates at the nation's elite colleges say they "have

---

*In early 2007, the U.S. Bureau of Labor Statistics issued its own updated study, "Trends in Labor Force Participation of Married Mothers of Infants." The government report found that while the proportion of married women with infants in the workforce had peaked in 1997 and fallen six percentage points in the following three years, that trend had actually halted in 2000 and "has been relatively stable" since then (Sharon R. Cohany and Emy Sok, "Trends in Labor Force Participation of Married Mothers of Infants," U.S. Bureau of Labor Statistics, *Monthly Review*, February 2007, p. 9).

already decided that they will put aside their careers in favor of raising children," Story wrote; "many" say they "will happily play a traditional fe-male role"; "many" say that staying home "is not a shocking idea among their friends," and so on for twelve "manys"—a proliferation that prompted *Slate* media critic Jack Shafer to wonder, in his online column, "Press Box," "How many 'many's' are too many for one news story?"[52]

The basis for Story's generalizations was an e-mail questionnaire sent to Yale students that drew 138 responses from female undergraduates. The survey, Story wrote, "found that 85 of the students, or roughly 60 percent, said that when they had children, they planned to cut back on work or stop working entirely. About half of those women said they planned to work part time, and about half wanted to stop work for at least a few years." It took a *Times* reader to point out the obvious. In a letter to the ed-itor, Robin Herman wrote:

> This is no death knell for elite, leadership careers for women. Do the math, and you have 70 percent planning to continue working through motherhood.
>
> How about this headline: "Majority of Women in Elite Colleges to Opt for Lifetime Careers Either Full Time or with a Short Pause for Children." That's exactly what my friends and I did (Princeton '73, the first class to admit women).[53]

The article was eventually debunked, but the dismantling had little effect on the larger media dialogue. "Opting out," "the infertility epi-demic," and "the marriage crisis" of single women had likewise proved hollow upon inspection. Yet they refused to die. The trend of a reconsti-tuted "traditional" womanhood seemed viral, immune to the antibiotics of common sense or statistical hard evidence. It existed in the spectral realm of myth, where its relationship to the illusion of security was sym-biotic and self-perpetuating—each ginned-up generalization validating the existence of the other, each providing its counterpart with a penum-bra of emotional authenticity.

The myth of American invincibility required the mirage of womanly dependency, the illusion of a helpless family circle in need of protection from a menacing world. Without that show of feminine frailty, the culture could not sustain the other figment vital to the myth, of a nesting America shielded by the virile and vigilant guardians of its frontier. As the pageant of domesticity played out on the lifestyle page, the spectacle of virility unfolded on the political stage. It would prove just as chimerical.

CHAPTER 6

President of the Wild Frontier

A FEW DAYS BEFORE MOTHER'S DAY IN 2004, PRESIDENT BUSH MADE
a brief campaign stop in the Republican stronghold of Lebanon,
Ohio. His handlers were hustling him down the crowded rope line outside the Golden Lamb Hotel when a voice cut through the din: "Mr.
President! This girl lost her mom in the World Trade Center on 9/11!"
Bush, according to the much-burnished retellings, wheeled around and
plunged back down the line.[1]

Linda Prince, the woman who belted out the summons, had arrived
many hours earlier to stake out a position up front for her neighbor, Lynn
Faulkner, and his fifteen-year-old daughter, Ashley, the girl who lost her
mom. The president "locked" eyes with the grieving teenager.

"I know that's hard," he said. "Are you all right?"

"I'm OK," she said.

Then he gave her "The Hug." The moment was captured by Ashley's
father, a marketing consultant and ardent Bush supporter, who had purchased a new digital camera for the occasion. After professedly averting

his eyes from the viewfinder to grant his daughter her "private moment" with the president, Lynn Faulkner went home and e-mailed the photograph to more than a dozen "friends and family" across the country. They must have been well-positioned intimates; by the next day, the photo was on prominent display on the Drudge Report and scores of conservative blogs. The day after that, The Hug ran in the *Cincinnati Enquirer* and soon thereafter was enjoying national news coverage. As various reverential accounts of this "emotion-packed encounter" later characterized it, the president had "stopped in his tracks" when he heard the call and fought his way "against the flow" of the rope line, and "without fanfare" and "in one of those huge solitary moments that speak legions" had "instinctively reached for the teenager, clutched her head, placed it on his chest—and just held her."[2]

The photo drew a record 1.6 million page views on the *Cincinnati Enquirer*'s Web site. In the echo chamber of the conservative blogosphere, the photo was said to reveal Bush as a man of "strength" with "the courage to do what needs to be done to protect our country." "The protective encirclement of her head by President Bush's arm and hand is the essence of fatherly compassion," said a particularly adoring post on FreeRepublic.com. To Bush's backers, the photo became the money shot. "Nothing speaks better to the compassion, the character, and the leadership of the president," Brian McCabe, the head of one of the biggest Republican funding groups, told CNNfn. Some weeks after Lynn Faulkner snapped that single frame, McCabe's group, the Progress for America Voters Fund, dispatched a camera crew to the Faulkners' home to film "Ashley's Story," a multimillion-dollar political commercial.[3]

"Ashley's Story" is told first by Ashley's father, who relates how his daughter "closed up emotionally" after her mother was killed (Wendy Faulkner was in a business meeting on the 104th floor of the World Trade Center when the planes hit), and then by Ashley's neighbor, Linda Prince, who relates how "our president took Ashley in his arms and just embraced her" and how "at that moment, we saw Ashley's eyes fill up with tears." Finally, Ashley gets to deliver her only line: "He's the most powerful man in the world, and all he wants to do is make sure I'm safe, that I'm OK." The scene then shifts to ground zero, where Bush embraces a New York City fireman, a shot altered to create a bright aura around the president and suggest "a tableau," an ad analyst remarked, "reminiscent of Christian saints." Then the camera returns to the bucolic Faulkner homestead, panning across family photographs and the languishing figure of young Ashley, recumbent on a hammock, genteelly turning the pages of a novel with a painting of a Victorian lady on its cover. Finally, "Ashley's Story" returns to its real protagonist. The commercial ends on a lingering shot of the president-protector, his head bowed prayerfully.[4]

In the post-9/11 effort to restore Americans' confidence in the country's impregnability, national politics would become increasingly deranged. The demonstrations, as often as not, were comically absurd, as witness the deskbound officeholders of the 2004 presidential campaign out in the woods, felling flora and blasting fauna to prove their virile bona fides. But the needs these staged exertions in the wild addressed ran deep in the American past, far deeper than the superhero fantasies we constructed around our leaders. The attack on home soil triggered a search for a guardian of the homestead, a manly man, to be sure, but one particularly suited to protecting and providing for the isolated American family in perilous situations. He was less Batman than Daniel Boone, a frontiersman whose proofs of eligibility were the hatchet and the gun—and a bloody willingness to wield them.

"The swinging of the ax and the singing of the chain saw," *National Review*'s Dave Shiflett wrote in "Bush vs. Brush," showed that Bush possessed "exactly the kind of disposition one would hope for in a wartime president." After all, "first and foremost, clearing brush is an aggressive act." There was "something refreshingly brutish" in the way "the president sizes up the situation and says, 'You're mine, sucker.' Not only that, he will probably saw up the victim's body and feed the piece into a fire, smiling as the flames dance before him." That sort of "brush-clearer's language," Shiflett continued, "is no doubt widely respected in the Arab street. . . . The hand that swings the ax, it seems, fits nicely on the tiller of the ship of state. If bin Laden ever goes to trial and is convicted, perhaps the president should be given the honor of chopping off his head."[5]

By the end of the 2004 campaign, Bush was declining almost all newspaper requests for interviews. But he made an exception for the hunting and fishing media. He offered long sessions to *Field & Stream* and *Outdoor Life*, publications that had never before been granted an audience with a president. The reporter for *Field & Stream* recalled getting a personal tour of Bush's Crawford, Texas, ranch in a pickup truck—the president at the wheel—before being ushered into his private study, where, without prompting, Bush hastened to a cabinet, "opened a gun safe and started handing me some of his favorites":

> President Bush: My favorite gun is the first gun that my dad gave me, which is a Winchester .22 pump, Model 61. Another gun that's one of my favorites is a Weatherby custom-made gun presented to me by the CEO of the company, Mr. Weatherby. I've probably got six or seven guns in a safe in my office there: two shotguns, two .22s, a couple of deer rifles and a varmint rifle. A .248.
>
> [*Field & Stream's* Sid] Evans: A .243, maybe?
>
> President Bush: A .243. I beg your pardon, a .243. Given to me by the former lieutenant governor of Texas, Bob Bullock, my old buddy, who on his deathbed said, "I want to give you a gun."

Bush was glad to elaborate on his backwoodsman exploits, past and future: the "great quail crop" he once encountered in Beeville, Texas ("My greatest day in the field"); an April fishing trip in Crawford, where he proved the star trawler ("I caught the biggest fish of the day"); the day he hooked his biggest bass ever ("Nine and a half pounds on Rainbow Lake in East Texas"); and intrepid wilderness expeditions that might be in the offing ("I'd love to go down to the Patagonia area. Maybe I'll get you to come with me and we'll do an article down there. That would be neat"). Just in case the point had not been driven home sufficiently, Bush invited photographers to watch him chop down trees and a film crew from the Outdoor Life Network to spend much of a day witnessing him fish on his ranch's lake. Regrettably, he caught only one small bass, which he allowed Barney, the presidential Scottish terrier, to lick several times before tossing it back in the water.[6]

The Democratic candidate might have made great sport of Commander in Chief Crockett. Instead, he joined the mountain-man match. Senator John Kerry offered himself up to *Field & Stream* and *Outdoor Life*, too, where he proved the president's equal in bragging rights. "I've been a hunter since I was about 12 years old," he told *Field & Stream*. "I started with a BB gun, moved up to a .22, then a .30/30, and a shotgun. And I've shot birds off and on through my life, some game, rabbits, deer—I've been on Massachusetts deer hunts." He recalled gunning down a stag with a marginally impressive rack—"an 8-pointer, something like that"—and once having "an incredible encounter with the most enormous buck—I don't know, 16 points or something." He had failed to pull the trigger that time, but just that past year, he informed *Outdoor Life*, he had succeeded in "bagging two pheasants with two shots on my first hunt in Iowa."[7]

Guns have always played an emblematic role in American public life, but the firearms preoccupations of the 2004 presidential race went far beyond previous political seasons. "It's remarkable how the gun issue is playing this year," a CNN political report noted as early as December 2003, observing that Democratic candidates were now acting as if gun control were "some sort of virus" and even Howard Dean was bragging about his "high marks" from the National Rifle Association. "America's political debate over guns is different this year," the *Philadelphia Inquirer* commented in the summer of 2004. "Four years ago, Democrats Al Gore and Bill Bradley argued the merits of licensing or registering gun owners and weapons. . . . Now, Kerry leads Democrats in championing gun rights. . . . Democrats have locked and loaded and changed their tune, their image, even their party platform." By fall, a penchant for armaments had become an obsession. "Political analysts say they've never seen anything quite like the tough-guy competition between President Bush and Massachusetts Sen. John Kerry," *USA Today* reported in late September. And while the presidential contenders were eager to win gun owners in midwestern battle states, a much deeper force—and fear—was driving the frenzy. As *USA Today* condensed the analysts' findings: "Voters everywhere are haunted by 9/11."[8]

When the candidates picked up their guns, they weren't just stalking the flannel-jacket set; they were hunting the vote of haunted America, a nation vulnerable to the enticements of protection fantasies. A Kerry campaign brochure spelled out the underlying agenda with a photograph of the candidate holding a shotgun, titled "John Kerry Will Defend Ohio." And, the promise implied, the forty-nine other states. Kerry devoted an inordinate amount of his campaign to peddling his coonskin-cap credentials. On a swing through the Midwest in July 2004, Kerry stopped to brandish a 12-gauge at the Gunslick Trap Club in Holmen, Wisconsin, before hurrying on to La Crosse, where he had the campaign bus pull over so he could demonstrate his shooting prowess at a clay pigeon skeet range. The following day, he stopped to expound on his deer hunting techniques with a group of midwestern journalists. "I go out with my trusty 12-gauge double-barrel, crawl around on my stomach," Kerry told them. "I track and move and decoy and play games and try to outsmart them. You know, I kind of play the wind. That's hunting." His eagerness to underscore his double-barrel talents would earn him the media moniker "John the Deerslayer." While sawing away at a steak dinner one night, he regaled *Washington Post* writer Laura Blumenfeld with the details of dove gutting: "Carve out the heart," he told the dismayed reporter, "pull out the entrails and cut up the meat. . . . You clean them. Let them hang. It takes three or four birds to have a meal. You might eat it at a picnic, cold roasted. I love dove."[9]

As soon as hunting season opened, a camo-coveralled Kerry could be found in one frost-laden duck blind after another. Bleary-eyed journalists rose before dawn to follow him. There was the pheasant hunt in Iowa (where Kerry inspected the neck of his fresh kill before a phalanx of photographers), the goose hunt in Ohio (where Kerry emerged from a cornfield with a hand "stained with goose blood" but empty of an actual carcass), and another clay pigeon hunt in Wisconsin (no blood, but the candidate reportedly plugged seventeen of his twenty-five marks). At a campaign appearance in West Virginia, Kerry hoisted a shotgun onstage and told an audience of miners that he'd like to go "gobble-huntin'." In Pike County, Ohio, Kerry dropped in on the Buchanan Village Gun Shop to inquire, in freshly acquired twang, "Can I get me a hunting license here?" It was a moment that inspired a *National Review* columnist to invoke the sodomy scene in *Deliverance*: "What will Kerry say if he goes on the campaign trail into deepest Appalachia? 'Squeal like a pig?' "[10]

For those who couldn't make Kerry's early-morning shoot-'em-ups, the campaign's Web site posted photographs of the candidate pursuing his prey and admiring the gory results; and before public appearances, his advance teams distributed 8×10 glossies of the senator in full hunting finery, clutching his "trusty" shotgun. Eventually, a "right to own firearms" plank was even added to the Democratic Party platform, for the first time ever.[11]

Kerry's camo cameos succeeded mostly in provoking the deep-pocketed ire of the National Rifle Association, which spent $20 million denouncing him during the campaign. "John Kerry's not a hunter," its thirty-minute television infomercial sneered. "He just plays one on TV." Vice President Dick Cheney, who delivered the keynote address at the NRA convention that year, made a point of noting that Kerry's camo jacket looked suspiciously "new." Bush ridiculed Kerry's sartorial strategy on campaign stops, albeit muffing his own joke, as he did in Hershey, Pennsylvania. "He can run," the president said, "he can even hide in camo, but he can't hide."[12]

Gun enthusiasts, who weren't going to vote for a Democrat, no matter what he did—especially not one with an F grade from the NRA and a 100 percent rating from the pro–gun control Brady Campaign—delivered microscopic deconstructions of the candidate's online action shots. "Notice Kerry's thumb wrapped firmly over the barrel blocking the sights," instructed SportsmenforKerry.com, one of several conservative Web sites dedicated to molecular scrutiny of the senator's hunting photos. (The Web site's deceptively pro-Kerry name was meant to mock the "Sportsmen for Kerry" signs and buttons the Kerry campaign had been distributing.) "There were no reports of Kerry burning his hand so he must not have fired." The picture of Kerry's hunting hound also came in for criticism; the dog evidently had his back to the prey. Other know-it-all critics were eager to note that no real hunter "hung" doves or slithered, shotgun in hand, on the ground while tracking deer. *National Review*'s Mark Steyn wrote that neither he nor any of his New Hampshire neighbors had "ever heard of anybody deer hunting by crawling around on his stomach, even in Massachusetts":

The trick is to blend in with the woods and, given that John Kerry already looks like a forlorn tree in late fall, it's hard to see why he'd give up his natural advantage in order to hunt horizontally. Possibly his weird Vietnam nostalgia is getting out of control. Still, if I come across a guy in the woods in deer season inching through the undergrowth with a mouthful of bear scat, at least I'll know who it is.

Conversely, if you're a 14-point buck and get shot in the toe this autumn, you'll know who to sue.[13]

Even Kerry's attempt to impress *Outdoor Life*—he told the magazine that one of his most treasured guns was a "Communist Chinese assault rifle"—misfired. Kerry's detractors promptly pointed out that it was a felony to own such a weapon without a $750 federal permit, which he didn't have. The Kerry campaign hastily issued a correction: the candidate's actual favorite rifle was a bolt-action, hundred-year-old "relic" from Russia.[14]

The Chinese assault rifle was an artifact from Kerry's real military service, as opposed to Bush's make-believe one. As Democratic pollster Celinda Lake pointed out to *USA Today*, Kerry had carried an actual M-16 into actual combat: "We're the only party that's had a candidate walk around with a fully automatic weapon in his hand. All those Vietnam rifles were fully automatic." But in the kabuki realm of American myth, such facts barely signified. The firearms fixation of the 2004 campaign had little to do with overseas battlefield experience or with the display of Cold War "relics" commandeered from commies. The candidates were engaged in a contest closer to home, a casting call to decide who would get to play the electorate's King of the Wild Frontier. Bush intuitively understood the role's requirements—perhaps because he, more than any other politician since Ronald Reagan, seemed to dwell in that flickering stage set. When he said of his plans for Osama bin Laden, "There's an old poster out West I recall that says, 'Wanted: dead or alive,'" some commentators mocked him for seeming to mistake a movie scene for an actual memory. But in the drama unfolding on the political hustings that year, the fictional recollection was the real thing. The point of the performance was to reconstitute an imaginary America that would always prevail over its swarthy "invaders" and an imaginary American man who would always repel them from his homestead door.[15]

In the months after September 11, dozens of media reports claimed that American heads of household were also reaching for their guns. They were said to be "taking matters into their own hands," applying for permits to carry concealed weapons and crowding weapons-training classes, determined to "keep them [terrorists] out of my backyard," as Mark Lawler, a shopper at Texas Guns in San Antonio, told the Associated Press. Suburbia was said to be in an arming frenzy: commuter dads were filling their "clothes closets" with assault rifles and machine guns; wives were gift wrapping ammunition "for their husbands as a Christmas stocking stuffer." Gun manufacturers hoping to capitalize on the new "home protection" trend issued 9/11-themed weaponry. The Ithaca Gun Company offered its new "Homeland Security model" for "our current time of national need," and Beretta rushed its "United We Stand" guns to stores; wholesalers put in two thousand orders in one day for the 9-millimeter pistol, which came with a holographic American flag.[16]

In fact, the increased traffic in gun stores didn't last long. By October, sales were back to normal.[17] But the underlying shame that a clothes closet full of guns was supposed to relieve did not abate. On September 11, a nation of television viewers had watched a massacre with the immediacy of being on the scene but with no ability to act. For so many spectators, the fact that they could do nothing but watch from a safe remove only added to the ignominy. In an article in the *New York Observer* a month after 9/11, Philip Weiss described, more honestly than most, the humiliation—and hence, the hollow bravado—that witnessing the World Trade Center's collapse had spawned in him and his male colleagues. He described various social gatherings he'd attended in the weeks after the terrorist attack in which all stripes of men invariably congregated in one corner to engage in compensatory chest-beating sessions:

"What do you think we should do?" I said to one friend. "Go over there and ice 'em," he said. We shook hands. At a birthday party, a biker told me about off-the-books assassination squads that roam free in mountains in the Far East. We both grunted with approval. A third friend and

I drank red wine before his stone fireplace and talked about how some action was required. An artist, but he seemed to be saying 'Love it or leave it,' and I found myself agreeing.[18]

Many of Weiss's fellow writers and thinkers seemed similarly eager to establish their creds through outlaw professions of murderous intent (professions that they left to others to fulfill). It was "time to think about torture," Jonathan Alter declared in *Newsweek*. "OK, not cattle prods or rubber hoses," but "we'll have to think about transferring some suspects to our less squeamish allies, even if that's hypocritical. Nobody said this was going to be pretty." *Time* columnist Charles Krauthammer believed it was time to think, too, about secret prisons, secret tribunals, and violent interrogations of terrorists—and if flouting the Geneva Conventions provoked "the gnashing of teeth and rending of garments" among human rights weenies, cowboy Krauthammer wanted it known that he for one did not care: "I myself have not gnashed a single tooth. My garments remain entirely unrent." *New York Times* columnist Thomas Friedman advised, "We have to fight the terrorists as if there were no rules." *New York Post* columnist Steve Dunleavy outlined his game plan for the new Old Wild West:

I don't mean hunt them, arrest them, extradite them and prosecute them in a court of law. I mean a far quicker and neater form of retribution for this cabal of cowards. A gunshot between the eyes, blow them to smithereens. . . .

Train assassins (we've done it before), hire mercenaries, put a couple of million bucks up for bounty hunters to get them dead or alive, preferably dead. As for cities or countries that host these worms, bomb them into basketball courts. . . .

Then we should go into the interior, hunt down the desert rat and execute him and his followers on the spot.

And if Saddam Hussein makes so much as a peep, do him, too.[19]

Pundit contemplation of cattle prods and "off-the-books assassination squads" would not keep the nation any safer than campaign photo ops of pheasant shoots or candidate promises to make firearms more available.

(Two congressional studies, in fact, found that terror suspects easily could—and easily *did*—take advantage of lax U.S. gun control laws to stock up on weaponry; an Al Qaeda training manual devoted a whole chapter to the benefits of shopping for assault rifles in the United States.) Nor were homeowners going to forestall terrorists by packing heat. "What are you going to do, shoot an envelope filled with anthrax or stop a 747 with a handgun?" a perplexed analyst at the Violence Policy Center told the press. "It's literally crazy." But the political rhetoric of the 2004 campaign, like so much of the cultural reaction to 9/11, spoke to more pervasive and phantasmagoric threats than the possibility of Islamic extremists storming suburban split-levels. Kerry's problem was that he never fully grasped his role in that national shadow play. Brandishing the gun was only half the protection script, and of little value without the other half: women and children who needed to be protected.[20]

Once again, the Bush campaign better understood the particulars of the underlying drama. The tale of Ashley's tears belonged to a larger narrative, one that demanded the display of female fear, of a cowering feminine populace in need of masculine support. Soon after 9/11, media reports began proliferating of a "worry gap" or "anxiety gap" between the sexes. The *Washington Post* heralded "the great worry divide," based on interviews with three couples and a poll that found women were more likely than men to say they felt depressed and had trouble sleeping immediately after 9/11. "When his wife feels jittery, Will Heyniger tries to reassure her with reason and information," the *Post* reported. "He's a voracious reader, and he's more up on the news than she is. He tries to place the present troubles in their proper geopolitical context." His wife, on the other hand, was "overwhelmed" and has been known to "break into tears" on her way to work. Another husband was described as "fearless," while his wife found the future "frightening." (In fact, she had good reason: a friend of hers had died in the bombing of Pan Am Flight 103 over Lockerbie, and she herself had worked only a few blocks from the World Trade Center when it was first bombed in 1993.) The *Post* jumped from the three couples to the existence of "perhaps a few million couples like them" and speculated that gender differences in reaction to 9/11 were "rooted in the varying size, chemistry and physiology of male and female brains."[21]

The insistence on an anxiety divide persisted for the next several years. "The worry gap remains as strong as ever," the *Philadelphia Inquirer* announced on March 23, 2003, as the invasion of Iraq began. "Not for nothing do we say that men are from Mars and women are from Venus." The *Washington Monthly* beat the same drum in its April 2003 article "Homeland Security Is for Girls": "Ever since September 11, there's been a steady stream of evidence that when it comes to the question of terrorism, men are from Mars and women are from Venus." Among the "evidence" the article's author offered: she saw more female than male shoppers in line when she went to Target in February 2003 to buy medical tape and bottled water—after Homeland Security director Tom Ridge recommended stocking emergency supplies in case of a terrorist biochemical attack.[22] "Even today, the disparity in anxiety level between the two sexes continues," *Time* asserted a couple of months later, pointing to its recent survey in which 37 percent of men said they feared another terrorist attack, compared with 47 percent of women. *Time* did not consider the possibility that, if women were more likely to fear a terrorist attack, perhaps they were being more realistic, or cynical, about their government's ability to protect them: a November 2001 poll by Greenberg Quinlan Research found that most women lacked confidence in the counterterrorism skills of their nation's law enforcement agencies. The media ignored those findings, preferring to read women's concerns as proof of a genetically jittery sex.[23]

The worry gap would find its most well-known expression in the figure of the "security mom," who made her appearance early in the 2004 election campaign. Her story premiered on the cover of *Time*.

"Goodbye, Soccer Mom. Hello, Security Mom," the magazine's June 2, 2003, headline declared. "Since 9/11, polls suggest [the soccer mom] has morphed into Security Mom," the magazine said. "She's worried, she wants answers and she likes toughness in a President." This once liberal-minded, anti–military spending, pro–gun control woman "now believes the Pentagon should have whatever it wants" and thinks "her civil liberties seem less important than they used to, especially compared with keeping her children safe." *Time* documented this "sea change" with quotes from an anonymous "senior Bush aide" and a few random women, who were interviewed in the midst of the fourth terrorist "orange alert" within a year: Debbie Creighton, mother of two, said, "Since 9/11, all I want in a President is a person who is strong." Jillian Kelly, single mother and proprietor of "a Chicago-area massage-therapy business," said she worried the Homeland Security Department wasn't getting enough money. Nancy Potter said she supported current antiterrorism initiatives.[24]

Pollster David Winston of the GOP-affiliated research firm the Winston Group, asserted that "most Americans see the 9/11 attacks as a defining moment in their lives—and no one group was more affected than women, especially married women with children." In an October 2004 column in the *New York Post* titled, a tad defensively, "Security Moms Are Real," Winston described the emergence of this new female perspective:

> My first inkling that 9/11 would have more than just a passing impact on women came only a month after the attacks. As Congress considered legislation to allow the arming of pilots, I did a survey for the Allied Pilots Association and United Seniors Association. One finding surprised a lot of people: Married women with children were the biggest proponents of putting guns in the cockpit—favoring the idea by a whopping 78 percent, five points higher than men.

To go from a narrowly defined question about cockpit security to a grand statement about the impact of 9/11 on women was something of a leap, and Winston offered only one other study to justify it: a 2004 poll conducted by his group just a few weeks after the Beslan school massacre that found that 26 percent of married women with children cited "defense/terror" as their top concern, narrowly beating out "economy/jobs," at 24 percent. (He did not offer comparable figures for men.) Nonetheless, pollsters on both sides of the party divide were ready to jump. The presidential candidates were playing the part of gun-toting sentinels to speak to the security mom's fears as much as to her husband's fury, as electoral analysts informed the press. "It's about getting men's votes, but this year it's also about getting women's votes," Democratic pollster Celinda Lake told *USA Today* in the fall of 2004. "What in the past seemed too arrogant, too macho, women really like this cycle. They want someone who will do what it takes to protect America."[25]

The Bush campaign's "W Stands for Women" initiative was based on that premise. Frontloaded with female volunteers and merchandised with pink baseball caps for sale on the WStandsforWomen Web site, the effort launched in May 2004—timed to coincide, of course, with Mother's Day. Mindy Tucker Fletcher, cochair of the W Stands for Women national steering committee, told the press that for the security mom the election would come down to one question: who would she want to protect her "if September 11 happened again?" To answer that question, the W promoters offered up two such mothers who were all in the family—literally. "You know, I'm a security mom," Vice President Dick Cheney's daughter Elizabeth told CNN. "I've got four little kids. And what I care about in this election cycle is electing a guy who is going to be a commander in chief, who will do whatever it takes to keep those kids safe." The second was Laura Bush, who quickly attained status as the Mother of All Security Moms. On the afternoon talk shows, in ads on the Web sites of women's magazines like *Ladies' Home Journal* and *Family Circle,* and, ultimately, from the dais of the Republican National Convention, she assured American mothers of "George's work to protect our country and defeat terror so that all children can grow up in a more peaceful world."[26]*

Predictably, the conservative female punditry fell into line. According to Kay Daly, a commentator and a lobbyist for Bush's federal judicial nominees, American housewives across the nation were quavering in

---

*W Stands for Women claimed reinforcements from newly hatched groups like Security Moms 4 Bush and Women in Support of the President (with the feminine-delicate acronym WISP), which were billed as independent efforts and part of a grassroots "movement" boasting explosive growth. "Security Moms 4 Bush are working hard, often late at night, at their computers, after tucking their children into bed," one of that group's many electronic press releases announced. "They are writing letters to the editor, calling in to talk radio, getting people registered to vote and hosting parties for the President. Most of these moms have never before been politically active. This time the stakes are too high." Security Moms 4 Bush claimed that it had membership in nearly forty states and was even drawing "registered

their kitchens. In a May 10, 2004, column titled "Happy 'Security' Moms Day!" she wrote:

> On a clear September morning in 2001, the most basic instinct of mothers—protection of home and family—took top priority over any other concerns. In an instant, all other concerns outside the realm of survival seemed trivial. Suddenly, the enemy had not only invaded our nation, but the realities of everyday life. Just turning on a kitchen faucet to mix formula for the baby was a seemingly dangerous act for fear that the water supply had somehow been contaminated.[27]

In *USA Today*, conservative columnist Michelle Malkin pointed to herself as proof of the phenomenon: "I am what this year's election pollsters call a 'security mom.' . . . Nothing matters more to me right now than the safety of my home and the survival of my homeland." Children, she implied, were among the main targets of the 9/11 attacks. "Security moms will never forget that toddlers and schoolchildren were incinerated in the hijacked planes on Sept. 11," she wrote. (Among the 2,973 victims were eight children, all on planes.) "Murderous Islamic fanatics will stop at nothing to do the same to our kids." And a Democratic president—or a compassionate Republican—would only encourage them. "As they plot our death and destruction, these enemies will not be won over by either hair-sprayed liberalism or bleeding-heart conservatism."[28]

Independent Women's Forum writer Anne Morse, likewise, declared herself a security mom. What "we" needed in the White House, she wrote, was a man who had "the same qualities we look for in a husband:

Democrats." If so, its foot soldiers were keeping a remarkably low profile. Media accounts of the group invariably featured the same lone mom, Nancy Kennon, who maintained the group's Web site from her Westchester County home—a Web site tethered by innumerable links to right-wing blogs, the *National Review*, Fox News, and the *Washington Times*. ("Media Reporting Is All about Security Moms," Security Moms for Bush, press release, Sept. 18, 2004, www.Moms4Bush.com; Liza Porteus, "Security Moms on a Mission," Oct. 15, 2004, www.FoxNews.com; Dan DeLuce, "Myth of the 'Security Moms,'" *New York Beacon*, Oct. 27, 2004; T. Shawn Taylor, "Woman News," *Chicago Tribune*, Oct. 13, 2004; Gayle White, "Republican Convention: GOP Urges Women to Join Party," *Atlanta Journal-Constitution*, Sept. 3, 2004.)

Someone who is strong and who will do his utmost to protect us." All that matters to the security mom is knowing "that this man would sacrifice his life for our children." Over and over, she struck the threat-to-our-children theme: security moms are "obsessed" with protecting their progeny "from those who think they'll receive 70 black-eyed virgins if they murder American kids"; "We're not going to let their killers get anywhere near our own kids if we can possibly help it"; "We want to see Tom Ridge out on the White House lawn at least once a week, saying, 'Here's what we're doing this week to keep your children safe'"; "Given a choice between having them attack our well-trained, well-armed soldiers in Iraq (who are quite good at shooting back), or mount an assault on the kindergarten down the street, we'll take attacks in Iraq, thank you"; and "Security Moms don't much care if we never locate weapons of mass destruction in Iraq, but . . . when we put our kids on the plane to visit Grandma, we want to know those planes are safe." To protect their kids, security moms looked to a particular kind of president, Morse said—a president who reminded them of "Marshal Will Kane in *High Noon*." "This is the kind of leader we want when outlaws ride into town—or fly planes into buildings." A president, that is, out of a Hollywood Western, who would "go it alone" to shield the frontier wife's young 'uns.[29]

By the fall of 2004, the existence of the security mom was mainstream media gospel. The press declared her the crucial bloc that would decide the election. A Media Matters for America review of the coverage just for late September yielded a bumper crop of such unsourced assertions: Security moms were "one of this election's hot categories" who were "displacing Democrat-friendly issues such as health care and education" (*Washington Post*). They were "weakening a traditionally Democratic base" (*Christian Science Monitor*). "Now, women in general are moving to Bush" (ABC News).[30]

There wasn't much data to back these claims. "We've been looking at security moms on and off," *Time's* pollster, Mark Schulman, confessed in the fall of 2004. "We honestly could not find much empirical evidence to support it." Pollsters for the *Washington Post* and ABC News were having trouble, too; married women with children didn't seem to be expressing national security concerns that distinguished them from other voters.

After scrutinizing a large repository of electoral research, Democratic pollster Anna Greenberg also began to wonder: in voter surveys, she noted, only about one woman out of four who belonged to the "security mom" category was citing terrorism and national security as her number one reason to support Bush — and that was about the same percentage for all women polled. Two months before the election, Greenberg issued this conclusion: the security mom was a "myth."[31]

But the relentless retailing of this mythical figure went on and on. Like the supposed post-9/11 trends of "baby fever," "nesting," "opting out," security motherhood seemed to have a life beyond the reality — in fact, independent of reality. The security mom was a character crucial to the restoration of that larger American myth of invulnerability, and documenting her existence mattered less than mobilizing her image in our dream life. It was in this illusory realm that the presidential contest would be fought — and won by the candidate who best deployed its spectral players and props. The victor didn't have to appeal to an actual security mom. He had to appeal to voters at large by manipulating her likeness in a convincing, if fictional, dramatization of our national protection fantasy.

Kerry and his advisers were engrossed in the same myth reenactment as the Bush administration. They were counting on the senator's decorated service in Vietnam to qualify him for the role, especially when contrasted with Bush's AWOL record. But they were missing the female part of the myth's equation. Having adopted the "reporting for duty" protective mantle, the Kerry campaign only belatedly went looking for women to protect. To that end, Kerry strategist Mike McCurry announced in the fall of 2004 that the candidate would be adjusting his "tonal quality" and seeking "softer" approaches, which mostly meant dispatching Kerry to media venues where security moms might be found. The candidate made the rounds of *Dr. Phil* and *Live with Regis and Kelly* and appeared at an event sponsored by *Redbook*. "No American mother should have to lie awake at night wondering whether her children will be safe at school," Kerry pronounced in a Philadelphia stump speech in September, seizing upon the Beslan school hostage crisis as an eleventh-hour opportunity to position himself as America's guardian father. "When we look at the images of children brutalized by remorseless terrorists in Russia, we know that this is not just a political or military struggle—it goes to the very heart of what we value most—our families. It strikes at the bond between a mother and child." As president, he said, he would regard it as "my sacred duty" to be able to say "I am doing everything in my power to keep your children safe."[32]

In the murk of this hallucinatory American wilderness, the Bush pathfinders were more surefooted. One of their political commercials was set in a dark forest invaded by a pack of wolves. A trembling female voiceover warned voters that Kerry would make cuts in U.S. intelligence "so deep they would have weakened America's defenses—and weakness attracts those who are waiting to do America harm." Kerry had no plans to make such cuts, but that fact hardly registered in the nation's electoral reverie. "Wolves" engaged America's terror dream, which the GOP hunter-in-chief would vanquish with a hug.[33]

"ASHLEY'S STORY" WAS ready by summer, but the Bush campaign held the commercial until the final weeks of the race. The subsequent $14 million to $17 million spent to buy airtime made "Ashley's Story" the single most expensive political ad of the race. The sixty-second commercial was broadcast more than thirty thousand times, achieving saturation level in the crucial swing states. In Ohio alone, the spot ran seven thousand times. The bombardment was intensified by an Internet, phone, and direct-mail campaign that distributed 2.3 million brochures featuring The Hug.[34]

Once again, the Kerry campaign struggled to catch up. One week prior to the unveiling of "Ashley's Story" (and after much internal disagreement), the candidate's advisers finally shot a political commercial featuring Jersey Girl Kristen Breitweiser, in which the 9/11 widow looked into the camera and said: "We are no safer today. I want to look in my daughter's eyes and know that she is safe." But they had yet to release the ad. The day The Hug came out, Jersey Girl widow Mindy Kleinberg offered to help the Kerry campaign counter its impact, and a second commercial was hastily shot, in which Kleinberg tartly noted that her three children needed more than a "hug" to feel safe. But when Kerry's strategists tried to air these two spots, they discovered they'd been trumped: the Bush campaign had bought up all the commercial time in the big swing states.[35]

It's doubtful the ads would have helped, anyway. Throughout the presidential race, the media largely ignored the Jersey Girls' efforts on behalf of the Kerry campaign: their grueling traveling and speaking tour yielded little coverage, and they were quickly deemed, as the *New Republic* observed, "virtual nonentities." By reminding Americans that their protectors had failed them—"We are no safer today"—the Jersey Girls' commercials exhumed the original trauma and violated the terms of the myth. Ashley Faulkner confirmed those terms when she said of President Bush, "He's the most powerful man in the world, and all he wants to do is make sure I'm safe." That one line returned us to the Western's most iconic scene: a passive girl falls into the embrace of an inarticulate Texan outrider whose deep emotion barely shows through his flint-eyed stoicism.[36]

Studies of exit polls later concluded that "Ashley's Story" was critical to the election results. Political analysts scored it "the most effective ad" of the political season and postelection surveys found it to be one of the two most remembered (the other being its evil twin, the Swift Boat Veterans for Truth ad attacking Kerry's combat credentials). The Bush administration would send Ashley a ticket to the inaugural ceremonies. On the morning the president was sworn in for another four years, Ashley appeared on the *Today* show to describe the "real, like, ballgown dress" she would be wearing to the capital galas that evening. If Bush was Ashley's frontier hero, she was his American Cinderella.[37]

Ashley was by no means the only girl cast for this fairy-tale part. The most promising contender had had her screen test—quite literally captured on film by a military video crew—one night more than a year earlier and half a world away, on a flag-draped gurney in Nasiriyah.

CHAPTER 7

Precious Little Jessi

I AM A SOLDIER, TOO: THE JESSICA LYNCH STORY, BILLED AS THE BOOK that finally "lets Jessica Lynch tell the story of her capture in the Iraq war in her own words," debuted at number one on the *New York Times* nonfiction best-seller list in November 2003. One of the readers curious to learn its contents was the subject herself. In a *Time* cover story that accompanied the book's release, Lynch told the reporter that she had taken a look at it but "skipped the parts" that might upset her. If this seemed like a peculiarly arm's-length relationship to one's own memoir, Lynch had her reasons. "The Jessica Lynch Story" wasn't hers — and hadn't been since the day eight months earlier when the nineteen-year-old private and fellow soldiers in the army's 507th Ordnance Maintenance Company had been ambushed on the outskirts of a desert town. Eleven of her thirty-three comrades — chefs, mechanics, requisition and supply clerks — died, five were held hostage for three weeks in a succession of houses, and Lynch, severely injured in an ensuing car wreck that knocked her unconscious for three hours, woke to find herself in a Nasiriyah hospital room, where she remained for nine days.

It would be more accurate to say that *I Am a Soldier, Too* belonged to its Boswell, Rick Bragg, a former *New York Times* correspondent who had recently left the paper under a cloud, after acknowledging that he had outsourced his reporting on an article to an intern who was neither paid nor credited for it. In this case, Bragg *had* interviewed Lynch, but she seemed strangely absent in the resulting account. The "I" in the title was missing from the text, which was told in the third person. The ghostwriter had ghosted his subject. And imposed on her an interpretation of the hours right after the accident that she didn't recall, having been out cold. Of these conjured memories, Lynch told *Time*, "It's like reading a book that really wasn't about me."[1]

Bragg's narrative was only the most recent in a line of rewrites—authored by the military, the media, docudrama script doctors, and a self-proclaimed Iraqi savior whom Lynch said she never met. "It seemed like I was doomed for scrutiny," Jessica Lynch told me when we talked four years later. "I was the one everyone wanted to dig into and pick apart." The only person not offering a Jessica Lynch chronicle, it seemed, was Jessica Lynch. She had packed a camcorder in her duffel bag, but during her deployment she never once removed it from its case. For months after her return, she uttered not one public word.[2]

The story of a helpless white girl snatched from the jaws of evil by heroic soldiers was the story everybody wanted.* "By now they are calling it 'Saving Private Lynch,'" CNBC's host Brian Williams told viewers less

---

*As opposed to the story of the five other soldiers taken hostage from Lynch's unit—four men and one woman, the first black female prisoner of war in U.S. military history—whose captivity was humiliatingly aired on Iraqi television and Al Jazeera. Three weeks later, these soldiers were essentially liberated by their last set of Iraqi guards, whom the POWs praised as kind and generous. The guards contacted the marines, asked them to come collect the captured soldiers, and supplied directions to the house where they were camped. Even armed with an exact street address, though, the marines had trouble finding the place and, suspecting a *"Black Hawk Down* situation," as one of the officers later put it, were about to beat a hasty retreat when an exasperated POW finally leaned out of a doorway and yelled, "I'm an American!" This was not the sort of drama the American military, or the American media, cared to enshrine in public consciousness, and it soon fell from view (Peter Baker, "Rescuers Nearly Called Mission Off," *Washington Post*, April 16, 2003).

than twenty-four hours after the night that more than one thousand "special ops" troops descended by helicopter to extract the wounded Lynch from an Iraqi hospital. "The story of her rescue is right out of a major motion picture: Blackhawks landing in the dark, a firefight on the way in and out, a diversion across town by the marines so they could slip in and get her out. The real life story is almost more incredible than that."[3]

Cognizant of the "right out of a major motion picture" potential, the U.S. military armed the commandos who stormed the Saddam Hussein Nasiriyah General Hospital about midnight on April 1 with night-vision video recorders. The film was rolling as the soldiers charged down the corridors. And was available for viewing about 180 minutes later. Before four that morning, the U.S. Central Command in Doha, Qatar, rousted war correspondents from their beds to screen a five-minute film clip in which a prostrate Jessica Lynch ("pretty, but stricken," as one press account described her) was hustled by gurney to a waiting helicopter, an American flag draped on her chest. The rescue of Lynch—who, according to anonymous "military sources" and one Iraqi lawyer, had been shot, stabbed, slapped by fedayeen interrogators, and possibly tortured—was a "classic" operation by "the nation's finest warriors," the army's spokesmen told the press, and "hot news." So hot that General Tommy Franks, the war's overall commanding officer, had monitored the operation on live video feed, keeping President Bush and Defense Secretary Rumsfeld apprised of the progress. When informed of the mission's outcome, the president was exultant, military spokesmen advised the media, and said, "That's great!"[4]

On April 5, the Central Command headquarters sent for the war's reporters once more. In an unusually long briefing, Major General Victor "Gene" Renuart personally provided the press corps with what amounted to the Lynch video's narration. An "assault force" of marines, Army Rangers, special forces, army aviators, U.S. Navy SEALs, air force pilots, and "combat controllers," Renuart said, had battled their way into the heavily fortified hospital that doubled as "headquarters" and "command-and-control facilities" for Hussein's Republican Guard "death squads." Once inside, the commandos cut the electricity and "persuaded" a doctor to guide them down the darkened corridors to the captive's chamber. "As the team entered the hospital room, they found

Private Lynch in a hospital bed," Renuart said. "The first man approached the door and came in and called her name. She had been scared, had the sheet up over her head because she didn't know what was happening. She lowered the sheet from her head. She didn't really respond yet because I think she was probably pretty scared. The soldier again said, 'Jessica Lynch, we're the United States soldiers and we're here to protect you and take you home.'" The title of Lynch's book comes from her response: "I'm an American soldier, too," she told him. But that was hardly how she would be cast, as Renuart's culminating anecdote suggested. "While the helicopter transported her to a nearby aircraft, who was then going to move her on to a field hospital," he said, "Jessica held up her hand and grabbed the Ranger doctor's hand, held on to it for the entire time and said, 'Please don't let anybody leave me.'"[5]

The media hung on every word. "First of all, thank you very much for giving us that level of detail about Jessica Lynch," *Newsweek* correspondent Martha Brant said when Renuart opened the floor to questions. The reporter was soon rushing, like the rest of her colleagues, to her computer. Evidently the speed with which Brant posted her "*Newsweek* Web exclusive" precluded translation of the insider army argot. "CENTCOM," the story said, referring to the U.S. Central Command, "had received HumInt"—human intelligence—of Lynch's whereabouts. After obtaining "intel" that the hospital was serving as "a military staging area," "the special-ops forces dropped in well outside the city and sneaked up on the compound in the dark for the 'snatch.'"[6]

"It sounded like one of those fanciful Hollywood scripts," *Newsweek* related, one of many media outlets to applaud the rescue effort's cinematic attributes. That the drama seemed straight out of a Schwarzenegger vehicle raised no eyebrows. The press was too busy providing its own whiz-bang sound track with headlines like "She's Alive," "Inside the Daring Nighttime Rescue," and "POW Jessica Saved in Just Six Minutes; Plucked from Death's Jaws," and breathless reenactments like these:

People: Around midnight on April 1 a few dozen Special Operations "doorkickers" piled into Black Hawk helicopters and headed for Nasiriya.

The southern Iraqi city was dark, lit only by scattered fires and the generator-powered lights of the Saddam Hussein Hospital, where Pfc. Jessica Lynch lay gravely injured. Suddenly one of the helicopters floundered, its landing gear snagged on the guy wire of a transmission tower. "The wire threw it into a 25-degree right roll and tossed the passengers around before the cable finally broke," says a colonel who was there. The pilot righted the chopper free and the team landed safely. Says the colonel: "God smiled on us that night." . . .

Washington Post: Commandos in blacked-out Blackhawk helicopters and protected by low, slow-flying AC-130 gunships, swooped toward the hospital grounds. Marines fanned out as an exterior perimeter, while Army Rangers made a second protective shield just outside the hospital walls. These forces took light fire from adjacent buildings, according to military sources. Commandos burst into the hospital, fired explosive charges meant to disorient anyone inside and headed for Lynch's room. . . .

Associated Press: On her hospital bed, Pfc. Jessica Lynch peered out from the sheet with which she'd been covering her head in fear. . . .

Daily News: Once more, as the commandos slipped out of the building, came the enemy gun blasts. And once more, the resistance was put down—as the rescuers in night-vision goggles loaded their wounded comrade into the bay of the waiting Black Hawk and escaped into the night. . . . [7]

Perhaps the soldiers who carried Lynch out regarded her as simply "their wounded comrade"—it's hard to say; they were forbidden from speaking publicly or even being identified by name—but from the start, the army command's spin and the media's coverage underscored the ways in which she was *not* their comrade. She may have been in uniform, but this wasn't a story about a soldier's return to her brothers in arms. It was a tale of a maiden in need of rescue. As General Renuart put it in his account at the briefing, the soldiers were able to "return" her to the homeland and "a reunion with her family." The good news, NBC journalist Kerry Sanders reported on April 2, was that "Jessica Lynch is no longer in harm's way," as if she weren't a soldier fulfilling her service but a civilian who had somehow wandered into a war zone. "This is obviously a wonderful story, and all of us feel very proud of the men who pulled off this mission and very pleased that this young woman has been—is going to come home," Mark Bowden, author of *Black Hawk Down*, said on *Larry King Live* the night after the rescue. "It's nice to see that she's safe," *Newsweek*'s Martha Brant, also a guest on the show, agreed, adding, "And I don't know whether the American people are ready to see women dying on the battlefields, as well as men." King turned to a panel of retired military brass—"five former servicemen, all heroes," he said—and invited two of them to recount their own heroic participation in a "rescue operation." The invitation backfired somewhat when one of them admitted that his rescue effort "didn't turn out well." Nonetheless, a gender line was being drawn in the Iraqi sand, where men were men because they saved women, and women were women because, once saved, they clung to their savior's hand and returned to the domestic fold.[8]

The story of Lynch's redemption had some evident problems. How did the U.S. forces manage to get in and out past the "headquarters" of Republican Guard "death squads" in six minutes flat? If the mission required such a fierce firefight, how come the rescue team didn't sustain a single casualty? These were questions the American media weren't eager to ask; they clung stubbornly to the military's version of virile heroism and vulnerable maidenhood and for more than a month sought no independent sources. Further investigation would fall to the foreign press corps, in particular the British.

On the day after the rescue, British Sky TV interviewed an Iraqi pharmacist at the hospital who had treated Lynch and who was baffled by the high-drama assault and the description of the hospital as a Republican Guard command post. While there had been some fedayeen in the basement at some point, he said, they were hiding from the American invasion and hardly patrolling the hallways. The pharmacist said he had attended to Lynch every day and never once saw a Republican Guard enter her room; it was "only me and the doctors."[9] In mid-May, the BBC and the *Guardian* reported on their more extensive findings from the field. They had gone to Nasiriyah and interviewed hospital staff and witnesses on the ground. The story the British journalists heard was very different from the version across the pond: the doctors who examined Lynch said she showed no signs of being shot or stabbed; her injuries all came from the accident when her Humvee had slammed into a jackknifed tractor trailer. Moreover, if Lynch was singled out for any unusual treatment during her hospital stay, the British journalists (and a few reporters who subsequently retraced their steps) found, it was unusually favorable.[10]

The medical staff told the British reporters that they had been inundated with about two thousand casualties from the American bombings, most of them civilians. Yet, the doctors had given Lynch the only specialty bed designed to ease bedsores, had used one of the only three platinum plates they had on hand to repair her shattered bones, had infused her with blood from their own veins when supplies ran out, had brought her American-style food and juice from their own homes when she recoiled at the hospital's native victuals, and had assigned her one of the only two nurses on the floor for full-time care. "I was like a mother to her and she was like a daughter," Khalida Shinah, the nurse, said, weeping at the memory of her charge's physical pain, which she did her best to ease. ("The nurses were wonderful," Lynch told me. "They really were there for me. They would rub my shoulders with talcum powder, and there was this one old lady who would sing to me and soothe me to sleep.") When the special-ops troops finally carried Lynch away, one of the medical staff members recalled, she was wearing a dress that a nurse had provided from her own closet.[11]

The hospital's doctors and nurses told reporters they were eager not just to cure their patient but to return her. Harith Hassona, Lynch's primary physician during her stay, had tried to send her back to the American military two days before her "rescue." He had bundled her into an ambulance and told the driver to deliver her to the U.S. checkpoint, but, when they drew near, American soldiers had opened fire, forcing the driver to retreat. Back at the hospital, when one of the doctors saw an American soldier on a nearby roof, Lynch recalled, her caregivers rolled her bed in front of the window in hopes that he would see her. And when the remaining Republican Guards hiding in the hospital's basement fled, a doctor and neighboring residents relayed the news to the Arabic interpreter for the U.S. military's advance team.[12]

Nonetheless, the "assault force" charged with guns blazing. "We heard the noise of helicopters," Anmar Uday, a doctor, told the BBC. "We were surprised. Why do this? There was no military, there were no soldiers in the hospital." Like so many American reporters, Uday regarded the drama as cinematic—though he was less enamored of the performance. "It was like a Hollywood film," he said. "They cried, 'Go, go, go,' with guns and blanks and the sound of explosions. They made a show— an action movie like Sylvester Stallone or Jackie Chan, with jumping and shouting, breaking down doors."[13]

Footage that cast the heroes in a less than flattering light either hit the cutting room floor or was never committed to film. Some action scenes that the hospital staff recalled but that were absent from the military video screened for reporters included American forces kicking down doors even as they were being handed keys, interrogating and handcuffing doctors, manacling patients to their bed frames (including one patient who was already immobile and tethered to an IV drip), seizing one of the hospital administrators for no apparent reason and penning him for several days in an outdoor prison camp, and slashing the special sand-filled bed the hospital staff had allocated to Lynch. "They took samples of sand out of it," a perplexed Hassona said. "It was the only bed like it that we have, the only one in the governorate."[14]

The heroic rescue story was an effort to counter an earlier humiliating episode, in which heroes were harder to locate. That episode was the ambush and surrender of much of Jessica Lynch's unit. Private Lynch would never have needed rescuing, would likely not even have been captured, if the superiors responsible for her safety and that of her fellow soldiers in the 507th Maintenance Company hadn't abandoned them. The abandonment took several forms. On March 22, 2003, in the first days of the invasion, the convoy's leaders had raced ahead, out of radio range, and failed to slow or send in combat unit reinforcements even when they knew their trailing end had fallen dangerously behind. The day before the ambush, the battalion commanders had informed the company's commanding officer, Captain Troy King, that they couldn't wait for the 507th to catch up, even though going ahead meant leaving the maintenance unit without protection.

Despite being armed with a map of the course and a detailed account of the route on a CD-ROM, King managed to take one wrong turn after another. He was supposed to have benefit of human direction, in the form of a military contingent standing at a fail-safe checkpoint outside Nasiriyah, guiding the convoy's stragglers to the detour that skirted the city. But these sentinels had evidently left their posts. Further up the wrong route, King came across a marine unit, but its members did nothing to alert the lost convoy to the impending danger. The route led directly into Nasiriyah. Once north of the city, King realized his mistake and ordered the company to reverse course and retrace the route, back into the town they were supposed to avoid. On the return, King again took the wrong road, requiring yet another U-turn. Many of the big trucks were having trouble swinging around on the narrow streets. And as they neared Nasiriyah, they came under fire. In all the ensuing confusion, the convoy splintered into three isolated processions. Lynch was with the last group, and as its lumbering vehicles threaded through town, they were ambushed—to devastating effect.[15]

Once under attack, the soldiers had no guidance from their superiors, who could not be raised on the radio. They also had trouble getting any clear instructions from their commanding officer, Captain King. They were left to fight their way out with little armament; the unit didn't even have grenades. The soldiers had only their M-16s, and the swirling sands quickly jammed the rifles. "We were like Custer," Sergeant James Riley, a member of the company, recalled woefully. "We were surrounded. We had no working weapons. We couldn't even make a bayonet charge." Less than fifteen minutes into the "battle," Riley had no choice but to order his unit's soldiers to surrender.[16]

"How do they let a whole convoy go past?" Lynch would wonder later of the marines that let her unit go by without a warning. "Not one person tried to stop us. They just sat there." Her question was never answered. The army conducted a desultory investigation and issued a report in July 2003 that blamed the whole debacle on a single "navigational error" and recommended no disciplinary action. Not one officer would be held accountable for the decisions that led to the U.S. military's deadliest day of the early ground war.[17]

• • •

FOR A MOMENT, it seemed as though the hero of the 507th Maintenance Company might be Jessica Lynch herself. Thanks to a mistaken pronoun by an Arabic translator in the National Security Agency, a counterversion to the Jessica Lynch story surfaced briefly. An intercepted Iraqi radio account of the Nasiriyah ambush described a blond soldier who had reportedly fired his weapon until he ran out of ammunition, even as he was shot multiple times and stabbed. In the botched translation, "his" became "her." Further confusion ensued when someone mistakenly characterized this report to the *Washington Post* as a description of Jessica Lynch. "She was fighting to the death," an unnamed U.S. official said. "She did not want to be taken alive." The *Post* published these quotes on April 3, two days after Lynch's rescue. The account of Lynch's heroics was hedged—the *Post* noted that its information "comes from monitored communications and from Iraqi sources in Nasiriyah whose reliability has yet to be assessed"—and Lynch's putative heroics were described with condescension, as charming Annie-get-your-gun pluck. "Talk about spunk!" Senator Pat Roberts said in the article. "She just persevered. It takes that and a tremendous faith that your country is going to come and get you."[18]

But even with all that, the story fell uncomfortably outside of the girl-in-need-of-rescue script. The media didn't have to be uncomfortable for long. Hours after the *Post* published its article, Lynch's father, Greg, was widely quoted as saying that the army doctor who was treating his daughter had seen no evidence of combat injuries: "He looked for the gunshot wounds, for the knife stabbing, and there is no entry whatsoever." The hospital's army commander confirmed the father's account and his remarks were also heavily reported. The *Post* itself ran a story quoting Lynch's father the following day, and quoting the commander the day after that. An army spokesman was soon assuring the press that Lynch hadn't fired a single shot, and a senior Pentagon official made the media rounds to deride the notion of "a female who fought to her last breath." He told reporters that the *Post*'s story "wasn't grounded in anything" and the *Post*'s "official" source was just "somebody grasping at straws." The media didn't seem dismayed by the new information: like the military, they far preferred the tale of an ailing girl rescued by burly commandos (however artificial) to the anxiety-producing tale of an American Amazon (however erroneous).[19]

Perhaps that anxiety explains the ferocity with which the media dismantled the *Washington Post's* initial account. Long after the *Post* had recanted the story and run a 5,600-word article correcting its original 1,000-word piece, and its ombudsmen had penned three apologias (more contrition than the *Post* and its brethren would ever exhibit over, say, the false reports of Hussein's WMDs), commentators would continue to condemn the brief portrayal of Lynch as "a female Rambo," as they invariably and sarcastically referred to her. "While Lynch's gruesome ordeal as a victim of war's brutality is celebrated as an Audie Murphy anecdote," an indignant Kate O'Beirne wrote in a cover story in the *National Review*, "the unambiguous heroism of the men who rescued her goes largely unmentioned." *Washington Post* media columnist Howard Kurtz berated his employer in print and on CNN's *Reliable Sources*, where he served as host. "Why did the media run so hard and so long with a story that we now know was largely bogus?" Kurtz wanted to know on his November 16 show—seven months after the press had quit running a story it had backed away from after one day. "The media went wild over their new heroine," Kurtz griped. His show's guests joined in the self-flagellation. "Yes, we willfully went along with this media hype," syndicated columnist and media ethics professor Steven Roberts said. "I think we wanted heroes." And Lynch was no hero, the show's guests all agreed. "Everyone around her was—may have been fighting heroically, but she couldn't do a thing," *Time's* Nancy Gibbs told Kurtz, as if that hadn't been established months before. "She didn't do any of the things that have been attributed to her."[20]

Over at Fox News, host John Gibson was still complaining at the end of 2003 about "the story about her, you know, being John Wayne at the Alamo and taking her gun and firing it off." He was joined in his ire by Elaine Donnelly, the director of the Center for Military Readiness, an organization devoted to reining in women's full participation in the armed forces. For months, Donnelly had been denouncing the *Post* for its "thinly sourced" story and the Defense Department for "staying silent when this Jessica as John Wayne story" was "captivating not only Americans, but around the world." In September 2003, Donnelly's lobbying group had filed a formal appeal with the White House to "find a way to allow military women, especially those in support units, to serve without undue exposure to 'a substantial risk of capture' in or near close combat units, to the greatest degree possible."

"Elaine, the big question," Gibson asked her. "Is Jessica Lynch a hero, a victim, or both?"

"I would say she certainly is a victim," Donnelly said. "We know that for sure."

Gibson agreed. Yet, he still seemed unsettled. "If Jessica Lynch is a hero, what do you call a soldier that actually goes out and kills the enemy, maybe saving an entire platoon?" he asked. "A lot of our soldiers have won medals for their heroic action in combat. But how many of them are we hearing about these days? Do we make war heroes out of the survivors instead of warriors?"[21]

Donnelly's sister conservative columnists were soon indicting the culprit that they believed lurked behind the gun-toting girl tale: feminists, they held, were trying to leverage bogus accounts of Lynch's heroics to force the military to open combat positions to women. "Much of this can be laid at the feet of feminists who want to use Lynch as their poster girl for the 'I can do anything better than you' feminized military," Betsy Hart wrote in the *Chicago Sun-Times*. That accusation was even more "thinly sourced" than the *Post* story that Donnelly had denounced. But it would resound in the conservative media's echo chamber, where feminists were chastised for "overplaying women's exploits" as a way to "discount the masculine traits that the history of warfare shows to be vital to military success." These feminists threatened to destroy our fighting forces. "Where are the male politicians and military commanders," antifeminism's éminence grise Phyllis Schlafly wrote the day Lynch's "rescue" was announced, "who will stand up and say out loud that feminist ideology, like G.I. Jane standing naked in the shower, is an empress who has no clothes?"[22]

On conservative Web sites, some went so far as to blame the empress's "poster girl" herself. "It's LONG past time for Jessica Lynch's 15 minutes of fame to be over," declared blogger Chuck Muth, who regarded

Lynch's presence in the war zone as the misbegotten result of the army's "stupid" decision "to placate loud-mouthed feminists." He shared these views in an online column on Veteran's Day. "Cash in on your book deal, Jessie, and move on with your life," he wrote. "It may sound cold, but we have bigger fish to fry." Lynch was a "political piranha and an economic opportunist" who "relishes" her fame and grandstands "on her liberal soapbox," online commentator Jon Christian Ryter pronounced. "Lynch should make a real political statement by declining her own military stipend." In Lynch's hometown, Helen Burns, a neighbor of the Lynch family, recalled having "almost to run a man off" who had showed up accusing Lynch of self-promoting deceit. "He said he didn't know why Jessi didn't tell the truth," she said. "And I told him Jessi didn't talk. Everyone else talked."[23]

With Jessica Lynch declared ineligible for hero status, the search proceeded for a proper, read male, replacement. "Well, now it turns out there was a hero that day, a recipient of neither fame nor fortune," Mike Wallace announced on 60 Minutes, after reminding viewers yet again that Lynch was a mere victim and never fired her gun. Wallace's hero was Private Patrick Miller, a repairman in the 507th Maintenance Company who was driving the last truck in the convoy. When his truck lost power, Miller jumped out and, encountering a fusillade of bullets, dived behind a berm and, as Wallace described it, "effectively put that mortar pit out of action." 60 Minutes showed a film clip in which Miller demonstrated his rifle skills—which, according to him, were limited; he had failed the army's marksmanship test. Miller was a mechanic, not a sharpshooter. Wallace moved on to what he evidently viewed as Miller's other act of valor: singing Toby Keith's hit country tune "Courtesy of the Red, White & Blue" after surrendering to Iraqi gunmen.

WALLACE: What are the words?

MILLER: "You'll be sorry that you messed with the US of A, because we'll put a boot in your ass. It's the American way."

"Everybody knows about Jessica," Wallace pointedly reminded Miller. "But nobody knows about Patrick." When Miller failed to rise to the bait,

Wallace prodded him further: "A million-dollar book deal and television [for Lynch]. Does it ground on you just a little bit?"

"Somewhat," Miller said. "But I don't want to get all into that."[24]

In early 2004, the media seized on another male hero prospect from Lynch's unit: Sergeant Donald Walters, the blond soldier whom the National Security Agency's Arabic translator may have mistakenly identified as female. "Lost in the Jessica hero hysteria," *Insight on the News*, a companion publication to the *Washington Times*, maintained, were "extraordinary efforts" by men like Walters "that challenge the best Hollywood could imagine about combat heroism." What Walters, a food service supervisor in the 507th Maintenance Company, actually did was unknown. The official army report, on which *Insight* based its account, could state with confidence only that the vehicle in which Walters had been traveling had broken down and he had climbed out with the other occupants:

> It is unclear whether SGT Walters was picked up by others in the convoy or remained in the area of the disabled tractor-trailer. There is some information to suggest that a U.S. Soldier, that could have been Walters, fought his way south of Highway 16 toward a canal and was killed in action. SGT Walters was in fact killed at some point during this portion of the attack. The circumstances of his death cannot be conclusively determined by available information.

The army granted Walters a posthumous Bronze Star and Purple Heart, which it upgraded, following congressional interference, to a Silver Star, its third-highest award for heroism. A month later, the results of a military forensic examination, based on DNA evidence obtained at the site where Walters was killed, were announced: Walters, the army concluded, was actually captured after suffering a leg wound and then shot twice in the back.[25]

In the effort to anoint a masculine hero for the Lynch story, the media grasped at ever thinner straws. A *Nightline* special in July 2003 pinned its hopes on Sergeant Robert Dowdy, whose contribution to "the frantic efforts that saved Private Jessica Lynch" was probably inadvertent: he had dropped his duffel bag at Lynch's feet when he climbed into her Humvee.

REPORTER JIM WOOTEN: In a way that probably saved her life.

KATHY DOWDY [Sergeant Dowdy's widow]: Probably did. Probably did. Yeah.

WOOTEN: Which strikes me as being, suggesting that even in those last moments your husband was the kind of a guy you always knew he was.

DOWDY: Right, yes.[26]

When *Primetime's* Diane Sawyer interviewed Lynch months later, the host revisited the subject:

SAWYER: [Dowdy's] wife has said that she was given a military briefing, that they told her he had put his bag in front of you.

LYNCH: Yeah. There was, one of his bags was actually kind of at my feet. So, it was kind of protecting me. But I mean it was full of clothes. I guess it was—enough to save my life.[27]

Lynch was dubious, though, that he had actually intended to offer her padded protection. "When we're all in the middle of fighting, would that have been one of his main goals?" she said to me. "I mean, I don't think with bullets whizzing by that was, like, his first priority."

In Nasiriyah, one local man stepped forward to claim the hero's badge. Mohammed Odeh al-Rehaief was a thirty-two-year-old former divorce lawyer with time on his hands—ever since a man had threatened bodily harm if Rehaief didn't withdraw divorce papers he had filed on behalf of the man's wife. Rehaief had complied, then, chagrined, quit his practice. Since then, he had been teaching kung fu part-time and hanging around the house, screening his large video stash of American action movies. "My favorites were Westerns with John Wayne," he said. Making a living was not a pressing concern; Rehaief came from a wealthy landowning family. Anyway, his wife worked as a nurse.[28]

On the morning of March 27, 2003, as Rehaief would recount time and again for the many journalists who sought out his story, he had gone to visit his wife, Iman, who, he said, was working then in the Nasiriyah hospital's kidney dialysis unit. Inside, he reported, the halls were "crawl-ing" with fedayeen in "black ninja-style dress, with hoods hiding all but their eyes." Overhearing talk among the medical staff about an American female soldier who was on the ward, Rehaief said, he decided to sneak past the ninjas and get a look. He described how he waited until one of the guards posted outside Lynch's door—"a hulking man with a black crew cut and a Fu Manchu mustache"—took a break and his replace-ment dozed off. Rehaief said he then peeked through a small glass panel in the door and saw the act that would turn him into a media celebrity. By the time he had written his own account in his 2003 book, *Because Each Life Is Precious: Why an Iraqi Man Risked Everything for Private Jessica Lynch*—for which HarperCollins paid him $300,000—Rehaief had honed that moment to a well-polished set piece:

> I took two steps forward to see inside that room.
>
> I registered a well-built man, easily six-foot-three, standing with his back to me. He was all in black, except for the glimmer of his gold epaulets: a fedayeen officer. I could see his face in profile: dark skin, thick hair, broad mustache like Saddam's. His left foot was propped on a chair, his arm resting on his knee. He was leaning out over the foot of the bed, menacing a pale figure who now stole my attention.
>
> I cannot say how I had pictured this American POW, but I never imagined her as quite so small or quite so young. She was a child, really. . . . She was mostly covered by a white blanket. Her forehead was bandaged. Her mouth was knit in pain. . . .
>
> I saw the officer look to the translator. Whatever he heard did not please him. Swinging from the shoulder, he slapped his captive with the palm of his right hand, then with the back of it. Her head jerked back and forth; she was a poor match for him.
>
> I could not hear the sound of those slaps, but I felt them at my core. My heart was cut. In that flash of violence I did not see an American, some captured combatant. I saw a helpless young girl.

And saw his chance to be her rescuer. "Minutes earlier, I'd been an ordinary man," Rehaief wrote. "I'd wanted only to escape a battleground with my family intact. But I now had seen something not meant to be seen, and it turned me upside down. . . . If I pretended this morning never happened, I would always be a small man. But if I seized my chance and went to the Marines, I would be a big man—in my own eyes—for the rest of my days." The next day, he said, he slipped into Lynch's room. "Don't worry," he recalled telling her. He would find a way to get her out of there. "The girl looked up at me and blinked back a tear."[29]

So began Rehaief's mission to save the "helpless young girl." His rescue operation, according to him, involved hours of spying on bloodthirsty fedayeen, several solo Bataan-worthy marches on bloodied feet to a marine outpost, numerous near-death experiences, a treacherous swim across the Euphrates past "poisonous water snakes and snapping turtles two feet long," an explosion that flung blinding shrapnel in one eye, and a high-speed car chase that was "like something out of 'Total Recall,' when Arnold repelled the Martian mutants." Nonetheless he persevered, even defying four guards with AK-47 machine guns in the hospital at one point. As he later told *People* magazine, "It was very important that I save Jessica's life."[30]

Rehaief reportedly endured all these adventures so he could hand off maps and details of the hospital's layout to the marines. He was well rewarded for this delivery: the U.S. Department of Homeland Security offered Rehaief and his immediate family "humanitarian parole," with the guarantee they could live almost anywhere in the world. Rehaief chose the United States and soon thereafter, the American government flew him and his wife and daughter out of the country, granted all three political asylum, and moved them into a home in a Virginia suburb. Rehaief was given a consulting job at the GOP-affiliated Livingston Group (the lobbying firm of former Republican congressman Bob Livingston, who had resigned during Clinton's impeachment hearings after word of his own marital infidelities surfaced).[31]

The marines later confirmed that Rehaief had provided their field officers with information about the hospital. But the rest of the ex-lawyer's dramatic tale was soon under dispute. If Rehaief imagined himself Arnold Schwarzenegger in *Total Recall*, others saw a resemblance to Walter Mitty. The Nasiriyah hospital's chief nurse told the *Washington Post* that she had never employed a nurse named Iman—Rehaief's wife's name—nor did she know of any nurse on her staff married to a lawyer. "This is something we would know," she said. Medical staff members who had maintained a twenty-four-hour vigil at Lynch's bedside told journalists that no Republican Guard officer, in black ninja costume or otherwise, had ever made an appearance in the room—and the sentinel at the door was no "hulking" fedayeen but just a low-level watchman. "Never happened," Harith Hassona, Lynch's primary physician, said of Rehaief's story. As for men in black slapping Lynch, Hassona told the *Post*: "That's some Hollywood crap you'd tell the Americans." Rehaief was "a big liar," a nurse told ABC. "He should be hung by his ears."[32]

Once in the States, Rehaief repeatedly sought an audience with the young woman he had "saved." Lynch, still in residence at Walter Reed Hospital, declined through relatives, who said there were "scheduling problems." After Lynch returned home to Palestine, West Virginia, Rehaief showed up in town and tried again to arrange a reunion. Lynch's family turned him away, explaining that she was "busy." Her failure to shower thanks on her "saviour," as one media account dubbed Rehaief, sparked local disapproval. "A lot of people thought that was disrespectful," a Palestine resident told the London *Times*. "She should have found the time. Some people think this whole experience might have changed her." Lynch finally agreed to a brief meeting with Rehaief—and without reporters—in April 2004. The reason for her reluctance became clear in the course of Lynch's interview on *Primetime*. Sawyer asked her if she recalled being slapped by a fedayeen officer, as Rehaief had claimed:

LYNCH: No. From the time I woke up in that hospital, no one beat me. No one slapped me. No one, nothing.

SAWYER: You're sure? How can you be sure?

LYNCH: When I was conscious, I know that did not happen. I know that did not happen. And maybe it did happen when I was unconscious. But why would you slap someone while they're unconscious, trying to give them answers, you know?

SAWYER: He [Rehaief] also says that at one point he came up to you and that he said to you that he was going to get you help. "Don't worry."

LYNCH: No. I don't remember that, either.[33]

Despite all the questions, NBC bought the rights to Rehaief's book. It served as the basis for the network's two-hour TV movie, which would, NBC promised, tell "a story of incredible courage": a young woman's rescue by "an Iraqi stranger and the American Special Operations team who brought her home" that "provided hope to the nation during Operation Iraqi Freedom." "This story is *Mission: Impossible*, but it's real," an NBC executive told *Daily Variety*. "It's as good a story as you can get from this war," he added, which was probably true. In any event, the real story wasn't what NBC was seeking, as was evident from the unusually long disclaimer the network appended to the final cut, which advised that "some characters, scenes and events in whole or part have been created for dramatic purpose." Or, as Lynch later remarked to me, "All the facts weren't straight. It was odd." Then again, at least the network made the disclosure, unlike Lynch's mythicizers in the military and the media.[34]

The director of *Saving Private Lynch* was Peter Markle, who would subsequently direct *Faith of My Fathers*, a cable drama about John McCain's ordeal as a POW, and *Flight 93*, the second such cable movie on the subject. The network premiered the Lynch movie during sweeps months in early November 2003, on the same night and at the same time as the CBS TV movie *The Elizabeth Smart Story*, another docudrama about the captivity of another helpless girl, the Salt Lake City teenager abducted from her bedroom in the summer of 2002 and held for nine months. Reviewers complained that there didn't seem to be much of Lynch in *Saving Private Lynch*. As the *Daily News*'s TV critic wrote, "Laura Regan, as Lynch, has so little to do here, she's almost like her own stand-in."[35]

A FEW REPORTERS finally got around to asking Lynch to name the soldier she thought deserved the hero's mantle. She was quick to answer. But her nomination didn't fit the media's gender specs. "Lori," she told *Rolling Stone*. "Lori is the real hero."[36]

Lori Piestewa, a twenty-three-year-old Hopi Indian and a single mother of two, had been Lynch's army roommate at Fort Bliss, outside El Paso, Texas, and the women had become close friends. Lynch recalled Piestewa's stoicism and self-reliance. "She didn't need help," Lynch said. "She was strong." When the unit deployed to Iraq, Piestewa was supposed to stay stateside; she had badly injured her shoulder in a training exercise and was still recovering from surgery. She insisted on going anyway; to stay behind, she believed, would be to abandon her unit and, in particular, her closest comrade, Jessica Lynch. Piestewa told Lynch: "You have to; I have to."[37]

On the afternoon of March 20, as the 507th Maintenance Company made its way north through the desert, the five-ton water truck Lynch was driving broke down. As she stood at the side of the road, one army vehicle after another sped by. The drivers were too worried about keeping up with the convoy to stop for the stranded. Then Piestewa drove up in her Humvee and pulled over. "Get in, roommate," she shouted. Lynch never forgot who rescued her that afternoon. "She stopped," Lynch marveled. "She picked me up. I love her."[38]

When the Humvee came under attack in Nasiriyah three days later, there was much screaming and praying inside. Lynch recalled one occupant who remained calm and firmly "in control": Lori Piestewa. As the long line of trucks started its 180-degree loop to head back into town, the lead vehicle, the Humvee transporting the commanding officer responsible for all those wrong turns, eventually met up with Piestewa's Humvee, which was near the rear. The commander's driver, Private Dale Nace, was a friend of Piestewa's and he offered to trade places with her. "I'm not getting out of this Humvee," she told him. She didn't want to desert her unit. Nace was struck by her composure. "She had this look on her face that was like: 'Something is about to happen, but we're going to be OK,'" Nace recalled. "It made me feel at ease with myself. She gave me this calmness. If it wasn't for her, I probably would have freaked out."[39]

Soon after, a huge tractor trailer ahead of Piestewa's Humvee jackknifed. She was attempting to steer around the mess when a rocket-propelled grenade hit her wheel well and hurled the Humvee into the stalled truck. She died of her catastrophic injuries a short while later, becoming the first Native American woman ever to be killed in an American war. On foreign soil, that is.[40]

Four months after that terrible accident, Lynch spoke publicly for the first time at a homecoming event in Elizabeth, West Virginia. She chose to focus her remarks on the soldier whose support had meant the most to her. Lori Piestewa, she said, "fought beside me, and it was an honor to have served with her. Lori will always be in my heart." Later, when reporters asked Lynch how she mustered the will to live in that hospital room thousands of miles from home, her body a mass of broken bones, she always told them, "Lori helped me get through." Lynch said there were moments when she saw her dead friend's spirit perched at the foot of her bed, assuring her that everything would be OK.[41]

The media, though, had little interest in the story of the Native American woman who had protected her sister in arms. The story in *Rolling Stone* was one of a very few exceptions, and that profile of Piestewa ran more than a year after the event. The headline read, accurately enough, "The Forgotten Soldier."[42]

WE CAST OUR male soldiers returning from the war zone as "battle-tested," seasoned, tougher, old beyond their years. But the postwar Lynch would be lauded not for her hard-won maturity but for having remained a girl. Her virtue lay in her preserved-in-aspic innocence. "She hasn't changed one bit," a typical media report assured, after consulting with her kindergarten teacher.[43]

The celebration of her perpetual childhood began immediately, with media accounts from the military hospital in Germany that described her as "the tiny girl" and the "blonde waif." She was said to be "clutching a teddy bear." She was said to favor applesauce and steamed carrots. She was said to be dreaming of washing her hair and styling it with the curling iron she "calls her magic wand." She was said to be "asking for her mother."[44]

Stateside, reporters flocked to Palestine, West Virginia, to harvest sugar-and-spice details from kindergarten teachers and grade school play-mates. Her grandmother called her "precious Little Jessi," the media reported. Little Jessi was, according to various dispatches, a "princess, laying out her clothes every night," a "part tomboy, part wannabe beauty queen" who liked her hair ribbons to match her outfits, and a "little girl who loved pink dresses and perfect hair." We learned that she "once fractured her arm and insisted on a pink cast to go with her pink shoelaces," liked to play with Barbies, "took pride in her appearance," presided as the Wirt County Fair's "Miss Congeniality," "couldn't hit the ball at all" in softball but "had a big smile on her face all the time when she was trying to do it," wore "small-waisted dresses," and was "every mother's dream of a teenager daughter." When Rick Bragg sat down to write his book on Lynch some months later, he devoted a chapter, titled "Princess," to the enumeration of her maidenly attributes. The chapter's first sentence is "Her bangs were always perfect." The biography of a good girl follows: She was born "tiny" and "beautiful," a "doll-like little girl" who was "almost as quiet as one" and "never any trouble." "She cried her first day or so in Linda Davies' kindergarten class because she missed her mom, and that was about the extent of her misbehavior for the next twelve years." In middle school, she was a cheerleader in "little pleated skirts"; even while playing school sports, "she was always perfectly made up." As Miss Congeniality, she was "radiant in her burgundy form-hugging gown."[45]

In other words, the "Princess" belonged in beauty pageants, not boot camp. "Her fatigues swallowed her like a big frog," Bragg wrote. "She looked like a child who had sneaked into her daddy's closet and tried on his uniform to play soldier." *I Am a Soldier, Too* seemed an ironic title for a book dedicated to proving the opposite. "In the macho world of the military," he wrote, "Jessi stood out like a lapdog in a pen of pitbulls." Bragg, like the many commentators before him, was annoyed by the way that, as he put it, "Jessi, damsel in distress, would be transformed into a kind of invincible action hero who absorbed bullets and just kept on fighting as the enemy closed in." He was eager to effect a reverse metamorphosis. Forgotten, by Bragg and the others, were Lynch's own choices: she had joined the military of her own free will—and reenlisted for four more years. As Lynch put it to me: "I definitely did not see myself as being passive and being a little girl. No, no, no. I signed up, I enlisted, I volunteered for this. It was my decision to go into the military. No one forced me. It was my job and I was there to try to do my part." Her chroniclers refused to believe that military service was what the real Little Jessi wanted. "All the while," *People* preferred to maintain, "she stayed true to her desire to one day be a teacher like her friend and former kindergarten teacher Linda Davies."[46]

The Jessica Lynch storytellers did allow their protagonist one other aspiration. Jessica Lynch, "In Love," *People* proclaimed in August 2003. While Lynch was stationed in Fort Bliss, she had met Ruben Contreras, "a 6-ft., 24-year-old sergeant" and "ex-high-school wrestling star from Colorado Springs," as he was invariably described. The media reported on the romance to follow in the breathless style of teen magazines: we learned of "the first time he laid eyes on her" (she was napping in the gym bleachers at Fort Bliss), the first time Mr. Right asked her out ("First date, 'Scooby Doo'"), the second time he asked her out (burritos at Taco Bell), and when they held hands ("only while in their civvies"). *People* had a full rundown on the couple's first-year anniversary:

> Contreras arrived at Lynch's bedside for a 10-day visit, bearing a special gift—a platinum "promise ring" with a solitary marquise-cut diamond. His mother, Lisa Latorre, helped him pick out the present. "Jessi says she never takes it off," reports Latorre, 46, who works for a computer firm. "She's a wonderful girl. Hopefully wedding bells are right around the corner."

People hoped so, too. "Rescued POW Jessica Lynch . . . starts planning a June wedding," the teaser to its November 2003 story announced. The pair wasn't actually engaged, but Lynch reportedly "coos" into the phone when chatting with "her not-quite-but-almost fiancé." A *People* reporter escorted her to Vera Wang's bridal boutique, "where she gazes dreamily at a cream satin gown," and talked about her plan to have "one to two children."[47] Lynch recalled the day differently. "Going to a big designer like that was certainly not something I would have ever thought of doing on my own," she told me. "*They* took me to Vera Wang's shop. They wanted me to actually try on dresses. I didn't want to do that. I finally just held one up in front of me, so they could get a picture."

By March 2004, the Associated Press was regretfully issuing this bulletin: "Jessica Lynch Not a June Bride." The news service still held out hope. "Lynch has been unable to focus on planning a wedding because of her busy schedule and continued therapy for injuries," but "she's still wearing an engagement ring." By August 2005, the ring was gone. Tucked into a brief AP article about Lynch starting college at West Virginia University came the disappointing verdict: Lynch had broken the engagement. She didn't have time for a wedding right now, a family member explained. The princess who only cared about her pink dresses was "totally focused on her education."[48]

One year later, on the fifth anniversary of 9/11, *People* made brief note of an update in Lynch's domestic affairs: "Former soldier and prisoner of war Jessica Lynch, 23, is expecting her first child in January." The two-sentence item seemed oddly perfunctory, given the magazine's previous obsession with Lynch's familial future. But then, Lynch had not held up her end of the deal: she was not marrying the father.[49]

On January 19, 2007, Lynch gave birth to a baby girl. She named her Dakota Ann, in honor of the Indian woman she regarded as her true protector and comrade. "Ann" was Lori Piestewa's middle name, and "Dakota" is Sioux for friend or ally.[50]

FOR JESSICA LYNCH to be regarded as virtuous, she had to be an innocent girl. And to be innocent, she had to be vulnerable. By becoming a soldier she had failed to adhere to those terms, and attempts to reassert her helplessness by describing her as a child in Daddy's uniform could only rehabilitate her so far. The ultimate proof of her vulnerability would be her despoliation. The ironic equation was that for Jessica Lynch to be virtuous, she had to be violated.

The media began pondering her possible defilement within hours of the rescue. "Many questions remain," *Newsweek*'s very first online report said, and the questions were not about the military's performance. "What did Lynch live through? The speculation is not pleasant." Within twenty-four hours, NBC News was intimating that a depraved act had taken place at the first field hospital where Lynch was treated. The evidence: "Her blood-soaked uniform was later found ripped up, her name patch torn off." The Iraqi physicians who first attended to Lynch would later tell the press that she arrived fully dressed; *they* were the ones who removed her flak jacket and cut away her clothing to expose the injured area, as is standard practice in a trauma ward. Three days later, the *Daily News* was insisting on interpreting Lynch's injuries as evidence of something more sinister than a major car wreck. "Officials have refused to say why so many of Lynch's bones were broken, but it's likely she was tortured."[51]

About two weeks after the rescue, *Newsweek* was back making murky allusions to "unsettling questions" and "the unpleasant implication" about Lynch's "treatment in captivity." "The possibility of mistreatment had been very much on the mind of President Bush," the magazine reported, "who, according to a senior administration official, had frequently raised concerns about American women's falling into Iraqi hands." By the following week, *People* was treating the "unpleasant implication" as a foregone conclusion. Lynch had suffered an unnamed form of "extensive torture," according to an unnamed "Capitol Hill source." The source told *People*, "Those people—the Iraqi captors—were barbaric. I have no doubt that with her injuries, and with what they had planned for her, she was going to die." By June, *People* was quoting some even more unlikely sources to support its suspicions of sexual torture: "Country singer Mark Wills, who recently stopped by for a 20-minute chat, doesn't believe the skeptics for a moment. 'You don't sustain injuries like she had from not being abused or mistreated,' he says."[52]

On June 17, the *Washington Post* weighed in with its own unverified insinuations:

> But she also appears to suffer from wounds that cannot be seen—and the story of her capture and rescue remains only partly told.
>
> Her family says she doesn't remember anything about her capture. U.S. military sources say she is unable—or unwilling—to say much about anything that happened to her between the morning her Army

unit was ambushed and when she became fully conscious sometime later at Saddam Hussein General Hospital in Nasiriyah.

The *Post* couldn't resist adding this nonconfirmation confirmation to the mix: "Two U.S. officials with knowledge of the Army investigation said Lynch was mistreated by her captors. They would not elaborate."[53]

In July, *Newsweek* claimed to have a lead. "U.S. military intelligence officers believe Lynch's injuries were inflicted after she and other survivors surrendered," *Newsweek* reported, citing three anonymous military sources who claimed Lynch was "standing when she surrendered, and had minor injuries at most." *Newsweek* also said that Mehdi Kafaji, the Iraqi orthopedic surgeon who was in charge of Lynch's treatment at the hospital in Nasiriyah, had told its reporters that she had "blunt-force trauma not consistent with what you'd expect from a car accident" and appeared to have suffered, in *Newsweek*'s words, a "severe beating, probably with numerous rifle butts." But Kafaji heatedly denied ever making such statements when other journalists contacted him. He said that Lynch's injuries from the car crash were so severe she would have died if she had been assaulted. "If she had been raped, there is no way she could have survived it," he said. "She was fighting for her life—her body was broken. What sort of an animal would even think of that?"[54]

What Lynch didn't remember would ultimately be redefined—as a memory *repressed* and willfully so. If she wouldn't cooperate, others would recover the buried trauma for her. The retrieval would constitute the second "rescue" of the missing private, a mission carried out on U.S. soil and in American letters. Its point man was Rick Bragg, the former *New York Times* reporter who had anointed her a "damsel in distress." The "distress" he had in mind is introduced midway through his book. It is one sentence long: "The records also show that she was a victim of anal sexual assault." Bragg did not say what these records contained or where they came from. In place of information, he provided lurid speculation: "The records do not tell whether her captors assaulted her almost lifeless, broken body after she was lifted from the wreckage, or if they assaulted her and then broke her bones into splinters until she was almost dead."

Lynch had no such memory of either alternative, or any other aspect of this alleged ordeal. "I didn't remember any sexual assault," she told me. "I still don't, to this day. I haven't had any flashback or memory of it or anything." Bragg declined to be interviewed for this book, citing a confidentiality agreement, but in *I Am A Soldier, Too*, he offered a psychological explanation for Lynch's lack of recall. In a chapter titled "Damaged," he asserted that Lynch couldn't bear to contemplate "those three hours of cruelty," so she "lost" the experience and sought "refuge" in a "retreat from reality." "The only way she could escape was to slip back into sleep and dream [of home]." Sleeping Beauty couldn't bring herself to remember, so her male rescuer would remember for her. "It all left marks on her," he wrote, "and it is those marks that fill in the blanks of what Jessi lived through on the morning of March 23, 2003." Lynch was adamantly opposed to including the rape claim in the book. "I definitely did not want that in there," she told me. But, she said, Bragg eventually wore her down. "He told me that people need to know that this was what can happen to women soldiers."[55]

By the time the book was published, Lynch's rescue was eight months old and had fallen out of the news. But that one sentence sent it roaring back. It inspired a nineteen-page *Time* cover story, an hour-long *Primetime* special watched by 16 million people, and screaming headlines in the United States and abroad: "Jessica's Rape Horror"; "Fiends Raped Jessica, Book Reveals Shocker"; and "Heroine Tells of Ordeal: I Was Raped by Saddam Beasts."[56]

Time, which had bought the first serial rights to the book, tried to flesh out Bragg's skimpy account. The magazine asked Greg Argyros, Lynch's primary physician at Walter Reed Medical Center, for more details. He said, "The exam in Landstuhl [the army hospital in Germany] indicated that the injuries were consistent with possible anal sexual assault." *Time* did not linger long over the word "possible." "Sometime after the crash," the magazine stated, "and before [Lynch] was delivered to Nasiriyah hospital—a period that could have been as long as three hours—she appeared to have been forcibly penetrated by someone or something." As the story circulated, what "appeared" to be true quickly became gospel truth. The same press that was so eager to broadcast Lynch's violation was not interested in investigating it. A Nexis database search yielded only one other media report that bothered to confirm *Time*'s conversation with Argyros, and none that conducted any other inquiries into the rape claim or called the original doctors who had examined her in Germany. When *Primetime*'s Diane Sawyer, the one journalist who placed the follow-up call, phoned Argyros, he was more equivocal. While the medical exam records indicated "peri-anal lesions," he told her, "there is, of course, an element of speculation."[57]

Speculation was the preferred mode of reportage in this instance. Bragg himself "chose not to report the story from Iraq," as *Time* forgivingly put it. "Given his deadline, he says, there wasn't time." After the book's publication, a few foreign correspondents in Iraq would do that reporting in his stead. They interviewed the doctors and nurses who had treated Lynch. Every one of them said they had seen no evidence that she had been sexually assaulted. Jamal Kadhim Shwail, the first doctor to examine Lynch, said: "Her injuries were consistent with severe trauma—a car crash, nothing else. Her clothes were not torn, her boots had not been removed. There is no way she could have been raped." The surgeons who subsequently operated on Lynch at the second hospital in Nasiriyah reported that they had carried out a full examination and turned up no indications of sexual trauma and no trace of semen. "It is just not possible that we would have not noticed," Aqil Maktuf, an anesthetist, said. "Why are they saying such things?" Khodheir al-Hazbar, the hospital's deputy director, said. "I just do not believe this. I can only think that these allegations are being made to promote her book. I would invite her back to visit us and hope that the memory of what really happened will return to her."[58]

Lynch wasn't making any allegations of rape to promote "her" book. "It was put in the book," she told me, "but I never said it." Nonetheless, she had promised Knopf she would help with the publicity. And so, with the publication of *I Am a Soldier, Too*, she began the media tour. Lynch's interviewers did their best to extract a confession. On *Primetime Live*, Diane Sawyer billed the upcoming show thusly: "They said she couldn't remember. They were wrong. Tonight, she answers the questions. Torture? Sexual assault? Injuries?" Actually, "they" (whoever they were) were right. When Sawyer asked Lynch to recall the day that the news of her violation had been "brought" to her, the following exchange transpired:

LYNCH: It was just, you know, like, they were speaking, but they weren't speaking to me.

SAWYER: [To viewers] The family asked if I approach the subject with her, to do it without graphic words. [To Lynch] What did you think when you heard it?

LYNCH: I just remember, you know, looking off in space, not— reacting to anything.

SAWYER: Was it a hard decision to put it in the book?

LYNCH: Yeah, it was. Because I have no memory of that. . . .

SAWYER: You really wonder whether it happened? You don't necessarily believe it?

LYNCH: It's all kind of questionable. . . .

SAWYER: Is it work to keep it from coming back? Do you think some, sometimes do you feel some memory you don't want coming back and you have to fight it away?

LYNCH: No, no.[59]

Later in the program, Bragg made an appearance on the set. Sawyer asked why he decided to override Lynch's "reservations" and include the assertion that she had been raped in the book. "We could have written a fairy tale about the princess goes off to war," he said. "That's like watching old war movies. When people get shot and they don't bleed. You know? Or people get hit in the jaw and they don't fall down. Jessica got hit in the jaw and fell down." But he *had* written a fairy tale, a cautionary one, in which the princess goes to war—and pays the price for not staying in the castle. Lynch's self-appointed amanuenses—from the special forces camera crew to the John Wayne–emulating divorce lawyer to the recovered-memory-theorizing writer—were all reenacting old war movies, where American boys win the battles and American princesses of war learn their lesson and go home. Lynch was hard-pressed to say why everyone was s insistent that she conform to a certain narrative, but she sensed that it ha nothing to do with concern for the real agonies she had faced. Wh

Diane Sawyer asked if the obsessive minute-by-minute recording of her rescue bothered her at all, Lynch replied: "Yeah, it does. It does, that they used me, as a way to, to symbolize all this stuff. I mean, yeah, it's wrong."[60]

After only a few days on the media circuit, Lynch had had enough. Sick with the flu, she canceled a much-hyped appearance on *Larry King Live*, along with the rest of her book tour, and returned to Palestine. Bragg, meanwhile, was showing increasing signs of touchiness about the challenge the Iraqi hospital staff had raised to his claim that Lynch had been raped. When a reporter at the *Birmingham News*, his hometown newspaper, brought up the subject, he bridled. "Asked about recent news stories in which the Iraqi doctors who examined Lynch disputed the book's contention that she was sexually assaulted," *Birmingham News* reporter Kathy Kemp said in her article, "Bragg asks to go off the record. Then, with occasional profanity, he lectures his interviewer about what he believes is the inappropriateness of that question." Kemp, who clearly didn't appreciate the rebuke, gave herself the last word. "At 44, Bragg is single again — having been dumped by a girlfriend during the Lynch project," she wrote. "By winter, he plans to be back home with his mother in Calhoun County."[61]

In the press, Bragg had to deal with the occasional skeptical reporter, but within the pages of his own book, he was the controlling authority. He could make the fairy tale end the way he wanted. He brought down the curtain with two endings, one feminine, one masculine. In the first denouement, which comes in the last paragraph of the last chapter, the heroine is dispatched to the domestic circle:

[Jessi] has had songs written about her, and poems, and even interpretive dance pieces. Artists from all over the country painted portraits and did sketches of her face. But they all used the same model: the picture of Jessi and her camouflage cap, the flag behind her. It is the likeness that they love.

But Jessi will never be in camouflage again, unless she marches in a Veterans Day parade. The next time she hides it will be behind a veil, as she begins that normal life.

In the second denouement, in the brief epilogue that followed, another hero took her place. "Among the millions of photographs and video images taken during the odyssey of Jessica Lynch," Bragg wrote, "one is a perfect metaphor for her legacy here in the mountains, and maybe beyond":

> It is not the green-tinged night-vision video of her being taken from Saddam Hussein General Hospital, or that first image of her face, stricken but trying to smile, as she was carried to a waiting helicopter.
>
> It is not in the boxes of snapshots of beauty queen pageants, softball games and senior proms, not on the cover of *People* magazine, not in the newspaper photographs of her victorious ride through her hometown in the convertible, medals on her chest.
>
> The photograph that best captured her story does not even include Jessi.

The photograph, Bragg continued, was published in the local *Parkersburg News and Sentinel,* and it "shows a Wirt County firefighter in his yellow slicker and helmet, holding an American flag over his head. . . . Looming behind and above him on the front of the courthouse is his shadow, in the shape of the young man but bigger, darker. It is two stories tall." That firefighter, Bragg wrote, was "the kind of man who would run into a burning building—or maybe drive a truck across the desert into the middle of a war." Bragg titled the epilogue "The Long Shadow of Jessica Lynch." But neither Lynch nor her shadow was present.[62]

PART TWO

PHYLOGENY

CHAPTER 8

Original Shame

"WHY IN THIS COUNTRY IS ALL THE ATTENTION PAID TO JUST ONE young girl?" Diane Sawyer wondered out loud, partway through her *Primetime* special on Jessica Lynch. It was a profound question, likely more than she knew. In a sense, it distilled all the other questions that swirled around the strangeness of our response to 9/11. Questions like: Why was the attack reconceived as a threat to the American home and family? Why were independent female voices censured and a bugle call sounded to return to Betty Crocker domesticity? Why were our political and cultural stages suddenly packed with Lone Ranger leaders, Davy Crockett candidates, and John Wayne "manly men"? Why, in short, when confronted with an actual danger, did America call rewrite?

Each rewrite required a girl in jep, whether a literal feminine dependent or a metaphorical minor in the form of a tremulous security mom. Without the girl, the cowboy president had no one to hug, the buckskin pol no one to protect, the urban outrider no one to rescue. In the resurrection drama of American might, this supporting actress was the essential dramatis persona, without whom the play could not go on.

That play, the domestic fantasy in which we have dwelled since the attack, wasn't improvised just to deal with 9/11. It was much older. The heroic ideal of the knight in shining armor and his damsel in distress is, of course, common to all cultures. But the monomyth (as Joseph Campbell called it) assumes a particular shape and plays a particular role in American life. After all, the British didn't invoke Lancelot or invent a Guinevere to weather the trauma of the terrorist bombing of London's mass transit in 2005. Nor did the Spanish reenact the chivalric romance of Amadis and Oriana after the 2004 Madrid train attack. America's wilderness history has given that hoary ideal a complexion and prominence it enjoys nowhere else. At pivotal moments in our cultural life extending back to the Puritans — moments when America was faced with a core crisis — we restored our faith in our own invincibility through fables of female peril and the rescue of "just one young girl." Jessica Lynch had a legion of historical sisters.

Among those siblings was an especially close twin, albeit a woman a century and a half older than her. Like Lynch, Cynthia Ann Parker was a young white woman who fell hostage during a bloody battle and was subsequently held in the desert by people her countrymen viewed as rapacious non-Christian murderers, until she was rescued in a gunfight trumpeted afterward as heroic, though it was not. As with Lynch, her plight was misconstrued, for her "captors" were people who did not harm her and for whom she held no animosity. As with Lynch, her fabricated rescue would be played and replayed in breathless newspaper accounts. Her ordeal is said to have inspired both Alan Le May's 1954 bestseller, *The Searchers*, and John Ford's legendary 1956 film of the same name (which is based on the novel).[1] And as with Lynch, those later accounts would eclipse Parker's actual experience, with concrete political benefits for a Texas politician (in Lynch's case a former governor, in Parker's case a future one) and with larger — much larger — consequences for an American culture eager for her myth, though not her truth.

Early on the morning of May 19, 1836, a band of Comanche warriors attacked Fort Parker, a family compound about fifty miles west of Houston, and abducted five settlers, among them nine-year-old Cynthia Ann Parker, daughter of Texas pioneer settlers, as well as her cousin, Rachel, and Rachel's two-year-old son, James. Cynthia Ann's father was killed in the raid and one of her brothers also taken captive. Within six years the others taken that day were ransomed, but Cynthia Ann would stay with the tribe for another quarter century, during which time she adopted the Comanche name Nautdah ("She carries herself with dignity and grace"), married Peta Nocona, the warrior who had led the raid on Fort Parker, and bore three children.[2]

Nautdah's subsequent life with her abductors was happy enough, at least judging by her reluctance to return to the settlers' world. In the spring of 1840, a white trader and Indian guide who encountered her at a Comanche camp on the Canadian River tried to exchange some mules and merchandise for her. She refused to speak to him. Five years later, federal agents again spied her, traveling with Comanches along the Washita River in Oklahoma. This time they offered an even larger ransom of cash and merchandise—and the Indian negotiators seemed amenable to the terms. But not Nautdah. "She would run off and hide herself to avoid those who want to ransom her," the federal agents later wrote in their report. "From the influence of her alleged husband, or from her own inclination, she is unwilling to leave the people with whom she associates."[3]

Attempts to buy Nautdah back continued, and she continued to rebuff them. Sporadically, over the decades, she was sought by her uncle, James W. Parker, the man who would serve as the model for John Wayne's Ethan Edwards in *The Searchers*. Parker was ill cast as an avenging angel, at least the angel part. His life was dogged by recurring allegations of venal and criminal behavior, including horse thievery, passing counterfeit money, refusing to pay his debts, attempting to collect on fake debts, claiming other people's slaves as his own, impeaching a woman's good character, and, a year after the Comanche raid on Fort Parker, murdering a woman and her daughter (in what was suspected to be a robbery staged to look like an Indian attack). For a period, Parker had to go into hiding to dodge a vigilante mob, and two different churches would excommunicate him for egregious misconduct. But in his quest for his captured relatives, Parker positioned himself as the model of manly virtue and familial devotion. "I have spared neither my purse nor my person," he declared of his search for his niece Cynthia Ann and his daughter

Rachel, who was also taken in the raid, "and so long as I have one acre of land, or one cow, and health and strength, I shall not give it up."[4]

In truth, Parker refused to tap into his own savings and large property holdings and demanded that the Texas treasury foot the bill. Hostage rescue was often a moneymaking endeavor, the equivalent of modern bounty hunting. Traders who purchased captives were known to pay one ransom to the Indians and then charge retail rates to government agents and desperate relatives. "The withering spirit of sordid avarice," captive Sarah Horn wrote in 1839 of Benjamin Hill, the man who bought her, "was the god at whose shrine he devoutly humbled himself." Still, Parker distinguished himself among his peers by his enthusiasm for making money off his own relatives. Five years after his daughter Rachel came out of captivity—her release largely negotiated by the first pioneer woman of Santa Fe—Rachel's young son was liberated from the Comanches by a member of the Kickapoo Indian tribe. By then, Rachel had fallen ill and died. Parker retrieved her son, then refused to turn the boy over to his father, L. T. M. Plummer—unless Plummer agreed to hand over hundreds of dollars in ransom money, which Parker (falsely) claimed he had paid out to redeem the child. The ensuing custody fight came before Sam Houston, president of the Texas Republic, who ordered Parker to relinquish his grandson at once. "Though I had some reason to suspect the professions of Mr. Parker," Houston wrote later to the boy's father, "yet, until this case was presented, I had not supposed him capable of practicing such scandalous fraud upon his kindred and connexions."[5]

Given all that, Parker's desire to promote himself as the indefatigable searcher of Cynthia Ann and Rachel was about rescuing his reputation as much as his kin. The published account of his labors, *Narrative of the Perilous Adventures, Miraculous Escapes, and Sufferings of Rev. James W. Parker,* was larded with histrionic hardships of a sort that news anchor Brian Williams might laud as "right out of a major motion picture." Like the time Parker said he set out to find a captive who fit Rachel's description rumored to be eighty miles away—without his horse, hunting rifle, or sufficient provisions—and within days, according to him, suffered near starvation, near death in a torrential thunderstorm, and near loss of his limbs in a freak freeze (this final ordeal requiring him to crawl, inch by excruciating inch, for fifty yards to the only dry log in the vicinity, which he shot with his pistol to start a fire). "The sun was now setting, and I almost hoped I would not live to see it rise," Parker wrote with typical self-martyrdom. "Darkness came on apace; and Oh, how horrible was the thought of having to spend another night in the wild wilderness, eight hundred miles from home, with the frozen ground for a bed, and the blue dome of heaven my only shelter." But he soldiered on: "The hope of soon seeing my lost child added a new vigor to my body, and summoning all my remaining strength, I pursued my journey."[6]

Eventually, on December 18, 1860, a thirty-four-year-old Cynthia Ann was reclaimed, not by her long-suffering, spotlight-hogging uncle but by a party of Texas Rangers. As with Jessica Lynch, the rescue, no matter its later portrayal, was a one-sided military assault. The Rangers had come across a small group of Comanches camped by the Pease River. Captain Sullivan "Sul" Ross ordered an attack, promising a Colt revolver to the first man who killed and scalped an Indian. As it happened, the camp's occupants were almost entirely women and children curing bison meat for winter; none of them was armed. Some desperately tried to flee, still clutching slabs of buffalo meat and camping gear; others tried to use their horses as shields. An officer who witnessed the massacre wrote that the regiment "killed every one of them, nearly in a pile." The camp was looted and the corpses were scalped. The official report, which the press dutifully reprinted, declared the assault a "victory," waged against hundreds of armed warriors, but there were no more warriors in the camp than there were Republican Guard fedayeen in the Nasiriyah hospital. A member of the shooting party later confessed: "I was in the Pease river fight, but I am not very proud of it. That was not a battle at all, but just a killing of squaws." They were not all killed. Cynthia Ann Parker was among the few survivors, spared when Ross saw that her eyes were blue and deduced that she was a white captive. The Rangers forcibly rode her back to white civilization, her infant daughter in her arms.[7]

Her return set off a new flurry of notoriety. Newspaper stories told tales of the whippings and torture she had supposedly endured at the hands of the "heathen savages." Her arms and body "bear the marks of having been cruelly treated," the *Clarksville Northern Standard* claimed. Her torments were sexualized—and likened to the ravages a woman might expect in a Muslim harem. Her "long night of suffering and woe," the *Dallas Herald* asserted, could "furnish the material for a tale more interesting than those found in the Arabian Nights Entertainment." Her manufactured agonies would provide justification for Indian removal for decades to come, and her rescue would become a brass-bright emblem of Texas pride. "All my men acquitted themselves with great honor, proving worthy representatives of Texas valor," Captain Sul Ross told the press. Ross rode the acclaim for Parker's restoration all the way to the governor's office.[8]

The newspaper accounts contributed to a fictionalization of the Cynthia Ann Parker story that would crescendo for a century. The original falsifications had clear motives—men like James Parker or Sul Ross were, respectively, escaping a checkered past or aspiring to an auspicious future. But the larger mythologizing was not meant to elevate any individual or exculpate an individual's guilt, the pecuniary motives of Cynthia Ann's uncle, or the murderousness of her actual rescuers. It was aimed more generally at a societal shame, the shame of the settlers' vulnerability, their inability to defend their community from terror.

That particular incapacity had been on vivid display on the day in 1836 when Cynthia Ann Parker was carried off. Her protectors proved themselves more bumblers than shining knights. The Parker men received numerous warnings that an attack was imminent. Like the later dire alert delivered to a Texas ranch on August 6, 2001, urgent advisories flooded in from scouts, traders, and several Comanches. One friendly Indian even pinpointed the exact date of the assault. Sam Houston counseled the family to evacuate. But the Parker patriarchs ignored all alarms. James W. Parker, he of the Perilous Adventures, Miraculous Escapes, and Sufferings, was the fort's designated Texas Rangers captain, but he disbanded the troops under his command because, as he bizarrely wrote later, "there appeared to be but little danger of an attack, and as the Government was not in a condition to bear the expense of supporting troops, unless the circumstances were of such nature as to imperiously demand it."[9]

The Parker men were proud of the heavy-duty "bullet-proof" gate they had installed at the fort's entrance, but on the day of the raid, they had left the gate open and the grounds largely undefended. Ten of the fort's fifteen adult men were off in the fields, and Silas Parker, Cynthia

Ann's father, was left to guard the homestead with a gun that he'd forgotten to load. As the raiders descended on the fort, some of the remaining putative defenders headed for the hills. "Good Lord, Dwight, you are not going to run?" Silas Parker called after settler G. E. Dwight. "Stand and fight like a man, and if we have to die we will sell our lives as dearly as we can." Dwight declined, and Silas died after getting off a few futile shots and, as his niece later recalled, a "triumphant huzza as tho' he had thousands to back him." James Parker, the compound's Rangers captain and, later, the glorified "searcher," spent the day hiding in a thicket by the river with his wife and one of his daughters. He never returned to the fort.[10]

Such was the man whose cinematic reincarnation filled the first and last frames of Chuck Workman's post-9/11 celebration of national resolve, *The Spirit of America*. John Wayne's Ethan Edwards in *The Searchers* bears little resemblance to the feckless James W. Parker, on whom he is thinly modeled; while they share a shady past, Edwards's outlawry is Confederate-heroic and, unlike his progenitor, Edwards is the consummate effective protector. The transition of the Parker story from tragedy to triumph to cause célèbre, from Sul Ross's massacre to Peggy Noonan role model, was achieved through a century of rewrites, beginning with the Texas newspaper dispatches of 1861 and proceeding through Le May's novel to Wayne's star turn.

The end result is regarded as totemic. "Ernest Hemingway once said that all of American literature could be traced back to one book, Mark Twain's 'Huckleberry Finn,' and something similar might be said of American cinema and 'The Searchers,'" *New York Times* movie critic A. O. Scott wrote on the fiftieth anniversary of the film in June 2006. Or, as a critic put it in *Maclean's*, "If imitation is the sincerest form of flattery, then 'The Searchers' is the most flattered movie of all time."[11]

Its imitators are legion and include, to name just a few, Steven Spielberg (who even made his own boyhood version of *The Searchers* in his suburban backyard, with Monument Valley painted on bedsheets), George Lucas (who credited the film as inspiration for several scenes and plot devices in *Star Wars*), Martin Scorsese (who reworked it as *Taxi Driver*), John Milius (ditto, *Dillinger*), Ron Howard (*The Missing*), and Paul Schrader (whose *Hardcore* restages *The Searchers* in the porn world). As one exhaustive survey of the film's influence concluded, "When one film obsesses so much talent, it won't do just to call it a cult movie. *The Searchers* is the Super-Cult movie of the New Hollywood." These film-makers didn't just appreciate *The Searchers*; they were consumed by it. John Milius watched the film sixty times, named his son Ethan after Wayne's character, and recalled his first screening of *The Searchers* as "such a seminal and primal experience that I was absolutely convinced I'd dreamed it—which was just right because that was in keeping with the movie. It almost should be dreamed."[12]

With the remaking of the Parker family story into the fictional *Searchers*, the connection between Cynthia Ann Parker and Jessica Lynch became more than two cases linked by coincidental parallels. The dream of the indomitable and devoted searcher, fashioned to obscure the shame of the original Parker family experience, became part of the boilerplate of the American security myth and provided the template for Jessica Lynch's rescue and her portrayal in the media. The public Jessica Lynch would have to exist within the parameters of the transformed Cynthia Ann Parker story, and those parameters relied on a division of the sexes into assigned roles: rescuing and stalwart men, vulnerable and grateful women.

The myth itself was vulnerable, especially to the possibility that women would repudiate their role. In Parker's case, she didn't want rescue at all. Pulled from the scene of the massacre at gunpoint, she tried for years to es-cape her repatriation into settler society. "Just going home," she called her attempts to leave. After a while, her relatives took to locking her in her room. Her lamentations for her lost family were punctuated by bouts of self-mutilation. She slashed her arms and breasts and chopped off her hair with a butcher's knife. In December 1863, on the third anniversary of her rescue, the redeemed captive suffered a final loss: her five-year-old daughter, Top-sannah, caught pneumonia and died. Cynthia Ann retreated behind a cur-tain of perpetual mourning. Toward the end, she refused to speak. Tom Champion, the one relative who had bothered to draw her out on her life among the Comanches, had a starkly different view of her "rescue" than his contemporaries: "To hear her tell of the happy days of the Indian dances and see the excitement and pure joy which shown [*sic*] on her face, the memory of it, I am convinced that the white people did more harm by keeping her away from [the Comanches] than the Indians did by taking her at first."

The Parker kin moved Cynthia Ann from one household to another, and finally to the home of her grown sister and brother-in-law in a tiny town in Texas with the same name as Jessica Lynch's birthplace: Palestine. They soon wearied of her and moved her once more to a small sawmill they owned outside of town. There, alone and despondent, she performed her final act of protest: she stopped eating. Starvation was followed by influenza. At an unknown date in 1870, Cynthia Ann Parker/Nautdah was found dead.[13]

Her protest was an insult to the pretension that she had been saved from torment by white intervention, and the mythmakers would do their best to expunge it from the record. In Le May's novel, her long despair is reduced to young captive Debbie's brief crisis of faith in the desert, as she resists—for a moment—the entreaty to return. ("I was better off with them," she says. "Now I have no place.") Her reluctance vanishes as soon as she receives a pledge of protection and an embrace from her rescuer, Martin Pauley, who as a boy witnessed his family's massacre by Indians. By that pledge, the young man redeems himself from the grip of his life-long nightmare of impotence, the "terror-dream" that has plagued him since boyhood. Two years later, Ford's movie would further shrink the captive's reluctance to return—this time to a split second's hesitation—and then flirt with an urge to punish her for her racial desertion. John Wayne's character suppresses his instinct to shoot the tainted Debbie for her (now barely discernible) conversion to the Indians.[14]

Neither version had room, of course, for the real drama of loyalty hidden in Nautdah's life. Her Comanche husband, Peta Nocona, would never marry again. Her younger son, Pecos, died young, of smallpox contracted from whites. Her elder son, Quanah, became the most important Comanche leader of his generation, and the last in the tribe's history. In 1875, Quanah led his people to Fort Sill in Oklahoma, where the Comanches would dwindle into a pathetic remnant on the reservations. Quanah, who never permitted his war parties to kill white women or children for fear he'd kill his mother and sister, spent many fruitless years searching for Nautdah and Topsannah. After he learned of his mother's death in 1877, he tried to arrange a meeting with the Parkers. They refused. In 1910, Quanah finally located his mother's gravesite and, after appealing all the way to the U.S. Congress, was granted permission to reinter her in a Comanche reservation cemetery near his Oklahoma home. At the funeral, witnesses recalled, he gave a speech about how we were "all same people, anyway," before falling silent for the rest of the ceremony, "in tears and deep agony." A few months later, he died and was buried next to his mother. But their bodies would not rest there. In 1957, one year after the premiere of *The Searchers*, the U.S. government ordered the seven hundred Comanche bodies exhumed and moved—to make way for a proving ground for guided missiles.[15]

Those missiles and the contemporaneous movie were kindred—both responses to national insecurity, one to the threat of our Cold War rivals, the other to a deeper fear reawakened by the Cold War. *The Searchers* was a tried-and-true formulaic attempt to allay societal fears by replaying a rendition of our oldest national myth, the rewrite with the happy ending in which we prevail over the terrorists and save the girl.

We perceive our country as inviolable, shielded from enemy penetration. Indeed, in recent history the United States has been, among nations, one of the most immune to attack on its home soil. And yet, our foundational drama as a society was apposite, a profound exposure to just such assaults, murderous homeland incursions by dark-skinned, non-Christian combatants under the flag of no recognized nation, complying with no accepted Western rules of engagement and subscribing to an alien culture, who attacked white America on its "own" soil and against civilian targets. September 11 was aimed at our cultural solar plexus precisely because it was an "unthinkable" occurrence for a nation that once could think of little else. It was not, in fact, an inconceivable event; it was *the* characteristic and formative American ordeal, the primal injury of which we could not speak, the shard of memory stuck in our throats. Our ancestors had already fought a war on terror, a very long war, and we have lived with its scars ever since.

On the tenth of *February*, 1675, came the *Indians* with great numbers upon Lancaster. Their first coming was about Sun-rising. Hearing the noise of some Guns, we looked out; several Houses were burning, and the Smoke ascending to Heaven. . . .

> At length they came and beset our own House, and quickly it was
> the dolefullest day that ever mine eyes saw.[16]

So began the firsthand account of Mary Rowlandson, a minister's wife, of the immolation of her village about thirty-five miles west of Boston and her subsequent time of captivity. With "the smoke ascending to heaven" on that terrible morning, the inhabitants of Lancaster who had gathered inside one of the village's six fortified "garrison" houses found themselves facing the same choice that so many years later would confront the occupants of the twin towers: burn within or "escape" outside to their deaths. Rowlandson, shot in the side the moment she stepped through the portal, would be one of about two dozen townspeople taken captive, most of them women and children, including Rowlandson's own three children; her youngest, a six-year-old girl badly injured in the attack, would die in her arms several days after the raid.[17]

The attack by five hundred Narragansetts came five months into King Philip's War (or Metacom's Rebellion, for those who preferred the Wampanoag chief's non-British appellation), the fearsome confrontation between white settlers and the New England tribes that would stand as "the great crisis" of Puritan America, presaging so many other traumas in early America. To this day King Philip's War remains, per capita, America's deadliest war: in the yearlong conflict, one in every ten white men of military age in Massachusetts Bay died; one of every sixteen in the northeastern colonies. Two-thirds of the New England towns were attacked, more than half the settlements were left in ruins, and the settlers were forced to retreat nearly to the coast; the war decimated the colonial economy, bankrupted its government treasuries, and brought the entire Puritan project to the edge of annihilation.[18]

The ordeal would shatter the Puritan psyche, and its reconstitution would have deep implications for the course of American identity. As Richard Slotkin and James K. Folsom observed in So Dreadfull a Judgment, their anthology of Puritan responses to King Philip's War:

> The spiritual and psychological immiseration caused by the war, the
> trauma to the Puritan colonists in their collective spirit, was as deeply

felt as the material and personal losses the colonies suffered. For a community that had conceived of itself as the new chosen people of the Lord, as the bearers of Christian light to heathen darkness, the ful-fillers of a divinely inspired "Errand into the Wilderness," the catas-trophe of the Indian war threatened their most basic assumptions about their own character and the relationship to God and to their new world. . . .

The process of reconstructing and explaining the history of their great calamity forced the Puritans to test the strength and validity of their central dogmas and structuring myths against overwhelming and unprecedented experience. In the process their myths and dogmas un-derwent transformations that marked the beginning of a new phase in the cultural history of the colonies.[19]

These "barbarous inhumane Outrages," Ipswich minister William Hubbard wrote in his account of King Philip's War in 1676, "no more de-serve the Name of a War than the Report of them the Title of an History." He could call them only the "troubles." The colonial leadership, of course, was hardly blameless—its offenses had been instrumental in pro-voking the war, to which it contributed its own inhumane outrages—and the devastation inflicted on the Indian communities by the conflict was far worse.* But such realities, which were instantly repressed anyway, could not mitigate the settlers' trauma. Like the "different kind of war" that Bush heralded before Congress on September 21, 2001, the "troubles" seemed to have no limits, no battlefield conventions, no stopping point. The bitterness unleashed in both camps by Metacom's Rebellion, a war in which no treaty was ever signed, foreclosed the possibility of peaceful relations between native and white Americans for all time and unleashed

---

*Most famous of those outrages was the Great Swamp Fight, two months before the Narragansett attack on Rowlandson's town, in which English soldiers slaughtered and burned alive six hundred Narragansetts in their winter retreat in Rhode Island, about half of them women and children. Puritan luminary Cotton Mather later crowed that the victims had been "Berbikew'd" (Richard Francis, *Judge Sewall's Apology* [New York: Fourth Estate, 2005], pp. 22–23; Annette Kolodny, "Among the Indians: The Uses of Captivity," *Women's Studies* 21 [1993]: 185).

a harrowing series of conflicts—King William's War, Queen Anne's War, King George's War, the French and Indian War—that dragged into the next century.[20]

Caught in these coils, early American settlers dwelled in a state of perpetual insecurity, in what they repeatedly described as an experience of "terror." Time and again, military attempts to guard frontier towns failed. Long after King Philip himself had been shot, quartered, and beheaded, long after his head was impaled on a pole and displayed in Plymouth's town square (where his father had dined with Pilgrims at the first Thanksgiving) for the delectation of white passersby for the next quarter century; and long after Cotton Mather, that famous scion of the dynastic Puritan ministry, broke off what remained of the putrefied jaw "from the Blasphemous exposed Skull of that Leviathan" and pocketed it (as if, historian Jill Lepore observed, to "shut Philip up"), the different kind of war roiled on, in the borderlands of the continent and the bitter hearts of its antagonists.[21]

The desire to silence a long-dead combatant suggested a deeper emotion: shame. That shame was largely a male burden, the result of recurring attacks in which the captivity of women and children served to spotlight male protective failures. More than sixteen hundred New England settlers were seized in raids between the start of King Philip's War in 1675 and the end of the French and Indian War in 1763. While more men may actually have been taken in Indian attacks in the colonial period, the captive was most frequently portrayed as female—and the subsequent feelings of disgrace fell on male shoulders.[22] What galled was the inability of these New World patresfamilias to shield their wives and dependents from "barbarian" assault. Over and over, the story repeated: When a settlement was invaded, its heads of household so often were out in the fields or present but taken hostage themselves—thereby reduced to impotent witnesses to their families' agonies—or laid waste by gunfire or hatchet blows. Surviving male settlers then suffered the further mortification of hearing female captives denounce bungled male efforts at protection or, worse, recount how they managed to protect themselves from abduction without male intercession. And finally, male attempts to rescue women and children from captivity frequently fell short of success.

In a study of New England colonists taken to Canada over four decades of the "troubles," more than a quarter of all female captives—and a whopping 60 percent of the female captives between the ages of twelve and twenty-one—never returned. (The comparable figures for men are 13 percent of all male captives and 23 percent of males between the ages of twelve and twenty-one.)[23] They remained with their captors-cum-adopted family. And even more humiliating, from their rescuers' point of view, some of these women—especially the women taken as *girls*—let it be known that they did not *want* to be redeemed, that over time they'd come to prefer their new Native American life and, ultimately, Native American husbands. Almost one-third of female captives are estimated to have refused, like Cynthia Ann Parker, to rejoin white society, compared with less than 10 percent of their male counterparts. This unsettling phenomenon was widespread enough to draw comment from several early American observers, among them Benjamin Franklin, who marveled at the "short time" it took for these captives to "become disgusted with our manner of life . . . and take the first good Opportunity of escaping again into the Woods, from whence there is no reclaiming them." A year after the close of the French and Indian War, Colonel Henry Bouquet demanded that the Shawnees hand over the eighty-eight captives who still had not come home; seventy were women and children. The reluctant contingent of captives finally arrived at Fort Pitt, where they had to be "closely watched and well Secured" to stop them from running back to their Shawnee loved ones. One young woman "cryed and roared when asked to come and begged to Stay a little longer," and "several women eloped in the night, and ran off to join their Indian friends."[24]

The specter of the white maiden taken against her will by dark "savages" became our recurring trope, riveting the American imagination from Jane McCrea's Revolutionary-era seizure and death at the hands of British-allied Algonquins to the fictional Alice and Cora Munro's Indian immurement in *The Last of the Mohicans* to Patty Hearst's kidnapping (and alleged rape) by members of the Symbionese Liberation Army helmed by escaped black convict "Field Marshal Cinque." That maiden's rescue, fantasized or real, became our reigning redemption tale. Many scholars of American culture see our national preoccupation with female rescue as mere cover story, a pretext employed to justify the sanguinary pleasure our pioneers took in the slaughter of the continent's natives and the decimation of the wilderness. That is: first we conquered, then we made up a fiction of defiled womanhood to rationalize it. The ethic implicit in that fiction "demands that the wilderness be destroyed so that it can be made safe for the white woman and civilization she represents," Richard Slotkin wrote in *Regeneration through Violence*, his magisterial 1973 exploration of the frontier myth's development. But what if the reverse is also true? What if the unbounded appetite for conquest derives not only from our long relish for the kill but from our even longer sense of disgrace on the receiving end of assault—assaults to our women in our own settlements and in our own homes? What if the deepest psychological legacy of our original war on terror wasn't the pleasure we now take in dominance but the original shame that domination seeks desperately to conceal?[25]

In her book *White Captives*, historian June Namias pondered the historical legacy of America's long grapple with domestic terror:

> Along America's moving frontier, not just one group but each vanguard of the white American population experienced the traumas of outbreaks of what appeared to be random violence, along with outbreaks that mushroomed into large-scale wars. In both situations, the loss of family members was indeed a possibility. The retelling of these stories of loss marked each American generation during the first three centuries of North American life. These tales constituted significant childhood memories, so significant that in their telling we find the education of the next generation of historians who pass the word along.

Struck by the longevity of these memories in the national psyche, Namias wondered if this was a case where, as Peter Loewenberg, a professor of history and political psychology, wrote in *Decoding the Past*, a "social trauma" haunts a nation the way a childhood ordeal can torment the life of an adult.[26]

Early on, the chronicling of those ordeals was given a name: captivity narratives. Mary Rowlandson's chronicle of the "dolefullest day" in Lancaster and the eleven weeks to follow was the premier model of the form.

In 1682, Mary Rowlandson composed her account of her trials in the wilderness. *A Narrative of the Captivity and Restoration of Mrs. Mary Rowlandson* went through four printings in its first year and became America's first best seller; by 1800, more than fifteen editions had been published. Its popularity was no freak occurrence. In the half century to follow Rowlandson's debut, the nation's best sellers, with the one exception of *Pilgrim's Progress*, were all captivity narratives. The trial of Indian bondage was the first story America told itself. Again and again. The New-berry Library's repository of captivity narratives lists more than two thousand such works published before 1880, and that excludes fictional accounts. In the early nineteenth century, every best-selling novel featured a captivity drama. The captivity narrative, the only genre indigenous to American literature, wasn't merely a recording of that ordeal. It was the medium through which these haunting memories would be contained, reconstructed, and effectively repressed in the centuries to come. By the nineteenth century, it had become the essential tool of domestic exorcism, the instrument by which so many self-reliant Mary Rowland-sons were reborn as rescued little Debbies. The captivity narrative, historian Roy Harvey Pearce wrote in his classic 1947 essay on the form, was America's "terroristic vehicle," our verbal armor against our oldest national nightmare.[27]

American culture spent three hundred years rewriting such accounts. Faced with bloody attacks from a hostile antagonist, attacks in which women often were not saved or refused to be saved or saved themselves, white America restored its sense of national security through the creation of a compensatory gender narrative. In the service of establishing a national story that would supplant intense humiliation with invincible invulnerability, the early captivity story would evolve through successive permutations, even into the twentieth century, where it would find expression in such iconic films as *The Searchers*. Or, in its most recent reissue, in the fanciful media tale of a girl soldier's ordeal in the desert. As American studies professor Melani McAlister observed in a *New York Times* op-ed piece in the spring of 2003, "Accounts of the Lynch rescue have depicted it, implicitly or explicitly, as the classic happy ending of a classic American captivity story."[28]

In the course of that evolution, the many resourceful captives who fended for themselves would disappear behind a chorus line of fictional frightened little girls with a thousand and one diminutive and forgettable names, girls whose passivity would always be rewarded in the end with rescue. And the many fathers and husbands who could not prevent their loved ones' captivity would be supplanted in our cultural consciousness by that ever-vigilant domestic guardian Daniel Boone, who handily rescues his girls and repels all incursions on the domestic compound of Boonesborough. Boone, in turn, would give way to his ever more impregnable cultural descendants, all of the Hawkeyes, Crocketts, Buffalo Bills, Deadwood Dicks, and Lassiters, all of the gunslingers who slayed, rescued, and prevailed in what frontier literary historian Henry Nash Smith called our "objectified mass dream," that long national reverie of Leatherstocking Tales, Wild West shows, Erastus Beadle dime novels, Zane Grey cowboy pulps, *Gunsmoke* television series, John Wayne Westerns, and hyperbolic White House nostrums. That mass dream conceals the shaming memory, as it was meant to, but can't expel it. The humiliating residue still circulates in our cultural bloodstream, awaiting provocation to bring it to the surface. And with each provocation, we salve our insecurities by invoking the same consoling formula of heroic men saving threatened women—even in provocations that have involved few women and no female captives, like the Revolutionary-era kidnappings of American sailors on the Barbary Coast. Or the terrorist attack of 9/11.[29]

Our cultural response to 9/11 brought into play many forces disinterred from our distant past. Prominent among them was a renewed subscription to an abiding American security myth that had its roots in the captivity narratives of our earliest national experience. The kinship between that myth and our reflexive reaction to the 2001 terrorist attacks is apparent in the genetic code shared by both. After September 11, our recovery passed through a series of phases that uncannily recapitulated the metamorphosis of captivity literature into the comforting myth of American impregnability. That myth held us in its protective thrall until the morning four hijacked planes exposed it as a sham. In our frantic effort to restore its credibility, we reconstituted, link by link, the formula that had served us so well in converting actual terror into an illusion of security. Of those phases, the first was our peculiar urge to recast a martial attack as a domestic drama, attended by the disappearance and even demonization of independent female voices. The second framed our suddenly vulnerable state as a problem between the sexes, in which the American man and the nation's vigor were sapped by female influence—and solved that "problem" with a media and political campaign that inflated male strength by artificially consigning women to a fearful and vulnerable position. A final phase would underscore and document that feminine vulnerability with the invention of a female rape-and-rescue drama, thereby reinstating "the classic happy ending of a classic American captivity story." Thus was the republic secured in our own day, as it had been before, following the outbreak of America's original war on terror.

CHAPTER 9

Heed the Mothers

IN THE ORIGINAL WAR ON TERROR, THE ORIGINAL FEMALE CAPTIVE DID not await the exertions of a male rescuer. To the Puritan Mary Rowlandson, only God could play that role, and while he tarried, she looked to her own ingenuity. Faced with starvation, she bartered her sewing skills with her captors in exchange for bear meat and favors and shrewdly knit the son of King Philip himself a shirt and cap. The latter needlework led to a dinner invitation from the Wampanoag leader, by which she won his approbation—and set the stage for liberation. Rowlandson even set the terms of her own release, naming her ransom price and, having called it right, clinching her deliverance.[1]

Nevertheless, what she celebrated in the famous account of her captivity was weakness, not strength. Weakness, that is, before God. Rowlandson interpreted her wilderness immurement as a divine opportunity for submission. She spelled out that essential revelation in the closing paragraphs of her 1682 narrative:

When I lived in prosperity; having the comforts of this World about me, my Relations by me, and my heart chearful: and taking little care for any thing; and yet seeing many (whom I preferred before my self) under many trials and afflictions, in sickness, weakness, poverty, losses, crosses, and cares of the World, I should be sometimes jealous least I should have my portion in this life; and that Scripture would come to my mind, *Heb. 12. 6. For whom the Lord loveth he chasteneth, and scourgeth every Son whom he receiveth:* but now I see the Lord has his time to scourge and chasten me. The portion of some is to have their Affliction by drops, now one drop and then another: but the dregs of the Cup, the wine of astonishment, like a sweeping rain that leaveth no food, did the Lord prepare to be my portion. . . .

And I hope I can say in some measure, as *David* did, *It is good for me that I have been afflicted.* The Lord hath shewed me the vanity of these outward things, that they are the *Vanity of vanities, and vexation of spirit*; that they are but a shadow, a blast, a bubble, and things of no continuance; that we must rely on God himself, and our whole dependence must be upon him.[2]

Her words expressed precisely the Puritan understanding of weakness and dependency. By our modern lights, it might seem more natural that settlers thrust into a "howling wilderness" and terrorized by "savages" would soothe their fears with a myth of supreme strength. But the Puritans began with a starkly different model. They did not try to hide their vulnerability. In fact, they highlighted it. From the Calvinist perspective, the travails the settlers suffered in the New World weren't signs that they were weak—rather, that they weren't weak *enough*. They had fallen from favor by committing a grave sin, independence from God. "In the earliest captivities the Indian is identified as an agent of God," Jay Fliegelman, a professor of American literature, observed in *Prodigals and Pilgrims*, "sent by Jehovah as he might send a storm or plague, to chasten his sinful creatures through affliction to a converting realization of the literal truth of man's absolute dependence on the Divine Will and of the necessity of surrendering to that Will." Mortal strength was their undoing, spiritual dependency their salvation—which goes a long way toward explaining how Puritan women came to play such a prominent role in the earliest response to "homeland" assault.[3]

The Puritans were hardly feminists. Women were proscribed from virtually all formal roles of authority in church and state, instructed to play the dutiful helpmeet at home and expected to maintain a dignified silence abroad. A "public woman" was a fallen woman. "Our Ribs were not ordained to be our Rulers," a Puritan maxim held. The good good-wife did not draw attention to herself, and she certainly did not write her memoirs. And yet, in the wake of King Philip's War, the Puritan patri-archs not only published but celebrated female captivity narratives, of which Rowlandson's was the first and most famous. The voices of women speaking directly about their own experiences were suddenly being am-plified in the church-controlled printing press and the Massachusetts Bay Colony's equivalent of the airwaves, the pulpit.[4]

A published female author was an aberration shocking enough to re-quire elaborate explanation, which it received in Rowlandson's account: her text was bracketed by a justificatory preface and a concluding sermon from, respectively, her minister and her minister husband. (The preface is signed "Per Amicam" ["For a Friend"] but is widely believed to have been written by the eminent Rev. Increase Mather; the sermon "Of the Possi-bility of God's Forsaking a People That Have Been Near and Dear to Him" was the final homily delivered by Rev. Joseph Rowlandson, whose domestic authority over his wife evidently still prevailed, though he had died more than three years before her work was published.)[5] "I hope by this time no one will cast any reflection upon this Gentlewoman, on the score of this publication of her Affliction and Deliverance," the preface advised the reader. "Though this Gentlewomans modesty would not thrust it into the Press," she had been persuaded by "friends," who be-lieved her account "deserves both commendation and imitation."[6]

The Puritan theocrats not only commended these women's writings but enshrined the women themselves as embodiments of the entire sainted community's ordeal. And the steadfastness of faith with which these women weathered their afflictions in the wilderness was deemed a model worthy of "imitation" by all congregants, regardless of sex. Increase Mather's powerful clerical son Cotton drove this point home when he likened the Puritan society's travails in the New World to an image on a Roman coin, an image he borrowed from the book of Isaiah. "On the Reverse of those Medals [coins]," he told his congregation, "which are to be seen unto this Day, there is, *A Silent Woman sitting upon the Ground and leaning against a Palm-tree, with this Inscription* JUDAEA CAPTA." Mather converted that emblem into more modern currency. "Alas, if poor *New-England*, were to be shown upon her old Coin, we might show her *Leaning* against her Thunderstruck *Pine tree, Desolate, sitting upon the Ground*." Mather, whose vision of captivity profoundly influenced New England Puritan society, repeatedly envisioned his New World flock in such female terms — as the exiled "Daughter of Zion," the "Daughter of my People," the "bondswoman" in Babylon, the "poor Maid, sitting in a Wilderness."[7]

Mather wasn't calling on his congregants to pluck this "poor Maid" from harm's way. To place human intervention before divine was a sin for imperiled women and men alike. Thus, when the "Utmost Frontier Town" of Deerfield, Massachusetts, faced imminent Indian attack, Rev. John Williams, the community's preacher (and in-law of Cotton Mather's), delivered back-to-back sermons on Jacob's wrestled submission to the angel, underscoring to his congregation the pertinence of Jacob's famous cry at dawn: "I will not let Thee go, except Thou bless me." The people of Deerfield understood that they should pray not to conquer their enemies but to be conquered themselves by God. Thus, too, did Mary Rowlandson perceive, and welcome, her captivity, invoking, twice, the passage from Amos 3:6 "Shall there be evil in the City and the Lord hath not done it?" Recalling "how careless I had been of Gods holy time: how many Sabbaths I had lost and misspent," she concluded: "How righteous it was with God to cut off the threed of my life, and cast me out of his presence for ever. Yet the Lord still shewed mercy to me, and upheld me; and as he wounded me with one hand, so he healed me with the other."[8]

Every terror the new settlers experienced in the wilderness was a divinely granted opportunity to be so wounded and healed, to surrender to His mercy. And nothing made the Puritan sense of divine dependence more vivid than the experience of captivity, which Slotkin described as "the hardest and most costly (and therefore the noblest) way of discovering the will of God in respect to one's soul, one's election or damnation." The captive's passage through the phases of separation, subjection, and ultimately "redemption" showed the way toward holy restoration for the entire populace, whether female or male. The early captivity narratives were, more often than not, women's stories, but they were embraced by both sexes—and consumed with such ardor that few first editions remain. As several colonial scholars have observed, they were literally "read to pieces."[9]

If the Puritans were able to blur the differences between the sexes, at least in this regard, it was because concepts like weakness and submission had very different connotations in Calvinist doctrine than in the liberal Protestant theologies that would supplant it by the middle of the nineteenth century. Dependency on God was not a passive enterprise. To determine whether one was, indeed, the chosen "bride" of Jesus—a term applied equally to Puritan women and men—required systematically searching one's daily life, even one's dreams, for portents of one's standing with God. Mary Rowlandson examined every event of her captivity for divine clues and embraced its hardships with a vigorous intensity. She regarded her ordeal as an enlistment into a sort of spiritual basic training. She understood, as did her coreligionists, that "weakness" before God, paradoxically, demanded one's full and energetic commitment. The believer must be in a simultaneous state of absolute humility before God's infinite and unknowable power and high readiness to leap through salvation's open door. Or, put in secular terms, the Puritan adherent was seeking to integrate two essential aspects of the human condition—the need for dependency and the desire for strenuous engagement—aspects that an audience of our age might imagine as, respectively, "feminine" and "masculine" qualities. In the mind of the New England Calvinist, helplessness and heroism were one.[10]

The captivity experience provided a constant and concrete reminder to the settlers of that struggle-toward-submission ideal. And by championing that experience, Puritan society wound up championing a vision of femininity in which the rigors of the frontier were confronted by a woman who, however humble and dependent on God, was active, enterprising, and rigorous in her pursuit of that humility and dependency. But stalwart womanhood would have only a limited run on the Puritan stage. The new ethic was soon demolished by the pressure of those same terrors that had given rise to it.

Up against the realities of the New World wilderness, the Puritan ideal of submission would soon be taking its knocks. Along with the spiritually ennobling exemplar of Judea capta, the captivity ordeal gave prominence to two secular character types troubling to the Puritan mind: men who couldn't mount a defense and women who could. Puritan men might be "brides" of Christ, but they were expected to be paternal protectors in their own households: as Christ guarded them, so they were expected to shield their wives and dependents. In a society that regarded the home as the "little commonwealth," the foundational model for the state, the effective performance of husbands was a matter of profound public import. Yet the story of the Indian raids was plagued by episodes of botched male protection—of sentinels who failed to sit sentry, of husbands who were absent when their wives and children were seized or slaughtered, of townsmen who hid in the woods, of militia who refused to give chase.

That unflattering drama was already evident in Rowlandson's celebrated case: only a dozen soldiers were guarding the town of Lancaster the morning of the raid, though Indian scouts had repeatedly warned the governor of an impending attack. (Rowlandson's husband and the town's chief military officer, her brother-in-law, were also both away in Boston, pleading unsuccessfully for military reinforcements.) And the colonial militia proved as incapable of rescuing the hostages in the woods as it had been of defending them in their homes. Rowlandson herself remarked on the lack of "courage or activity" of one such unit of soldiers, who got within yards of the fleeing Narragansetts and the captives, only to turn back before a river that the Indian group had no trouble crossing—even though, Rowlandson noted tartly, that group included "old and young, some sick, and some lame" and many with "Papooses at their backs," and "the greatest number (at this time with us) were *Squaws*."[11] In between tributes to her heavenly father-protector, Rowlandson took a few well-placed jabs at his earthly counterparts:

224 | THE TERROR DREAM

d with the remembrance of my sleepy neighbours at Deerfeild
d that all that came to their assistance could not make out snow
follow a drunken, loaden, tyred enemy, of whom they might have
asters to our honour." He may have been joined in that assessment
. Williams's young captive daughter, Eunice, who famously quit
g for her father and his brethren to rescue her, married an Indian
and refused to come home. In his classic account of the Deerfield
l, *The Unredeemed Captive*, historian John Demos ruminated on her
ns: "Her sorrow for him [her father] had turned to pity, and finally to
e." Eunice's thoughts, Demos suspected, ran thus: "*Faithless, forget-
ther: protector who could not protect, comforter who could not comfort,
aker who did not care.*" Such weakness in the face of travail may have
religious expectations, but it hardly fulfilled the security needs of New
gland settlements or the secular obligations of Puritan manhood.[14]

All of which served to highlight the other pressure troubling Puritan
iety: like Mary Rowlandson, captive women were often failing to await
d's intervention and were taking control of their destinies, at times
th a notable lack of humility, by outfoxing or even assaulting their cap-
rs. It was one thing to ply knitting needles to placate one's captors, quite
nother to take up arms. Some women were showing little remorse for
heir bellicosity and little acknowledgment that their plight was just
esserts for unacceptable independence. The church clerics would have
ifficulty making these stories fit the captive ideal. In one famous instance, Boston's most illustrious minister would be reduced to some remarkable verbal gymnastics.

In the spring of 1697, Cotton Mather honored the return of a female
captive with a "humiliation" sermon. "Humiliations Follow'd with Deliv-
erances," as his homily was titled, was a celebration of the Judea capta
type, albeit a cautionary one. On the surface, the homily appeared to conform to the doctrine of spiritual abasement and regeneration, beginning
with his subtitle ("A *Brief Discourse On the Matter and Method, Of that
HUMILIATION which would be an Hopeful Symptom of our Deliverance
from Calamity*"), continuing with his prefatory "Lecture" on the biblical
text from the second book of the Chronicles ("*They have HUMBLED
themselves, I will not destroy them but I will grant them some Deliver-*

I cannot but remember how the *Indians* der
ness of the *English* army, in its setting out. I
Lancaster and *Medfield*, as I went along with ti
I thought the *English* army would come after ti
not tell: It may be they will come in May, said tl
at us, as if the *English* would be a quarter of a ye

Three decades later in Deerfield, where t
urged his congregants to grapple like Jacob with tl
masculine earthly protection was still wanting. For
that Massachusetts village had been full of dread. T
reports that the town, which had already been attac
ing King Philip's War, was about to be assaulted agai
fered nocturnal hallucinations: they heard "a trampli
Fort" one night, "as if it were beset by Indians" (though
found the next morning), and they saw a "black cloud
ning over the neighboring town, which "on a sudden
blood." Despite all the human warnings and otherworld
field's guardians were no more prepared for assault on
February 29, 1704, than the Bush administration was on
September 11. The stockade fence was rotting. Many tov
bothered to move their families to the fort, and so they were
defended, in outlying homes. The twenty "muskiteers" a
town by the state legislature were too few and too dispers
watchman had fallen asleep. When the war party of two hun
and Indians descended, Deerfield was overwhelmed. About
residents would be killed, including two of Rev. Williams's so
others taken captive, including Williams ("seized by 3 Indians,
and bound . . . naked, as I was in my shirt") and the rest of h
(Williams's wife, still recovering from childbirth, would die on tl
march north.) Soon after the invaders departed with their captive
men from the surrounding towns arrived, but they decided to p
their pursuit because they lacked snowshoes and feared that even
did catch up, "we should too much Expose our men."[13]
Governor Joseph Dudley wrote later of the whole sorry affair,

ance"), and concluding with his "Improvement" message to the congregation ("The *Use* which you are to make of [the experience] is, To Humble your selves before the Lord Exceedingly"). But divine "Deliverance from Calamity" did not exactly describe what had actually transpired on an island at the confluence of the Merrimack and Contoocook rivers, in an incident involving the forty-year-old woman who now sat before Mather in a church pew, presumably humbled by the high honor of having inspired a sermon. Her name was Hannah Duston (or Dustan or Dustin; spellings vary).[15]

Early on the morning of March 15, 1697, several weeks before Mather's sermon, a group of Abenaki Indians had attacked the village of Haverhill, Massachusetts. They'd been promised French bounties for British scalps. Hannah Duston was lying in her bed, her midwife, Mary Neff, in attendance. Five days earlier, Duston had given birth to her twelfth child. Thomas Duston, Hannah's husband, a prominent citizen in the town—the constable and town brickmaker—was working in his clay pits when the attack came. He called to his children to head for a garrison, and he himself ran inside the house, as Mather would relate in his account, to "inform his Wife of the horrible Distress come upon them. E'er she could get up, the fierce *Indians* were got so near, that utterly despairing to do her any Service, he ran out after his Children; resolving that on the Horse which he had with him, he would Ride away with *That* which he should in this Extremity find his Affections to pitch most upon, and leave the rest unto the Care of the Divine Providence." In plainer terms, Constable Thomas Duston skedaddled, leaving his wife and her nurse behind.[16]

Abenaki warriors seized the two women and murdered Duston's infant by smashing her head against a tree. Then they marched their several hundred captives north at breakneck speed. A few days and more than a hundred miles later, Duston (who was said to have made the winter's trek wearing only one shoe) and Neff were turned over to an Abenaki family on Contoocook Island in the Merrimack River (now part of New Hampshire). The Indian family had twelve members; its domestic circle on the island also included another white captive, a British boy named Samuel Lennardson who had been taken eighteen months earlier. Learning that the family intended to remove the three of them to Canada, where, they were told, they would have to run a gauntlet of whips and blows—a ritual that was often the prelude to Indian adoption—Duston resolved to take matters into her own hands. Late on the night of March 30, 1697, as the members of the Abenaki family lay sleeping, she instructed her fellow captives to each grab a hatchet and go to work: Lennardson was able to knock off one slumbering Indian; Duston brained the other nine. "Only one *Squaw* Escaped sorely wounded, and one *Boy*," Mather recounted. (That "squaw" later showed up at an Indian camp, according to a deposition years later from a white captive woman who witnessed her bloody arrival, bearing seven hatchet gashes on her head.) The body count around the Abenaki campfire: two men, two women, and six children.[17]

If freeing herself by means of massacre did not go far enough in violating the tenets of virtuous submission, what Hannah Duston did next was sure to divest her of any hint of humble grace. The three escapees had not fled far in a purloined canoe when Duston insisted on going back. She was toting a dripping tomahawk and a gun she had liberated from one of the slaughtered men, but her booty was incomplete. Returning to the corpse-strewn campsite, she seized a knife and, with the assistance of her two colleagues, scalped all ten victims. She carefully wrapped the flesh in a square of linen cloth, a bit of homespun from her own loom. Duston, like the Indians who had attacked her home, intended to collect a bounty: she remembered that the Massachusetts legislature was offering £50 an Indian scalp. (In fact, that offer had lapsed some months earlier, but after some protest, a reduced bounty was eventually remitted—albeit to Hannah's husband, Thomas.)[18]

Back in Massachusetts, Duston regaled the General Court and leading citizens with her story. Judge Samuel Sewall (who was later to preside over the Salem witch trials) invited her to dinner. Cotton Mather graced her with a private hearing and took down her tale. The governor of Maryland sent her "a very generous Token of his Favour," an inscribed pewter tankard. But the reception, however laudatory, was also laced with unease. Duston was hardly the "*Silent Woman sitting upon the Ground.*" Moreover, by taking up the scalping knife, she'd practically gone native. Nor was the murder of children the sort of "extraordinary action" that the Puritan clergy generally applauded. Only four years earlier, Mather himself had delivered a verbal thrashing to Duston's own sister, Elizabeth Emerson, an unwed mother accused of (and eventually hung for) killing her newborn twins. How then to praise sister Hannah's bloody act? Perhaps the need to preserve the mythology of the female captive ideal trumped the clerical impulse to condemn a woman who had stepped beyond the bounds. Or perhaps the Puritan belief in divine will explained the forbearance of the authorities: if Duston had returned unscathed despite her transgressions, it must be God's doing, not hers. Whatever the reason, Cotton Mather would have to labor greatly to return the Duston genie to the Judea capta bottle.[19]

Mather tried invoking Jael from the book of Judges, "blessed above women" for her murder of Canaan's military leader, Sisera, an assassination that delivered the Israelites from oppression. Jael had lured Sisera to her tent with promises of hospitality and a good night's sleep; once he dozed off, she grabbed a mallet and hammered a tent peg into his temple with such force that she nailed his head to the ground. Mather proposed that Duston must have "took up a resolution to imitate the action of Jael upon Sisera." In all other regards, Mather did his best to argue, Duston and her midwife, Mary Neff, were just "poor Women" who "had nothing but fervent prayers to make their Lives Comfortable or Tolerable"—and anyway, Duston's actions were legally acceptable because "she thought she was not forbidden by any *Law* to take away the *Life of the Murderers* by whom her *Child* had been Butchered." That last strained bit of logic only served to highlight the contradiction: Duston herself had "butchered" six Abenaki children, who were hardly "the murderers" of her own progeny.

Mather's suspicion that he might be endorsing self-reliant hubris instead of dependent humility was apparent, too, in the chastisement he felt obliged to deliver to Duston and her cocaptives in the closing lines of his sermon. "You are not now the Slaves of *Indians*, as you were a few dayes ago," he warned, "but if you continue Unhumbled, in your Sins, You will be the Slaves of *Devils*." As a further corrective, when Mather published the sermon some months later, he appended to it the captivity narrative of Hannah Swarton, whose account comported better with the humbled ideal. Swarton scored extra points for describing her ordeal as proper punishment for having moved with her family to a frontier settlement "where there was no Church, or Minister." These instructional messages, however, did not seem to have the intended humbling effect on Duston, who wouldn't get around to seeking formal admission to the church for another quarter century.[20]

Rev. Mather's choice of Jael as the vehicle for his sermon was doubly telling. That biblical woman's story offered, along with a qualified reprieve to Duston, an implicit reproach to her male contemporaries—and the lack of courage they appeared to be displaying of late. The authors of Judges, writing in a time of declining Israelite male leadership, made much of instances of male quavering and female decisiveness. They showcased women not to exalt their Amazonian exploits but to shame the men who should have occupied the defender's place. The military saga that ends with Jael killing Sisera begins with Deborah, a judge and prophet, dispatching orders from beneath a palm tree (under which she does not sit silent) and instructing the Israelite military commander Barak to raise an army to fight Sisera. Barak dithers. "If thou wilt go with me, then I will go," he finally says, "but if thou wilt not go with me, *then* I will not go." Deborah agrees to accompany him but advises Barak that the victory "shall not be for thine honour; for the LORD shall sell Sisera into the hand of a woman." A similar admonition seemed to lurk behind the words of Mather's sermon.[21]

By Duston's time, the Indian wars had induced a full-bore spiritual crisis. Puritan leaders sought desperately to explain the "terror" afflicting them in the New World. Why were they no longer "under the Hand" of God's blessing? What, as Rev. Jerry Falwell asked three hundred years later, had "caused God to lift the veil of protection"? The answer they conceived was one that, recast in modern terms, Falwell might well endorse.

As early as King Philip's War, the settlers of New England had tried to make sense of the scourge that seemed to have no limits and no end. In his 1676 "Earnest Exhortation to the Inhabitants of New-England," Increase Mather had asked:

Is it nothing that so many have been cut off by a bloody and barbarous Sword? Is it nothing that Widdows and Fatherless have been multiplyed among us? that in a small Plantation we have heard of eight widows, and six and twenty fatherless children in one day? And in another of the Villages of our Judah, of seven Widows and about thirty fatherless children, all at once: How can we speak of such things without bleeding Lamentation! Shall not such solemn strokes at last awaken us? . . . Alas that *New-England* should be brought so low in so short a time.[22]

God "hath seemed to cast us out, and put us to shame," Mather wrote, but why? The minister called for a deeper investigation into the source of their sufferings. *"Let an enquiry be made into the cause of the Lords controversie with us"*:

He would not have given us to the Spoil, and to the Robbers, if we had not sinned against him. But some one will say, *how shall we know what sin it is that the Lord now contends with us for?*[23]

To Mather and his Puritan brethren, that sin lay in large measure in the spiritual decline of the sons of the second generation, who seemed to be setting aside a muscular religious devotion for the enchantments of worldly goods and property accumulation in the land-rich New World. Young men had fallen into a "strange degeneracy," Mather worried. They lacked the fortitude and spiritual rigor of their fathers, liquored up at the taverns, and gadded about in "monstrous and horrid *Perriwigs.*" They "hath the form," Mather said, "but little of the power of *Religion.*" His choice of words implied a judgment not only on the young men's religiosity but on their manhood. Singling out an instance from King Philip's War where eighteen men toting weapons ran off, abandoning two women and several children to the Indian marauders, he wrote, "We have cause to think of Joshuahs words, who said, O Lord What Shall I say When Israel turns their backs before their Enemies?"[24]

What Mather intimated about the new generation's masculinity, other theologians would make explicit. "Intemperance, Luxury, filthiness, and uncleanness in the world doth so debauch men, they are not like to breed up Souldiers for Christ," Samuel Nowell, the presiding military chaplain during King Philip's War and later a chief magistrate and the treasurer of the Massachusetts Bay Colony, lamented in a 1678 sermon to the newly elected officers of the provincial artillery. It is "a strange piece of dotage befallen this crazy-headed Age that man should not use the sword." Young men were dodging their military duties, he complained; they were "effeminate and wanton" and "not so bold." Nowell urged Puritan fathers to toughen up their sons by following the example of Isaac, who taught Jacob to "endure *Hardness*" by sending him into the world without a servant or a pillow. "A tender, softly, effeminate People is a curse and misery," Nowell concluded.[25]

What was behind this outbreak of supposed effeminacy? How had the New England colony become so vulnerable? And who was causing the vulnerability? Until these questions could be resolved, the Puritan establishment feared descent into greater and greater ruin. Early on, there would be scattered hints of a possible answer. Mather's "Earnest Exhortation" contained one such clue. When he enumerated the colonial sins most offending to God, number one in his inventory, under the heading of "*Manyfold Abuses of Peace and the Blessings of God in this good land*," was female arrogance:

> And now behold how dreadfully is God fulfilling the third chapter of Isaiah. *Moreover the Lord saith,* (if the Lord say it who dare slight what is said) *because the Daughters of Zion are haughty, therefore he will discover their Nakedness.* Hath not the Lord fulfilled this threatening, when the *Indians* have taken so many and stripped them naked as in the day that they were born. . . . *Thy men shall fall by the Sword & the Mighty by the War.* Hath not that word been fulfilled upon us when so many have fallen by the Sword, yea so many Captains in the War, and this is because of the pride of the Daughters of Zion.[26]

The community's emblem of virtuous humility had been a woman. Yet her sex was threatening now to become a symbol of that weightiest of sins, pride, and the evil that it begat. Were the Daughters of Zion shaping up to be Judea captas or female Judases?

• • •

The powers of the state, so ineffective against an external threat, were aimed at an internal culprit, with a notable consequence: the leadership ducking its culpability was entirely male, its newly identified antagonists overwhelmingly female. Many theories have been floated over the years to explain the witch trials, ranging from internecine community tensions to rising commercial pressures to nutritional deficiencies (a lack of calcium, one anthropologist postulated, made the bewitched go into spasms and become hysterical). Before the recent onset of feminist scholarship the various speculations made little of the overwhelming presence of women among the defendants: 141 of the 185 people accused, 52 of the 59 tried, 26 of the 31 convicted, and 14 of the 19 hung were female. And the male "witches" may have been collateral damage more often than primary target: nearly half of the men were kin or closely associated with women who had already been charged with witchcraft.[31]

Important to the profile of these women was their agency, their free will. Satan could not enter a person without the individual's consent, and that fact made the crime of witchcraft all the more heinous. "Her soul specifically chose the devil, rather than passively waiting for Christ, and she purposefully allowed the devil to use her body," historian Elizabeth Reis noted. "Thus, the witch acted assertively, while the mere sinner, after falling, suffered passively."[32]

Significantly, there was a definite character to the women singled out for witchcraft accusations in New England. Previously in Europe, women accused of witchcraft had tended to be poor villagers, easy to scapegoat because they were without resources, and generally charged with perpetrating specific acts of mischief on their neighbors. In her pioneering 1987 analysis of the demographics of Salem witchcraft, *The Devil in the Shape of a Woman*, historian Carol Karlsen found the opposite to be true of Salem's so-called coven, many of whose suspected members came as well from the middle and higher social ranks. Even when not affluent, these women seemed to enjoy an economic and personal liberty that allowed the impression that they were beyond the dictates of patriarchal family and society and, especially damning, were inclined to defend their unfettered state. A substantial majority of the accused were older women who had no brothers, sons, or children; of the executed female

234 | THE TERROR DREAM

witches, 89 percent were women from families with no male heirs. That is to say, they stood to inherit and so disrupted male control of the purse strings. And these were not just any women without male heirs: they were so often women who had shown themselves unwilling to relinquish their economic independence, even going to court to mount a public challenge to the rules of male inheritance. The "common thread running through the many sins of witches," Karlsen wrote, was a "lack of deference." It was "not just pride that most fundamentally distinguished witches from other people; it was female pride in particular."[33]

Female pride could well lead to female rebellion. And "rebellion is as the sin of witchcraft," as Cotton Mather stressed.* In the Salem drama, so often the witches seemed to be women who refused to submit to the authorities, whether religious, civil, or domestic. In a society where the family relationship was the template for state hierarchy, and at a time when the political and religious establishment, looking for evidence of male effectiveness, was struggling to reinstate an image of womanly weakness, such female impudence would almost certainly have ensured a collision: the campaign to buttress a patriarchy unable to defend its homeland inevitably ran headlong into demonstrations of female assertiveness.[34]

The Salem crisis also departed from previous European witchcraft hysterias by foregrounding the testimony of "possessed" girls. For women, much less girls, to be allowed to hold forth in church and court was remarkable. And there was nothing in Puritan theology to justify it. Yet, the elevation of the girls made sense in a society struggling to contain New World opportunities for female insubordination. Economic, legal, and demographic changes were beginning to loosen the reins, ever so slightly, on women's engagement in public life. By the 1690s, women were starting small businesses, filing (and winning) lawsuits, having fewer children, and, especially in the frontier outposts, asserting themselves in nontraditional

---

*That rebellion, or rather the fear of that rebellion, was also showing up in a dramatic increase in prosecutions of women for fornication and infanticide. Such arrests spoke to the same suspicion—that women were shucking off the yoke of feminine and maternal submission (Mary Beth Norton, "The Evolution of White Women's Experience in Early America," *American Historical Review* 89 [June 1984], pp. 610–11).

ways. At the same time, a counter female wilderness narrative was threatening to emerge—a narrative in which women either scalped Indians or ran off with them, and in either case made the choice themselves. Against that backdrop, perhaps society instinctively sought another outlet to channel female discontent into safer territory—an outlet that rewarded female submission. The bewitched girls enjoyed a faux rebellion: they got to spew invective and make outrageous and unfounded accusations in public forums, and for this bad behavior, they enjoyed the rapt attention and approval of the highest male authorities. That is, as long as they ranted at the designated targets. In Salem, the moment the girls' tantrums posed a threat to the power structure, the game was up. Late in 1692, a few girls overstepped and accused the kin of colonial leaders, including the governor's wife. Soon thereafter, the prosecutions were shut down.[35]

The possessed girls also served to recast that other crisis besetting the New England establishment: the seeming powerlessness of the male leadership to shelter the settlements from Indian invasion. These suffering girls appeared to be, and were described as being, under assault by an invisible enemy and so became prime candidates for a spiritual "rescue," often by the same protectors who had previously proved incapable of shielding them and their families from wartime atrocity. Many of the possessed girls had been orphaned by the Indian war. Of the twenty-one bewitched young women whose backgrounds are known, seventeen had lost one parent or both. In that regard, they provided a face-saving opportunity to the Puritan authorities. And Cotton Mather, for one, would seize it, most famously in the case of a possessed teenage girl named Mercy Short.[36]

Mercy Short had been orphaned and taken captive in King William's War. On March 18, 1690, Wabanaki Indians attacked the undefended frontier settlement of Salmon Falls, New Hampshire. Mercy, the daughter of Clement and Faith Short, watched the slaughter of her parents and three of her siblings, who were among the roughly one hundred villagers killed that morning. Then, on the forced march to Canada, she witnessed a series of horrors, culminating with the dismemberment and burning alive of an adult man. After the Indians "bound him to the Stake," wrote Cotton Mather, who composed an account of the attack based on his personal interview with Mercy, they "brought the rest of the Prisoners, with their Arms tied each to other, so setting them round the Fire." The captives had "their Friends made a Sacrafice of Devils before their Eyes," but they dared not react, "lest it should, upon that provocation, be next their own Turn, to be so Barbarously Sacrificed."[37]

Ransomed eight months later, Mercy Short, like many of the surviving female orphans of the Indian raids, became a servant, a maid to Margaret Thacher, a well-off Salem widow who had managed to maintain her claim to family property throughout New England. In late May 1692, Thacher (who herself would eventually be accused of witchcraft) sent Mercy on an errand to the Boston jail where several accused witches were being held and where, after a verbal tiff with one of them, Mercy fell into fits.[38] Cotton Mather promptly diagnosed her condition: "Fits as those which held the Bewitched people then Tormented by Invisible Furies," he wrote in his account of Short's possession, "A Brand Pluck'd Out of the Burning." The eminent minister himself took charge of the girl's exorcism, maintaining a vigil over her prostrate body, praying for her "no less than Ten Times," and meticulously recording her prolonged spells of wailing, screaming, and convulsions, along with the manifold afflictions that were visited upon her by invisible spirits who pinched and bit her, stuck her with needles, and tried to force poison down her throat. Mather took note of the pleasure she seemed to take in lashing out not only at the "invisible furies" but at the visible and pious churchgoers gathered at her bedside — but that latter behavior he wrote off to the devil's noxious influence:

Her Tortures were turned into Frolicks; and Shee became as extravagant as a Wild-cat. Shee now had her Imaginacion so strangely disordered, that shee must not Acknowledge any of her Friends; but tho' shee Retained a Secret Notion, Who wee were, yet shee might by no means confess it. Shee would sometimes have diverse of these Fitts in a Day, and shee was always excessively Witty in them; never downright Profane, but yet sufficiently Insolent and Abusive to such as were about her. And in these Fitts also shee took an extraordinary Liberty (which I have likewise noted in some other possessed Persons) to animadvert upon all People, that had any thing in their Apparrel that savoured of Curiosity or Ornament.[39]

By his ministrations, Mather aimed to redeem Mercy—or, perhaps, himself. If the establishment he represented had failed to save her parents from the terror, he might yet save her from the terror dream. Mather explicitly cast the battle for the girl's soul in the terms of the Indian wars. She was, he wrote, "in a Captivity to Spectres." And Mercy Short, traumatized so recently by an actual Indian captivity, provided all the right words for that drama. She told Mather that the witch specters chained her and dragged her to meetings where she saw "French Canadiens and Indian Sagamores among them." She said she was being held at an Indian camp, where French Canadian priests were trying to force her to take communion. She described the devil as "A Short and a Black Man" who was "not of a Negro, but of a Tawney, or an Indian colour." She reprised, too, the horror of witnessing her neighbor burned. "But Burning seem'd the cruellest of all her Tortures," Mather reported of Mercy's sufferings at the hands of the invisible furies. "They would Flash upon her the Flames of a Fire. . . . The Agonies of One Roasting a Faggot at the Stake were not more Exquisite, than what Shee underwent." By such characterizations, Mather subtly refurbished his own prowess: his exorcism was relieving her of an agony even more "exquisite" than the actual ones she had witnessed.[40]

On the actual failures of male protectors to prevent the Indian invasion of Salmon Falls, Mercy maintained a politic silence, focusing her wrath instead on culprits "in the Shape of a Woman." Mercy reserved her most bitter outbursts for her female elders. "Must the Younger Women, do yee say, hearken to the Elder?" Mather recorded her screaming to the unseen shades in her bedroom. "What a dreadful Sight are You! An Old Woman, an Old Servant of the Divel! You, that should instruct such poor, young, Foolish Creatures as I am, to serve the Lord Jesus Christ, come and urge mee to serve the Divel! Tis an horrible Thing!"[41]

THE WITCH TRIALS were a spasm—a hysterical reflex that seemed to owe much of its impetus to the shock of terrorist attack and its shape to the domestic tensions those attacks unmasked. But like later spasms involving gender and terror, their unplanned nature didn't deprive them of

a certain utility. The institution of the witch trials, and especially the useful agonies of young women like Mercy Short, allowed the colonial authorities to forestall an indictment of their own performance—and redirect that
anger into a condemnation of "prideful" and "rebellious" women. The
trials have often been characterized as excesses of their time and place, as
the Puritan ethic run amok. But it may be more accurate to say they mark
the early premonitions of a more modern sensibility and the premature
death throes of a nascent Puritan invention. The Puritan ethic had given
rise in the New World to a feminine ideal, the Judea capta, that exalted a
forceful spiritual struggle toward submission to God, whether that struggle
was waged by a feminine or a masculine soul. And the Puritan experience
had fleshed it out with real-life demonstrations of female resourcefulness,
ingenuity, and strength, as women like Mary Rowlandson and her sister
captives endeavored to preserve their lives in the wilderness and gain
their freedom. But that ideal would soon be dealt a devastating blow, delivered by a male leadership desperate to shore up its masculine credentials. In the process, an archetype of national womanhood that was
culturally central and individually strong gave way to the figure of a hysterical, marginal dependent requiring male salvation, a girl whose neediness better served the psychological needs of a people at war with terror.
With that passing, the possibilities contained in the Puritan ideal passed, as
well. Mary Rowlandson might have been the progenitor of a new female
type, an authentic original forged on the fluid frontier of a new continent.
Instead, she would take her place in history as a fading artifact of a lost opportunity, a distant glimmer of the American woman who never evolved.

One of the last women to be championed by the New England establishment as a Judea capta exemplar, though her bellicose actions simultaneously threatened to undermine that type, would continue to trouble the
American imagination. Hannah Duston seemed to be Mary Rowlandson
unbound and unhinged, a formidable dynamo of female force and a potential rival to the later American frontier vigilante. She, far more than
Rowlandson, would haunt a future America. An apparition of aggressively
independent womanhood, her spirit had to be contained whenever it
threatened a comeback. Even a comeback in inanimate form.

In the latter half of the 1800s, well into the century that enshrined the cult of true womanhood, three efforts were launched to commemorate the very un-Victorian exploits of Hannah Duston. The first was attempted by a handful of residents in Duston's old parish in Haverhill in 1852. This "Committee of 15" commissioned a stone masonry to construct an Italian marble monument to her memory, adorned with tomahawk and scalping knife. But the citizens of Haverhill proved unenthusiastic and the committee couldn't raise the funds to cover the $1,200 bill. By 1862, the matter was in the courts, and three years later, the unfinished statue was repossessed, crowbarred from the designated half-acre site where the Duston homestead once stood, and shipped to the public square of Barre, Massachusetts, where it would be refashioned into a monument to Union soldiers. The disappointed Committee of 15 marked the bare spot the statue left behind with what a local newspaper at the time described as "a fine boulder."

The next attempt, another venture by private citizens in New Hampshire, enjoyed better fortunes. In 1874, a statue was unveiled on Contoocook Island, in the woods where Duston had committed her notorious deed, and the womanhood it celebrated had a conqueror's stature. The thirty-five-foot-high granite monument displayed a massive woman with a steely gaze, undulating coils of Medusa hair, and a no-frills drape that billowed over formidable thighs. Beneath her giant feet, a poem to her heroism was etched in the stone. Its last stanza read:

> That Pilgrims here may heed the Mothers,
> That truth and faith and all the others
> With banners high in glorious colors
> May stand forever.

This fearsome figure clutched a tomahawk in her right hand, and a bouquet of scalps in her left. Almost two centuries after Duston's bloody self-liberation, a memorial to her militancy had made its debut.[42]

But few "pilgrims" would pass through the out-of-the-way atoll, and this Mother stood largely unheeded. (To this day, the statue is barely visible from the road and "often overlooked by locals," as the *Concord Monitor* remarked in 2005.) For the next half century, no one bothered to maintain the statue and the state legislature declined to allot the funds needed for its upkeep; the granite Duston soon fell into shabby decay.

While this tribute to American womanhood might be tolerated in a neglected corner of a forest, displaying such a female Titan on a city street was quite another matter. Five years later in 1879, Haverhill's civic fathers erected *their* monument to their town's most famous former citizen. This endeavor was the first avowedly public representation of Hannah Duston, for it was the first built with public funds. The statue would also come to be officially recognized as the first statue ever erected to honor a woman in the United States—as if its Contoocook predecessor had never been built. The bronze sculpture the Haverhill authorities commissioned for the commons was a more modest fifteen feet—and its honoree more demure, her gown buttoned up, her waist cinched tight. But there was a more notable change: Duston's scalps were gone.[43]

In the terms that would later be applied to Jessica Lynch, the Haverhill statue showed a woman who had "spunk"—she retained, after all, her tomahawk (albeit not raised) and a determined look in her eye—but lacked the unseemly trophies of retributive aggression. She had been frozen pre-mayhem, her tomahawk as martial but as virginal as the jammed M16 that Lynch carried but never fired. Hannah may have gotten her ax, but in her new reincarnation she wouldn't be allowed to use it. Her feistiness would be untainted by ferocity. The distinction between her and her bloody granite sister less than fifty miles away would be crucial to the gender evolution of Victorian America and to the myth that has guided us ever since.

CHAPTER 10

Here Is Our Father!
Now We Are Safe!

BY THE MID-EIGHTEENTH CENTURY, AS THE POWER OF PURITAN theology waned and the French and Indian War set off a whole new round of invasions and abductions of frontier settlements, the captivity narrative underwent a quiet but striking transformation. More and more, colonial anxieties revolved around an earthly instead of a satanic enemy. The Indians were now in league not with the devil but with the French — who recruited large numbers of native warriors to their side in that nine-year conflict — and later with the English, who enlisted Indian forces in their efforts to stamp out colonial challenges to British authority. In these secular combats, the colonists desired to crush their opponents, not struggle toward submission to God. That change in attitude found its reflection in the cultural marketplace, as the captivity tale of the stalwart Puritan woman in the wilderness was increasingly shouldered aside by a new frontier literature featuring battle-hardened and wilderness-savvy men, frontier fighters, and scouts who, even when they had been taken captive (like soldier-adventurers

James Smith and Tom Brown, who both penned popular accounts in the 1750s), proved that they could take on the Indians, the French, and eventually the British. In pursuit of this new hero, eighteenth-century publishers also scoured the previous century's Indian wars, cherry-picking examples of triumphal martial exploit from that grim era. Their rummaging yielded such works as Benjamin Church's popular 1716 tome, *Entertaining Passages Relating to Philip's War*, in which the independent ranger recalled his successful attacks on Indians of almost a half century earlier, and John Mason's *Brief History of the Pequot War* (1736), which exhumed the account of that colonial military commander's immolation of a Pequot village in 1637.[1]

Where did this new ardor for the hard-charging Indian fighter leave the Judea capta? Starting in the early decades of the 1700s, the familiar female captivity narrative would be reengineered to inflame settlers' antipathies toward their human antagonists. The captive woman's role was now propagandistic; she was to demonstrate the enemy's brutality with increasingly lurid accounts of her victimization. One of the most reprinted—and rewritten—captivity narratives of the eighteenth century was Elizabeth Hanson's *God's Mercy Surmounting Man's Cruelty, Exemplified in the Captivity and Redemption of Elizabeth Hanson*. Or rather, it was a narrative that purported, upon first publication in 1728, to be written by Hanson; by the 1760 edition, its title page promised only to have been "Taken in Substance from her own Mouth, by Samuel Bownas," an itinerant preacher. With every new version, Hanson, a Quaker farmer's wife who was abducted in 1724 along with four of her children and a maid from her home in New Hampshire, became more passive and fragile, her docility serving to amplify the malignant capacities of her captors; by the 1760 account, she was declaring herself to be "in a poor weak condition" and "very unfit to endure the hardships I afterward met with."* Where Mary Row-

---

*None of the various Hanson narratives mentioned the circumstances that occasioned her captivity, which cast a rather unflattering light on her household protector: Hanson's husband, John, had refused to place the family in the fortified garrison, despite warnings of an imminent Indian raid. At the time of the attack, he was off at a Quaker meeting and his wife and children faced the Indians alone (Kathryn Zabelle Derounian-Stodola, ed., *Women's Indian Captivity Narratives* [New York: Penguin, 1998], p. 65).

landson had used the drama of captivity to highlight not only her spiritual struggle to salvation but also her survival capabilities, Hanson (or the men who were writing Hanson's story) used it to exaggerate her infirmities and, hence, her jeopardy. Hanson also invoked God, but her spiritual quest was decidedly secondary. Roy Harvey Pearce succinctly summed up the tendencies of the eighteenth-century captivity narrative:

> Religious concerns came to be incidental at most. French and Indian cruelty, not God's Providences, was the issue. The writing of the hack and the journalist, not the direct outpourings of the pious individual, became the standard of, and the means to, this new end. By 1750 the captivity narrative had become the American equivalent of the Grub Street criminal biography.[2]

THE INDEPENDENT URGINGS of the American Revolution brought with them a brief swan song for the vigorous woman of agency. Mary Rowlandson's captivity narrative, which had begun to languish by the turn of the century, suddenly ran through five new editions between 1770 and 1773. The frontispiece of the 1771 reissue displayed Rowlandson in a three-cornered hat, gripping her rifle and a powder horn. The 1773 edition had a title-page woodcut of Rowlandson defending her own home, leveling her musket at a row of "Indian" attackers who, standing in formation and wearing long coats, looked suspiciously like British soldiers. (In fact, the illustration was probably a knockoff of Paul Revere's popular print *The Bloody Massacre Perpetrated in King Street*, which was itself a copy of Henry Pelham's engraving *The Fruits of Arbitrary Powers*.)[3] Rowlandson's Revolutionary-era printers even omitted from their editions the preface by Increase Mather and the closing sermon by the Reverend Joseph Rowlandson, as though, in the spirit of the times, they were inclined to liberate a sister-in-captivity from patriarchal spin.[4]

Readers also relished a 1779 account of an Indian raid at Dunkard's Creek, Kentucky, and the martial exploits there of Mrs. Experience Bozarth, who with "one blow cut out the brains" of one attacking Indian, "clove in two with her axe" another, and gave yet another "several large cuts, some of which let his entrails appear." A Mrs. Merril bested that record in 1791 by knocking off seven Indians, including two who tried to climb down her chimney, only to be smoked out by a feather bed she tore up and lit in the hearth. The "smoke and heat occasioned by the burning of the feathers brought the two Indians down, rather unpleasantly," the account reported, and added the testament putatively given by the lone surviving marauder when he made it back to camp: "Bad news for poor Indian, me lose a son, me lose a brother,—the squaws have taken the breech clout, and fight worse than the Long Knives."[5]

Other women were exalted for Hannah Duston–style triumphs. Mary Smith stabbed and hacked to death her sleeping Kickapoo Indian master. Hannah Dennis gave her kidnappers the slip and was said to have marched three hundred miles home on a mauled foot. The exertions of Frances Scott's getaway supposedly included dealing a death blow to "a venomous snake," climbing "impassable" mountains, and leaping from twenty-five-foot rocks. In 1792, Mercy Harbison related her marathon passage through the wilderness without shoes, her baby carried inside a coat she clenched in her teeth. A military surgeon reportedly later removed 150 thorns from her feet and legs.[6]

In the late eighteenth and early nineteenth centuries, strong and independent heroines were also taking their stand in fictional captivity dramas, most of them penned by female authors. "Women, not men, popularized the wilderness of fiction," Christopher Castiglia pointed out in his study of the captivity narrative's evolution, *Bound and Determined*: before Charles Brockden Brown ("the father of the American novel") wrote *Edgar Huntly*, Ann Eliza Bleecker wrote *The History of Maria Kittle*; before James Fenimore Cooper published his Leatherstocking Tales, Susanna Haswell Rowson penned *Reuben and Rachel*. The women in these popular novels by female writers were physically fit and psychically autonomous—they freed themselves not only from the torments of Indian masters but from "the tyranny of fathers and husbands." Indeed, by the early nineteenth century, Castiglia noted, some of these female authors were devoting an alarming amount of space to their heroines' struggles for freedom *post*captivity. *A Narrative of the Life, Occurrences, Vicissitudes, and Present Situation*, an 1809 captivity tale by the pseudonymous K. White, barely bothers with the heroine's Indian internment; most of the pages are concerned with K.'s triumphs against a cavalcade of white male hypocrites, liars, cheats, philanderers, and bigamists. The last straw is a spendthrift husband whose debts bankrupted the mercantile business she launched to establish what she calls her "independency." She leaves town and, being of a "masculine form" and "a robust strong complexion," decides to live as a man. Challenging a man to a duel, she declares, "I am content to wa[i]ve the distinction with which society has marked the walks in life of the two sexes."[7]

But for all that, the Revolution's promise of equality for women was fleeting. There would be no waiving of distinctions between the sexes. The nation's architects were careful to spell out women's secondary status in the Constitution, the legal code, and the popular debates of the day. The vaunted mantle of Republican Motherhood turned out to mean little more than staying home and raising one's sons to be virtuous and civic-minded American patriots. "The ambivalent relationship between motherhood and citizenship would be one of the most lasting, and most paradoxical, legacies of the Revolutionary generation," historian Linda Kerber observed in *Women of the Republic*.[8]

Post-Revolutionary heroism would come to require feminine peril, especially when it had to be derived, post facto, from male haplessness, as in the first deployment of the U.S. Navy. On Halloween of 1803, the U.S. frigate *Philadelphia* ran aground in Tripoli harbor and hundreds of American sailors were taken hostage and held for nineteen months. The botched launch of the Tripolitan War, an engagement celebrated in the Marine Corps anthem, was one of many such episodes in a century-long "sea-borne jihad," as it was called, in which Barbary Coast privateers repeatedly seized American merchants on the high seas and exacted onerous ransoms for their release. In one particularly ignominious instance, the U.S. government had to shell out $1 million, or one-sixth of the federal budget, to redeem eighty-eight sailors. Such affronts were widely perceived not only as "public humiliation" and distressing evidence of the young nation's pregnable state but as high-sea replays of America's earliest home-soil travail. As Cotton Mather raged of the Barbary Coast humiliations in 1703, "the Filthy Disciples of *Mahomet*" had perpetrated "the most horrible *Captivity* in the world."[9]

On the Barbary Coast, captivity was an all-male experience, and the personal chronicles of these ordeals were written by men. The specter of American manhood in manacles was unsettling, and seemed to call for a counternarrative. Converting male victimization into heroism would require a transference: "authentic" firsthand accounts of (fictional) captive women and their redemption by robust American heroes were soon rushed into publication. They were instant best sellers. These bogus female testaments borrowed liberally from the actual male versions; whole paragraphs from Captain James Riley's account were lifted, word for word, and presented as the experience of an "Eliza Bradley"—with pronouns changed and the captives reimagined as inept and frail ladies whom the men could save. In one of the most popular of these works, *History of the Captivity and Sufferings of Mrs. Maria Martin* (which went through twelve editions with nine different publishers between 1807 and 1818), the captive, an inveterate swooner who proudly proclaims her genteel inability to work in any field, is seized by an Algerian "bashaw," chained, and forced to perform menial work in a "dark and dismal dungeon." She remains a slave of Barbary for six years, "wretched and helpless," until she is discovered by an intrepid American sailor, who (after persuading her master to relieve her from further labor) pulls off a daring midnight rescue. As Maria alternately weeps, faints, and clings to his coat hem, he whisks her to a waiting American ship. "My deliverer," she anoints him, "my generous and noble benefactor." For his gallantry, an Algerian tyrant has him seized and sentenced to a torturous death. But the hero is unfazed: "If I suffer thus inhumanly," he proclaims, "it is a consolation that I suffer for no other crime than that of attempting to liberate from unjust and cruel slavery an innocent woman." Thus was the nation's nascent gender myth first put to foreign policy purpose.[10]

In the earlier captivity narratives, women had periodically remarked on the *lack* of male liberators. But in the new form that took shape in the post-Revolutionary chill into gender convention, and that prevailed over the long freeze of the nineteenth century, the abducted women were enlisted into a new duty: their job now was to defend their men from suspicions of insufficiency, to buttress America's frail sense of security by amplifying American masculinity. Amplification was achieved by contrast.

For the American man to become the larger-than-life domestic rescuer, the American woman had to be knocked down to pint-sized rescuee.

The long uneasiness over Hannah Duston's facility with a hatchet, as evidenced in her far-from-identical twin statues, made her an ideal candidate for dethronement. The issue wasn't what Duston had done to her captors but what she had done to her husband, Thomas. By her fierce stand in the forest, she had set in high relief his feeble defense—and that of the larger male protectorate. The apprehension of national vulnerability was to be framed as a domestic problem, a problem of strong women weakening their husbands' and their nation's manhood. And the solution increasingly seemed to be an insistence on a clear division of heroes and victims, sorted by sex. Women and men in real life might not fit such tidy categories, but their cultural simulacra could be made to comply. The literary censors set to work with their shears and bellows.

Valorizing Thomas would require some adept revisionism. Yale University president Timothy Dwight may have been the first to try his hand. In his 1821 account, *Travels in New England and New York*, he depicted Thomas Duston as vigilant protector. "Upon the first alarm," Dwight wrote, "he flew to the house" and "ordered" his seven children "to flee with the utmost expedition in the course opposite to that in which the danger was approaching." Hurrying past the moment when Thomas abandoned his wife and her nurse, Dwight focused instead on the father's "rescue" of his seven children. Dwight plucked his evidence not from the historical record but from his imagination.

> He was unable to make a choice [between his children], or to leave anyone of the number. He therefore determined to take his lot with them and to defend them from their murderers, or die by their side. A body of the Indians pursued and came up with him, and from near distances fired at him and his little company. He returned the fire and retreated, alternately. For more than a mile he kept so resolute a face to his enemy, retiring in the rear of his charge, returned the fire of the savages so often and with so good success, and sheltered so effectually his terrified companions that he finally lodged them all, safe from the pursuing butchers, in a distant house.

Hannah Duston's dispatch of her savages in the wilderness, by contrast, inspired no such exaltations. "Precedents innumerable and of high authority may indeed be urged in behalf of these captives, but the moralist will equally question the rectitude of these," Dwight opined. Perhaps, he mused, the unhinging effects of her infant's murder, her home's destruction, and the threat of "torture and indecency more painful than torture" might explain her unfortunate behavior. "But, whatever may be thought of the rectitude of *her* conduct, that of her husband is in every view honorable," he said, launching into a second round of hosannas to the mighty Thomas:

> A finer succession of scenes for the pencil was hardly ever presented to the eye than is furnished by the efforts of this gallant man, with their interesting appendages. The artist must be destitute indeed of talents who could not engross every heart, as well as every eye, by exhibitions of this husband and father flying to rescue his wife, her infant, and her nurse from the approaching horde of savages; attempting on his horse to select from his flying family the child which he was the least able to spare, and unable to make the selection; facing, in their rear, the horde of hell hounds; alternately and sternly retreating behind his inestimable charge, and fronting the enemy again; receiving and returning their fire; and presenting himself equally as a barrier against murderers, and a shelter to the flight of innocence and anguish. In the background of some or other of these pictures might be exhibited, with powerful impression, the kindled dwelling, the sickly mother, the terrified nurse with the newborn infant in her arms, and the furious natives, surrounding them, driving them forward, and displaying the trophies of savage victory and the insolence of savage triumph.[11]

With a few such pencil strokes—and eraser rubbings—Dwight had turned the male head of household into an invincible shield of armor and his female dependents into a nineteenth-century triptych of feminine frailty, the central panel devoted to the ailing angel of the house supine on her lying-in bed, enhanced by flanking portraits of cowering nursemaid and innocent helpless babe. No less an enforcer of the era's mores than Sarah Josepha Hale, editor of *Godey's Lady's Book* (the *Ladies' Home Journal* of its day, only far more influential), contributed to that realignment with her own poem, "The Father's Choice," hailing Thomas Duston's paternal valor ("He saves his children, or he dies/The sacrifice of love") and consigning his wife to the shadows. The verse was published, among other places, in the 1832 *History of Haverhill*, whose author shared Hale's sentiments. "Let what will be said of her conduct," B. L. Mirick wrote of Hannah, "there is something in the actions of the father and husband, disinterested perhaps, beyond comparison and noble beyond example." The formidable Hannah of 1697 was an affront to the emerging new era of separate spheres, in which women were to be the repositories of all piety and purity, while the men went to battle in the new industrializing workplace. In such a century, there would be no room for women wielding hatchets, unless—like Carrie Nation—they were winging them at liquor bottles. Hannah Duston's motives did not pass muster. As George Chase concluded in his own *History of Haverhill*, dated 1861, "It was not with her a question of life or death, but of *liberty and revenge*."[12]

Appeals of such verdicts (reflecting the importance of the case) reached the highest literary offices. John Greenleaf Whittier looked for extenuating circumstances in his 1831 rumination, "The Mother's Revenge," proposing that Duston's "insatiate longing for blood" might be explained away as a momentary maternal derangement: after witnessing the violent death of her newborn, "an instantaneous change had been wrought in her very nature; the angel had become a demon." As for the scalps, Whittier suggested that Duston's trophies might be the product not of bloodlust but simple worry that "the people of her settlement would not credit her story, unsupported by any proof save her own assertion."[13] But Duston's most prominent judge responded with the most virulent condemnation yet. Literary dean Nathaniel Hawthorne let loose in the May 1836 issue of *American Magazine of Useful and Entertaining Knowledge*, a periodical to which he had recently been appointed editor in chief. His harangue, which would enjoy repeat publication in a variety of venues and versions, including a book for the edification of schoolchildren, was unvarnished:

Would that the bloody old hag had been drowned in crossing Contoocook River, or that she had sunk over head and ears in a swamp, and
been there buried, till summoned forth to confront her victims at the
Day of Judgment; or that she had gone astray and been starved to death
in the forest, and nothing ever seen of her again, save her skeleton, with
the ten scalps twisted round it for a girdle!

"Goodman Duston," on the other hand, was a model of masculine
rectitude. Having "immediately set off fullspeed to look after the safety of
his family," Hawthorne wrote, Thomas arrived at the family manse just as
the Indians were descending:

> At this terrible instant, it appears that the thought of his children's dan-
> ger rushed so powerfully upon his heart, that he quite forgot the still
> more perilous situation of his wife; or, as is not improbable, he had such
> knowledge of the good lady's character, as afforded him a comfortable
> hope that she would hold her own, even in a contest with a whole tribe
> of Indians.

In other words, Thomas knew what his "bloody old hag" could do when
provoked.

> However that might be, he seized his gun and rushed out of doors again,
> meaning to gallop after his seven children, and snatch up one of them
> in his flight, lest his whole race and generation should be blotted from
> the earth, in that fatal hour. With this idea, he rode up behind them,
> swift as the wind. . . .
>
> Hearing the tramp of hoofs in their rear, they looked round, and es-
> pying Goodman Duston, all suddenly stopped. The little ones stretched
> out their arms; while the elder boys and girls, as it were, resigned their
> charge into his hands; and all the seven children seemed to say, "Here is
> our father! Now we are safe!"

Father Thomas had saved the day. "This awful woman, and that tender
hearted, yet valiant man, her husband, will be remembered as long as the

deeds of old times are told round a New England fireside," Hawthorne concluded. "But how different is her renown from his!"[14]

Her deeds, if not his, would be remembered for longer than Hawthorne might have imagined. In the late summer of 2006, a booster group in Haverhill, Massachusetts, hoping to attract tourists to their depressed mill town, proposed a rebranding scheme—with Hannah Duston as the new community emblem. As a first gambit and to advertise the "Haverhill Rocks!" music festival, the promoters printed up posters, T-shirts, and bumper stickers of Duston blasting away at an electric guitar. The chair of Team Haverhill tried to bill her as "a symbol of Haverhill's courage, resourcefulness, and history." A furor ensued, in which Duston was denounced all over again as a "vigilante murderess," a "shameful woman," and a model of "insanity, lust and greed." She was likened to Bull Connor and death-row convict Karla Faye Tucker. Demands were issued not only to remove Duston's statue but to "bury" it.

A columnist in the local *Eagle-Tribune* labored to sanitize Duston's image with further confection: "She had to be certain the men were not warned of what was going on, so she killed the women and children, preventing them from running to the men." S. J. Reidhead, a distant descendant of Duston's, also struggled to recast (and so, redeem) her as the helpless woman in letters to the local newspaper and the Haverhill Chamber of Commerce and in editorial commentary on his conservative-minded blog, The Pink Flamingo. On September 11, 2006, he dedicated his online column to her memory. "Hannah was the victim of a terrorist attack back on March 15, 1697," he wrote. "Let's be honest here. What was done to her by the Abenaki Indians, if done today by Islamic militants, would be called terror." Even so, to return her to victim status, Reidhead felt compelled to explain away her unfeminine behavior—and did so by imagining the most female of ordeals. His was the same explanation that Jessica Lynch's biographer, Rick Bragg, would employ. Hannah Duston must have been "a rape victim," Reidhead concluded, who was "taking revenge on her rapist."[15]

• • •

HANNAH DUSTON WASN'T the only audacious heroine, nor Thomas Duston the only straw hero, caught up in the thresher of literary revisionism that began not long after the Revolution and escalated throughout the nineteenth century. The national imperative to mint male credentials in the post-Revolutionary era, and the decades of literary recobbling it required, was apparent in the respective fates of two significant captivity narratives published three years apart in the wake of the Revolutionary War. The first was a story appended to a 1784 tract promoting real estate on the Kentucky frontier, penned by a schoolteacher hoping to cash in on western land fever. It was titled *Adventures of Col. Daniel Boon.* The second narrative, which came to be known as "The Panther Captivity," was written under the pseudonym of Abraham Panther and published in *Bickerstaff's Almanack* in 1787. Its full title, unwieldy but descriptive enough, was, "A surprising account of the Discovery of a Lady who was taken by the Indians in the year 1777, and after making Her escape, she retired to a lonely Cave, where she lived nine years." Of those two competing tales, the first would be refashioned into the reigning fable of American male heroism. The second, a parable of female autonomy, would be exiled from cultural memory.

That "The Panther Captivity" would lose the publishing war could hardly have been deduced by its debut. The story was an instant hit, savored less for the literal truth of the events it recounted than for the possibilities it imagined. It dramatized a set of freedoms that the mutable new nation might extend to its young citizens—its young women in particular. It made the rounds of periodicals and, as a stand-alone text, went through at least twenty-five editions between 1787 and 1814, making it, by some estimates, the best-selling short fiction of post-Revolutionary America. Few of the early copies remain; most were worn to crumbs and dust.[16]

The story recounts an expedition undertaken by Panther and his hunting partner, who, after trekking west into the wilderness for two weeks and shooting a "very great variety of birds and wild beasts" along the way, have their manly adventure interrupted by the sound of singing. They search out its source and, as Panther relates, "to our inexpressible amazement, we beheld a most beautiful young LADY sitting near the mouth of a cave." When this apparition recovers from the shock of unexpected visitors, she tells the men she was born near Albany in 1760 and raised an only child by her father, a wealthy merchant. At fifteen, she fell in love with a lowly clerk in the household. Her father forbade the marriage but, in keeping with the Revolutionary spirit of that year, she paid him no mind. As she eloped with her lover to the countryside, her father "threatened vengeance to us both." Fleeing from the posse deeper and deeper into the woods, the two were captured by an Indian war party. Her lover was "barbarously murdered," mutilated, then burned at a stake, but the young woman managed to escape into the forest, where she subsisted on nuts and berries until the afternoon of the fifteenth day, when "a man of a gigantic figure" suddenly appeared, spoke to her in a language she couldn't comprehend, and led her to this cave, where he fed her Indian cake. His benevolence turned to rage when she rebuffed his sexual overtures. She freed herself from his walnut-bark restraints as he slept, and "as I expected that he would use violence when he awaked, to make me partake of his bed," she "took up the hatchet he had brought, and summoning resolution I with three blows effectually put an end to his existence."

The "beautiful young lady" wasn't done yet. "I then cut off his head," she continued, "and next day having cut him into quarters drew him out of the cave about half a mile distance, when after covering him with leaves and bushes I returned to this place." She claimed the giant's domicile as her own, planted a patch of Indian corn outside, and, along with a "faithful dog" that she found, "here have I existed for nine long years, in all which time . . . you are the only human beings who ever heard me tell my tale." Not keen to return to civilization, she "refused to quit her cave," and it took the men five days of "some persuasion" to change her mind. Several weeks later, the hunters delivered her to the house of her father, who begged her forgiveness and then promptly expired, leaving "a handsome fortune to his daughter." There ends the story, with our heroine a wealthy woman with no betrothal in sight. Abraham Panther does not claim her hand in marriage; his final act is simply to assure readers that he has presented this "most singular and extraordinary" adventure "as it really happened, without addition or diminition."[17]

This "lady," never named, personified the Revolutionary charter: upending paternal tyranny, demanding liberty, insisting on equal and inalienable rights. She emerges from the womb of the wilderness cave as a self-reliant pioneer of the American frontier, returning to civilization not to submit to authority but to claim a fortune that will guarantee her independence. She is a woman without male heirs whose freedom, unlike that of her Salem forebears, doesn't condemn her to the gallows. She could have been the symbol of the new nation, as the Judea-capta daughters of Zion had been the emblem of the Puritan experiment in the New World. That is, if her society had been willing, as the Puritans briefly were, to recognize her as central to the nation's identity and mission. It was not to be. Despite its popularity, "The Panther Captivity" had no hope of enshrinement as national myth.

A culture forges myths for many reasons, but paramount among them is the need to impose order on chaotic and disturbing experience—to resolve haunting contradictions and contain apprehensions, to imagine a way out of darkness. A young nation was struggling to make sense of a troubling legacy of episodic rampant terror in the homeland, a terror that its male settlers and soldiers had not been able to check at the familial front door. This was the experience that a national myth was called to address—by remaking its shame into triumph. "The Panther Captivity" held a sly reference to that shame: "Panther" was the name of the actual Indian warrior who, in the service of the British, shot and scalped Jane McCrea, a young woman in upstate New York who had stayed behind after the Revolutionary partisans had gone, in hopes of rejoining her Loyalist fiancé. Her murder kicked off a torrent of outrage and humiliation, became the subject of many poems and paintings (the most famous of which portrays McCrea beset by bloodthirsty braves, while her tardy beau is reduced to a dot on the horizon), and served as a primary recruiting tool for the American army. It was probably no coincidence, as Jay Fliegelman observed in *Prodigals and Pilgrims*, that the author of "The Panther Captivity" had its heroine elope from Albany with her lover "exactly the month and year the rebel population of Albany left Jane McCrea behind."[18]

As a historical palliative, "The Panther Captivity" didn't fit the bill. That a woman had so capably protected herself in the wilderness only highlighted the reverse: that her male partner hadn't. What the nascent American culture craved was a narrative that would redeem the benighted

brothers of skedaddling Thomas Duston from their century-long ignominy. And for that, *Adventures of Col. Daniel Boon* would serve nicely.

In 1853, a massive marble statuary was unveiled with much pomp in
Washington, D.C.—far in literal and metaphoric distance from the Duston memorial's lonely isle—that celebrated an archetype that had already,
by then, squared off against that female colossus, supplanted in popularity
"The Panther Captivity," and secured the ground of American valor once
and for all as a male preserve. Where else to honor this homegrown
Apollo than at the American Acropolis? *The Rescue,* as the sculpture was
named, was installed on the main staircase to the U.S. Capitol. The monument displayed a gigantic white man in a buckskin coat (and what appeared to be a combination of a Roman helmet and Renaissance cap, an
embellishment by the sculptor, Horatio Greenough, who, despite his glorification of the American frontier, preferred the expat life in Florence).
The mighty frontiersman loomed over a nearly naked Indian. There was
an ax in the Indian's hand, but it had already been rendered impotent;
the gargantuan pioneer had a death's grip on the Indian's arms. At the pioneer's feet, and so disproportionately tiny as to appear to belong to another tableau, was the figure of his wife, hunched over their infant.*[19]

The unveiling elicited ecstatic reviews. "You see the exposure and
suffering of the female emigrant, the ferocious and destructive instinct of
the savage, and his easy subjugation under the superior manhood of the
new colonist," one appraisal read. "He, the type of your own glorious nation, stands before you." The sculptor gave the rescuer no name, but the

---

*In assembling the statuary on the Capitol steps, workers mistakenly placed the
woman and child at the pioneer's side instead of up front, much to the outrage of
Greenough's family members, who understood the underlying message of the monument all too well. As the sculptor's brother-in-law wrote in a letter of protest: "The
mother and child were before the Indian and she in her maternal instinct was
shielding her child from his grasp, to prevent which the husband seizes both arms of
the Indian and bears him down. . . . Now all this is perverted, the mother and child
are removed from the peril, which is the *causa causans* of the action of the piece"
(Nathalia Wright, *Horatio Greenough: The First American Sculptor* [Philadelphia:
University of Pennsylvania Press, 1963], pp. 163, 175–76).

public recognized him at once. The statuary was soon widely known as "Daniel Boone Protects His Family."[20]

This ultimate marbled expression of male heroism—the Simplicity pattern for every Rudy Giuliani and Donald Rumsfeld to follow—would come at the tail end of a long metamorphosis. In none of its many mutations along the way to its final perfection did the myth quite reflect the individual on whom it was putatively based. As the man himself protested at one point: "Many heroic actions and chivalrous adventures are related to me which exist only in the regions of fancy. With me the world has taken great liberties, and yet I have been but a common man."[21]

Daniel Boone was raised a Quaker in a Pennsylvania settlement of Friends that had achieved a remarkably affable coexistence with the neighboring Indians. His grandfather distinguished himself with this chivalric act: in 1728, he rescued two *Indian* girls from violation by *white* men. Boone himself was no Indian hater: he killed three Indians in his life but took no pleasure in their deaths. Nor was he the vaunted patriot-soldier that he was later made out to be. His contributions to the Revolutionary cause were limited, and his overly friendly relations with British military officials and their Indian operatives made him a figure of great suspicion in Boonesborough and got him court-martialed for treason (he was eventually cleared). Nor did he hold himself out as a devout partisan of the new republic. At the first offer of land in Spanish Missouri, Boone was happy to abandon his American homeland and relocate.[22]

Nor was Boone a great provider. He rarely put his shoulder to the plow (several contemporaries denounced him as a man "who didn't like to work") and repeatedly failed at the various vocations he attempted, from land surveyor (where he developed "a reputation for unreliability") to assemblyman (he was absent so often that the Virginia assembly speaker ordered the sergeant at arms to "take in his custody Daniel Boone"). His wife, Rebecca Bryan Boone, was the family's primary supporter. She was a skilled markswoman—she was said to have once shot seven deer in a row while perched in a tree—and fended for herself and her family while her husband was out on his extensive hunting expeditions, which, fabled as they became, yielded little income. Boone's land speculations met a catastrophic end; he lost vast acreage through faulty claims and litigation and would have been landless if not for an act of government welfare: in 1814, Kentucky legislators convinced Congress to grant this "worn-out man" one-tenth of his original holdings. His repeated removes west were impelled not just by a spirit of adventure but by a quest, never satisfied, for land he could call his own. The quest put his children in harm's way. He managed, famously, to save his daughter and two of her young girl-friends from Indian capture, but two of his sons died at the hands of Indians, one after a hideously prolonged round of torture, the memory of which would haunt Boone for the rest of his life.[23]

That there was scant material here for a tale of Olympian mettle hardly seemed to matter. The lionizing of Daniel Boone (and his literary descendants) was pursued not in spite of the dolorous facts but because of them. Boone's life would be reworked to give birth to the "Achilles of the West," as one hagiographer anointed the new Boone. His mythmakers were not, by and large, men of the frontier themselves. They were urban Easterners—a Harvard graduate, a banker, ministers, and aspiring writers. The first was a schoolteacher from Brandywine, Pennsylvania. John Filson was no rugged pioneer figure, judging by a self-portrait in which he depicted himself as a chinless nebbish in a cravat and by contemporary descriptions that recalled a man who was easily scammed and once fell out of his own wagon. His own biographer would later refer to him as "this melodramatic little man." Nevertheless, in about 1782, Filson left his schoolroom to try his luck at wilderness land speculation. His scheme was to snap up some forest acreage, then hurry back home and market it with a pamphlet exalting Kentucky real estate. He needed a guide to pick out the choice tracts, and a grizzled Daniel Boone, still struggling to make a living at fifty, offered his services. After some weeks spent listening to Boone's recollections, Filson got the inspiration to append the old frontiersman's story to his sales brochure. Thus was born *Adventures of Col. Daniel Boon*, a promotional addendum to *The Discovery, Settlement, and Present State of Kentucke*. In the *Adventures*, Filson imposed a narrative on the pioneer's rambling tales, but his conceptual contribution to the Boone myth and to the American liturgy went deeper: he reprised the sermon format that had for so long showcased the female captive's test of faith and altered it to dramatize the

male settler's dominance over his surroundings. Jacob was no longer sub-
mitting to the angel; he was making it submit and taking its place. As
Slotkin noted in *Regeneration through Violence*, Filson organized Boone's
stories into "a series of initiations": Boone blazes a trail to Kentucky and returns for his family; Boone defends the fort and emerges a leader; Boone is
captured by Indians and escapes; Boone pursues Indian assailants and rescues his daughter and two little girls. In the process, the aging backwoodsman is transformed into the "chief architect" of the American frontier.[24]

Long after Filson's premature death in 1788—at the hands of Indians,
no less—the Boone story would receive generations of further inflation.
Key to that enlargement was his relationship to women. Boone was no
foppish "Squire of Dames," William Gilmore Simms assured in his 1845
account; he was their strapping protector who "risked his scalp more than
once to rescue beauty from the clutches of the savage." If it were still the
"age of chivalry—during the Crusades," Simms opined, "Boon would
have been a knight-errant, equally fearless and gentle." Timothy Flint's
1833 account claimed that Boone stopped to issue a chivalric oath before
charging into the wilderness to save his daughter and her friends from the
Indian ravagers, which he scripted thusly: "By the Eternal Power that
made me a father, if my daughter lives, and is found, I will either bring
her back, or spill my life blood."[25]

John Trumbull, a Connecticut printer, pirated the Boone section of
Filson's pamphlet and issued his own version, which would in turn be
copied and reissued in many different forms for the next half century. Trumbull replaced one fiction with another, stripping away Filson's florid prose
(in which the schoolteacher-pedant had Boone wax on about "gentle gales,"
"sylvan shade," and "beauteous tracts"), and refashioning Boone into a
tight-lipped action hero. By way of instructional contrast, Trumbull appended a second narrative to the text—the story of a helpless woman taken
captive by Indians. In later amendations by other imaginative biographers,
Boone was increasingly portrayed as a he-man loner fleeing the fey comforts
of settled society and, beating Tarzan to the punch, even swinging through
the forest on a vine. Boone's Boswells claimed he was revolted by the "luxury and effeminacy" of East Coast urban life and "read a lesson to shrinking
and effeminate spirits, the men of soft hands and fashionable life."[26]

These literary concoctions made the rounds of printers and magazines over the next half century, and celebrations of a leviathan Boone
sprang up in other genres, including the Georgia two-dollar bill, where
he was depicted as Saint George slaying the dragon, and in the 1813 epic
poem "The Mountain Muse," in which a bevy of angels anoints Boone to
conquer the West. Daniel Bryan, its author and a relative of Boone's by
marriage, inserted as Boone's first act of fortitude the imaginary rescue of
a young woman whom he returns to her betrothed, a remake of the Jane
McCrea tragedy with a happy ending.[27]

"The Mountain Muse" also turned Boone's wife into a quivering
ninny. When her husband sets out for Kentucky, Rebecca falls apart
prettily—and endlessly:

> *The tenderest eloquence of mourning love*
> *At length broke from the sweet impassion'd lips*
> *Of his affectionate spouse. "My Boon!" She cried,*
> *And press'd him to her groaning breast; "My Boone!"*
> *How can you leave your Home, your Wife and Babes,*
> *Your life in bloody woods to jeopardize,*
> *Among the murdering Indians' cruel tribes?*
> *My God! The horrid thought I cannot bear!*
> *How shall I rest in peace, when dangers watch*
> *To take away my dear Companion's life?*
> *How, when the dreadful, silent, solitude*
> *Of dark and cheerless Night, surrounds my Bed;*
> *When Fancy's gloomy spectres flit along*
> *My dreary chamber, and your bleeding Corpse*
> *By grinning Savages or glare-eyed Beasts,*
> *Before my sleepless eyes is rudely drag'd;*
> *How shall I then support my sinking heart?*
> *How then the bodings of my rueful thoughts*
> *Endure? O then! . . .*
> *Oh, do not go! MY HUSBAND! Do not go!*[28]

Not for nothing did Boone say he'd like to sue Bryan for slander.[29]

The demotion of Rebecca Boone from capable frontier wife to dependent helpmeet was widespread and popular. Filson had merely erased her, allowing his Boone only a passing mention to "my wife," unnamed, whose "only happiness," allegedly, was her husband. In later accounts, a rehabilitated Rebecca would return, "meek," "faithful," and mute. John Mason Peck's *Life of Daniel Boone* reduced her from skilled hunter to docile seamstress: "His affectionate wife, who was an excellent household manager, kindly and quietly consented to this separation, and called into requisition her skill as a housewife in assisting to provide the necessary outfit." Boone's actual daughters, adventurous and raucous souls in their own right, likewise were turned into delicate maidens. Gone was the resourcefulness displayed by thirteen-year-old Jemima Boone and her two girlfriends when they were taken captive: the real-life young women had invented ingenious ruses to slow their captors' flight, pinched and kicked one of the Indians' horses so it couldn't be mounted, and deposited hot coals on their kidnappers' feet. Their cunning enterprise won them the admiration of the leader of the raiding party, who told one of the rebellious girls she was "a fine young squaw." A mutual respect pervaded the brief captivity. Jemima praised her captors' "honorable conduct." She told her niece later, "The Indians were really kind to us, as much so as they well could have been, or their circumstances permitted." Jemima's account, however, was rewritten by Boone's mythicizers to portray the girls as incapable weaklings, paralyzed at the mere thought of molestation by their chief captor. "They were terrified almost out of their senses," famed dime-store novelist Edward S. Ellis wrote in his Boone biography. "They could only huddle together in terror, and await his pleasure, whatever it might be." Boone had arrived just in time, readers were led to believe, to rescue his daughter's chastity.[30]

Jemima Boone's captivity threatened to make her less pure a woman; her father's abduction, two years later, promised to make him more virile a man. In February 1778, Boone was seized by Shawnees along the banks of the Licking River, where he and twenty-seven other men had camped while gathering salt for the settlements. Boone, unable to outrun his pursuers, put down his gun and surrendered. Brought to the Indian encampment, he agreed to the surrender of his twenty-seven compatriots—in exchange for the Shawnees holding off an intended raid on Boones-borough until spring. Boone remained with the Shawnees through June, was adopted into the tribe—the chief called him "my son"—and, although eventually permitted to hunt alone, passed up several opportunities to escape. Boone's chroniclers would cast their hero's time with the Shawnees as a transformational drama, in which Boone emerged even more skilled in Indian ways than his uncivilized tutors—their better as pathfinder, hunter, and warrior of the wilderness. "In the knowledge of wood-craft, and in powers of endurance, no Indian surpassed him," John S. C. Abbott wrote typically in his 1898 biography, and Boone's eventual flight from Shawnee captivity proved that superiority. "Though he would be pursued by sagacious and veteran warriors and by young Indian braves, a pack of four hundred and fifty savages following with keener scent than that of the bloodhound," Abbott wrote, Boone was "yet undismayed. . . . The history of the world perhaps presents but few feats so difficult and yet so successfully performed." Captivity followed by self-liberation would become the manly American rite of passage in so many subsequent accounts, real and fictional, about white men seized by Indians.[31]

In 1833, Timothy Flint published *The Biographical Memoir of Daniel Boone, the First Settler of Kentucky*, reissued in 1847 with a new title: *The First White Man of the West*. The book would become the best-selling biography of antebellum America and assure Boone's place in the pantheon. "He presents himself to us as a new man," Flint wrote of his subject, "the author and artificer of his own fortunes, and showing from the beginning rudiments of character, of which history has recorded no trace in his ancestors." Boone was the self-birthed begetter of a new race of American men imbued with "herculean vigor" and "manly beauty," "noble, square, erect forms, broad chests, clear, bright, truth-telling eyes, and of vigorous intellects." Boone's most distinguishing trait, however, was his ability to dominate and to kill. Under Flint's hand, Boone became a veritable shooting machine. From an early age, Flint claimed, Boone had "waged a war of extermination" on the animal kingdom. The author lingered in particular on one fanciful hunting triumph of Boone's youth, an encounter with a terrifying panther, which Boone dispatches with one shot to the heart, "at the very moment it was in the act to spring upon him. It was a striking instance of that peculiar self-possession, which constituted the most striking trait in his character in after life." Flint's Boone demonstrated the same power over savages as over savage beasts—in one case, subduing an Indian brave with his bare hands and slaughtering him with a knife while standing on the body of one he'd already knocked out. Flint wasn't alone in his eagerness to remake the real Boone—a man who had taken no pride in the three braves he'd slain—as an unapologetic Indian killer. In the fantasized recastings of many other memorialists, Boone became a man who "smote the savage man" and "could take a scalp with the rest." Poet Bryan maintained that Boone "had killed a host of Indians," and when the real Boone begged to differ, another biographer wrote off his demurrals as the memory lapses of a hero in his dotage.[32]

The mythic Boone was morphing into a darker male avatar. There wasn't much to distinguish him now from the sanguinary "fiends" of the frontier—other than his willingness, as Simms had put it, "to rescue beauty from the clutches of the savage." Boone's rescue of Jemima Boone and the two other girls, which Filson described in two sentences, received the better part of a chapter in Flint's book. But even that chivalric moment was not enough. For the "new man" of the West to prove himself more than a degenerate desperado, the vulnerability and need of the weaker sex had to be placed front and center—and would have to be dire.

What was good for Daniel Boone was good for the country: his coronation as rescuer of captive girls reflected a culture-wide desire to measure national male strength by female peril. Such a formula, when applied in insecure times, would demand that women be saved from more and more gruesome violation to prove their saviors' valor. Ultimately, as with Jessica Lynch, no rescue drama could be sufficient without the specter of rape. The Boone legend would become a proving ground for this ultimate refinement of the American security myth.[33]

CHAPTER 11

Touch Me Not

JAMES FENIMORE COOPER MAY HAVE BEEN ONE OF AMERICA'S MORE
wooden men of letters, but he had an instinctive understanding of
his culture's deepest needs. Little wonder that he became the first
American to earn a living writing fiction and that we are living his fiction still. In his Leatherstocking Tales, of which *The Last of the Mohicans*, published in 1826, is the second and the most enduring, Cooper
transformed Daniel Boone into Nathaniel "Natty" Bumppo, with the
Indian-bequeathed name of Hawkeye. The character he created—a
man who lives a largely solitary life in the wilderness, unmarred by familial or romantic attachments—would have been unpalatably uncivilized
were it not for his involvement in the *Mohicans* with the two imperiled
Munro half sisters: the blond and helpless Alice and the raven-haired and
headstrong Cora (whose dangerously willful nature is said to be the result
of a few drops of African blood on her mother's side). Hawkeye's defense
of their sexual purity forms the narrative's essential core.

Set during the French and Indian War, the story opens with the two young women traveling through the woods to Fort William Henry, where their father presides as commanding officer. They are accompanied by Major Duncan Heyward, a naïf to the ways of the woods and a suitor to the pale Alice, and David Gamut, a ludicrous singing psalmist. The group is guided by a sullen Indian scout named Magua, decked out ominously in war paint. Unbeknownst to his charges, Magua blames the girls' father for his misfortunes and has arranged for the traveling party to be ambushed by fellow savages. Fortunately, just before the ambush, the group encounters Hawkeye, who is camping in the woods with his two Indian soul mates, Chingachgook, who is Hawkeye's "adopted" father, and Chingachgook's son, Uncas, the last descendant of the Mohican tribe. For the next many endless pages, the young women will be repeatedly kidnapped by Magua and his forces and repeatedly saved by Hawkeye and his good-natured Mohican sidekicks. Early on, Magua offers Cora a sexual deal: marry him and he will release her sister, Alice, and the other captives. With ample lachrymosity, Cora relates the offer to her sister and Major Heyward:

> "He would have me," she continued, her accents sinking under a deep consciousness of the degradation of the proposal, "follow him to the wilderness; go to the habitations of the Hurons; to remain there; in short, to become his wife! . . . Major Heyward, aid my weak reason with your counsel. Is life to be purchased by such a sacrifice? . . .
> "Would I!" echoed the indignant and astonished [Heyward]. "Cora! Cora! you jest with our misery! Name not the horrid alternative again; the thought itself is worse than a thousand deaths."[1]

The "horrid alternative," and how both sexes should respond to it, would become a prevailing idée fixe of the Victorian imagination. That fate worse than death provided the necessary firewall, dividing men from women and heroes from victims. In the effort to shore up male strength with female weakness, the threat of rape would provide the crucial buttress. Vulnerability to rape was the feminine Achilles heel, the special weakness that women possessed and their male rescuers allegedly didn't. In The Last of the Mohicans, which drew on and heavily altered the

story of Jemima Boone's captivity and rescue, the sisters' sexual vulnerability provides the counterweight to the fictionalized Daniel Boone's
impregnable virility, repositioning in perfected form the essential parameters of American frontier literature. By the end of the nineteenth
century, that literature, for all its individual and private authorship,
would amount to a cultural public-works project, an engineering feat of
national mythology.[2]

Even Cora's display of revulsion at the prospect of a coerced marriage to Magua is not enough to clear her name; she has already be-
smirched her reputation by betraying an attraction to Hawkeye's Indian
friend, the handsome young Uncas. Though the infatuation is uncon-
summated, her breach is irreparable. She pays the price, stabbed "in the
bosom" by one of Magua's deputies and, still evidently tainted by her
appetite for those "swarthy males," consigned to an Indian burial. Only
Alice, who has expressed unadulterated disgust toward Indian men, is
permitted to return to white society. Alice has no discernible adult sexuality; she is all innocent girl. That's her appeal to Major Heyward, who
casts an adoring gaze "on the beautiful form of Alice, who was clinging
to his arm with the dependency of an infant." And that would be the appeal of her many likenesses in Victorian society. The virginal child-
woman was the caryatid supporting the edifice of male effectiveness and
thus of national psychological security; without her vulnerability, the
structure collapsed. Helplessness and the feminine need for protection
was the new female force, as Cooper himself advised readers in 1849. "If
women thoroughly understood how much of their real power and influence with men arises from their seeming dependence," he wrote, "there
would be very little tolerance in their own circles for those among them
who are for proclaiming their independence and their right to equality
in all things."[3]

By the second half of the nineteenth century, the most popular captivity stories would be riddled with ever more outlandish protestations of
feminine delicacy, infirmity, and all the prissy timidities that urban Victorian America had glamorized with its angel-of-the-house ethos. These
anemic female captives flaunted their feebleness and their fear of deflo-
ration as white badges of uncourage. As Dawn Lander Gherman wrote

despairingly in her classic (and regrettably unpublished) 1975 University of Massachusetts dissertation, "From Parlour to Tepee," "Victimization and martyrdom are the bone and muscle of every statue, picture and word portrait of a frontier woman." What had happened to the society that had put a musket in Mary Rowlandson's hands and that had thrilled to the tale of the giant-slaying, cave-dwelling, "beautiful young lady"? Occasional attempts to revive that spirit notwithstanding—like the 1874 Duston statue in the Contoocook woods—female initiative in defense of herself or her family was now a character defect.[4]

"Woman, as an Amazon, does not appear to advantage," John Frost, the editor of several volumes of captivity narratives, pronounced in 1854. "Something seems to be wanting in such a character; or perhaps it has something too much." Frost expressed stern disapproval of one Mrs. Porter, who had whacked two Indians with her husband's sword and shot a third before successfully fleeing her assailants, and chose to single out for exaltation instead a Mrs. Rowan, whose only deed was handing the hatchets to her male protectors. "That mother of the west should have a monument," Frost enthused. Other editors were similarly reworking women's frontier narratives. Mercy Harbison's captivity was one of many that went through repeated rewrites to make it comply with the new model. The original 1792 account, *Capture and Escape of Mercy Harbison*, was an unadorned first-person report. By 1825, the now titled *Narrative of the Sufferings of Massy Harbison* itemized the many miseries of this "poor widow," who was given to purple eruptions of self-pity like this one: "Some seem to pass over the seasons of life, without encountering those awfully agitating billows which threaten their immediate destruction; while to others, the passage to the tomb is fraught with awful tempests and overwhelming billows."[5]

The refurbishment of Mercy/Massy as a "poor widow" was typical. The image of the Puritan-era widow, a formidable figure who maintained her independence and parlayed her economic wherewithal into propertied influence (traits that, by the end of the seventeenth century, opened her up to charges of demonic power), had been supplanted by the destitute veiled lady in a state of perpetual bereavement, ideally at a shockingly young age. As long as she maintained a front of fainthearted neediness, the John Frost hagiographers deemed her worthy of tribute. The wholesale reduction of widows in the nineteenth century to "pitiful charity cases" was emblematic of a larger downgrading of the female sex in the Victorian imagination. As Ann Douglas remarked in *The Feminization of American Culture*:

> In common nineteenth-century conception, the widow waited for a man—a brother, a son, a new lover—to help her; any show of self-reliance was valuable chiefly as evidence of her worthiness of such aid. She had no communal tasks deemed appropriate to her widowed state; she was obligated to undertake nothing but the heavily self-involved business of mourning. The process of adjustment was seen as a private and psychological one. The widow had become a source of sentimentality; a woman without a man was an emblem of frailty and unproductivity.[6]

The demotion of one nineteenth-century female captive from self-defending heroine to defenseless sexual victim bears particular note—that of Rachel Plummer. Her father was James Parker, the man whose search for Cynthia Ann and her captive kin would so inspire Hollywood. As is evident in Plummer's literary metamorphosis from an autonomous and aggressive spirit to a sniveling weeper, Cynthia Ann wasn't the only woman in that family to receive a personality overhaul.

In the account that Rachel Plummer wrote herself immediately after her 1836 captivity, she made some attempts to conform to the femininity requirements of her era, like the choice of title, *Narrative of the Capture and Subsequent Sufferings of Mrs. Rachel Plummer*. Nonetheless, the adventures she described had more in common with the escapades of the "Panther Captivity" heroine—and the pugnacity of Hannah Duston—than the sexualized apprehensions of Alice Munro. Plummer was, for one thing, not afraid of combat with her female Indian overseers, knocking one out with a length of wood after the woman tried to prevent her from investigating a cave she had discovered. ("I cared not for her cries, but firmly told her that, if she attempted again to force me to return until I was ready, I would kill her.") On another occasion, when Plummer refused to fetch a tool, the same "mistress," furious, charged her. Plummer knocked her down and, having "got hold of a large buffalo bone," she "beat her over the head with it," determined "to make a cripple of her." Finally, after "I had cut her head in several places to the skull," Plummer gathered up her victim and carried her back to the camp, where she washed her face and gave her some water. After this bloody set-to, mistress was "remarkably friendly" and one of the chiefs praised Plummer for her "brave" performance. Soon thereafter, she had another violent showdown with another Indian woman, who tried to burn her with a straw torch. Plummer knocked her into the fire and held her there "until she was as badly burned as I was." When the woman tried to hit her with a club, Plummer seized it and the two began to wrestle so violently that "we had broken down one side of the house, and had got fully out into the street." In the end, Plummer won the fight. Summoned by the Indian council of chiefs the next day, she delivered an impassioned defense of her own actions and won them over. "This answered me a valuable purpose afterwards, in some other instances," Plummer wrote. "I took my own part, and fared much the better by it."[7]

Plummer's account was soon reworked, by a male author, and reissued as *Narrative of the Captivity and Extreme Sufferings of Mrs. Clarissa Plummer*. Its frontispiece is illustrated with a sobbing young woman on her knees in a sleeveless and flowing white gown, a child in her alabaster arms. Looming over her is a dark, half-naked Comanche warrior, hatchet in hand. Behind them, more Indians dance malevolently around a raging bonfire, where a white settler burns at the stake. Despite an accompanying publisher's note attesting to the narrator's "fair character of truth and veracity," Clarissa Plummer did not exist. Her words were a bowdlerized clip-and-paste job from Rachel Plummer's text and that of another captive woman. None of the episodes where Plummer "took my own part" made the cut. The only assertive stance in this version is assumed by the white husbands, who gallantly sacrifice their lives in an attempt to rescue their wives. Clarissa, a poor widow given to reiterations on "the feeble state of my health," collapses a few days into her abduction, so "overcome by the shocking spectacle" that she "felt unable longer to stand or help myself."

Clarissa spends the ensuing two years in that mental posture. "Never, no never, could a human being of my sex be reduced to a more wretched condition," she wails. She and another woman are both forced into "a mock ceremony of marriage" with two Indian chiefs, and "notwithstanding the object of our hatred and disgust, the most beastly liberties were to be taken with us!" She cringes before his advances. Her master, who is "in person, as well as disposition, the most ugly and disgusting of the human race," forces her to carry heavy packs, denies her food for days at a time and dresses her in "the meanest kind" of clothes—"for no other reason than because I declined gratifying a savage brute in his unreasonable and wicked request." She can think of no way to fight back, because he "had me completely in his power." Finally, a fur trader arrives and, vowing to "spare no time or pains," speedily buys her release. Four days later, he is escorting the grateful widow back to "that beloved land of liberty and peaceful home." This fictional act of male heroism is verified by an official-looking "certificate" displayed in the book's preface, which the text asserts is written by Clarissa's savior: "I, Ebenezer C. Elfort, a native of Madison, State of Georgia, hereby certify, that early in the fall of 1837, being in company with others at Santa Fe for the purpose of purchasing furs, I was there informed by a Camanche Indian of the captivity of two of my unfortunate countrywomen . . . whom, (as stated by Mrs. Plummer) I succeeded in redeeming out of their hands and restoring to liberty."[8]

THE MASS MIGRATIONS across the Great Plains in the middle of the nineteenth century revived old terror fears. Between the 1840s and 1870s, when the cross-continental railroad took the place of covered wagons, a quarter to a half million settlers made the arduous two-thousand-mile journey across the Overland Trail from the Missouri River to the Pacific Coast. The move west was accompanied by highly embroidered, salacious reports from newsmen and their literary fellows about female captives who "suffered all the cruelties that the fiend-like malignity and heartlessness of their cowardly captors could invent." Half-baked stories peddled by "old settlers" associations and retired cavalrymen clubs were seized upon by overeager journalists, who weren't inclined to check the facts. The *New York Times* trafficked in tales of "outrages" perpetrated by Indians on women and children. "The very sight of Indians were terrible to many women on the frontier," John Frost reported in yet another tome he issued on the subject in 1875.[9]

The reality of the Overland Trail experience was quite different, as direct accounts from the migrants themselves suggest. In *Women and Indians on the Frontier*, historian Glenda Riley reviewed 150 journals, memoirs, and letters by women—and found only 10 percent recorded any major difficulties with Indians; 75 percent reported no problems at all. Historian Lillian Schlissel's survey of more than 100 overland diaries by women turned up only 7 percent that reported Indian attacks. Historian John D. Unruh's extensive investigation of the overland migration uncovered an epidemic of "mythical massacres"; he concluded that reports of hundreds of cases of Indian "rapine and slaughter" in the mid-nineteenth century were made up and that far more Indians perished at the hands of white pioneers than vice versa. As pioneer Caroline Richardson confided in her journal in 1851, "We are continually hearing of the depredations of the Indians but we have not seen one yet." After being subjected to one false alarm after another, sounded by male "protectors," some female settlers began to suspect a protection racket. Julia Sinks, who settled in Austin, Texas, concluded that "ladies' men" were ginning up "a host of fears for the pleasure of allaying them." These wannabe gallants "fought windmills diligently," she wrote, "bringing in their somber visages as if laden with the news of terrible calamity"—a calamity that never seemed to materialize.[10]

Despite a paucity of documented accounts, the culture's literary guardians insisted on foregrounding the threat of rape—and garnishing it with ever more explicit and graphic descriptions of despoliation as the century wore on. In an era that confined women to a separate sphere, the possibility of rape provided a pretext for that confinement. And the portrayals of women cringing from sexual contact with the Indians also relieved a specific male fear: that white women might *choose* the company of their enemy, whether as intimates or friends. That concern wasn't unwarranted. Pioneer women in the Far West tended to have far more convivial relations with their Indian neighbors than pioneer men. Two-thirds of the diaries of frontier women that Riley examined showed a shift over time to favorable attitudes toward the native Americans they encountered—many with a heartfelt intensity—while "the dominant tone of the men's writings in this sample was one of acrimony and hostility." Female literary preferences seemed inclined in that direction, too—that is, in the few instances when women book buyers were offered an alternative. Catharine Maria Sedgwick's 1827 novel, *Hope Leslie; or Early Times in the Massachusetts*, which featured what may have been the one happy marriage between a white woman and an Indian man to appear in nineteenth-century American fiction, was wildly popular among female readers and launched the author's career. Another instant best seller (with a hundred thousand copies sold in its first year, and twenty editions published in the next hundred years) was the 1824 nonfiction captivity account *A Narrative of the Life of Mrs. Mary Jemison*, in which Jemison recalled her 1758 abduction by Shawnees at age fifteen—and her subsequent loving marriages to two consecutive Indian husbands, her delight at the greater liberties bestowed upon her as a woman by her adopted tribe, and her lifelong and adamant refusal to return to white society.[11]

In part to counteract such troubling reality, rape in Indian captivity would become a fixation by the mid-nineteenth century in newspapers and periodicals, literature, and art. The fear was not a response to a clear and present danger: Indian rape of captives was actually fairly uncommon, as it had been since the earliest abductions. Rowlandson was one of many captives to remark on its absence: "Not one of them ever offered the least abuse of unchastity to me, in word or action." She attributed the restraint to God, but numerous North American tribes subscribed to an ethic of strict chastity while on the warpath and an incest taboo afterward. While this was particularly true of the eastern tribes (some of whom regarded rape as a capital offense), North American Indians in general took captives, particularly younger ones, to adopt them, not to turn them into love slaves; the point was to replace family members lost in battle. (The Europeans introduced, of course, a second motive: money. Taking captives to collect a ransom was the byproduct of the colonial era.) When historian Susan Armitage searched first-person accounts by nineteenth-century pioneer women in the Far West, she found no reports of rape, or even expressions of fear of rape. Nor have frontier scholars found evidence of coerced marriage. "Not only were younger captives and consenting adults under no compulsion, either actual or perceived, to marry, but they enjoyed as wide a latitude of choice as any Indian," James Axtell wrote in *The European and the Indian*. In fact, "so free from compulsion were the captives that several married fellow white prisoners."[12]

Nonetheless, the image of the bound and barely clad virgin begging for mercy as she is about to be ravished by a lascivious brave became the centerpiece of the Victorian-era captivity drama. The phrases "passed over the prairie" and the "lost" daughter entered common parlance as euphemisms for sexual ruin at the hands of Indians. "In the last twenty-five years no woman has been taken prisoner by any plains Indians who did not as soon as practicable become a victim to the lust of every one of her captors," Richard Irving Dodge maintained in 1877 in *The Plains of the Great West and Their Inhabitants*. He took pains to spell out what that entailed:

> If she resists at all her clothing is torn off from her person, four pegs are driven into the ground, and her arms and legs, stretched to the utmost, are tied fast to them by thongs. Here, with the howling band dancing and singing around her, she is subjected to violation after violation, outrage after outrage, to every abuse and indignity, until not infrequently death releases her from suffering.[13]

One of the most popular American statues of the Victorian period was Erastus Dow Palmer's 1859 *The White Captive*, which portrays a pubescent girl—"the young daughter of the pioneer," the sculptor called her—who has been abducted from her bed, stripped of her nightgown, and tied to a tree stump by "Indian savages"; her white marble purity is on the verge of desecration by unseen Indian assailants. The statue was greeted with a "gush of melodramatic prose," as religion scholar James R. Lewis noted in his analysis of captivity rape images. When the statue went on exhibition in New York City, drawing thousands of visitors, the *New York Post* raved: "No more suggestive incident can be imagined for either poetry, romance or art, than the fair, youthful and isolated hostage of civilization surrounded by savage captors. . . . Virgin purity and Christian faith assert

themselves in her soul, and chasten the agony they cannot wholly sub-
due. . . . The White Captive illustrates the power and inevitable victory of
Christian civilization." A reviewer in *Atlantic Monthly*'s January 1860 issue,
whose article was subsequently reproduced as a handout to guide visitors
through the exhibit in New York, proved an even more prodigious gusher:

> They stripped her naked, and bound her to a stake, as the day was break-
> ing. But the Christian heart was within her, and the Christian soul up-
> held her, and the Christian's God was by her side. . . . "Touch me not!"
> she says, with every shuddering limb and every tensely-braced muscle,
> with lineaments all eloquent with imperious disgust, — "Touch me not!"
> Among her thronged emotions we look in vain for shame. Her naked-
> ness is a coarse chance of her overwhelming situation, for which she is
> no more concerned than for her galled wrists or her dishevelled hair.
> What is it to such a queen as she, that the eyes of grinning brutes are
> blessed by her perfect beauties?[14]

Just as chaste resistance exempted the Victorian "queen" from
shame, so any departure from the gender code of conduct risked very real
public retribution. When Sarah Wakefield, a Minnesota physician's wife,
returned from six weeks in captivity in 1862, she credited a Dakota Sioux
Indian, Chaska, with saving her and her infant from certain murder.
Chaska was among a contingent of 400 Sioux men who voluntarily returned the 269 captives taken during the Dakota War to the safety of
white territory. For their pains, 303 of them were sentenced to death in a
kangaroo court. The proceedings before a military commission of dubious authority were absent any binding jurisprudence, defense lawyers,
right to cross-examination, or, in many cases, specific charges or real evidence. In this fashion, thirty to forty defendants were tried a day. Writing
a century and a half later on the frantic search for case-law precedent to
justify the Bush administration's treatment of "illegal enemy combatants," scholar Marouf Hasian Jr. noted ironically that the modern quest
had "neglected one of the most pertinent historical parallels to the
post–September 11 era": the U.S. military tribunal procedures against the
Dakota Sioux Indians in 1862.[15]

Upon her return, Wakefield told army officers that Chaska was "the Indian who had saved me" and recounted "how kind he had been." Her remarks were instantly seen as suspect. She would be the first captive called up for questioning by a military court of inquiry, where she was pressed to reveal Indian threats to her sexual purity. "They thought it very strange that I had no complaints to make," she wrote, and "did not appear to believe me." Making no headway, her interrogators urged her to retire to another room to talk to a minister, to whom she might confide "anything more of a private nature." She had nothing to reveal, but Chaska was arrested anyway, and Wakefield soon found herself the object of a vilification campaign by the military. Rumors spread that she was embroiled in an adulterous love affair with Chaska. When she protested, the commanding officer of the Minnesota troops attributed her "hysteria" to entanglement with a "dusky paramour." Witnessing her humiliation, some of the other captive women summoned before the tribunal changed their stories and claimed to have suffered grievously at the hands of their captors. "It shocked me," Wakefield wrote of these sudden spasms of recovered memory. "I do not know of but two females that were abused by the Indians. I often asked the prisoners when we met, for we were hearing all kinds of reports, but they all said they were well treated." She suspected the women of spinning tales "to excite the sympathies of the soldiers."[16]

By the time of the trial, the claims of molestation and rape had been vastly inflated. "The female captives were, with very few exceptions, subjected to the most horrible treatment," testified one man, a white clerk. (More than four hundred men, and four women, spoke before the commission.) "In some cases a woman would be taken into the woods and her person violated by 6, 7, and as many as 10 or 12 of these fiends at one time." The state's newspapers and politicians contributed to the furor; a Minnesota congressman contended that although "these savages" had "sometimes spared the lives of the mothers and daughters, they did so only to take them into a captivity which was *infinitely worse than death*."[17]

At the trial, Wakefield was one of the few who took the stand on behalf of a defendant, but her testimony that Chaska had "saved [her] life three times," protected her children from harm, and arranged for his mother to hide her from marauders didn't seem to register. Nor did a ruling from President Abraham Lincoln, who personally pardoned 265 of the 303 condemned men. (Lincoln also found only two cases that presented any evidence of a Dakota man "violating females.") Chaska's name was on the presidential pardon list. Nonetheless, on December 26, 1862, he was hanged at Mankato, Minnesota, along with thirty-seven other Dakota men, in the largest mass execution in American history. After Wakefield demanded an explanation, the Reverend Stephen Return Riggs, who had participated in the transfer of the prisoners to the gallows (and earlier had urged Wakefield to testify that she'd been raped), wrote her a letter claiming that Chaska's hanging had been an instance of mistaken identity: he and the other officials that morning had just "forgotten" that another Indian convict in the prison had a similar name and confused Chaska with the other condemned man. Riggs's story was flimsy: he and the group of clergy and soldiers who rounded up the men for execution had gotten to know the prisoners well over the many months of detention—and, with all the ruckus over Wakefield's "dusky paramour," they especially knew Chaska. Wakefield, for one, didn't buy it. "Now I will never believe that all in authority at Mankato had forgotten what Chaska was condemned for," she wrote, "and I am sure, in my own mind, it was done intentionally."[18]

Wakefield published her narrative in hopes that a written testament might finally, if posthumously, clear Chaska's name—and her own. She would not succeed in either case. The tale of the ravished white women of the Dakota War was the version that would prevail. Wakefield's account would soon be eclipsed by a fictional account, the 1875 *Miss Annie Coleson's Own Narrative of Her Captivity among the Sioux Indians*. This sentimental fabrication provided the acceptable admixture of brave male defenders, hysterical women, and despoiling Indians. The virginal "Miss Annie" is ultimately rescued by a white woodsman named "Webb," her knight in shining buckskins. "He was dressed in hunting costume which well became his athletic form," the putative Miss Annie reports, "he had a Roman nose, with a fine intelligent countenance and his thick black hair was brushed off his high and expansive forehead." Her hero genteelly addresses her as "madam," assures her he will take care of her henceforth, and—shades of John Wayne's Ethan Edwards—scalps her dead captor.

As Webb leads the trembling Miss Annie to safety, they are attacked once more by Indians. She makes a halfhearted attempt at self-defense—"I never had skill in fire-arms"–and, having missed her target in her lone attempt to pull the trigger, she "quickly repented my temerity" and "ran away through the bushes," while her protector dispenses with her assailant in one shot.[19]

The American masculine archetype that emerged by the end of the nineteenth century was a detached figure of the frontier, with no wife or children, no companions beyond a subordinate Indian sidekick, and no possessions besides his gun. He populated the "penny dreadful" cowboy novels that dominated the late Victorian marketplace—juvenile potboilers with mind-numbing rounds of Wild West shoot-'em-ups and maiden rescues. Only the titles seemed to change: *Daredeath Dick, King of the Cowboys; Goldglove Gid, the Man of Grit; Hurricane Hal, the Cowboy Hotspur.* The hero of these interchangeable plots was a loner who could handle torture and, when necessary, deliver it. He had one calling above all others: to shield helpless girls from the monster of grown-up male sexuality. Which is to say, the American hero had become a boy engrossed in a prepubescent cartoon fantasy. He would "go backwards, from old age to golden youth," as D. H. Lawrence said in another context, describing the hero trajectory of the Leatherstocking novels. "That," Lawrence concluded, "is the true myth of America." The myth of a secure America, patrolled by vigilant boys and populated by virginal maidens, would attain its full expression in the same years that saw the closing of the American frontier. From 1860 to 1890, the "clearing" of the continent moved to its grand finale. By 1890, vast Indian populations had been wiped out and their remnants consigned to reservations. America had quarantined its remaining illegal enemy combatants and, along with them, centuries-long contagions of shame. Or so it imagined. The myth was now in final form—and ready to be reactivated whenever a homeland threat might call for its protective services.[20]

One of the earliest and most searing of these deployments would arise in the climate of the defeated South. Shamed by their inability to protect their homeland from incursion and destruction and their homes and families from harm, the region's guardians refashioned longstanding racial hatred into a morality play of dark invader and chivalrous white male protector, with an imperiled white maidenhood caught between. The cause of action was one James Fenimore Cooper could have penned: the "horrid alternative" of rape of white women by "savages." The solution was lynching, a ceremony that, however imaginary the particular crimes it redressed, conferred a robe of knighthood on humiliated masculinity. That drama, as retold in a postwar proliferation of racist "plantation novels" and infamously reenacted in real life by the white-robed men of the Klan, recapitulated all the elements of the captivity and rescue myth in a black-white context: heroic Southern gentlemen on horseback came to the rescue of virginal young women, terrorized by marauding troupes of "barbaric" black freedmen amassed at the "lonely, isolated farmstead" door. "The southern woman with her helpless little children in a solitary farm house no longer sleeps secure," the president of the University of North Carolina declared typically in 1901. "The black brute is lurking in the dark, a monstrous beast, crazed with lust. His ferocity is almost demonical."[21]

Thousands of black men would be lynched in the years following the Civil War, cresting at the turn of the century and persisting into the 1930s—and the number one justification offered was rape of white women. Never mind that less than 25 percent of lynching victims had actually been accused of rape or attempted rape (and many of that group were either falsely accused or "guilty" of no more than a consensual relationship or a friendly greeting to a white woman). Never mind that interracial sexual assaults were far more likely to run in the other direction, perpetrated on black women by white men. "By the late nineteenth century," Nancy MacLean wrote in *Behind the Mask of Chivalry*, "large numbers of white Americans, particularly in the South, believed that black men had acquired an incorrigible desire to rape white women."[22]

Sexual predation was anointed the "new Negro crime" and black men were declared insatiable when white female flesh came in view, moved "to gratify their lust at any cost and in spite of every obstacle," as one Southern historian wrote. According to the postwar's cultural overseers, a greater horror could scarcely be imagined than that of the black "ravenous brute" stalking the white "young virgin," who fled her despoiler with a "scream of beauty and innocence." Newspaper scribes of the time called it the "most frightful crime which negroes commit against the white people," "many times more brutal that death itself," and "THE MOST TERRIBLE CRIME ON THE FACE OF THE EARTH." In Atlanta in 1906, hyperbolic newspaper accounts of a fabricated rape epidemic set off violent riots. As historian Jacquelyn Dowd Hall observed, the stories of black sexual assault that made the rounds were tarted up in ever more lurid garb. One alleged accoster was said to have raped a pregnant woman so violently her unborn child died; another was said to have infected a six-year-old girl with syphilis; still another was described as "so large he could not assault her until he took his knife and cut her, and also had either cut or bit on her breast [sic] off."[23]

In the early twentieth century, a powerful new mode of mass media dramatically inflamed the rape hysteria. The 1915 Birth of a Nation — D. W. Griffith's masterwork and tribute to the men in white, based on Thomas Dixon's bestselling novel, The Clansman — drew millions of enraptured viewers, remained the nation's most popular film for more than half a century, and helped launch the "second" Ku Klux Klan, which, unlike its earlier informal incarnation, forged a national organization that claimed a membership of as many as five million white men by the mid-1920s. The Klan's original "Prescript" of 1868, embraced with renewed ardor by the men who orchestrated the group's twentieth-century revival, vowed "to protect the weak, the innocent, and the defenseless" from the "brutal" machinations of black molesters — and spelled out its primary protectees: "the widows and orphans of Confederate soldiers."[24]

In filming Birth of a Nation, Griffith was keenly conscious of building on the national protection myth purveyed by so many earlier Western dime novels, Wild West shows, and cowboy-and-Indian horse operas. "Now I could see a chance to do this ride-to-the-rescue on a grand scale," he said. "Instead of saving one little Nell of the Plains, this ride would be to save a nation." And, like his literary forbears, Griffith understood the essential role that these helpless little Nells played in restaging a mythic victory. In a clear echo of the earliest homeland assaults, Birth of a Nation embodies the fallen South in the figure of a feeble plantation patriarch, a sickly member of the old gentry who fails to shield his wife and daughters from

Union and black troops who invade his once grand manse. But his robust sons, both literal and metaphoric, erase the humiliating specter of his ineptitude, replacing his shame with their triumphal redemption of fragile white femininity, here represented by two beautiful young women, one Southern, one Northern, facing a common sexual peril. Rather than submit to the advances of a black freedman, the Southern girl leaps from a cliff to her death (a plunge to mortal purity that is reprised in both the 1936 and the 1992 film versions of *The Last of the Mohicans*, where, respectively, Cora and Alice jump off woodland precipices to escape the lustful Indian warrior Magua). The dead girl's brother founds the Klan and vows retribution for her death. "Brethren," he tells his fellow night riders, holding up a blood-soaked cloth, "this flag bears the red stain of the life of a Southern woman, a priceless sacrifice on the altar of an outraged civilization." After killing the girl's libidinous pursuer, the Klansmen come to the rescue of her Northern female counterpart, who is about to be "forced" into marriage with a "mulatto" Reconstruction leader. Not only does the South rise again, but it saves the North and restores national unity in the process. Then the white-sheeted brothers ride off to a final and glorious mission—saving a brood of women and children, along with some ineffectual Northern transplants and the Klan founder's own sickly plantation father, all of whom are trapped in a "Settler's Cabin" that appears to be lifted straight from a Western stage set.[25]

DECADES LATER, THE fantasy of the protector male and the helpless female would resurface in modern form. The 1950s witnessed its own terror dream and demonstrated how a myth cemented a century earlier to deflect that horror could operate in a setting very distant from the defeated South and at a great remove from Indian captivity. Though the United States was newly enshrined as a world power, postwar Americans perceived themselves as more vulnerable than ever before, in this instance, precisely because our own inventions—the atomic bomb, combined with the long-range bomber and the guided missile—seemed to remove our defensive isolation. The homeland was now susceptible to annihilation from any Communist madman or from the insidious internal forces of fifth-column subversives or even from the genetic mutations induced by invisible penetrating rays. Dropping the A-bomb on Hiroshima and Nagasaki may have ended the war, but it left the nation feeling newly endangered. News commentaries and government reports after our attack on Japan fixated on our own anxiety, describing a nationwide mood of "hysteria," "fear psychosis," "primordial apprehensions," a "poisonous fog" of fear, and a "new pitch of terror." The *New Republic* wondered at the "curious new sense of insecurity, rather incongruous in the face of military victory," and CBS's Edward R. Murrow remarked on his August 12, 1945, broadcast, "Seldom if ever has a war ended leaving the victors with such a sense of uncertainty and fear, with such a realization that the future is obscure and that survival is not assured."[26]

That anxiety, as historian Paul Boyer documented in *By the Bomb's Early Light*, only worsened as the years went by, resurging in 1949 when the Soviets exploded their first atomic bomb, in the early to mid-fifties when atmospheric testing sprayed radioactive ash across the Pacific and dropped irradiated rain in Chicago, and again in the late fifties when strontium-90 was found in milk. The Gallup Poll tracked a rising fear of imminent nuclear war; by the late forties, 77 percent of Americans believed we'd be facing an atomic third world war within twenty years, 57 percent within a decade.[27]

Our sense of vulnerability immediately revived the old fear of masculine insufficiency. We were vulnerable because our nation and its men had "gone soft," the latter-day Increase Mathers warned; a feminized male populace had opened the door to nuclear-tipped Communist penetration. In the *Vital Center*, Arthur Schlesinger Jr.'s celebrated 1949 anti-Communist manifesto of the new liberal "fighting faith" (and a book much reinvoked by post-9/11 liberal hawks), the Harvard historian and social critic couldn't seem to get off the subject of effeminacy's contagion. Its vector was the "progressive" American male, Schlesinger advised, who was "soft, not hard," a "doughface" with a "weakness for impotence," a "need for prostration," a "feminine fascination" with the downtrodden, and a "sentimentality" that "has softened [him] up" for "Communist permeation and conquest." Schlesinger returned to this theme through the decade. In a 1958 *Esquire* article, "The Crisis of American Masculinity," he warned of "the unmanning of the American man." The characteristic American male hero had been "castrated" and the other sex was grabbing the reins. "Women seem an expanding, aggressive force, seizing new domains like a conquering army, while men, more and more on the defensive, are hardly able to hold their own and gratefully accept assignments from their new rulers." Schlesinger yearned for the days of "the frontiersmen of James Fenimore Cooper," who "never had any concern about masculinity; they were men, and it did not occur to them to think twice about it."[28]

Beneath the anxieties of the Communist-infested atomic age lay different perturbations. Fears that a "castrated" America would not be able to shield its homeland were intertwined with suspicions that a female "conquering army" had performed the castration. Psychiatrist Edward Strecker was one of many social analysts making the connection. In his much-quoted 1946 book, *Their Mothers' Sons*, based on his study of young men rejected for military service for psychological reasons, Strecker concluded that overly dominant mothers were the force behind a new male generation's supposed lack of battle readiness; the "somewhat devious" methods of these women had left their sons "forever enwombed." The following year, psychiatrist Marynia Farnham and sociologist Ferdinand Lundberg published the best-selling *Modern Woman: The Lost Sex*, which charged that power-hungry moms, who were "afflicted very often with penis envy," were the prime culprits in the "rather extensive psychological castration of the male." The plots of innumerable anti-Communist Hollywood films and paperback best sellers revolved around sexually aggressive sister travelers who took advantage of their weak brothers (or sons) to slip atomic secrets to the Soviets. The suspicion that behind any pinko man was a conniving, controlling woman would have its real-life applications. "Julius is the slave and his wife, Ethel, the master," American Civil Liberties Union cocounsel Morris Ernst concluded of the Rosenbergs, a belief that was enshrined in the "psychological study" of the couple submitted to the White House. Upon denying clemency, President Eisenhower wrote that Ethel was "the more strong-minded and the apparent leader of the two."[29]

The Cold War culture set out to resolve this crisis in much the way Victorian literature did. In that regard at least, Schlesinger wasn't wrong to invoke James Fenimore Cooper's imaginary frontiersmen. The fifties media and advice industry maintained that men would regain their virility once women reclaimed their feminine delicacy. For men to be brave Cold Warriors, women had to be compliant homemakers. As a postwar Ford Foundation study concluded, the nation wouldn't be able to confront the threats of the atomic age until it had defeated the threats to domestic traditionalism at home. "The world approaches this critical period with a grave disruption of the family system," the study's authors, two Harvard sociologists, maintained. "The new age demands a stronger, more resolute and better equipped individual. . . . To produce such persons will demand a reorganization of the present family system and the building of one that is stronger emotionally and morally." FBI director J. Edgar Hoover put it more succinctly: women should marry early and have children to fight "the twin enemies of freedom—crime and Communism."[30]

That connection between nuclear insecurity and the securing of American domesticity was on display in the anointment of the era's symbolic bulwark and bunker: the nuclear family's suburban "ranch" home. And spelled out by the chief of the Federal Civil Defense Administration, who warned that the Cold War's home front "actually exists in our homes, right in our living rooms," and that the failure to pursue "home protection" was akin to a " 'fifth-column' action which undermines our national defense." That protection would be achieved by men doing the protecting, women the helping—as the agency's civil defense posters made clear, dividing the duties by sex. In case of a nuclear attack, the government placards instructed, men should handle "fire-fighting," "rescue work," "police auxiliary," and "rebuilding," while women saw to "child care," "social work," and "emergency feeding." The agency's brochures urged high school girls to start honing their fallout-shelter decorating skills in home ec class. In army "training" films on nuclear wartime responsibilities, women were told to stock their shelters with canned goods and dishware, while men were counseled to resist succumbing to "nuclearosis" and to start stockpiling firearms—in case unwanted strangers tried to seek refuge in the family hideout. The media underscored the same sex divisions. A CBS series on civil defense featured a "Mrs. Brown" who stressed that a woman's job was to beautify the shelter and encourage family "togetherness." In *Time*, a Mrs. Kathleen MacDonald worried that, "being a widow," she was especially vulnerable to the bomb. "It's different when you have a man to lean on," she said.[31]

A renewed obsession with female sexual purity—and the menace of its violation—marked the era. "Touch me not!" was the anthem playing behind every fifties advice manual for girls, teen magazine dating column, and sex education course, albeit draped in more modern euphemisms about the dangers of "going all the way" and the importance of "saving" oneself for marriage. The Touch Me Not girl was Hollywood's new favorite, requiring actresses like Sandra Dee and Debbie Reynolds to play, with numbing repetition, the sexless bobby-soxer and eternally pure girl next door—and saddling poor Doris Day, as film critic Molly Haskell noted in *From Reverence to Rape*, with the pathetic image of "a forty-year-old virgin defending her maidenhead into a ripe old age." Sexually voluptuous starlets, from Jayne Mansfield to Jane Russell to Ava Gardner to Jennifer Jones, were put out to pasture or assigned roles as nymphomaniacs whose promiscuity had to be neutralized and punished. (Not even Marilyn Monroe was exempt from the era's new rules: as film critic Peter Biskind observed, she was now allowed to play only a benign scatterbrain in comedies; otherwise, she was cast as a psycho or husband killer in dramatic features like *Don't Bother to Knock* and *Niagara*.)[32]

The virginal girl required vigilant protection, lest she fall prey to the clutches of the "sex psychopath," a fifties bogeyman who soon became a national fixation. "How Safe Is Your Daughter?" asked Hoover in the July 1947 issue of *American* magazine, in a story illustrated with a picture of three little girls in pinafores and pigtails running for their lives from a gigantic hand that fills the sky behind them. The picture's caption read, "The nation's women and children will never be secure . . . so long as degenerates run wild." Hoover warned that "the most rapidly increasing type of crime is that perpetrated by degenerate sex offenders," who are "more savage than beasts" and "rove America almost at will." As historian Estelle Freedman chronicled, a "sex crimes panic" consumed the media and political culture from the late 1940s to the mid-fifties. Publications from *Time* to *Parents* to *Better Homes and Gardens* rang the alarm ("Sex Psychopaths," "What Shall We Do about Sex Offenders?"); the *New York*

Times was averaging forty articles a year on sex crimes; and *Collier's* ran a long series titled "Terror in Our Cities." Twenty-one states and the District of Columbia passed "sexual psychopath" laws; city, state, and federal commissions launched investigations into the threat of sex crimes; and a half dozen states built multimillion-dollar institutions to incarcerate sex offenders (and treated them with electroshock therapy, lobotomies, and sterilization). The furor wasn't in response to a new surge in sex crimes; in fact, arrests for rape and other sex offenses had fallen after the war. (Nor was the outcry driven by a new respect for the women so violated. As Freedman pointed out, the crusaders regarded raped women as suspect—one official sex crimes report said most rape victims were "seductive" and "flirtatious"—and changed rape laws to require additional witnesses and permit probes into the victim's sexual past.) When vice squads across the country fanned out in search of the predators behind that giant hand, the "sex psychopaths" they netted were mostly gay men drinking at bars or cruising parks, men who could hardly be blamed for the deflowering of America's girls (though the national guardians of sexual morality certainly held them responsible for the "sissification" of the American male).[33]

That gender anxieties were tangled up with atomic-age fears was apparent in the multitude of fifties science fiction films that reenvisioned nuclear terrors as mutant monsters and insects, whose sex was invariably female—like the giant radiated queen ants who go on a reproductive rampage in the 1954 blockbuster *Them!* The alien invasions in these films take place on a frontier—whether the New Mexico desert or the North Pole—and that is just one clue to their provenance. In the 1953 *War of the Worlds,* a square dance is under way as the Martians descend, a modern-day hoedown that justifies the astrophysicist hero wearing Western attire through much of the film. *Them!* opens with an orphaned little girl wandering across the sands of a southwestern American landscape, clutching a doll, voiceless from the horror of having her trailer home invaded, her family massacred. The assailants may be ants, but they are also replicants of an earlier trauma, as a lecture from the investigating "myrmecologist" makes clear. "As you can see, ants are savage, ruthless, courageous fighters," Dr. Medford tells the New Mexican lawmen. "They campaign, they are chronic aggressors, and they make slave laborers of the captives they don't kill."

By the early fifties, a more literal American frontier was on display in virtually every cultural venue. The "penny dreadful" Westerns of the late nineteenth century had long ago lost their allure and fallen out of print. The cowboy's sudden ubiquity perplexed some of the nation's leading literary critics. In "Ten-Gallon Hero," a 1954 essay in the *American Quarterly*, historian David B. Davis wondered at the lone rider's remarkable return:

> More than a half-century after the passing of the actual wild and woolly cowboy, we find a unique phenomenon in American mythology. Gaudy-covered Western or cowboy magazines decorate stands, windows, and shelves in "drug" stores, bookstores, grocery stores and supermarkets from Miami to Seattle. Hundreds of cowboy movies and television shows are watched and lived through by millions of Americans. Nearly every little boy demands a cowboy suit and a Western six-shooter cap pistol. Cowboys gaze out at you with steely eye and cocked revolver from cereal packages and television screens. Jukeboxes in Bennington, Vermont, as well as Globe, Arizona, moan and warble the latest cowboy songs. Middle-age folk who had once thought of William S. Hart, Harry Carey, and Tom Mix as a passing phase have lived to see several Hopalong Cassidy revivals, the Lone Ranger, Tim McCoy, Gene Autry, and Roy Rogers. Adolescents and even grown men in Maine and Florida can be seen affecting cowboy, or at least modified cowboy garb, while in the new airplane plants in Kansas, workers don their cowboy boots and wide-brimmed hats, go to work whistling a cowboy song, and are defiantly proud that they live in the land of lassos and sixguns.[34]

Significantly, the fifties Western concentrated on an extremely narrow band of American history. "The crucial period of settlement in which most Westerns take place lasted only about thirty years, from 1860 to 1890," sociologist Will Wright wrote in his *Sixguns and Society*. "In contrast, the settling of the eastern frontier—from the Atlantic to the Great Plains—required at least 130 years." (Or longer: westward expansion from Plymouth Rock to the eastern banks of the Mississippi River took nearly two centuries.) That lengthier epoch constitutes the terror years, which our national memory has placed in cold storage. Postwar Hollywood preferred to confine itself to that thirty-year bracket of the nineteenth century, playing over and over the moment when we finally routed our homeland "invaders," or, rather, exterminated them.[35]

The Cold War nation retreated to the old compensatory fiction. Fifties America dressed up in buckskins for its debut on the superpower stage. As time passed, the cowboys' progeny would become ever more grotesque— as *Dirty Harry*'s Harry Callahan and *Death Wish*'s Paul Kersey and all the other avenging vigilantes who patrolled the late-twentieth-century celluloid landscape sought retribution in the name of murdered and violated wives and young women. In the 1971 *Dirty Harry*, the template for many imitations to follow, a serial killer named "Scorpio" (modeled on the Zodiac Killer, who was never caught) vows to lay waste to innocents in San Francisco until he's paid a "ransom." After Scorpio abducts and rapes a fourteen-year-old girl, holding her captive in an underground dugout, police inspector Callahan throws off all lawful niceties, stabbing, torturing, and finally obliterating the stalker with that famous "lucky" sixth shot from his .44 Magnum. Callahan's brutality is justified by the line he delivers to the district attorney about the captive girl: "She's raped and left in a hole to die. Who speaks for her?"[36]

In fixing only on the moment of conquest, Cold War America turned its back on the earliest chapters of our history and the insights they might yield. One potential insight, which would seem all the more essential in a postatomic age, involves learning to live with insecurity, finding accommodation with—even drawing strength from—an awareness of vulnerability. It entails struggling, as the earliest Puritans once struggled, to perceive the message in Jacob's story of strength and dependency, to fathom the distinction between wrestling with angels and slaying them. But the postwar nation refused to venture down that path. Presented with a chance to free itself from the thrall of a dangerous myth, the country balked and summoned John Wayne and his avenging brethren instead. That same refusal would doom our response to the catastrophe that struck our home soil on 9/11, when, called to forge a mindful future, we succumbed to the hauntings of a fabricated past.

What If?

FOR A MOMENT ON THE MORNING OF SEPTEMBER 11, WE WERE AWAKened to the reality of our weakness and vulnerability. The revelation was too disturbing to bear and we soon turned away. What if we hadn't?

Ruth Sergel, like many other New Yorkers, found herself in the days after the attack "wandering around downtown in a state of shock," looking for a way to be of use. A photo editor, she wound up volunteering at Here Is New York, an art gallery in Lower Manhattan that opened its doors immediately after 9/11, where she sorted and scanned photos of the World Trade Center disaster. Over the weeks she spent there, Sergel began to suspect she was archiving 9/11 history in the wrong medium. "It was the *voices* we were losing," she told me when we talked some years later. "People came in with these extraordinary stories to tell, and I thought we should preserve them. Because these stories were already getting edged out by the media narrative." Already the media had imposed on "the pile" the name ground zero; already the media categorizing of the heroes and the helpless, the masculine rescuers and the feminine cringers, was eclipsing what actual people had thought, seen, done.[1]

Sergel recalled the firefighters and rescue workers who had stumbled into the gallery after a shift digging in the ruins, desperate to put words to their experience. "They would come in and just stand in the middle of the room and start talking to the air." One firefighter described feeling as "isolated as a moonscape." Another talked about studying a bright red blotch on the ground, only to realize he was examining a human heart. A traumatized construction worker assigned to the excavation effort recounted how he had tried to "hug" parts of a body back into a living whole. He had tried to explain this impulse to his family over the dinner table, he said, but they just shut him down and changed the subject. "They didn't have a whole lot of places to explore their own stories," Sergel said. "At first, they were happy to speak to the media, but then they stopped. They felt betrayed by their portrayal. Someone would present them as a 'hero,' and they would say, 'What the fuck is that?' And then they'd hear, 'Well, that's what they're saying on X or Y talk show.'"

Sergel tried to counter the media juggernaut with a modest act of preservation. She arranged for a video booth to be installed in the gallery. Immediately, visitors began slipping inside to confide their stories to the soundproofed closet. "Voices of 9.11," as the project was dubbed, eventually traveled to the Pentagon and Shanksville, Pennsylvania, collecting more than five hundred personal stories.

What struck Sergel most strongly about these earliest testimonials, both the ones recorded in the booth and the ones she heard in the gallery and on the streets as she wandered around Lower Manhattan, was how few distinctions there were between heroes and victims, men and women. "The real reaction to 9/11 was to make everyone more *human*." Both sexes spoke of a bond forged by a common experience of "weakness," "fear," and "vulnerability." In the booth, an office worker from the World Trade Center described her colleagues calming one another's trepidations, guiding one another through the darkness, making it at last to a stairwell where they witnessed the drawn faces of the firefighters ascending the stairs. "We saw the fear in their eyes," the woman said, "the fear in their faces." A Pentagon survivor who had brought her son that day to enroll in the building's day care center recalled how two officers, a man and a woman, helped her to extricate her buried, unconscious son; and how she helped in turn to dig out several of her colleagues trapped under rubble. An ironworker at the pile broke down in the booth as he described finding at his feet the copper column covers he had installed on the World Trade Center's rooftop antennae in 1996: "I told everybody—I just tried to say, 'This is Windows on the World, right here where we're standing.' . . . I cried a million tears." A male choreographer a few blocks from the twin towers remembered watching people jump, hand in hand, pirouetting through space, as if they were performing a macabre ballet. "What I saw were people holding each other and then leaning forward and falling out of the building, and the thing that struck me was"—he paused and tried to bring his trembling voice under control—"that they didn't struggle."[2]

Sergel had hoped to turn Voices of 9.11 into an online "public archive," an electronic repository where the tapes would be readily accessible to everyone. But after the project's completion and the arrival of new management, the Voices tapes were warehoused for the foreseeable future. As of early 2007, only eight video testimonials had been posted on the Voices of 9.11 Web site. The authentic version of what people had actually experienced and felt sat in a box in storage.[3]

By September 12, our culture was already reworking a national tragedy into a national fantasy of virtuous might and triumph. No doubt, the fantasy consoled many. But rather than make us any safer, it misled us into danger, damaging the very security the myth was supposed to bolster. There are consequences to living in a dream.

Even the designated heroes were ill served as their honorary status precluded any inspection of what they'd gone through and any comprehension of what that experience might mean to the larger nation. Such was the story of the Fire Department of New York. Two and a half years after the FDNY's darkest day, the 9/11 Commission tried to examine the decisions that had led to the deaths of 343 firefighters. One city official after another protested such an inquiry. Simply to ask the question was to dishonor "the heroes." A deaf ear was turned to the many reports from surviving firefighters and other witnesses who said that the command structure had failed, that the evacuation order went unheard, that the radios malfunctioned just as they'd done during the 1993 World Trade Center bombing, that the department's brass had failed in the eight long years since the earlier attack on the twin towers to remedy this deadly problem, and that public officeholders had known and taken no action. The city authorities would have none of it. "We know for a fact that many firefighters continued their rescue work [in the North Tower] despite hearing Maydays and evacuation orders and knowing the South Tower had fallen," Mayor Michael Bloomberg maintained in a letter to the 9/11 Commission. Former mayor Rudy Giuliani made the same categorical assertion during a commission hearing, a claim he characterized as "the reality." Giuliani wasn't addressing reality. He was defending the myth, as was evident in his final remarks. "Rather than giving us a story of men, uniformed men fleeing while civilians were left behind, which would have been devastating to the morale of this country; rather than an *Andrea Doria*, if you might remember that," he said, "we got a story of heroism and we got a story of pride and we got a story of support that helped get us through." Faced with a choice between therapeutic fiction and useful reality, Giuliani made his preference explicit.[4]

The media, like the mayors, clung to the image of the New York City firefighter as cavalryman charging willingly, knowingly, to certain death. "The firefighters knew the second, closer tower would fall, too," *Newsweek*'s Jonathan Alter asserted. "Instead of moving backward, many, including the senior men, held their position, all but certain they would perish." "Some firefighters are recalling the words of Tennyson's 'Charge of the Light Brigade,'" *Newsweek* said in a December 31, 2001, story. The article quoted no such firefighters, just a few lines from that famous poem: "Was there a man dismay'd? / Not tho' the soldier knew, / Someone had blundered: / Theirs not to make reply, / Theirs not to reason why, / Theirs but to do and die." The refusal to be "dismay'd" was the FDNY's maxim, too, *Newsweek* assured readers. "Most firefighters just shrug and say, 'Heaven has some fire department now.'"

In truth, someone had decidedly blundered, and the many firefighters who did wish, fervently, to reason why, who did feel that an accounting of the debacle was important to the repair of the city's defenses, were offered hero status as a substitute. "It's a disgrace," said firefighter Steve Modica, who had tried to radio a warning to a colleague in the North Tower, only to be thwarted by the bad equipment. "The police are talking to each other. It's a no-brainer: Get us what they're using. We send people to the moon, and you mean to tell me a firefighter can't talk to a guy two floors above him?" In 2004, veteran FDNY battalion chief John Joyce published *Radio Silence F.D.N.Y.: The Betrayal of New York's Bravest*, a densely documented eye-opener (which reproduced more than a hundred internal memos, letters, and legal records) on the years-long failure to provide firefighters with a functional communications system. His revelations barely registered.[5]

Years after 9/11, New York's fire crews would find themselves still saddled with radio troubles and inadequate or antiquated safety equipment, still struggling to get the medical treatment they needed for illnesses from ground zero's toxic fumes, still limping along on wages so shockingly low that a newly hired officer with two children is eligible for welfare. A 2004 Cornell University survey of New York City firefighters found more than 50 percent of them complaining of inadequate to nonexistent training for terrorist attacks and 61 percent experiencing problems with the communications system in critical situations. Promised wage increases, which had already been deferred for two years before the attacks, were postponed time and again; a salary raise came only in 2006, after a long union fight. The federal government assigned New York's fire department onerous new homeland security duties, but not the funds to support them. Meanwhile, the city began cutting the department's budget. A half year after the attacks, medical leaves were up 35 percent at New York's fire department, 144 men were off duty with breathing ailments, and hundreds more were retiring. In the next few years, hundreds more would quit. Everyone wanted a piece of what Giuliani had called the firefighters' "story of heroism" and "story of pride," but no one wanted to deal with the reality of their afflictions. For their sacrifice, New York's firefighters were being asked to sacrifice further. For their courage, they had received a "zeros for heroes" contract, as firefighters acidly called it. "The city said it would remember us when times were flush," a fire union official told *New York*. "Guess what? They forgot!"[6]

In that regard, the real story of the New York firefighters may have been better captured by a second, less celebrated poem about the Charge of the Light Brigade, written thirty-seven years after Tennyson's panegyric. In 1891, Rudyard Kipling penned "The Last of the Light Brigade," a castigation of his countrymen for ignoring the plight of the surviving soldiers. Kipling imagined the ragged veterans, destitute and sick, shambling into an audience with the "Master-singer who had crowned them all in his song":

> The old Troop-Sergeant was spokesman, and "Beggin' your
>   pardon," he said,
> "You wrote o' the Light Brigade, sir. Here's all that isn't dead.
> An' it's all come true what you wrote, sir, regardin' the mouth of
>   hell;
> For we're all of us nigh to the workhouse, an' we thought we'd call
>   an' tell.
>
> "No, thank you, we don't want food, sir; but couldn't you take an'
>   write
> A sort of 'to be continued' and 'see next page' o' the fight?
> We think that someone has blundered, an' couldn't you tell 'em
>   how?
> You wrote we were heroes once, sir. Please, write we are starving
>   now."[7]

ON THE LARGER stage of national and international politics, as in New York, the need to pursue concrete concerns would be bartered for ceremonial scrip. In Afghanistan, our fantasies of female rescue actually got in the way of female security. Not only did White House vows to safeguard the rights of Afghan women prove hollow, our woefully inadequate attempts at "reconstruction" only served to make their conditions worse.

By 2006, the news was bleak: honor killings were dramatically on the rise (with 185 women and girls killed in the first nine months of the year), about 40 percent of women reported that they had been forced into marriage, about 50 percent had been beaten by their husbands, three hundred girls' schools had been set on fire in the last year and several teachers killed, as little as 3 percent of girls were enrolled in schools in some regions and many had retreated to secret home classes, no women were appointed to the new Afghan cabinet, and the director of the women's affairs ministry in Kandahar had been gunned down in her own front yard.[8]

The pattern would repeat in Iraq, a nation that had made significant progress in advancing women's rights from the sixties to the eighties. Once more, the United States promised heightened security and freedom for Iraqi women, and once more our policies helped accomplish the opposite. By 2005, human rights organizations were reporting a sharp rise in rapes, abductions, and sexual slavery; severe restrictions on women's ability to travel, go to school, and work; and the return of Sharia law in a U.S.-brokered constitution that also restricted women's reproductive, employment, marital, and inheritance rights. "Misery gangs" roamed the streets, tormenting and beating women who did not dress or behave "properly." In Basra, it became a capital crime for a woman to wear pants or appear in public. By 2005, several women's rights activists and female political leaders, along with one of the three female members of the Iraqi Governing Council, had been murdered, and even Bush's former female supporters in Iraq were in despair. "I want the American people to know that our dreams are gone, our work was in vain," wrote Raja Kuzai, an obstetrician and former member of the Iraqi assembly's constitution-drafting committee, who once hailed Bush as "My Liberator." "There will be no future for our children and our grandchildren in the new Iraq," she said. "The future is for the clerics."[9]

Our inept intervention in Afghanistan and our disastrous prosecution of the war in Iraq proved devastating to the general population, not only to women and not only in those two countries. The lawlessness we unleashed compromised security around the globe and within our own borders. By living in a myth, we made the world and ourselves less secure. By refusing to grapple with the actual failures that led to 9/11 and by refusing to listen to the people who tried to call attention to those failures, the nation denied its citizenry any real accounting of the missteps that led to catastrophe and any real assurance that we were any better equipped to prevent or repel another terrorist attack. Our ports, borders, rail and mass transit, and chemical and nuclear power plants would remain highly vulnerable, and our government showed little will to make the necessary changes. Bush requested no money for port security in the first three years after 9/11, and Republicans in Congress repeatedly blocked legislation to guard our infrastructure. As we moved into the second half of the 2000s, 95 percent of cargo containers were still entering U.S. ports without inspection; 70 percent of air cargo was still unchecked; and government security watchdogs were easily carrying prohibited goods past airport screeners (at rates similar to those before 9/11) and ferrying radioactive materials across our northern and southern borders. Meanwhile, a report by the federal Government Accountability Office found that the Department of Homeland Security had yet to act on more than half the steps identified as critical to the nation's safety, and other investigative bodies found that some of the department's grants were financing such "protective" measures as leather jackets for District of Columbia employees and self-improvement seminars for sanitation workers.

In 2005, the final report of the 9/11 Commission graded the nation's security improvements: most of the marks were Cs, Ds, and Fs. What it all added up to, as the commission's chairman and vice chairman put it in a *New York Times* op-ed, was "a formula for disaster." A disaster that few seemed inclined to forestall. In 2006, Jersey Girl activist Kristen Breitweiser wrote that she was "probably more scared than I was immediately after 9/11"—because she could now see how little was being done to protect the nation, and how little anyone seemed to care. "The American public fails to confront the truth about anything," she concluded in despair.[10]

Instead, we dwelled in a dream state that allowed certain political choices to unfold unimpeded. These choices and their consequences would play out in increasingly shameful and cruel forms: in the curtailing of civil liberties, the authorization of torture, the scandal of Abu Ghraib, the creation of secret prisons, the "extraordinary rendition" of detainees to foreign regimes where brutality was guaranteed, and, most of all, our reckless fool's errand into Iraq. The media-inflamed need for a virile "victory" drove our stampede to war, while the domestic assault on dissenters as traitors and "moral idiots" foreclosed any rational prewar discussion about the wisdom of attacking a country that had no connection to 9/11. In the end, the only real victor to emerge from our response was Al Qaeda, which was soon staging a comeback.

THE QUESTION REMAINS. What if the nation had responded to 9/11 differently? What if we hadn't retreated into platitudes and compensatory fictions? What if we had taken the attack as an occasion to "confront the truth"?

We would, of course, have found much to confront, from malfunctioning radios to inept intelligence to impeachable dishonesties reaching to the highest offices of government. But beyond all these particulars a larger deception begs to be met head-on. When an attack on home soil causes cultural paroxysms that have nothing to do with the attack, when we respond to real threats to our nation by distracting ourselves with imagined threats to femininity and family life, when we invest our leaders with a cartoon masculinity and require of them bluster in lieu of a capacity for rational calculation, and when we blame our frailty on "fifth column" feminists—in short, when we base our security on a mythical male strength that can only measure itself against a mythical female weakness—we should know that we are exhibiting the symptoms of a lethal, albeit curable, cultural affliction. Our reflexive reaction to 9/11— fantastical, weirdly disconnected from the very real emergency at hand— exposed a counterfeit belief system. It reprised a bogus security drill that divided men from women and mobilized them to the defense of a myth instead of the defense of a country. That is why, summoned by an hour of danger to unity of purpose, we clung to the fallacy that only a house divided against itself can stand. That self-delusion, so deeply ingrained in our history, so heavily defended by our culture, calls out for refutation.

We live at a moment of great possibility. By returning us to the original trauma that produced our national myth, the attacks on 9/11 present us with a historic watershed: faced with a replay of our formative experience, we have the opportunity to resolve the old story in a new way that honors the country and its citizens. We never really lacked that capacity. We just buried it under a fantasy. September 11 offers us, even now, the chance to revisit that past and reverse that long denial, to imagine a national identity grounded not on virile illusion but on the talents and vitality of all of us equally, men and women both.

Notes

INTRODUCTION: THE TERROR DREAM

1. Judith Greenberg, "Wounded New York," *Trauma at Home: After 9/11*, ed. Judith Greenberg (Lincoln: University of Nebraska Press, 2003), p. 26.
2. Judith Greenberg, Introduction, *Trauma at Home*, p. xvii; Dori Laub, "September 11, 2001—An Event without a Voice," *Trauma at Home*, p. 214.
3. Laub, "September 11, 2001," *Trauma at Home*, p. 209.
4. Dana Stevens, "United We Fall," *Slate*, April 27, 2006, http://www.slate.com/id/2140690/; Alessandra Stanley, "Once Again, the Tragedy You Can't Avoid," *New York Times*, Aug. 11, 2006.
5. Peter Beinart, *The Good Fight* (New York: HarperCollins, 2006), p. 115; Jonathan Alter, "Time to Think about Torture," *Newsweek*, Nov. 5, 2001, p. 45; Lance Morrow, "The Case for Rage and Retribution," *Time*, Sept. 12, 2001, p. 1; Bruce Hoffman, "A Nasty Business," *Atlantic Monthly*, Jan. 2002, p. 49; Charles Krauthammer, "The Jackals Are Wrong," *Washington Post*, Jan. 25, 2002; Charles Krauthammer, "The Truth about Torture," *Weekly Standard*, Dec. 5, 2005, p. 21; Charles Krauthammer, "Not Enough Might," *Washington Post*, Oct. 30, 2001;. David Brooks, "The Age of Conflict," *Weekly Standard*, Nov. 5, 2001, p. 19.
6. Peggy Noonan, "Welcome Back, Duke," *Wall Street Journal*, Oct. 12, 2001; Edna Gundersen, "John Wayne Tells Us Again Why He Loves America," *USA Today*, Nov. 23, 2001; "TV Turns on Marathon of Holiday Themes," *Grand Rapid Press*, Dec. 24, 2001.
7. Rob Long, "America's Turn," *National Review*, Oct. 15, 2001, p. 49; "President Bush Holds First Prime-Time Press Conference," CNN.com/Transcripts, Oct. 11, 2001; John Brown, "Our Indian Wars Are Not Over Yet," TomDispatch.com, Jan. 19, 2006; Patricia Cohen, "When Repetition Is Helpful Rather Than Annoying," *New York Times*, Sept. 17, 2001; Barton Gellman and Mike Allen, "The Week That Redefined the Bush Presidency," *Washington Post*, Sept. 23, 2001; "Ready for Battle," *Dallas Morning News*, March 20, 2003; Roxanne Dunbar-

Ortiz, "Indian Country," *Counterpunch*, Oct. 11, 2004; Max Boot, "Everything You Think You Know about the American Way of War Is Wrong," Foreign Policy Research Institute, Sept. 12, 2002; Robert D. Kaplan, "Indian Country," *Wall Street Journal*, Sept. 25, 2004; Robert D. Kaplan, *Imperial Grunts* (New York: Random House, 2005), p. 4.

8. Charlotte Allen, "Return of the Guy," *Women's Quarterly*, Winter 2002; "Horror at Home," *Newsweek*, Sept. 13, 2001, p. 52.

9. The final frame in Cagle's cartoon predicted what Americans would probably "remember" most of all: under the title "The American Idol," a cleavage-baring contestant belts out a tune. "President's Address to the Nation: The Fifth Anniversary of September 11," transcript, Sept. 11, 2006, in http://www.whitehouse .gov/news/releases/2006; "Presidential Address to the Nation," transcript, Oct. 7, 2001, in http://www.whitehouse.gov/news/releases/2001; "September 11th Remembered in Cartoons," *Daryl Cagle's Professional Cartoonists Index*, http://cagle .msnbc.com/news/9-11Remembered/main.asp.

10. Rick Lyman, "White House Takes Steps to Renew Tie to Hollywood," *New York Times*, Nov. 11, 2001; Gregg Kilday, "H'wood Meets White House at War Summit," *Hollywood Reporter*, Nov. 12, 2001; Dana Calvo, "Hollywood Signs On to Assist War Effort," *Los Angeles Times*, Nov. 12, 2001; Megan Garvey, "Studios to Put on a Show of Support, Patriotism," *Los Angeles Times*, Dec. 7, 2001; Jill Feiwell and Pamela McClintock, "White House Sez H'W'D True Blue," *Daily Variety*, Dec. 7, 2001; Rick Lyman, "3 Minutes of Patriotism on Film," *New York Times*, Dec. 20, 2001; "The Spirit of America Study Guide," http://www.filmclipsonline .com/downloads.lasso; "Entertainment," *Los Angeles Times*, Dec. 7, 2001; personal interview with Chuck Workman, Dec. 8, 2006; *The Spirit of America*, Calliope Films, 2001.

11. Kelly Bulkeley, "Reflections on the Dream Traditions of Islam," *Sleep and Hypnosis* 4 (2002): 5; Anthony Stevens, *Private Myths: Dreams and Dreaming* (Cambridge: Harvard University Press, 1997), pp. 23–24; "Scenes of Rejoicing and Words of Strategy from bin Laden and His Allies," *New York Times*, Dec. 14, 2001; Sigmund Freud, *The Basic Writings of Sigmund Freud*, trans. and ed. A. A. Brill (New York: Modern Library, 1995), p. 517.

12. David Brooks, "After Pearl Harbor: None of Today's Self-Doubting Gloominess Troubled America as It Entered World War II," *Weekly Standard*, Dec. 10, 2001, p. 25; "Vice President Dick Cheney Discusses a Possible War with Iraq," *Meet the Press*, NBC News, March 16, 2003; Emily Bittner, "Real Men Are Back," *Orange County Register*, Dec. 18, 2001; Sally Jenkins, "Company of Heroes," *Washington Post*, Sept. 20, 2001; Dan Neal, "Real Men Fight Fires, Win Wars, Push Pencils," *Palm Beach Post*, Oct. 21, 2001; Linda Cagnetti, "America's New Heroes," *Cincinnati Enquirer*, Nov. 25, 2001; Jeff Gordinier, "The Pussification of the American Man," *Details*, Oct. 2005, p. 97; Phil McCombs, "Comeback of the Alpha Male," *Washington Post*, March 16, 2003.

13. "The Land of the Smoldering Vagina," Men's Action to Rebuild Society, http://www.mensaction.net.

14. Seymour Hersh, "The Gray Zone," *New Yorker*, May 24, 2004, p. 38; Dexter Filkins, "The Plot against America," *New York Times*, Aug. 6, 2006; Lawrence

Wright, *The Looming Tower: Al Qaeda and the Road to 9/11* (New York: Knopf, 2006), pp. 9, 38–39, 107.

15. Alan Le May, *The Searchers* (New York: Harper and Brothers, 1954), p. 148.

16. Erik H. Erikson, *Childhood and Society* (New York: W. W. Norton, 1963), pp. 252–53.

17. Kelly Bulkeley, *Dreams of Healing* (New York: Paulist Press, 2003), p. 56; James Gibbons, The September 11 Dream Project, http://www.hungryghost.net/dream/dreampjtinnt.html.

18. "Fighting Back," Sept. 14, 2001, Electric Dreams, vol. 8, issue 10, Oct. 2001, http://www.dreamgate.com/dream/ed-backissues/ed8-10.txt; Jason Tarricone, The September 11 Dream Project, http://www.hungryghost.net/dream/dream17 .html; "Pogo.com," Sept. 17, 2001, Electric Dreams, vol. 8, issue 10, Oct. 2001, http://www.dreamgate.com/dream/ed-backissues/ed8-10.txt.

19. "Woiseu," Sept. 12, 2001, Electric Dreams, vol. 8, issue 10, Oct. 2001, http://www .dreamgate.com/dream/ed-backissues/ed8-10.txt; Jill Gregory, "The Death Factory," Sept. 11, 2001, Electric Dreams, vol. 8, issue 10, Oct. 2001, http://www .dreamgate.com/dream/ed-backissues/ed8-10.txt; The September 11 Dream Project, http://www.hungryghost.net/dream/dream9.html.

20. Irvin D. Yalom, *Love's Executioner* (New York: Basic, 1989), p. 6; Stevens, *Private Myths*, p. 254.

21. Sharon Begley, "The Toll on Our Psyche," *Newsweek*, Sept. 13, 2001, p. 40; Nancy Gibbs, "If You Want to Humble an Empire," *Time*, Sept. 14, 2001, p. 32.

1: WE'RE AT WAR, SWEETHEART

1. Suzanne Fields, "Yesterday's Laughs; Once Edgy, Now Cliché," *Washington Times*, April 25, 2002; Amy Holmes, "Feminism Goes to Battle," *Washington Post*, Oct. 14, 2001; Kay S. Hymowitz, "Why Feminism Is AWOL in Islam," *City Journal*, Winter 2003, p. 36; Philip Weiss, "When It Comes to War, the Sexes Still Split," *New York Observer*, Oct. 29, 2001, p. 1; Manon McKinnon, "No Place for Feminist Victims in Post 9-11 America," *Houston Chronicle*, Dec. 10, 2001.

2. Cathy Young, "Feminism's Slide since Sept. 11," *Boston Globe*, Sept. 16, 2002; Martin van Creveld, "A New World Is Coming," *Newsday*, Sept. 30, 2001; Mona Charen, "Hooray for Men," *Washington Times*, Jan. 1, 2002; John Tierney, "GI Stands Tall Again (12 Inches)," *New York Times*, Dec. 11, 2001.

3. Jaan van Valkenburgh, "Are Women Being Relegated to Old Roles?," *Christian Science Monitor*, Nov. 7, 2001.

4. "Falwell Apologizes to Gays, Feminists, Lesbians," CNN.com, Sept. 14, 2001.

5. B. Drummond Ayres Jr., "Abortion Foes Cite Terror Attack in Ad," *New York Times*, Dec. 2, 2001; "Interview with Karen Hughes," *CNN Late Edition with Wolf Blitzer*, CNN, April 25, 2004; "Dr. Dobson Responds to September 11," 2001, Focus on the Family, http://web.archive.org/web/20030824043312/http:/www.family.org/docstudy/excerpts/A0018615.html.

6. John O'Sullivan, "Their Amerika," *National Review*, Oct. 15, 2001, p. 28; Theodore Dalrymple, "The Conflict at Home: How Do You Like Your Multiculturalism Now?" *National Review*, Oct. 15, 2001, p. 24; "This Week," *National Review*, Oct. 15, 2001, p. 10; Mark Steyn, "Fight Now, Love Later: The Awfulness

of an Oprahesque Response," *National Review*, Oct. 15, 2001, p. 45. Continuing the theme, the same issue included two articles that claimed a feminine touchy-feely culture was threatening American vigor and two book reviews denouncing feminism for destroying the family and increasing poverty: Florence King, "The Misanthrope's Corner," p. 88; Rob Long, "America's 'Turn,'" p. 49; William Tucker, "In an Anti-Family Way," p. 62; Carol Iannone, "All in the Family," p. 74.

7. CNN *Live at Daybreak*, CNN, Dec. 8, 2001; Ahmed Rashid, *Taliban: Militant Islam, Oil, and Fundamentalism in Central Asia* (New Haven: Yale University Press, 2001), p. 111.

8. Lance Morrow, "The Case for Rage and Retribution," *Time*, Sept. 12, 2001, p. 48; James Poniewozik, "What's Entertainment Now?" *Time*, Oct. 1, 2001, p. 108; Joe Garofoli, "Will America Answer the Call to Sacrifice," *San Francisco Chronicle*, Sept. 23, 2001; Howard Swindle, "All of America Drafted in War on Terrorism," *Dallas Morning News*, Oct. 7, 2001; Thomas J. Kesolits, "Americans Need to Change Mind-Set," *Asbury Park Press*, Dec. 29, 2001; Karen Breslau, Eleanor Clift, and Evan Thomas, "The Real Story of Flight 93," *Newsweek*, Dec. 3, 2001.

9. John Strausbaugh, "Don't Cry for Us, Oklahoma," *American Spectator*, Jan–Feb. 2002, p. 33; "Men on Men: Intellectual Locker Room Talk. The State of Modern Manhood—What Men Think," *American Enterprise*, Sept. 1, 2003, p. 24.

10. William J. Bennett, *Why We Fight: Moral Clarity and the War on Terror* (New York: Doubleday, 2002), pp. 14, 32, 41–42, 60–61, 66, 168.

11. Steyn, "Fight Now, Love Later."

12. Mike Rosen, "Bands of Brothers Don't Need Girls," *Rocky Mountain News*, Dec. 7, 2001; Ann Coulter, "Women We'd Like to See . . . in Burkas," Townhall.com, Dec. 6, 2001, http://www.townhall.com/columnists/AnnCoulter/2001/12/06/women_wed_like_to_see__in_burkas.

13. "Women Facing War," Independent Women's Forum, April 1, 2002, http://www.iwf.org/issues/issues_detail.asp?ArticleID=356.

14. Charlotte Allen, "Return of the Guy," *Pittsburgh Post-Gazette*, March 17, 2002; Kate O'Beirne, "Men of the Hour," *National Review Online*, Sept. 21, 2001; Paul Bedard, "Pentagon Slows Clinton's Bid for Women in Combat," *U.S. News & World Report*, Oct. 29, 2001, p. 2; personal interview with Feminist Majority Foundation national coordinator Kathy Spillar, Dec. 5, 2005; "Missing: Information about Women's Lives," National Council for Research on Women, April 28, 2004; Bret Ladine, "Army Units to Bar Women; Pentagon Shift Triggers Debate on Roles, Limits," *Boston Globe*, June 13, 2002.

15. Rod Dreher, "Painful to Live in Stricken N.Y.," *New York Post*, Sept. 20, 2001; Susan Sontag, "Talk of the Town," *New Yorker*, Sept. 24, 2001, p. 32; Lawrence F. Kaplan, "No Choice: Foreign Policy after September 11," *New Republic*, Oct. 1, 2001, p. 21; Andrew Sullivan, "America Drops the Little Issues to Face the Real World," *Sunday Times*, Sept. 23, 2001; John Podhoretz, "America-Haters Within," *New York Post*, Sept. 19, 2001; Jay Nordlinger, "The Terrible Truth, a Book to Borrow, a Backstreet Boy, &c," *National Review Online*, Sept. 19, 2001; Jonathan Alter, "Blame America at Your Peril," *Newsweek*, Oct. 15, 2001, p. 41.

16. Steve Chapman, "Lunacy on the Left—and Some Sanity," *Chicago Tribune*, Oct. 21, 2001.

17. John McCaslin, "Half Empty," *Washington Times*, Sept. 26, 2001, p. A6; Joe Kovacs, "Rush Limbaugh: Bill Maher 'Was Right,'" *WorldNetDaily.com*, Nov. 9, 2001, http://www.wnd.com/news/article.asp?ARTICLE_ID=25267; Michael Schneider, "Wearing Happy Face," *Daily Variety*, May 15, 2002, p. 6; Paul Brownfield, "'Politically Incorrect' Canceled," *Los Angeles Times*, May 15, 2002, VI, p. 3.

18. Ed Koch, "Commentary: Support of Israel," Bloomberg Radio, Dec. 20, 2002.

19. Katha Pollitt, "Put Out No Flags," *Nation*, Oct. 8, 2001, p. 9.

20. Personal interview with Katha Pollitt, Jan. 9, 2007; Katha Pollitt, "Where Are the Women?" *Nation*, Oct. 22, 2001, p. 10; Michael Kazin, "A Patriotic Left," *Dissent*, Fall 2002, p. 41; Peter Carlson, "Still Pictures That Are Far More Moving than Words," *Washington Post*, Sept. 25, 2001; Steve Chapman, "Lunacy on the Left—and Some Sanity," *Chicago Tribune*, Oct. 21, 2001; Greg Pierce, "Inside Politics," *Washington Times*, Sept. 25, 2001; Steve Dunleavy, "Crybabies Have 'Left' Common Sense Behind," *New York Post*, Oct. 3, 2001; "Idiocy Watch," *New Republic*, Oct. 8, 2001, p. 10; "Chattering Asses, I," *Weekly Standard*, Oct. 8, 2001, p. 2; "Oh Shut Up," *Chicago Sun-Times*, Sept. 28, 2001; Leslie Bennetts, "One Nation, One Mind?" *Vanity Fair*, Dec. 2001, p. 176.

21. Personal interview with Pollitt, Jan. 9, 2007.

22. Personal interview with Barbara Kingsolver, Feb. 6, 2007; Barbara Kingsolver, "A Pure, High Note of Anguish," *Los Angeles Times*, Sept. 23, 2001; Barbara Kingsolver, "No Glory in Unjust War on the Weak," *Los Angeles Times*, Oct. 14, 2001; Barbara Kingsolver, "And Our Flag Was Still There," *San Francisco Chronicle*, Sept. 25, 2001; Barbara Kingsolver, "It's My Flag, Too," *San Francisco Chronicle*, Jan. 13, 2002; Letter from William A. H. Stafford, The Stafford Company, to John S. Carroll, editor, *Los Angeles Times*, Oct. 15, 2001, from Barbara Kingsolver's personal file; Gregg Easterbrook, "Free Speech Doesn't Come without Cost," *Wall Street Journal*, Nov. 5, 2001; John O'Sullivan, "Patriotism of Sept. 11 Faded Quickly," *Chicago Sun-Times*, Sept. 5, 2006; "Notebook," *New Republic*, Oct. 22, 2001, p. 10; Noemie Emery, "The Crybaby Left," *Weekly Standard*, Dec. 17, 2001, p. 25; Ross Douthat, "Kumbaya Watch: Kingsolver, Again," *National Review Online*, Oct. 16, 2001; Jonah Goldberg, "Patriot Games," *National Review Online*, April 21, 2004; Leo W. Banks and Jim Nintzel, "What a Riot!" *Tucson Weekly*, Dec. 27, 2001; Mark Jurkowitz, "Media Notes: WGBH Moves to Shed a Sponsor's Baggage," *Boston Globe*, Jan. 23, 2002; Letter from Stuart D. Karle, associate general counsel, Dow Jones, to Michael J. Meehan, attorney, Quarles & Brady Streich Lang, Dec. 21, 2001, from Barbara Kingsolver's personal file.

23. Arundhati Roy, "The Algebra of Infinite Justice," *Guardian*, Sept. 29, 2001; Ian Buruma, "The Anti-American," *New Republic*, April 29, 2002, p. 25; Victor Davis Hanson, "Our Spoiled and Unhappy Global Elites," *National Review Online*, May 27, 2005; "Babblers," *Weekly Standard*, Nov. 26, 2001, p. 42; Bennett, *Why We Fight*, p. 35; Bennetts, "One Nation, One Mind?" p. 176; personal interview with Leslie Bennetts, Nov. 29, 2006.

24. Michele Landsberg, "Unmasking Bigotry behind the Hysteria," *Toronto Star*, Oct. 14, 2001; Sunera Thobani, "Women's Resistance: From Victimization to Criminalization," speech transcript, Ottawa, Oct. 1, 2001, http://www.casac .ca/english/conference01/conf01_thobani.htm; Glenn Bohn and Kim Bolan, "Thobani Accused of Hate Crime against Americans," *Vancouver Sun*, Oct. 10, 2001; "More Anti-War Remarks from Thobani," *CBC News*, Oct. 21. 2001, http://www.cbc.ca/canada/story/2001/10/21/thobani011021.html; "Just Another Chance to Berate the Americans, *Globe and Mail*, Oct. 3, 2001; Licia Corbella, "They're Revolting and We're Paying for It," *Ottawa Sun*, Oct. 4, 2001; Cathy Young, "Multiculturalism vs. Feminism," *Boston Globe*, Oct. 17, 2001; "Over and Under Achievers: The Week of Bogus Borders," *Maclean's*, Oct. 15, 2001, p. 10; T. Y. Ismael and John Measor, "Racism and the North American Media Following 11 September: The Canadian Setting," *Arab Studies Quarterly* 25 (2003): 101.

25. Personal interview with Kingsolver, Feb. 6, 2007; Jonathan Alter, "Blame America at Your Peril," *Newsweek*, Oct. 15, 2001, p. 41.

26. *Readers' Guide to Periodical Literature: March 1973–February 1974* (New York: H. W. Wilson Co., 1974); *Readers' Guide to Periodical Literature: March 1974–February 1975* (New York: H. W. Wilson Co., 1975).

27. *Readers' Guide to Periodical Literature: 2004* (New York: H. W. Wilson Co., 2005); Allan Carlson, "The Curious Case of Gender Equality," *Society*, Sept.–Oct. 2004, p. 63; Sam Schulman, "How the Feminists Saved Marriage," *Commentary*, July–Aug. 2004, p. 25.

28. *Readers' Guide to Periodical Literature: 2004*.

29. Geneva Overholser, "Domination of Op-Ed Page by Men since September 11th," National Public Radio, Sept. 27, 2001; Geneva Overholser, "After 9/11: Where Are the Voices of Women?" *Columbia Journalism Review*, March–April 2002, p. 67; personal interview with Geneva Overholser, Jan. 25, 2007.

30. Overholser, "After 9/11"; "Op-Ed Echo Chamber: Little Space for Dissent to the Military Line," Fairness & Accuracy in Reporting, Nov. 2, 2001, http://www .fair.org/index.php?page=1669; "A Just Response," *Nation*, Oct. 8, 2001.

31. "Who's Talking? An Analysis of Sunday Morning Talk Shows," White House Project, Dec. 2001, http://www.thewhitehouseproject.org/v2/researchandreports/ whostalking/who_talking_full-report.pdf.

32. Caryl Rivers, "Pro-Feminist Media Bias? Show Me the Women!" *Women's eNews*, Feb. 20, 2002, http://www.womensenews.org/article.cfm/dyn/aid/822/con text/archive.

33. Caryl Rivers, "Knock. Knock. Who's There? Same Ol' Editor-Guys," *Women's eNews*, April 9, 2003, http://www.womensenews.org/article.cfm/dyn/aid/1285/ context/archive.

34. Quoted in Laura Zimmerman, "Where Are the Women? The Strange Case of the Missing Feminists," *Women's Review of Books*, Oct. 2003, http://www.wellesley .edu/womensreview/archive/2003/10/highlt.html.

35. "Who's Still Talking?" The White House Project, 2002, http://www.thewhite houseproject.org/v2/researchandreports/whostalking/whos_talking_2002.pdf; Mary Hemlinger and Cynthia Linton, "Women in Newspaper 2002: Still

Fighting an Uphill Battle," Media Management Center at Northwestern University, June 2002; "Minority Newsroom Employment Inches Up in 2003," American Society of Newspaper Editors, April 8, 2003, http://www.asne.org/index.cfm?id=4446; David H. Weaver, Randal A. Beam, et al., *The American Journalist in the 21st Century* (Mahwah, N.J.: Lawrence Erlbaum Associates, 2007), pp. 10–11, 186–87.

36. Julie Hollar, "Women Hard to Find on Op-Ed Page," FAIR, May–June 2005, http://www.fair.org/index.php?page=2597; Ruth Davis Konigsberg, *WomenTK .com*, Sept. 2006. *Alternet* editor Ann Friedman also found dramatic gender imbalances of contributing writers and editors in progressive magazines. At the *Nation*, for instance, the ratio was 26:4; at *Washington Monthly*, it was 30:5. See Ann Friedman, "The Byline Gender Gap," *Alternet*, Oct. 10, 2006. Alessandra Stanley, "A Historic Event for Women, Still Largely Covered by Men," *New York Times*, Nov. 9, 2006.

37. Jennifer L. Pozner, "Missing Since 9-11: Women's Voices," *Common Dreams*, Dec. 13, 2001, http://www.commondreams.org/views01/1213-04.htm; "Who's Talking: An Analysis of Sunday Morning Talk Shows," White House Project, Dec. 2001, http://www.thewhitehouseproject.org/v2/researchandreports/whostalking/who_talking_full-report.pdf.

38. Jennifer L. Pozner, "Look Who's Not Talking," *Chicago Tribune*, Dec. 12, 2001; Lynn Sweet, "Talk Shows Need Balance," *Chicago Sun-Times*, Dec. 6, 2001; Monica Collins, "Clickers; Cable Merger Could Split Subscribers," *Boston Herald*, Jan. 6, 2002.

39. Jodi Enda, "Since Sept. 11, Bush Has Forged New Alliances with Feminists," Knight Ridder News Service, Feb. 2, 2002.

40. Personal interview with Eleanor Smeal, Dec. 7, 2005; "The Bushies Unveil the Women's Issue," *Newsweek*, Nov. 26, 2001, p. 7; "President Signs Afghan Women and Children Relief Act," Office of the Press Secretary, White House, Dec. 12, 2001, http://www.whitehouse.gov/news/releases/2001/12/20011212-9.html; "Radio Address by Mrs. Bush," Office of the Press Secretary, White House, Nov. 17, 2001, http://www.whitehouse.gov/news/releases/2001/11/20011117.html; "Afghan Women: Secretary Colin L. Powell Remarks," transcript, U.S. State Dept., Nov. 19, 2001, http://www.state.gov/secretary/former/powell/remarks/2001/6229.htm; "Report on the Taliban's War against Women," U.S. State Dept., Nov. 17, 2001, http://www.state.gov/g/drl/rls/6185.htm; "Report on the Taliban's War against Women: Quotes by and about Women in Afghanistan," U.S. State Dept., Nov. 17, 2001, http://www.state.gov/g/drl/rls/6186.htm; "Humanitarian Relief of Afghanistan," transcript, Joint Hearing of the Senate Foreign Relations Committee, Near Eastern and South Asian Affairs Subcommittee, and International Operations and Terrorism Subcommittee, Federal News Service, Oct. 10, 2001.

41. Janelle Brown, "'Beneath the Veil' Redux," *Salon*, Nov. 17, 2001, http://archive.salon.com/mwt/feature/2001/11/16/veil_two/; "Taliban Documentarian," *On the Media*, Sept. 29, 2001, WNYC, http://www.onthemedia.org/yore/transcripts/transcripts_092801_taliban.html; "Best of the News: Taliban's Treatment of Women," Feminist Majority Foundation internal memo, Oct. 6, 2001; Nicholas D. Kristof, "The Veiled Response," *New York Times*, Dec. 11,

2001; Abigail Van Buren, "Dear Abby: Rescue Afghan Women Who Are Buried Alive," *Times-Picayune*, Feb. 26, 1999; Amy Waldman, "Reporters in Afghanistan: Fear, Numbness, and Being a Spectacle," *New York Times*, Dec. 29, 2001; John Otis, "Afghan Women Remain in Flux," *Houston Chronicle*, Dec. 30, 2001; "Zora Rakesh Discusses the Plight of Afghan People Under the Taliban," *Today*, NBC News, Oct. 9, 2001; Barry Bearak, "Kabul Retraces Steps to Life Before Taliban, *New York Times*, Dec. 2, 2001; "Afghan Refugees Try to Get into Pakistan from Kandahar Area," *CNN Sunday Morning*, CNN, Oct. 21, 2001.

42. Personal interview with Feminist Majority Foundation national coordinator Kathy Spillar, Dec. 16, 2005; personal interview with Eleanor Smeal, Dec. 7, 2005; Alessandra Stanley, "Women in Authority: Walking a Fine Line in Showcasing Women and Dealing with Muslim Allies," *New York Times*, Oct. 27, 2001.

43. Quoted in Jocelyn Guest, "Extreme Makeover Freedom Edition: An American Beauty School Sets Up Shop in Afghanistan," *Iris: A Journal about Women*, Spring 2005, p. 12; Hamida Ghafour, "Beauticians without Borders Teach Basics to Afghan Women," *Globe and Mail*, Feb. 24, 2004; Sharon Krum, "Beauty Unveiled," *Times* (London), Oct. 8, 2002; Hamida Ghafour, "Opening Afghani Eyes with Mascara and Beauty Classes," *Los Angeles Times*, April 4, 2004; Julia Stuart, "Beauty and the Burqa," *Independent*, Sept. 9, 2004; Louise Roug, "City of Angles," *Los Angeles Times*, Nov. 1, 2001.

44. Ramesh Ponnuru, "What We're Not Fighting For," *National Review*, Nov. 5, 2001, p. 20; quoted in Greg Pierce, "Stunning Turnabout," *Washington Times*, Jan. 10, 2002.

45. Sarah Wildman, "Arms Length; Why Don't Feminists Support the War?" *New Republic*, Nov. 5, 2001, p. 23; Kay S. Hymowitz, "Feminist Fog," *New York Post*, Feb. 9, 2003; Kay S. Hymowitz, "Why Feminism Is AWOL in Islam," *City Journal*, Winter 2003, p. 36.

46. Nicholas D. Kristof, "Back to the Brothel," *New York Times*, Jan. 22, 2005; Kristof, "Leaving the Brothel Behind," *New York Times*, Jan. 19, 2005; Kristof, "Girls for Sale," *New York Times*, Jan. 14, 2004; Kristof, "Bargaining for Freedom," *New York Times*, Jan. 21, 2004; Kristof, "Going Home with Hope," *New York Times*, Jan. 24, 2004; Kristof, "Loss of Innocence," *New York Times*, Jan. 28, 2004; Kristof, "Stopping the Traffickers," *New York Times*, Jan. 31, 2004.

47. Melinda Liu, "Now I See the Sunlight," *Newsweek*, Nov. 26, 2002, p. 46; Ron Moreau, "Delivered from Evil," *Newsweek*, Nov. 26, 2001, p. 52; "American Aid Workers Held News Conference Following Captivity in Afghanistan," *Mornings with Paula Zahn*, CNN, Nov. 16, 2001; http://transcripts.cnn.com/TRANSCRIPTS/0111/16/ltm.02.html; "President Welcomes Aid Workers Rescued from Afghanistan," transcript, White House, Office of Press Secretary, Nov. 26, 2001, http://www.whitehouse.gov/news/releases/2001/11/20011126-1.html; "Journalists Behind *Beneath the Veil* and *Unholy War* Tell Their Stories," *Larry King Live*, CNN, Dec. 26, 2001.

48. "President's Remarks to the Nation," transcript, White House, Office of the Press Secretary, Sept. 11, 2002, http://www.whitehouse.gov/news/releases/2002/09/20020911-3.html.

49. Bob Edwards, "Secretary of Defense Donald Rumsfeld on the War in Afghanistan and the War on Terrorism," National Public Radio, Feb. 14, 2002.

50. Personal interview with Eleanor Smeal, Dec. 7, 2005.

51. "Building a New Iraq: Iraqi Women Step Forward in Partnership," transcript, U.S. State Dept., Sept. 27, 2004, http://www.state.gov/g/rls/rm/2004/36654.htm; *National Review*, cover, Dec. 17, 2001; William Saletan, "Rape Rooms: A Chronology," *Slate*, May 5, 2004, http://www.slate.com/id/2100014/; "President's Press Conference," White House Press Releases, *Federal Information and News Dispatch*, March 16, 2005.

2: THE RETURN OF SUPERMAN

1. "Secretary Rumsfeld Message to U.S. Forces, DoD Civilians," transcript, U.S. Dept. of Defense, Office of the Assistant Secretary of Defense, Sept. 12, 2001, http://www.defenselink.mil/transcripts/2001/t09122001_t912sdmg.html; "Special Report: America United," Fox News, Sept. 13, 2001.

2. "Sexiest Man Alive: Donald Rumsfeld, Sexiest Cabinet Member," *People*, Dec. 2, 2002, p. 92; Miles O'Brien, "Profiles in Leadership," CNN, Jan. 1, 2002, http://transcripts.cnn.com/TRANSCRIPTS/0201/01/se.05.html; "Interview with Dick Cheney," *Fox Special Report with Brit Hume*, Fox News, Dec. 11, 2001, http://www.foxnews.com/story/0,2933,40619,00.html; Jay Nordlinger, "The Stud: Don Rumsfeld, America's New Pin-Up," *National Review*, Dec. 31, 2001, p. 24; Midge Decter, *Rumsfeld: A Personal Portrait* (New York: Regan Books, 2003), pp. 1, 14, 17, 22, 134, 213.

3. Howard Fineman, "Succeeding When It Matters Most," *Newsweek*, Sept. 27, 2001, p. 66; Fred Barnes, "Man with a Mission," *Weekly Standard*, Oct. 8, 2001, p. 4; David Brooks, "Bush's Patriotic Challenge," *Weekly Standard*, Oct. 8, 2001, p. 26.

4. Peggy Noonan, "The Right Man," *Wall Street Journal*, Jan. 30, 2003, http://www.opinionjournal.com/columnists/pnoonan/?id=110002995; Peter Roff, "The Return of the Evildoer," UPI, Oct. 18, 2001; James Carney and John F. Dickerson, "Person of the Year: Inside the War Room," *Time*, Dec. 31, 2001–Jan. 7, 2002, p. 112; Howard Fineman, "A President Finds His True Voice," *Newsweek*, Sept. 24, 2001, p. 50; Howard Fineman, "This Is Our Life Now," *Newsweek*, Dec. 3, 2001, p. 22.

5. "War and Destiny," *Vanity Fair*, Feb. 2002, p. 78.

6. Lacie Sooter, letter to the editor, *Vanity Fair*, April 2002, p. 136.

7. Graydon Carter, "The War Room," *Vanity Fair*, Feb. 2002, p. 38.

8. Jonathan Alter, "Grit, Guts, and Rudy Giuliani," *Newsweek*, Sept. 24, 2001, p. 53; Eric Pooley, "Mayor of the World," *Time*, Dec. 31, 2001–Jan. 7, 2002, p. 40.

9. Jonathan Alter, "The Spirit of America," *Newsweek*, Sept. 27, 2001, p. 62; "Person of the Year," *Time*, Dec. 31, 2001–Jan. 7, 2002, cover.

10. *DC 9/11: Time of Crisis*, dir. Brian Trenchard-Smith, 2003; J. Hoberman, "Lights, Camera, Exploitation," *Village Voice*, Aug. 27, 2003–Sept. 7, 2003, http://www.villagevoice.com/news/0335,hoberman,46558,1.html.

11. "Joe Quesada and Adam Kubert of Marvel Comics Discuss a New Poster Book," *Today*, NBC, Oct. 17, 2001; Kenn McCracken, "Heroes," *ComicsReviewlution*, Oct. 18, 2001, http://www.revolutionsf.com/article.html?id=516.

12. "Joe Quesada Discusses Their New Comic Series," *Today*, NBC, June 4, 2002; Paul Levitz, "Introduction," *9-11: The World's Finest Comic Book Writers & Artists Tell Stories to Remember*, vol. 2, DC Comics, 2002, p. 11.

13. "Silver Linings in a Big Dust Cloud," *9-11*: vol. 2, cover and pp. 134–35; J. Michael Straczynski, *The Amazing Spider-Man: Revelations*, vol. 2, Marvel Comics, 2001; "Unreal," *9-11*, p. 16.

14. Ann Wlazelek, "Freedom Under Attack," *Morning Call*, Sept. 23, 2001; Matthew Klam, "Waiting," *New York Times Magazine*, Sept. 23, 2001, p. 84; Dan Barry, "Pictures of Medical Readiness, Waiting and Hoping for Survivors to Fill Their Wards," *New York Times*, Sept. 12, 2001; Sandeep Jauhar, "They Had Everything They Needed, Except Survivors to Treat," *New York Times*, Sept. 18, 2001; "U.S. Healthcare Responds," *American Health Line*, Sept. 12, 2001; "America under Attack," CNN, Sept. 11, 2001; "Precious Mettle," *People*, Oct. 1, 2001, p. 22.

15. Klam, "Waiting"; Barry, "Pictures of Medical Readiness"; "Special Report," ABC News, Sept. 12, 2001.

16. Jane Fritsch, "Rescue Workers Rush In, and Many Do Not Return," *New York Times*, Sept. 12, 2001; *In Memoriam*, HBO Films, 2002.

17. "Precious Mettle," *People*, Oct. 1, 2001, p. 22; Barton Gellman, "In a Mountain of Dust, Fire, 'We Didn't Even Find People,'" *Washington Post*, Sept. 13, 2001; Nancy Gibbs, "If You Want to Humble an Empire," *Time*, Sept. 14, 2001, p. 32.

18. Stephen J. Dubner, "Looking for Heroes—and Finding Them," *New York Times*, Oct. 6, 2001; Shepard Smith, Brit Hume, et al., "Terrorism Hits America," Fox News, Sept. 11, 2001; "America under Attack, Attack Shuts Down Financial Markets," CNN, Sept. 12, 2001; "Daybreak on Second Day of Terror," CNN, Sept. 12, 2001; "America under Attack," ABC News, Sept. 13, 2001.

19. Julie Jette, "A Company Survives; After Attacks, Leaders, Fate Guide Network Plus," *Patriot Ledger*, Dec. 29, 2001; "Michael Benfante and John Cerqueira Discuss Carrying Wheelchair-Bound Woman to Safety," *Good Morning America*, ABC News, Sept. 25, 2001; "A New Lease on Life," *48 Hours*, CBS News, Oct. 19, 2001; Rick Hampton, Martha T. Moore, et al., "One Day Seared into Memory," *USA Today*, Sept. 17, 2001; Dennis Cauchon, "Four Survived by Ignoring Words of Advice," *USA Today*, Dec. 19, 2001; Jim Dwyer and Kevin Flynn, *102 Minutes: The Untold Story of the Fight to Survive Inside the Twin Towers* (New York: Times Books, 2005), pp. 98–99, 154–56.

20. "The Necessary Courage," *New York Times*, Sept. 13, 2001; "The Horror and the Heroes," *Washington Post*, Sept. 13, 2001; "Common Valor," *Wall Street Journal*, Sept. 14, 2001.

21. Jonathan Alter, "America Unchanged," *Newsweek*, Sept. 13, 2001, p. 50; Alter, "The New Shape of Patriotism," *Newsweek*, Oct. 1, 2001, p. 63; Alter, "Patriotism," *Newsweek*, Sept. 27, 2001, p. 78; Nancy Gibbs, "Mourning in America," *Time*, Sept. 24, 2001, p. 14.

22. Josh Tyrangiel, Michele Orecklin, et al., "Facing the End," *Time*, Sept. 24, 2001, p. 68; "Aftermath of Yesterday's Terrorist Attacks," CBS News, Sept. 12, 2001; "America under Attack, CNN Live Event," CNN, Sept. 12, 2001; Charles Lane and John Mintz, "Bid to Thwart Hijackers May Have Led to Pa. Crash," *Washington Post*, Sept. 13, 2001.

23. Jere Longman, *Among the Heroes* (New York: HarperCollins, 2002), pp. 111, 204, 206–7; Matthew L. Wald, "New Details in Battle of Hijackers and Passengers to Control Plane," *New York Times*, July 23, 2004; Josh Tyrangiel, Michele Orecklin, et al., "Facing the End," *Time*, Sept. 24, 2001, p. 68; Charlotte Faltermayer, "The Team Player, Todd Beamer," *Time*, Dec. 31, 2001–Jan. 7, 2002, p. 108; "Lyz Glick and Lisa Beamer Talk about Their Husbands," *Good Morning America*, ABC News, Sept. 18, 2001.

24. Tyrangiel, Orecklin, et al., "Facing the End"; Margie Mason, "Gay Hero Emerges from Hijackings," Associated Press, Oct. 22, 2001; Charlotte Faltermayer, "The Team Player, Todd Beamer," *Time*, Dec. 31, 2001–Jan. 7, 2002, p. 108; "Jere Longman, Author of *Among the Heroes*, Discusses New Details about Passengers on United Flight 93," *News with Brian Williams*, CNBC News, July 9, 2002.

25. Longman, *Among the Heroes*, pp. 157, 171–72, 176, 177–78; "Heroes of Flight 93," *Dateline*, NBC, Dec. 8, 2003; Evan Thomas, "A New Date of Infamy," *Newsweek*, Sept. 13, 2001, p. 22; "Alice Hoglan, Mother of United Flight 93 Hero Mark Bingham, Discusses the Calls She Made to Her Son the Morning of September 11th," *Good Morning America*, ABC News, March 29, 2002; Jon Barrett, *Hero of Flight 93: Mark Bingham* (Los Angeles: Advocate Books, 2002), p. 158; Paul Chadwick, "Sacrifice," *9-11 Artists Respond*, vol. 1 (Milwaukee, Ore.: Dark Horse Comics, Jan. 2002), pp. 15–18.

26. "No Greater Love," *Dateline*, NBC, Oct. 2, 2001.

27. Longman, *Among the Heroes*, pp. 123, 144.

28. *The 9/11 Commission Report* (New York: W. W. Norton, 2004), p. 14; Karen Breslau, Eleanor Clift, and Evan Thomas, "The Real Story of Flight 93," *Newsweek*, Dec. 3, 2001, p. 54; Lenore Skornal, *Heroes: 50 Stories of the American Spirit* (Philadelphia: Running Press, 2002), p. 12.

29. "President Discusses War on Terrorism in Address to the Nation, World Congress Center," transcript, Office of the Press Secretary, White House, Nov. 8, 2001, http://www.whitehouse.gov/news/releases/2001/11/20011108-13.html; Rena Pederson, "Todd Beamer's Gift for Others," *Dallas Morning News*, Dec. 23, 2001; Alexander Lane, "Flight 93 Hero's Fame Snowballs," Newhouse News Service, May 3, 2002; Charlotte Faltermayer, "The Team Player, Todd Beamer," *Time*, Dec. 31, 2001–Jan. 7, 2002, p. 108; "Debate over Use of a Phrase Tied to 9/11," *CBS Evening News*, Sept. 4, 2002.

30. Bryan Burrough, "Manifest Courage: The Story of Flight 93," *Vanity Fair*, Dec. 2001, p. 266.

31. Rachel Graves and Karen Masterson, "It Feels Like He's Here," *Houston Chronicle*, Sept. 11, 2002; Lisa Friedman, "Congress Awards Medals for 9/11 Heroism, Service," *Oakland Tribune*, Dec. 24, 2001; "Legislation Would Recognize Passengers' Bravery," *Rocky Mountain News*, Sept. 21, 2001; Debra Erdley, "Families Say All on Plane Should Be Declared Heroes," *Pittsburgh Tribune-Review*, Sept. 11, 2002, http://www.pittsburghlive.com/x/pittsburghtrib/news/specialreports/oneyearlater/s_90856.html.

32. Charles Krauthammer, "The Greater the Evil, the More It Disarms," *Time*, Sept. 24, 2001, p. 78; Nancy Gibbs, "Shadow of Fear," *Time*, Oct. 22, 2001, p. 24.

33. Bennett, *Why We Fight*, pp. 161–62.
34. Mark Steyn, "Local Heroes," *National Review*, Nov. 19, 2001, p. 34; Mike Carey, "Hellblazer: Exposed," *9-11*, vol. 2, p. 85.
35. Lisa Beamer with Ken Abraham, *Let's Roll!* (Wheaton: Tyndale House, 2002), pp. 100–101, 125, 127, 128, 307–8.

3: THE COWBOYS OF YESTERDAY

1. Dan Janison, "Minorities Not Out in Force," *Newsday*, May 4, 2001; Jane Latour, "Looking for a Fire Department That Looks Like New York," Dec. 3, 2001, Gothamgazette.com, http://www.gothamgazette.com/iotw/firedepartment/doc1 .shtml.
2. Stephen J. Dubner, "Looking for Heroes—and Finding Them," *New York Times*, Oct. 6, 2001; "The Firefighter: An American Hero," *People*, Dec. 31, 2001, p. 54.
3. Sally Jenkins, "Company of Heroes," *Washington Post*, Sept. 20, 2001; *The 9/11 Commission Report* (New York: W.W. Norton, 2004), p. 316; Tony Hendra, *Brotherhood* (New York: American Express, 2001), p. xvii.
4. "World Trade Center Task Force Interview, Firefighter Derek Brogan," Dec. 28, 2001, p. 24; "World Trade Center Task Force Interview, Firefighter James Murphy," Dec. 12, 2001, p. 12, *The Sept. 11 Records*, in http://graphics8.nytimes.com/ packages/html/nyregion/20050812_wtc_graphic/met_wtc_histories_full_01.html; Jim Dwyer and Michelle O'Donnell, "9/11 Firefighters Told of Isolation amid Disaster," *New York Times*, Sept. 9, 2005.
5. Jim Dwyer, Kevin Flynn, and Ford Fessenden, "Fatal Confusion: A Troubled Emergency Response; 9/11 Exposed Deadly Flaws in Rescue Plan," *New York Times*, July 7, 2002; Wayne Barrett and Dan Collins, *Grand Illusion: The Untold Story of Rudy Giuliani and 9/11* (New York: HarperCollins, 2006), p. 52; Dwyer and O'Donnell, "9/11 Firefighters Told of Isolation amid Disaster"; "World Trade Center Task Force Interview, Lt. Brian Becker," Oct. 9, 2001, p. 11, "World Trade Center Task Force Interview, Firefighter Nicholas Borrillo," Jan. 9, 2002, p. 6, "World Trade Center Task Force Interview, Lt. Neil Brosnan," Dec. 12, 2001, p. 9, "World Trade Center Task Force Interview, Lt. Robert Bohack," Jan. 9, 2002, p. 12, *The Sept. 11 Records*.
6. Michael Cooper, "City Told to Release Much of 9/11 Oral History," *New York Times*, March 25, 2005; "Eleventh Public Hearing," National Commission on Terrorist Attacks on the United States, May 19, 2004, http://www.9-11commis sion.gov/archive/hearing11/9-11commission_hearing_2004-05-19.htm; "Former NYC Mayor Testifies before 9/11 Commission," May 19, 2004, CNN, http:// transcripts.cnn.com/transcripts/0405/19/se.01.html.
7. Terry Golway, *So Others Might Live* (New York: Basic, 2002), p. xiii.
8. Patricia Leigh Brown, "Heavy Lifting Required: The Return of Manly Men," *New York Times*, Oct. 28, 2001; Olivia Barker, "The Hunk Factor," *USA Today*, Nov. 26, 2001; "Common Valor," *Wall Street Journal*, Sept. 14, 2001; Dermot McEvoy, "Demystifying the FDNY," *Publishers Weekly*, Sept. 9, 2002, p. 21.
9. Hendra, *Brotherhood*, p. 2.
10. "America Unites, Saving Lives and Helping the Victims," *Hannity & Colmes*, Fox News, Sept. 13, 2001.

11. Suzanne Herel, "The Latest Superhero—U.S. Firefighters," *San Francisco Chronicle*, Aug. 18, 2002.

12. Lloyd Robertson, "Firefighters Are a Hot Commodity in the Dating Game," *CTV News*, March 5, 2002; Valerie Gibson, "Firefighters Are Hot, Hot, Hot; Unprecedented Female Admiration," *Toronto Sun*, May 5, 2002; Catherine Townsend, "Hearts on Fire," *New York*, Oct. 22, 2001; Barker, "The Hunk Factor"; Tanya Corrin, "Forget *Sex and the City*; All the Nice Girls in New York Love a Fireman," *Observer*, Oct. 14, 2001, p. 5; Emily Bittner, "Looking for Mr. Real," *Orange County Register*, Dec. 7, 2001.

13. Barker, "The Hunk Factor"; Robertson, "Firefighters Are a Hot Commodity in the Dating Game"; Townsend, "Hearts on Fire"; Maureen Dowd, "Hunks and Brutes," *New York Times*, Nov. 28, 2001.

14. Lisa Birnbach, "How Singles Are Thinking since 9/11," *The Early Show*, CBS News, Nov. 7, 2001.

15. Bittner, "Looking for Mr. Real."

16. Gibson, "Firefighters Are Hot, Hot, Hot"; Chris Smith, "Smoldering Fires of 9/11," *New York*, March 18, 2002.

17. "Firefighters: America's Real-Life Superheroes," CNN, Nov. 1, 2001, http://archives.cnn.com/2001/US/11/01/rec.firefighter.heroes/index.html; Andrew D. Arnold, "Will Superheroes Meet Their Doom?" *Time*, Oct. 2, 2001; Herel, "The Latest Superhero—U.S. Firefighters"; "Joe Quesada Discusses Their New Comic Series," *Today*, NBC, June 4, 2002; Chuck Austen and David Finch, *The Call of Duty: The Brotherhood* (New York: Marvel Comics, 2002).

18. "A Collection of 30-Something Political Firefighter Cartoons Related to the World Trade Center Disaster," Postroad.com, http://postroad.com/9-11/; Hendra, *Brotherhood*; "September 11th Remembered in Cartoons," *Daryl Cagle's Professional Cartoonists Index*, http://cagle.msnbc.com/news/9-11Remembered/main.asp.

19. Lisa Rosetta, "Scores Fear Escape Means Losing All," *Salt Lake Tribune*, Sept. 6, 2005; "The American Heroes Fund of the Polo Ralph Lauren Foundation," advertisement, *Time*, Oct. 8, 2001, pp. 48–49.

20. Frank H. Boehm, "When the Hero Wept," *New York Times*, Dec. 5, 2001; 9/11, dir. James Hanlon, Gédéon Naudet, and Jules Naudet, 2002.

21. William Langewiesche, *American Ground: Unbuilding the World Trade Center* (New York: North Point Press, 2003), pp. 69, 70, 71, 96.

22. Jenkins, "Company of Heroes"; Patricia Leigh Brown, "Heavy Lifting Required: The Return of Manly Men," *New York Times*, Oct. 28, 2001.

23. James Wolcott, "Over, Under, Sideways, Down," *Vanity Fair*, Dec. 2001, p. 158; Christopher Hitchens, "For Patriot Dreams," *Vanity Fair*, Dec. 2001, p. 148; Steyn, "Local Heroes."

24. Kate O'Beirne, "Men of the Hour," *National Review*, Sept. 21, 2001, http://www.nationalreview.com/kob/kob092101.shtml; Charlotte Allen, "Return of the Guy," *Women's Quarterly*, Winter 2002; "What Women Think about Modern Manhood," *American Enterprise*, Sept. 2003, http://www.taemag.com/issues/issueid.152/toc.asp.

25. Peggy Noonan, "Welcome Back, Duke," *Wall Street Journal*, Oct. 12, 2001.

26. Lou Marano, "Maleness Makes a Comeback," UPI, Oct. 17, 2001.

27. John Kass, "As War Looms, It's OK to Let Boys Be Boys Again," *Chicago Tribune*, Nov. 10, 2002.

28. Phil McCombs, "Comeback of the Alpha Male," *Washington Post*, March 16, 2003.

29. Dan Neal, "Real Men Fight Fires, Win Wars, Push Pencils," *Palm Beach Post*, Oct. 21, 2001.

30. "To Our Readers," *Time*, Sept. 14, 2001, p. 1; "The Heroes," *Newsweek*, Sept. 27, 2001, p. 46; "Pain and Suffering," *Newsweek*, Sept. 13, 2001, p. 17.

31. "Women at Ground Zero Honored at Awards Dinner," Legal Momentum [formerly NOW LDEF] news release, Nov. 20, 2001; Susan Hagen and Mary Carouba, *Women at Ground Zero* (Indianapolis: Alpha, 2002), pp. 87, 92–95, 110–13, 212–15.

32. Personal interview with Maureen McFadden, Oct. 12, 2005.

33. Ibid.; *The Women of Ground Zero: A Documentary*, NOW Legal Defense and Education Fund, 2001; Hagen and Carouba, *Women at Ground Zero*.

34. Anne Nelson, *The Guys* (Dramatist's Play Service, 2003); J. R. Moehringer, "Response to Terror," *Los Angeles Times*, Oct. 1, 2001; Dan Rather, "Band of Brothers," *60 Minutes II*, CBS News, Nov. 21, 2001; Jim Ritter, "Heart, Lungs and Stairs," *Chicago Sun-Times*, Feb. 25, 2002; Barbara Stewart, "Capturing for Generations the Agony of a Single Day," *New York Times*, Feb. 23, 2002; Suzanne C. Ryan, "TV & Radio," *Boston Globe*, Feb. 22, 2002; "Alarm," *Rescue Me*, FX Networks, Sept. 15, 2004; "Justice," *Rescue Me*, FX Networks, Sept. 13, 2005.

35. Terese M. Floren, "Too Far Back for Comfort," *Firework*, Oct. 2001, http://www.wfsi.org/resources/archive/article_archive.php?article=12.

36. Philip Shenon, "2 Women Win Bias Suit against Fire Dept.," *New York Times*, Dec. 9, 1983; Jan Jarboe Russell, "Fire'men' Weren't the Only Heroes Risking Lives on Sept. 11," *San Antonio Express-News*, Nov. 25, 2001.

37. Beth Henary, "Identity Politics at Ground Zero," *Weekly Standard*, Jan. 10, 2002, http://www.weeklystandard.com/Content/Public/Articles/000/000/000/758tarhz.asp; Jonathan Turley, "Airbrushing History with Divisiveness," *Los Angeles Times*, Jan. 18, 2002.

38. Juliet Eilperin, "Sept. 11 Video Launches Effort for Recovery Funds for Women," *Washington Post*, Dec. 28, 2001.

39. Wendy McElroy, "NOW Grabs for WTC Funds," ifeminists.com, Jan. 8, 2002, http://www.ifeminists.com/introduction/editorials/2002/0108.html; John Elvin, "Vultures Gather Over $11 Billion Disaster Relief," *Insight on the News*, Feb. 18, 2002.

40. "Interview with Kim Gandy," *Hannity & Colmes*, Fox News, Jan. 8, 2002.

41. E-mails received by NOW LDEF, Jan. 2002.

42. Pro-Life America also announced its intention to counter with a "'Ground Zero' LoveMatters Project," which would inundate hundreds of schools with *LoveMatters*, an antiabortion periodical featuring celebrity endorsements. "When college and high school students pick up *LoveMatters.com*," the solicitation letter advised, "it's almost impossible for them not to be drawn to the famous faces and pro-morality words of celebrities such as Mel Gibson, supermodels and actresses Kim Alexis and Kathy Ireland, pro basketball star A. C. Green, actor Kirk Cameron, Grammy-winning vocalist Rebecca St.

James, and more." "Planned Parenthood of New York City Offers Free Reproductive Health Care," Planned Parenthood of New York City, press release,
Sept. 19, 2001, http://www.ppnyc.org/homepage.html; "Planned Parenthood Offered Free Abortions to Women Traumatized by the Sept. 11 Terrorist Attack,"
Pro-Life America, http://www.prolife.com/FrPavoneNYCrisis.htm.

43. "Interview with Kathy Rodgers," *The O'Reilly Factor*, Fox News, Jan. 22, 2002.

44. Deborah L. Rhode, "Job Bias Persists," *National Law Journal*, March 5, 2002,
p. A21; "Annual Report 2004: Women in the Industry," New York Building Congress, 2004; Kay Miller, "It's Hard to Be a 24/7 Hero," *Star Tribune*, Jan. 13, 2002;
Seth Stern, "Women Firefighters Struggle for First Rung," *Christian Science Monitor*, Dec. 3, 2001; Barry Adams, "Female Firefighters Are Not Rare in City Department; Madison Contrasts Sharply with New York City," *Wisconsin State Journal*,
March 22, 2002; "Snapshots of New York: 1993 and 2003," *New York Times*, Dec 14,
2003; Latour, "Looking for a Fire Department That Looks Like New York."

45. Joseph A. Slobodzian, "Women Lose Key Ally in Bias Suit vs. SEPTA, *Philadel-
phia Inquirer*, Oct. 3, 2001; Vanessa Blum, "The Fight Within; Equality in the
Justice Department," *Recorder*, Sept. 19, 2003; "Slip-Sliding Away: The Erosion
of Hard-Won Gains for Women under the Bush Administration," National
Women's Law Center, April 2004, http://www.nwlc.org/pdf/AdminRecordOn
Women2004.pdf; Doug Huron, "No More Enforcers?" *Legal Times*, May 19,
2003; Dan Eggen, "Civil Rights Focus Shift Roils Staff at Justice," *Washington
Post*, Nov. 13, 2005; "Under Scrutiny: The Effect of Consent Decrees on the
Representation of Women in Sworn Law Enforcement," National Center for
Women and Policing, Spring 2003.

46. Floren, "Too Far Back for Comfort"; personal interview with Margie Moore, director, National Center for Women and Policing, Dec. 7, 2002; personal interview with Penny Harrington, Dec. 11, 2005.

47. See, for instance, the responses to the March 18, 2002, *Boston Globe* story,
"Women Firefighters Say Sept. 11 Has Made Their Profession Wrongly Seem
All Male," on FreeRepublic.com and Boston.com; http://www.freerepublic
.com/focus/f-news/648654/posts; http://www.boston.com/dailynews/075/nation/
Women_firefighters_say_Sept_11P.shtml.

48. Nancy MacLean, "The Hidden History of Affirmative Action," *Feminist Studies*
25 (Spring 1999): 43–44; Suzanne Daley, "Sex Bias Lingers in Firehouses of
New York," *New York Times*, Dec. 8, 1986; Miller, "It's Hard to Be a 24/7 Hero";
Hagen and Carouba, *Women at Ground Zero*, pp. 216–17.

49. James Taranto, "Best of the Web," *Wall Street Journal*, March 18, 2002, http://
www.opinionjournal.com/best/?id=105001783; "Comments from 'Best of the
Web,'" March 18, 2002, http://www.freerepublic.com/focus/f-news/648654/posts.

50. Hagen and Carouba, *Women at Ground Zero*, pp. 301–3, 311–12; Mike Kelly,
"Stories from the Wreckage," *Record*, Feb. 17, 2002; "9/11 Mother's Day Tribute,"
Oprah Winfrey Show, May 10, 2002.

4: PERFECT VIRGINS OF GRIEF

1. "Sudden Tragedy: Fiancées and Wives Left Behind," *Montel Williams Show*,
Paramount, syndicated, April 24, 2002.

2. Jeff Glasser, "Coming to Grips with the Pain," *U.S. News & World Report*, Sept. 16, 2002, p. 27; "Invisible Mourners," *Boston Globe*, Nov. 17, 2002.

3. Greg Barrett, "For Families of Victims, No Holiday from Pain of 9-11," Gannett News Service, Nov. 16, 2001; Katie Couric, "Wives and Mothers of Victims of Flight 93 Discuss Loved Ones," *NBC Nightly News*, March 11, 2002; Deborah Petersen Swift, "She's Raising Her Daughter; She's Overseeing the Building of Their New House; and She's Getting Used to the Rest of Her Life," *Hartford Courant*, Jan. 27, 2002; Diane Sawyer, "Looking Back at the Victims and Families and Victims of the 9/11 Terrorist Attacks," *Good Morning America*, ABC News, March 11, 2002; Barbara Walters, "Families Left Behind, Effects of 9/11," ABC News, Sept. 11, 2002.

4. Personal interview with Marian Fontana, Dec. 13, 2006.

5. Ibid.

6. Gail Sheehy, *Middletown, America* (New York: Random House, 2005), p. 88; Bill O'Reilly, "Interview with Lynda Fiori and Elizabeth MacDonald," *The O'Reilly Factor*, Fox News, Oct. 4, 2001. See also "Talking Points," Oct. 5, 2001; "Personal Stories," Oct. 9, 2001; "Interview with Michael Taylor," Oct. 9, 2001; "Personal Stories," Oct. 16, 2001.

7. Meryl Gordon, "The Lives Left Behind," *New York*, Sept. 15, 2002.

8. Lesley J. Gordon, "Cupid Does Not Really Give Way to Mars: The Marriage of LaSalle Corbell and George E. Pickett," in *Intimate Strategies of the Civil War: Military Commanders and Their Wives*, ed. Carol K. Bleser and Lesley J. Gordon (New York: Oxford University Press, 2001), pp. 73, 76–78, 84–86. See also "Inquiring Minds: Michael Vorenberg on Lisa Beamer and Widow Activism," *George Street Journal*, Brown University, Feb. 1, 2002.

9. Diane Sawyer, "Lyz Glick and Lisa Beamer Talk about Their Husbands," *Good Morning America*, ABC News, Sept. 18, 2001.

10. Galina Espinoza, Thomas Fields-Meyer, et al., "Small Blessings," *People*, Feb. 25, 2002, p. 48; Carol Wallace, "Behind the Scenes," *People*, Feb. 25, 2002, p. 1.

11. Diane Sawyer, "63 Reasons to Hope," *Primetime Live*, ABC News, Aug. 29, 2002.

12. Katherine Roth, "102 Widows Gave Birth after Terrorist Attacks," Associated Press, Sept. 11, 2002; "Infant Care Project," Independent Women's Forum, Dec. 1, 2002, IWF.org, http://www.iwf.org/archives/archive_detail.asp?ArticleID=354; "Bringing Up Baby," *Wall Street Journal*, Sept. 6, 2002, http://www.opinion journal.com/taste/?id=110002223; Maggie Gallagher, "War Widows of 9/11," uExpress.com, Sept. 10, 2002, http://www.uexpress.com/maggiegallagher/index .html?uc_full_date=20020910.

13. "Lisa Beamer: A Young Widow's Profile in Courage," *People*, Dec. 31, 2002, p. 89; Rena Pederson, "Todd Beamer's Gift for Others," *Dallas Morning News*, Dec. 27, 2001; "Interview with Lisa Beamer," *Larry King Live*, CNN, Feb. 22, 2002; "Lisa Beamer Discusses Her New Book," *Larry King Live*, Aug. 23, 2002; "Lisa Beamer at Christmas Tree," *Larry King Live*, Dec. 24, 2001.

14. "America Fights Back," ABC News, Sept. 18, 2001.

15. Mark Shields, "Public Servants Personify Heroism," *Seattle Post-Intelligencer*, Sept. 17, 2001.

16. "Lisa Beamer at Christmas Tree."

17. "Lisa Beamer Talks about How She Feels about Her Husband Being Praised for His Courage aboard Flight 93 by President Bush," *Good Morning America*, ABC News, Sept. 21, 2001.

18. Beamer, *Let's Roll!*, p. 222.

19. Gina Piccalo, "A Widow's Story," *Los Angeles Times*, Aug. 26, 2002; Beamer, *Let's Roll!*, pp. 241, 264–70, 275–77, 303; "Panel Discusses Terrorist Attacks," *Larry King Live*, CNN, Sept. 18, 2001; "The 25 Most Intriguing People 2001," *People*, Dec. 31, 2001, p. 89; Bob Minzesheimer, "Lisa Beamer: Mom First, Author Second," *USA Today*, Aug. 19, 2002; "Interview with Lisa Beamer," *American Morning with Paula Zahn*, CNN, Aug. 23, 2002; "Lisa Beamer at Christmas Tree"; Sawyer, "63 Reasons to Hope"; "Interview with Lisa Beamer," *Larry King Live*.

20. "Lisa Beamer at Christmas Tree," *Larry King Live*; "Interview with Lisa Beamer," *Larry King Live*; "Lisa Beamer Discusses Her New Book," *Larry King Live*.

21. "Interview with Lisa Beamer," *Larry King Live*; Longman, *Among the Heroes*, p. 244.

22. "Lisa Beamer at Christmas Tree"; "Interview with Lisa Beamer," *Larry King Live*.

23. Beamer, *Let's Roll!*, p. 221; Piccalo, "A Widow's Story."

24. A. R. Torres, "The Reluctant Icon," *Salon*, Jan. 25, 2002, http://archive.salon .com/mwt/feature/2002/01/25/widow_speaks/print.html; Longman, *Among the Heroes*, p. 248.

25. Lyz Glick and Dan Zegart, *Your Father's Voice* (New York: St. Martin's Press, 2004), pp. 30–31, 60–62.

26. Steve Fishman, "The Dead Wives Club, or Char in Love," *New York*, May 31, 2004, http://nymag.com/nymetro/news/sept11/features/9189/; Jeane MacIntosh and Matthew McDermott, "New Heartache for Hero's Dad—Fights Son's Gal over 9/11 Cash," *New York Post*, Jan. 19, 2004; "9/11 Widow in the Eye of a New Storm," UPI, Jan. 8, 2004.

27. Jeane MacIntosh, "FDNY Wives Get Burned—Many Dumped for 9/11 Widows," *New York Post*, Dec. 1, 2003; Jeane MacIntosh and Andy Geller, "Boob Implants and Vacations? 'I'd Like to Knock in Her 40G Teeth,'" *New York Post*, Jan. 8, 2004; Susan Dominus, "One Very Tangled Post-9/11 Affair," *New York Times Magazine*, May 23, 2004, p. 36.

28. MacIntosh and Geller, "Boob Implants and Vacations?"; Jeane MacIntosh, "Kids 'Lost' Firefighter Dad," *New York Post*, Dec. 1, 2003; Jeane MacIntosh, "Firing Away at Dad," *New York Post*, Dec. 17, 2003; Jeane MacIntosh, "I Needed New Beginning," *New York Post*, Jan. 9, 2004.

29. "Meet 9/11 Merry Widow," *Sunday Herald Sun*, Jan. 11, 2004; George Gordon, "Outrage as the Merry Widow of 9-11 Buys a New Bust and Facelift," *Daily Mail*, Jan. 9, 2004; "Hero's Widow in Spending Furore," *Western Daily Press*, Jan. 9, 2004; Paul Vitello, "Parents of 9/11 Victims Torn from Grandchildren," *New York Times*, Jan. 19, 2007; personal interview with Marian Fontana, Dec. 13, 2006.

30. Dominus, "One Very Tangled Post-9/11 Affair"; MacIntosh and Geller, "Boob Implants and Vacations?"; MacIntosh, "Kids 'Lost' Firefighter Dad"; MacIntosh, "Firing Away at Dad."

31. Dominus, "One Very Tangled Post-9/11 Affairs"; Kate Sheehy, "Why Flames of Passion Are Stoked," *New York Post*, Dec. 1, 2003; Jeane MacIntosh, "FDNY Wives Get Burned."

32. "The Dead Wives Club, or Char in Love," *New York*, May 31, 2004, http://nymag.com/nymetro/news/sept11/features/9189/; "Letters to the Editor," *New York*, June 14, 2004, p. 10.

33. "Just Four Moms from New Jersey," SourceWatch.com, http://www.source watch.org/index.php?title=just_four_moms_from_new_jersey.

34. Gail Sheehy, *Middletown, America* (New York: Random House, 2005), pp. 31, 33; "Unanswered Questions: 9/11 Widows Speak," *NOW with David Brancaccio*, PBS, Sept. 12, 2003, http://www.pbs.org/now/politics/911widows.html.

35. Sheehy, *Middletown, America*, p. 4; Kristen Breitweiser, *Wake-Up Call: The Political Education of a 9/11 Widow* (New York: Warner Books, 2006), pp. 22–23; "Unanswered Questions."

36. "Interview with Michael Moore, Jean Charles Brisard, Kristen Breitweiser," *Donahue*, MSNBC, Aug. 13, 2002; Gail Sheehy, "Four 9/11 Moms Battle Bush," *New York Observer*, Aug. 25, 2003.

37. "Unanswered Questions"; Sheehy, "Four 9/11 Moms Battle Bush"; "Testimony Prepared for the National Commission on Terrorist Attacks upon the United States; Testimony Secretary of Defense Donald H. Rumsfeld," transcript, March 23, 2004, U.S. Dept. of Defense, http://www.defenselink.mil/Speeches/Speech .aspx?SpeechID=105; Kristen Breitweiser, "A 'Mind-Numbingly Boring' Propaganda Film," *Salon*, Sept. 8, 2003, http://dir.salon.com/story/ent/tv/feature/2003/09/08/dc911/index.html.

38. "Unanswered Questions."

39. Breitweiser, *Wake-Up Call*, pp. 102–3.

40. Sheehy, "Four 9/11 Moms Battle Bush."

41. Mary Jacoby, "Attack Clues Ignored, Panel Says," *St. Petersburg Times*, Sept. 19, 2002; Breitweiser, *Wake-Up Call*, pp. 110–11, 202.

42. Sheehy, "Four 9/11 Moms Battle Bush."

43. Sheehy, *Middletown, America*, p. 310; Breitweiser, *Wake-Up Call*, pp. 122, 202–4; Shaun Waterman, "Sept. 11 New Jersey Widows Endorse Kerry," UPI, Sept. 14, 2004; Charlotte Hays, "Another Reason (If One Is Needed) to Love Dorothy Rabinowitz," *Inkwell*, Independent Women's Forum, May 13, 2004, http://www.iwf.org/inkwell/archive.asp?start=5/9/2004&end=5/15/2004; Charlotte Hays, "Dorothy Rabinowitz on Jersey Girls Fatigue," *Inkwell*, Independent Women's Forum, April 14, 2004, http://www.iwf.org/inkwell/archive.asp?start =4/11/2004&end=4/17/2004; Charlotte Allen, "Where's Our 9/11 Movie?" *Inkwell*, Independent Women's Forum, April 15, 2004, http://www.iwf.org/inkwell/archive.asp?start=4/11/2004&end=4/17/2004.

44. Dorothy Rabinowitz, "The 9/11 Widows: Americans Are Beginning to Tire of Them," *Wall Street Journal*, April 14, 2004, http://www.opinionjournal.com/medialog/?id=110004950; Julian Coman, "Families of 9/11 Are the 'Rock Stars of Grief,' Says Sister of Pentagon Pilot," *Telegraph*, June 27, 2004, http://www .telegraph.co.uk/news/main.jhtml?xml=/news/2004/06/27/wsept27.xml&sSheet=/news/2004/06/27/ixworld.html; Debra Burlingame, "Divided We Fall," *Wall*

    Street Journal, June 22, 2004, http://www.opinionjournal.com/editorial/feature .html?id=110005251; Burlingame, "Right War, Right Place, Right Time," *Wall Street Journal*, Oct. 2, 2004, http://www.opinionjournal.com/extra/?id=110005706; "CNN Live Event: John McCain, Rudy Giuliani Address Republican National Convention," transcript, CNN, Aug. 30, 2004, http://transcripts.cnn.com/ transcripts/0408/30/se.01.html.

45. Ann Gerhart, "Driven by Their 9/11 Fears, Widows Pin Hopes on Kerry," *Washington Post*, Sept. 15, 2004; Breitweiser, *Wake Up-Call*, p. 213; "Personal Story—9/11 Widows Get Political," *The O'Reilly Factor*, Fox News, Sept. 22, 2004; Mark Steyn, "Ann Coulter: America's Fiery, Blond Commentatrix," Macleans.ca, http://www.macleans.ca/culture/books/article.jsp?content=2006 0626_129699_129699; "The Politics of 9/11," *Wall Street Journal*, March 10, 2004, http://www.opinionjournal.com/editorial/feature.html?id=110004797; Ann Coulter, *Godless* (New York: Crown Forum, 2006), pp. 103, 112.

46. Jerry Seper, "Survivor Groups Hit for Use of 9/11," *Washington Times*, May 25, 2004; "The Politics of 9/11"; "Anti-Bush 9-11 Families Backed by Heinz Foundation," *Rush Limbaugh*, March 9, 2004, http://www.rushlimbaugh.com /home/daily/site_030904/content/see_i_told_you_so.guest.html; Allan P. Duncan, "A Not So Mighty Wind," March 10, 2004, http://www.opednews. com/duncan031004_limbaugh.htm.

47. Colleen Kelly and David Potorti (codirectors of September 11th Families for Peaceful Tomorrows), letter, *Washington Times*, May 28, 2004; "Reader Responses—'The 9/11 Widows,' Dorothy Rabinowitz," *Wall Street Journal*, http://www.opinionjournal.com/medialog/responses.html?article_id=110004950; "Where Are the 9/11 Widows?" Wizbangblog.com, July 22, 2004, http://wiz bangblog.com/2004/07/22/where-are-the-911-widows.php; "Understanding of 9/11," FreeRepublic.com, June 24, 2005, http://www.freerepublic.com/focus/f-news/ 1430250/posts; "Bush-Bashing 9/11 Widow is Hillary Clinton's SOTU Guest (Monica Gabrielle)," FreeRepublic.com, Jan. 31, 2006, http://www.freerepublic.com/ focus/f-news/1568669/posts.

48. Personal interview with Marian Fontana, Dec. 13, 2006.

49. Marian Fontana, *A Widow's Walk* (New York: Simon and Schuster, 2005), p. 91.

5: NESTING NATION

1. "Angel or Devil? Viewers See Images in the Smoke," ClickonDetroit.com, http://urbanlegends.about.com/gi/dynamic/offsite.htm?site=http://www.clickon detroit.com/sh/news/stories/nat%2Dnews%2D96283920010917%2D120936.html; Virginia Heffernan, "The Way We Live Now," *New York Times Magazine*, Oct. 14, 2001, p. 30.

2. Heffernan, "The Way We Live Now."

3. Nancy Gibbs, "Life on the Homefront," *Time*, Oct. 1, 2001, p. 10.

4. Ginia Bellafante, "Being Single in New York Is a Little Lonelier Now," *New York Times*, Sept. 30, 2001.

5. Ibid.; Joel Stein, "Nation on the Couch," *Time*, Oct. 1, 2001, p. 98; "How Singles Are Thinking Since 9/11," *The Early Show*, CBS, Nov. 7, 2001; Nancy Gibbs,

"We Gather Together," *Time*, Nov. 19, 2001, p. 28; Mimi Avins, "Out of the Rubble Comes a Need to Connect: Like a Big-Screen Romance, Finding a Long-Term Relationship Has Taken on a New Urgency since Sept. 11," *Los Angeles Times*, Nov. 25, 2001.

6. Dan Parker, "Tragedy Spawns Resolve," *Corpus Christi Caller-Times*, Jan. 1, 2002; Avins, "Out of the Rubble."

7. "How Stars' Lives Have Changed," *Star*, Oct. 26, 2001, p. 2, cited in S. Elizabeth Bird, "Taking It Personally," *Journalism after September 11*, ed. Barbie Zelizer and Stuart Allan (New York: Routledge, 2002), pp. 148–49; Ariel Levy, "Single in the New City: Serious Fun," *New York*, Feb. 11, 2002, p. 28.

8. Avins, "Out of the Rubble."

9. Amy Sohn, "The Convert," *New York*, Nov. 12, 2001, http://nymag.com/nymetro/nightlife/sex/columns/nakedcity/5364/index.html.

10. Gibbs, "We Gather Together"; Kimberly Stevens, "What to Do in a Crisis? Wed," *New York Times*, Sept. 23, 2001; Anne D'Innocenzio, "Weddings on the Rise since 9/11," Associated Press, Nov. 21, 2001; "Americans Not Terrified of Marriage," *Townsville Sun*, Nov. 22, 2001.

11. "Tower of Strength," *People*, Oct. 1, 2001, p. 59; Katharine Q. Seelye, "Tragedy Shifts Focus of Weddings," *New York Times*, Oct. 14, 2001; John Kass, "Without a Doubt, It's Time for Us to Applaud Mayor," *Chicago Tribune*, Sept. 20, 2001; Keith Morrison, "The Road to Recovery," *Dateline*, NBC, Oct. 1, 2001.

12. Seelye, "Tragedy Shifts Focus of Weddings"; Ann Curry, "Millie Martini Bratten of *Brides* Magazine Discusses More Weddings as a Result of the September 11 Attacks," *Today*, NBC News, Oct. 16, 2001.

13. "*Brides* Magazine's Latest Issue Advises Readers, 'A Wedding Sends a Powerful and Comforting Signal to the World,'" PR Newswire, Nov. 7, 2001; Leonard McCants and Rosemary Feitelberg, "Bridal Overcomes 'For Worse,'" *Women's Wear Daily*, Oct. 2, 2001.

14. Levy, "Single in the New City: Serious Fun"; "New York Magazine: Single in the New City," Topline Data Report, Global Strategy Inc., Jan. 8, 2002–Jan. 12, 2002, http://nymag.com/personals/articles/02/02/singles/topline.PDF.

15. Levy, "Single in the New City: Serious Fun."

16. Sarah Bernard, "Baby Talk," *New York*, Oct. 29, 2001, p. 17.

17. Gibbs, "We Gather Together"; Bernard, "Baby Talk."

18. "Interview with Nancy Taylor," *Larry King Live*, CNN, Sept. 21, 2001; "Nancy Taylor Talks about Life after the Death of Her Husband," *CBS Evening News*, Nov. 30, 2001.

19. Gibbs, "We Gather Together."

20. "American Society for Reproductive Medicine Launches First Ever National Public Health Campaign for Infertility Prevention," American Society for Reproductive Medicine, U.S. Newswire, Aug. 6, 2001.

21. Hilary E. MacGregor, "A New Ad Campaign Is Telling Many Women in Their 30s What They Already Know and Don't Want to Hear: Their Biological Clocks Are at the 11th Hour," *Sun-Sentinel*, Oct. 21, 2001; "American Society for Reproductive Medicine Launches"; "Misconceptions and Missed Conceptions,"

Washington Post, Nov. 6, 2001; "*Glamour's* Be-Fertile Guide for Women Who Want to Be Pregnant Someday . . . or Ever?" *Glamour*, Feb. 2002, p. 74.

22. "American Infertility Association to Provide Educational Program to Address Dire Need for Fertility Information," American Infertility Association, U.S. Newswire, Oct. 24, 2001; Rebecca Theim, "Study Reveals Fertility Misconceptions," *Chicago Tribune*, Oct. 24, 2001.

23. Sylvia Ann Hewlett, *Creating a Life: Professional Women and the Quest for Children* (New York: Miramax Books, 2002), pp. 25–26, 85; Nancy Gibbs, "Making Time for a Baby," *Time*, April 15, 2002, p. 48.

24. Hewlett, *Creating a Life*, pp. 86, 87, 126–27, 201; Stephanie J. Ventura, Joyce A. Martin, Sally C. Curtin, et al., "Births: Final Data for 1999," National Center for Health Statistics, *National Vital Statistics Reports* 49 (April 17, 2001).

25. "When Should I Have a Baby?" *Oprah Winfrey Show*, Harpo, Inc., syndicated, May 1, 2002; "The Biological Clock," *60 Minutes*, CBS, June 30, 2002; Nancy Gibbs, "Making Time for a Baby."

26. Vanessa Grigoriadis, "Baby Panic," *New York*, May 20, 2002, http://nymag.com/nymetro/urban/family/features/6030/index1.html.

27. Julie Scelfo, "A 9-11 Baby Boomlet," *Newsweek*, June 3, 2002, p. 42; "Post-9/11 Baby Boom," *The Early Show*, CBS, June 11, 2002; Jan Galletta, "Hospitals Bracing for 9-11 Baby Boom," *Chattanooga Times Free Press*, June 9, 2002; Hector Saldana, "Post–Sept. 11 Baby Boom Hits Due Date; Area Hospitals Are Preparing for a Radical Increase in Deliveries," *San Antonio Express-News*, June 11, 2002.

28. Alisa DeMao, "Baby Boom Is Just Beginning," *Augusta Chronicle*, June 25, 2002; Michelle Wagner, "9/11 Baby Boom May Come Months Later Here," *Virginian-Pilot*, June 30, 2002; "Interview with Ellie Krieger," *Saturday Morning News*, CNN, Aug. 17, 2002.

29. Elizabeth Hays, "Post-9/11 Baby Boom Up for Debate," *Daily News*, June 16, 2002; Amy Kelley, "No Post–Sept. 11 Baby Boom Expected," *Journal News*, July 4, 2002; Maia Davis, "Hopes Dashed; Sept. 11 Didn't Spur Baby Boom," *Record*, Aug. 27, 2002; "Report Shows Birth Rate Reaches Record Low," National Center for Health Statistics, U.S. Newswire, June 25, 2003; "Health Statistics: U.S. Teen Birth Rate Continues to Decline," *Medical Letter on the CDC & FDA*, Jan. 11, 2004, p. 31.

30. Rebecca Gardyn, "The Home Front," *American Demographics*, Dec. 2001.

31. Peggy O'Crowley, "More Women Are Choosing to Make a Career Out of Raising Their Children," *Newhouse News Service*, April 18, 2002; Ann Marsh, "Mommy, Me and an Advanced Degree," *Los Angeles Times*, Jan. 6, 2002.

32. Nancy Dillon, "Analyst Makes Kids New Career; More Women 'Opting-Out,'" *Daily News*, March 29, 2004.

33. "Appreciating Your Life," *Oprah Winfrey Show*, Nov. 21, 2001.

34. Stacey Colino, "How Have You Changed Since 9/11," *Shape*, Sept. 1, 2002, p. 32.

35. Veronica MacDonald, "Enticing Uninspired Consumers: After Sept. 11, Challenges Remain on How to Get Women to the Fragrance Counter," *Household & Products Industry*, July 1, 2002, p. 56.

36. Gardyn, "The Home Front."

37. Kenneth Auchincloss, "We Shall Overcome," *Newsweek*, Sept. 24, 2001, p. 18; Gardyn, "The Home Front"; Levy, "Single in the New City: Serious Fun"; State

Farm Insurance ad, *Time*, April 15, 2002, p. 55; Kenneth Cole ad, *Vanity Fair*, April 2002, pp. 62–63.

38. Gibbs, "We Gather Together"; Cathleen McGuigan, "Nesting Instincts," *Newsweek*, Nov. 26, 2001, p. 72; Megan Sexton, "Furniture Designers Emphasize Comfort, Cocooning," *Orlando Sentinel*, Nov. 1, 2001; "The Changing Structure of the Home Remodeling Industry," Joint Center for Housing Studies of Harvard University, 2005, http://www.jchs.harvard.edu/publications/remodeling/remodeling2005.pdf.

39. David Ignatius, "Crisis Couture," *Washington Post*, Dec. 2, 2001; Sarah Baxter, "America Gets Back into Bed with the Bombshell," *Sunday Times*, Dec. 2, 2001; Cheryl Lu-Lien Tan, "White Out; the Seasons's 'It' Color Is White," *Baltimore Sun*, 2001, March 17, 2002; Anne Bratskeir, "A Kinder, Gentler Spring," *Newsday*, March 25, 2002, p. B19; Marylin Johnson, "A Clean Slate for Spring," *Atlanta Journal-Constitution*, March 24, 2002; Ginia Bellafante, "Sell That Dress; Back to Basics in Spring Advertising," *New York Times*, Feb. 5, 2002.

40. Mary Tannen, "Jingo Belle," *New York Times Magazine*, Oct. 10, 2004, p. 60; Baxter, "America Gets Back into Bed with the Bombshell."

41. Hector Saldana, "All Things Military Are Cool," *San Antonio Express-News*, Dec. 16, 2001; Melissa Grace and Emily Guest, "FDNY Items Big Sellers," *Daily News*, Nov. 2, 2001; FDNY Fire Zone Store online, http://firezone.stores.yahoo.net/; "Still Got Legs; Fashion Week Draws to a Close, Proving That Men's Wear Still Has a Home in New York," *Daily News Record*, Feb. 24, 2003; Nadra Kareem, "Army Gear; Military Fashions Make Comeback after Start of Iraq War," *El Paso Times*, March 26, 2003; David Brooks, "Hummers to Harleys," *New York Times*, Oct. 4, 2003.

42. Steve McClellan, "Prime Time Is Family Time," *Broadcasting & Cable*, April 15, 2002, p. 26; James Poniewozik, "Look Back in Angst," *Time*, Sept. 23, 2002, p. 73.

43. Warren St. John, "What Men Want: Neanderthal TV," *New York Times*, Dec. 11, 2005; Johnny Diaz, "Metrosexuals Are So Last Year; We're in the Middle of a Menaissance," *Boston Globe*, June 20, 2006; Lizzie Skurnick, "Chick Lit, the Sequel: Yummy Mummy," *New York Times*, Dec. 17, 2006; Jane Mayer, "Whatever It Takes," *New Yorker*, Feb. 19–26, 2007, p. 66.

44. Kati Marton, "A New Chapter for Laura Bush," *Newsweek*, Oct. 8, 2001, p. 33; Martha Brant, "The Chief Caretaker," *Newsweek*, Sept. 27, 2001, p. 69; Lesley Stahl, "Opinions of Laura Bush on How People Should Handle the Terror Attacks on America," *60 Minutes*, CBS News, Sept. 23, 2001; "How to Talk to Children about America under Attack," *Oprah Winfrey Show*, Sept. 18, 2001.

45. Marilyn Gardner, "Changing Career Values Make Room for Family," *Christian Science Monitor*, May 1, 2002; Richard Reeves, "Hughes' Changed Priorities," *Charleston Gazette*, April 28, 2002; Fran Spielman, "Hughes Quits for Something Even Better," *Chicago Sun-Times*, April 28, 2002; Richard Dunham, "Karen Hughes and the Courage to Quit," *BusinessWeek Online*, April 29, 2002; "Karen Hughes's Wise Decision," *Providence Journal-Bulletin*, May 4, 2002; Carl Wernicke, "It's Sometimes Good to Take a Step Back," *Pensacola News Journal*, April 28, 2002; John Rolfe, "There's No One like Mom for the Home," *Pough-*

keepsie Journal, May 12, 2002; Maureen Dowd, "No, Karl Didn't Ice Her," *New York Times*, April 24, 2002.

46. Peggy Noonan, "Back to Life," *Wall Street Journal*, April 26, 2002, http://www.opinionjournal.com/columnists/pnoonan/?id=105001978.

47. Rolfe, "There's No One Like Mom for the Home"; John Kasich, "Interview with Susan Estrich and Nancy M. Pfotenhauer," *The O'Reilly Factor*, April 24, 2002; Bill Plante, "Presidential Adviser Karen Hughes Discusses Her Decision to Leave the White House to Spend More Time with Her Family," *The Early Show*, CBS News, July 8, 2002.

48. Barbara Downs, "Fertility of American Women: June 2002," *Current Population Reports*, U.S. Census Bureau, Oct. 2003, http://www.census.gov/prod/2003pubs/p20-548.pdf; Cheryl L. Reed, "'Supermoms' Draw Line in Sandbox," *Chicago Sun-Times*, Oct. 10, 2004; Jerry Miller, "Giving Up Careers for Their Kids," *Union Leader*, May 9, 2004; Claudia Wallis, "The Case for Staying Home," *Time*, March 22, 2004, p. 50.

49. Lisa Belkin, "The Opt-Out Revolution," *New York Times Magazine*, Oct. 26, 2003, p. 42.

50. Heather Boushey, "Are Women Opting Out? Debunking the Myth," Center for Economic and Policy Research, Dec. 2005, http://www.cepr.net/publications/opt_out_2005_11.pdf.

51. Louise Story, "Many Women at Elite Colleges Set Career Path to Motherhood," *New York Times*, Sept. 20, 2005; Louise Story, "Background-Reporting on the Aspirations of Young Women," nytimes.com, Sept. 23, 2005.

52. Ibid.; Jack Shafer, "Press Box: Weasel-Words Rip My Flesh," *Slate*, Sept. 20, 2005, http://www.slate.com/id/2126636/.

53. Robin Herman, "A Revived Debate: Babies, Careers, 'Having It All,'" letter, *New York Times*, Sept. 22, 2005.

6: PRESIDENT OF THE WILD FRONTIER

1. Marsha Kranes, "Bush Opens His Arms and His Heart to WTC Teen," *New York Post*, May 7, 2004.

2. C. K. Rairden, "Bush Photo with Teen Shows Conviction and Compassion," *Washington Dispatch*, May 10, 2004, http://www.washingtondispatch.com/opinion/article%5F9003.shtml; "Ashley's Story," transcript, Oct. 19, 2004, Political Advertising Resource Center, http://www.umdparc.org/adanalysisashleysstory.htm; Judy Keen and Mark Memmott, "Most Expensive TV Campaign Goes for Emotions," *USA Today*, Oct. 19, 2004; Marsha Kranes, "Bush Opens His Arms and His Heart to WTC Teen"; Les Csorba, "Let Bush Be Himself," *Chicago Tribune*, Aug. 25, 2004.

3. John Kiesewetter, "Huggins Story Big Draw on Internet," *Cincinnati Enquirer*, Aug. 25, 2005; "Bush Photo with Teen Becomes Internet Phenomenon," postings on June 24, 2004, FreeRepublic.com, http://www.freerepublic.com/focus/news/1159791/posts?page=1; "Election Analysis," *Dolans Unscripted*, CNNfn, Oct. 29, 2004; Eric Boehlert, "Ad Blitz," *Salon*, Oct. 25, 2004; Howard Kurtz, "Ads Aiming Straight for the Heart," *Washington Post*, Oct. 27, 2004.

4. Susan Allen, "Ad Analysis," Political Advertising Resource Center, University of Maryland, Nov. 10, 2004, http://www.umdparc.org/AdAnalysisAshleysStory.htm.

5. Dave Shiflett, "Bush vs. Brush," *National Review*, Jan. 28, 2002, p. 28.

6. Sid Evans and Bob Marshall, "A Sporting Debate," *Field & Stream*, Oct. 2004, http://www.fieldandstream.com/fieldstream/columnists/article/ 0,13199,702716,00.html; "Bush vs. Kerry," *Outdoor Life*, Oct. 2004, http:// www.outdoorlife.com/outdoor/news/article/0,19912,696240-4,00.html; Charles Duhigg, "Gutsy by Nature?" *Los Angeles Times*, Oct. 12, 2004.

7. Evans and Marshall, "A Sporting Debate"; "Bush vs. Kerry."

8. "Guns and Candidates: The Silent Issue," *Judy Woodruff's Inside Politics*, CNN, Dec. 4, 2003; James Kuhnhenn, "Kerry, Party Court Gun Owners' Votes," *Philadephia Inquirer*, Aug. 15, 2004; Jill Lawrence and Judy Keen, "Election Is Turning into a Duel of the Manly Men," *USA Today*, Sept. 22, 2004.

9. Carl Weiser, "Campaigns Have Gun Issue in Their Sights," Gannett News Service, Oct. 21, 2004; Craig Gilbert, "Bringing the Candidate to Life," *Milwaukee Journal Sentinel*, July 5, 2004; Laura Blumenfeld, "Hunter, Dreamer, Realist," *Washington Post*, June 1, 2003.

10. Todd J. Gillman, "Hunter Kerry Targets Voters," *Dallas Morning News*, Oct. 22, 2004; Jodi Wilgoren, "Kerry on Hunting Photo-Op to Help Image," *New York Times*, Oct. 22, 2004; Kuhnhenn, "Kerry, Party Court Gun Owners' Votes"; Duhigg, "Gutsy by Nature?"; Julie Hirschfeld Davis, "Kerry Aims to Bag Gun Owners," *Baltimore Sun*, Sept. 15, 2004; Andrew Stuttaford, "The Deer Hunter," *National Review Online*, Oct. 26, 2004.

11. Kuhnhenn, "Kerry, Party Court Gun Owners' Votes"; Dan Frosch, "Gunning for the White House," *AlterNet*, April 27, 2004, http://www.alternet.org/story/ 18531/; Craig Gilbert, "Open Season," *Milwaukee Journal Sentinel*, Sept. 19, 2004.

12. Pat Robertson, "Politicians Targeting 'Sportsment,'" *State*, Oct. 31, 2004; Matea Gold, "Kerry Aims for Disparate Voters," *Los Angeles Times*, Oct. 22, 2004; Wilgoren, "Kerry on Hunting Photo-Op to Help Image"; Elisabeth Rosenthal, "The Gun Culture Counts in Presidential Politics, *International Herald Tribune*, Aug. 18, 2004; Katherine Mangu-Ward, "Trigger Happy," *Weekly Standard*, Sept. 27, 2004, p. 13; Paul Magnusson, "Stalking Deer Hunter Dads," *BusinessWeek*, Oct. 18, 2004, p. 112; Gillman, "Hunter Kerry Targets Voters."

13. "Kerry & Hunting," Fall 2003, http://www.sportsmenforkerry.com/jkhunting .htm; Harold Hough, "John Kerry, Hunter?" May 24, 2004, http://www.enter stageright.com/archive/articles/0504/0504kerryhunter.htm; Mark Steyn, "Kerry Can't Shoot Deer or Stop Terror," *Telegraph*, July 27, 2004, http://www.tele graph.co.uk/opinion/main.jhtml?xml=/opinion/2004/07/27/do2702.xml.

14. "Bush vs. Kerry"; Magnusson, "Stalking Deer Hunter Dads."

15. Lawrence and Keen, "Election Is Turning into a Duel of the Manly Men."

16. "Americans Turn to Guns Following Terror," Associated Press, Nov. 5, 2001; Al Baker, "Steep Rise in Gun Sales Reflects Post-Attack Fears," *New York Times*, Dec. 6, 2001.

17. Lee Hill Kavanaugh, "Number of Gun Sales Change Little since Terrorist Attacks," *Kansas City Star*, Oct. 21, 2001.

18. Philip Weiss, "When It Comes to War, the Sexes Still Split," *New York Observer*, Oct. 29, 2001, p. 1.

19. Jonathan Alter, "Time to Think about Torture," *Newsweek*, Nov. 5, 2001, p. 45; Krauthammer, "The Truth about Torture"; Krauthammer, "In Defense of Secret Tribunals, *Time*, Nov. 26, 2001, p. 104; Thomas L. Friedman, "World War III," *New York Times*, Sept. 13, 2001; Steve Dunleavy, "Simply Kill These Bastards," *New York Post*, Sept. 12, 2001.

20. Dan Eggen, "FBI Curbed in Tracking Gun Buyers," *Washington Post*, Nov. 18, 2003; Eric Lichtblau, "Terror Suspects Buying Firearms, U.S. Report Finds," *New York Times*, March 8, 2005; Baker, "Steep Rise in Gun Sales Reflects Post-Attack Fears."

21. Paul Farhi, "The Great Worry Divide," *Washington Post*, Nov. 29, 2001.

22. Jane Eisner, "Sexes' Anxiety Gap Might Save Us All," *Philadelphia Inquirer*, March 23, 2003; Garance Franke-Ruta, "Homeland Security Is for Girls," *Washington Monthly*, April 1, 2003, p. 10.

23. Karen Tumulty and Viveca Novak, "Goodbye, Soccer Mom. Hello, Security Mom," *Time*, June 2, 2003, p. 26; "The Impact of Terrorist Attacks on American Women," Greenberg Quinlan Rosner Research poll commissioned by the Center for Gender Equality, *Newswise*, Dec. 8, 2001, http://www.newswise.com/arti cles/view/?id=WOMEN2.CE2.

24. Tumulty and Novak, "Goodbye, Soccer Mom. Hello, Security Mom."

25. David Winston, "Security Moms Are Real," *New York Post*, Oct. 19, 2004; Siobhan Gorman, "The Issue That's AWOL," *National Journal*, Dec. 20, 2003; Lawrence and Keen, "Election Is Turning into a Duel of the Manly Men."

26. Mike Allen, "The Five (or More) W's," *Washington Post*, May 13, 2004; Alexandra Starr, "Desperately Seeking Single Women Voters," *BusinessWeek*, June 21, 2004, p. 126; Katherine M. Skiba, "Undecided Women Voters Vital to Bush," *Milwaukee Journal Sentinel*, Aug. 10, 2004; Nancy Gibbs, "What Do Women Want?" *Time*, Oct. 11, 2004, p. 30; "Interview with John Edwards," *Late Edition with Wolf Blitzer*, CNN, Oct. 10, 2004; "Laura Bush Delivers Remarks at the Republican National Convention," FDCH Political Transcripts, Aug. 31, 2004.

27. Kay R. Daly, "Happy 'Security' Moms Day," May 10, 2004, *GOPUSA*, http://www.gopusa.com/commentary/kdaly/.

28. Michelle Malkin, "Candidates Ignore 'Security Moms,' at Their Peril," *USA Today*, July 21, 2004; "September 11: A Memorial," CNN.com, http://www .cnn.com/SPECIALS/2001/memorial/lists/by-age/.

29. Anne Morse, "Mothers against Tolerating Terror," Independent Women's Forum, March, 4, 2004, http://www.iwf.org/issues/issues_detail.asp?ArticleID=524.

30. "Media Unskeptically Promote 'Security Moms' as Pivotal Constituency in 2004," Media Matters, Sept. 28, 2004, http://mediamatters.org/items/2004092 80004.

31. Richard Louv, "Myth of 'the Security Mom,'" *San Diego Union-Tribune*, Oct. 3, 2004; Noam Scheiber, "Mothers of Invention," *New Republic Online*, Sept. 24, 2004, http://www.tnr.com/doc.mhtml?i=express&s=scheiber092404; Dan DeLuce, "Myth of the 'Security Moms,'" *New York Beacon*, Oct. 27, 2004; Anna Greenberg, "Re: The Security Mom Myth—Updated," Greenberg Quinlan Rosner Research, Sept. 29, 2004, http://www.greenbergresearch.com/arti cles/1240/2019_security%20mom%20myth.pdf.

32. Steven Thomma and James Kuhnhenn, "Kerry's Message Misses Women," *Kansas City Star*, Sept. 25, 2004; Gibbs, "What Do Women Want?"; Charles Hurt, "Kerry Losing Ground with Women," *Washington Times*, Sept. 29, 2004.

33. Boehlert, "Ad Blitz."

34. Ibid.; Deborah Orin, "9/11 Ad Battle," *New York Post*, Oct. 20, 2004; Carl Weiser, "First Hug, Now Trip to Inaugural," *Cincinnati Enquirer*, Jan. 18, 2005; Breitweiser, *Wake-Up Call*, p. 224.

35. Breitweiser, *Wake-Up Call*, pp. 223–24.

36. Jason Zengerle, "False Dawn," *New Republic*, Oct. 31, 2004, http://www.tnr.com/doc.mhtml?i=20041108&s=zengerle110804.

37. Weiser, "First Hug, Now Trip to Inaugural"; "Ashley Faulker Discusses Her Role in Re-Election of President Bush by Appearing in Campaign Ad," *Today*, NBC, Jan. 20, 2005.

7: PRECIOUS LITTLE JESSI

1. Rick Bragg, *I Am a Soldier, Too: The Jessica Lynch Story* (New York: Vintage, 2004), back cover; Anna Cock, "Unmaking the Myth of Jessica Lynch," *Sunday Mail*, Nov. 30, 2001; Nancy Gibbs, "The Private Jessica Lynch," *Time*, Nov. 17, 2003, p. 24; Howard Kurtz, "Rick Bragg Quits at New York Times," *Washington Post*, May 29, 2003; Jack Shafer, "Rick Bragg's 'Dateline Toe Touch,'" May 23, 2003, *Slate*, http://www.slate.com/id/2083539/.

2. Gibbs, "The Private Jessica Lynch"; personal interview with Jessica Lynch, March 11, 2007.

3. "PFC Jessica Lynch's Rescue like Something out of a Movie," *News with Brian Williams*, CNBC, April 2, 2003.

4. Martha Brant, "She's Alive," *Newsweek Web Exclusive*, April 2, 2003, http://www.msnbc.msn.com/id/3068433/site/newsweek/; John Kampfner, "The Truth about Jessica," *Guardian*, May 15, 2003, http://www.guardian.co.uk/Iraq/Story/0,2763,956255,00.html; Susan Schmidt and Vernon Loeb, "She Was Fighting to the Death," *Washington Post*, April 3, 2003; Jim Garamone, "More Details on Lynch Rescue, 11 Bodies Found," American Forces Press Service, April 2, 2003, http://www.defenselink.mil/news/Apr2003/n04022003_200304023.html; Arnold Hamilton, "Military Details Daring Rescue," *Dallas Morning News*, April 3, 2003; Rory McCarthy, "War in the Gulf: Saving Private Lynch," *Guardian*, April 3, 2003.

5. "Central Command Briefing Transcript, Jessica Lynch/More Details of Her Rescue," U.S. State Dept., *Federal Information and News Dispatch*, April 5, 2003.

6. Ibid.; Brant, "She's Alive."

7. Brant, "She's Alive"; Jose Martinez, "Inside the Daring Nighttime Rescue," *Daily News*, April 3, 2002; Tim Shipman, "POW Jessica Saved in Just Six Minutes; Plucked from Death's Jaws," *Express*, April 3, 2002; Patrick Rogers, Peter Mikelbank, Rose Ellen O'Connor, et al., "Saved from Danger," *People*, April 21, 2003, p. 54; Dana Priest, William Booth, and Susan Schmidt, "A Broken Body, a Broken Story, Pieced Together," *Washington Post*, June 17, 2003; Nicole Winfield, "'I'm an American Soldier, Too,'" Associated Press, April 5, 2003.

8. "Central Command Briefing Transcript"; "The Capture and Rescue of U.S. Private 1st Class Jessica Lynch in An Nasiriya," *Today*, NBC, April 2, 2003; "POW Jessica Lynch Rescued by Marines," *Larry King Live*, CNN, April 1, 2003.

9. Kate Bishop, "Jessica in Safe Hands after Daring Midnight Rescue," *Birmingham Post*, April 3, 2003; Jillian Goold, "Saving Private Lynch," *Irish Examiner*, April 3, 2003.

10. Kampfner, "The Truth about Jessica"; "War Spin," BBC, May 18, 2003, http://news.bbc.co.uk/2/hi/programmes/correspondent/3007953.stm.

11. Kampfner, "The Truth about Jessica"; Azmi Bishara, "Casualty of Truth," *Al-Ahram Weekly*, June 5–11, 2003, http://weekly.ahram.org.eg/2003/641/op2.htm; Richard Lloyd Parry, "So Who Really Did Save Private Jessica?" (London) *Times*, April 16, 2003; Richard Beeston, "Rape Claim Nonsense, Say Lynch Doctors," (London) *Times*, Nov. 11, 2003; Bragg, *I Am a Soldier, Too*, pp. 115–16.

12. Kampfner, "The Truth about Jessica"; Bragg, *I Am a Soldier, Too*, pp. 119–20.

13. "War Spin," BBC; Kampfner, "The Truth about Jessica"; Priest, Booth, and Schmidt, "A Broken Body, a Broken Story."

14. Parry, "So Who Really Did Save Private Jessica?"; Patrick Rogers, Kurt Pitzer, et al., "Jessica Lynch's Rescue: What Really Happened?" *People*, June 16, 2003, p. 87.

15. "Attack on the 507th Maintenance Company, 23 March 2003, An-Nasiriyah, Iraq," U.S. Army, http://www.army.mil/features/507thMaintCmpy/; "The Lost Convoy," *Nightline*, ABC, July 15, 2003; Diane Sawyer, "Jessica Lynch: An American Story," *Primetime*, ABC, Nov. 11, 2003.

16. "Attack on the 507th Maintenance Company"; Ben English and Anna Cock, "Iraq War Rescue Mission; Back from the Dead, 'Like Custer, We Were Surrounded,'" *Advertiser*, April 15, 2003, p. 7.

17. Bragg, *I Am a Soldier, Too*, p. 67; "Attack on the 507th Maintenance Company."

18. Mike Wallace, "Jessica Lynch's Hero," *60 Minutes*, CBS News, Nov. 9, 2003; Schmidt and Loeb, "She Was Fighting to the Death"; Priest, Booth, and Schmidt, "A Broken Body, a Broken Story."

19. "Live from the Front Lines," *CNN Live Event*, CNN, April 3, 2003; "Advancing on Baghdad," *NewsHour with Jim Lehrer*, PBS, April 3, 2003; "Rescued POW Jessica Lynch in Good Spirits after Back Surgery," *Early Today*, CNBC News, April 4, 2003; "Lynch's Parents Deny Reports of Wounds," *Los Angeles Times*, April 4, 2003; Peter Whoriskey, "W.Va. Soldier's Parents Revel in Small Town Talk Over the Phone," *Washington Post*, April 4, 2003; Daniel LeDuc, "Pentagon Identifies 8 Soldiers Killed in Ambush," *Washington Post*, April 5, 2003; Joseph Coleman, "Jessica Lynch Health Better," *Long Beach Press-Telegram*, April 4, 2003; Michael Getler, "Reporting Private Lynch," *Washington Post*, April 20, 2003; Gibbs, "The Private Jessica Lynch."

20. Michael Getler, "According to Someone," *Washington Post*, May 25, 2003; Getler, "A Long, and Incomplete, Correction," *Washington Post*, June 29, 2003; Getler, "Reporting Private Lynch"; Gibbs, "The Private Jessica Lynch"; Priest, Booth, and Schmidt, "A Broken Body, a Broken Story"; Michele Orecklin, "The Controversy over Jessica Lynch," *Time*, June 9, 2003, p. 33; Bob Minzesheimer, "'Soldier' Tries to Sort Myth from Fact," *USA Today*, Nov. 17, 2003; Kate

O'Beirne, "An Army of Jessicas," *National Review*, May 19, 2003, p. 40; "Luring Private Lynch," *Reliable Sources*, CNN, June 22, 2003; "Are Media Merchandising Jessica Lynch?" *Reliable Sources*, CNN, Nov. 16, 2003.

21. "Interview with Elaine Donnelly, Bob Scales," *The Big Story with John Gibson*, Fox News, Nov. 11, 2003; Elaine Donnelly, "Jessica Lynch Reality Shatters Amazon Myths," *San Diego Union-Tribune*, Nov. 30, 2003; Betsy Hart, "Keep Women out of Combat," Scripps Howard News Service, Sept. 4, 2003.

22. O'Beirne, "An Army of Jessicas"; Betsy Hart, "Lynch Shows Pitfalls of Women in Combat," *Chicago Sun-Times*, Sept. 7, 2003; Betsy Hart, "Jessica Lynch Week," *National Review Online*, http://www.nationalreview.com/comment/hart200311121020.asp; Phyllis Schlafly, "Female U.S. Prisoners of Sadaam Hussein Less than Equal," Copley News Service, April 1, 2003.

23. Chuck Muth, "This Is Really Starting to Tick Me Off," *News & Views*, Nov. 9, 2003; Eric Boehlert, "Selling Pvt. Lynch," *Salon*, Nov. 15, 2003, http://www.mega.nu/ampp/military_erosion.html; Jon Christian Ryter, "Pfc. Jessica Lynch . . . War 'Hero,' Anti-Patriot and 'Author' Badmouths the U.S. Military," *News & Views*, http://www.newswithviews.com/Ryter/jon4.htm; Bragg, *I Am a Soldier, Too*, p. 160.

24. Wallace, "Jessica Lynch's Hero."

25. Kelly Patricia O'Meara, "The Real Hero in the Ambush at Nasiriya," *Insight on the News*, Jan. 19, 2004, p. 22; "Attack on the 507th Maintenance Company"; Alex Pulaski and Dan Hortsch, "Salem War Hero Was Captured, Shot in Back," *Oregonian*, May 28, 2004.

26. The Lost Convoy."

27. Sawyer, "Jessica Lynch: An American Story."

28. Mohammed Odeh al-Rehaief, *Because Each Life Is Precious: Why an Iraqi Man Risked Everything for Private Jessica Lynch* (New York: HarperCollins, 2003), pp. 41, 52, 125, 133–34.

29. Rehaief, *Because Each Life Is Precious*, pp. 30–33, 38, 184; Richard Beeston, "Rape Claim Nonsense, Say Lynch Doctors," (London) *Times*, Nov. 11, 2003, p. 12.

30. Rehaief, *Because Each Life Is Precious*, pp. 144–52, 155–57, 179–81, 187–93; Rogers, Mikelbank, O'Connor, et al., "Saved from Danger"; Beeston, "Rape Claim Nonsense."

31. Rehaief, *Because Each Life Is Precious*, p. 206; Adam Ashton, "Iraqi Who Aided Lynch Rescue Now a Washington Lobbyist," Associated Press, Nov. 10, 2003.

32. Priest, Booth, and Schmidt, "A Broken Body, a Broken Story"; Sawyer, "Jessica Lynch: An American Story"; Edward Helmore, "Private Jessica Says President Is Misusing Her Heroism," *Observer*, Nov. 9, 2003, p. 2.

33. Rose Ellen O'Connor, "Jessica's New Start," *People*, Nov. 24, 2003, p. 58; Beeston, "Rape Claim Nonsense"; Sawyer, "Jessica Lynch: An American Story"; Bob Withers, "Iraqi Who Helped Lynch Has Book," *Herald-Dispatch*, April 30, 2004.

34. "NBC's 'Saving Jessica Lynch' Tells Dramatic Story of the Ambush and Rescue of 19-Year-Old Pfc. Lynch during Operation Iraqi Freedom," NBC Entertainment Publicity, press release, Oct. 17, 2003; Josef Adalian, "Peacock Eyes POW's Rescue," *Daily Variety*, April 10, 2003, p. 1; Brian Lowry, "Sweeps Pix Proviso: The Truth Is Out There," *Variety*, Nov. 10–16, 2003, p. 38; Boehlert, "Selling Pvt. Lynch."

35. Tom Shales, "A&E's 'Flight 93': From Tragedy to Tripe, Nonstop," *Washington Post*, Jan. 30, 2006; Alessandra Stanley, "Battle of the Network Docudramas," *New York Times*, Nov. 7, 2003; David Bianculli, "Facts AWOL in 'Jessica Lynch,'" *Daily News*, Nov. 8, 2003.

36. Osha Gray Davidson, "The Forgotten Soldier," *Rolling Stone*, May 27, 2004, http://www.rollingstone.com/politics/story/6085435/the_forgotten_soldier/.

37. Ibid.; Bragg, *I Am a Soldier, Too*, p. 50.

38. Davidson, "The Forgotten Soldier"; Bragg, *I Am a Soldier, Too*, p. 11.

39. Davidson, "The Forgotten Soldier"; Bragg, *I Am a Soldier, Too*, p. 73.

40. Davidson, "The Forgotten Soldier."

41. Richard Jerome, J. D. Heyman, et al., "The Long Road Home," *People*, Aug. 4, 2003, p. 48; Bragg, *I Am a Soldier, Too*, p. 161.

42. Davidson, "The Forgotten Soldier."

43. Rogers, Mikelbank, O'Connor, et al., "Saved from Danger."

44. Sawyer, "Jessica Lynch: An American Story"; Kathy Kemp, "Clinching the Lynch Story, Author Bragg Finally Connects with Soldier," *Birmingham News*, Nov. 20, 2003; Winfield, "'I'm a Soldier, Too'"; Rogers, Mikelbank, O'Connor, et al., "Saved from Danger."

45. Niles Lathem, "Midnight Raiders Rescue Teen POW," *New York Post*, April 2, 2003; Sawyer, "Jessica Lynch: An American Story"; Rogers, Mikelbank, O'Connor, et al., "Saved from Danger"; Jodie Morse, "Saving Private Lynch," *Time*, April 14, 2003, p. 66; "POW Is Scooped out of Captivity," *Detroit Free Press*, April 2, 2003; Bragg, *I Am a Soldier, Too*, pp. 14, 23, 24, 27.

46. Bragg, *I Am a Soldier, Too*, pp. 37, 38, 157; Tamara Jones, "In Palestine, West Virginia, All Is Joyful," *Washington Post*, April 2, 2003; Rogers, Mikelbank, O'Connor, et al., "Saved from Danger."

47. Jerome, Heyman, et al., "The Long Road Home"; O'Connor, "Jessica's New Start"; Sawyer, "Jessica Lynch: An American Story."

48. "Jessica Lynch Not a June Bride," Associated Press, March 12, 2004; "Former POW Lynch Starts College," Associated Press, Aug. 22, 2005.

49. "Passages," *People*, Sept. 11, 2006, p. 105.

50. "Jessica Lynch Names New Baby Girl after Fallen Comrade," Associated Press, Jan. 20, 2007.

51. Brant, "She's Alive"; "The Capture and Rescue of U.S. Private 1st Class Jessica Lynch"; Rosalind Russell, "Iraqi Doctors Deny Jessica Lynch Raped," Reuters, Nov. 11, 2003; Owen Moritz, "Jessica Took Awful Beating," *Daily News*, April 5, 2003.

52. Jerry Adler et al., "Jessica's Liberation," *Newsweek*, April 16, 2003, p. 42; Rogers, Mikelbank, O'Connor, et al., "Saved from Danger"; Rogers, Pitzer, et al., "Jessica Lynch's Rescue: What Really Happened?"

53. Priest, Booth, and Schmidt, "A Broken Body, a Broken Story."

54. Rod Nordland, "Iraq: What Happened to Jessica Lynch," *Newsweek*, July 21, 2003, p. 7; "Lynch Rape Impossible," *Australian*, Nov. 12, 2003, p. 11; Gary Younge, "Private Lynch's Media War Continues as Iraqi Doctors Deny Rape Claim," *Guardian*, Nov. 12, 2003, http://www.guardian.co.uk/Iraq/Story/0,2763,1083110,00.html; Russell, "Iraqi Doctors Deny Jessica Lynch Raped."

55. Bragg, *I Am a Soldier, Too*, pp. 79, 96, 98–99.
56. Gibbs, "The Private Jessica Lynch"; Sawyer, "Jessica Lynch: An American Story"; "Jessica's Rape Horror," *Western Daily Press*, Nov. 7, 2003; Paul D. Colford and Corky Siemaszko, "Fiends Raped Jessica, Book Reveals Shocker," *Daily News*, Nov. 6, 2003; Tony Leonard, "Heroine Tells of Ordeal: I Was Raped by Saddam Beasts," *Daily Star*, Nov. 7, 2003.
57. Gibbs, "The Private Jessica Lynch"; Sawyer, "Jessica Lynch: An American Story."
58. Gibbs, "The Private Jessica Lynch"; "Lynch Rape Impossible"; Younge, "Private Lynch's Media War Continues"; Russell, "Iraqi Doctors Deny Jessica Lynch Raped"; Beeston, "Rape Claim Nonsense."
59. Sawyer, "Jessica Lynch: An American Story."
60. Ibid.
61. "Jessica Lynch Has Flu, Postpones Book Tour," *Seattle Times*, Nov. 18, 2003; Kathy Kemp, "Clinching the Lynch Story, Author Bragg Finally Connects with Soldier," *Birmingham News*, Nov. 20, 2003.
62. Bragg, *I Am a Soldier, Too*, pp. 201–3.

8: ORIGINAL SHAME

1. Arthur M. Eckstein, "Introduction: Main Critical Issues in *The Searchers*," *The Searchers: Essays and Reflections on John Ford's Classic Western*, ed. Arthur M. Eckstein and Peter Lehman (Detroit: Wayne State University Press, 2004), p. 1; Larry Swindell, "Yes, John Ford Knew a Thing or Two about Art," *John Ford Interviews*, ed. Gerald Peary (Jackson: University Press of Mississippi, 2001), p. 47; Nick Redman, dir., *A Turning of the Earth: John Ford, John Wayne, and the Searchers*, documentary, 1999.
2. Margaret Schmidt Hacker, *Cynthia Ann Parker: The Life and the Legend* (El Paso: Texas Western Press, 1990), pp. 1, 7, 9, 11, 12–15, 18–19; Jo Ella Powell Exley, *Frontier Blood* (College Station: Texas A&M University Press, 2001), p. 133.
3. Hacker, *Cynthia Ann Parker*, pp. 17–18.
4. Exley, *Frontier Blood*, pp. 99, 100–101, 104, 110, 113–15, 118, 128; Hacker, *Cynthia Ann Parker*, p. 19.
5. Exley, *Frontier Blood*, pp. 76–77, 82–84, 97, 98, 114, 115, 117; Christopher Castiglia, *Bound and Determined* (Chicago: University of Chicago Press, 1996), p. 38.
6. Exley, *Frontier Blood*, pp. 66–67, 120.
7. Hacker, *Cynthia Ann Parker*, pp. 24, 26–27; Exley, *Frontier Blood*, pp. 155, 158.
8. Hacker, *Cynthia Ann Parker*, pp. 30, 33, 40.
9. Exley, *Frontier Blood*, p. 52.
10. Ibid., pp. 53–55, 59–60; Hacker, *Cynthia Ann Parker*, pp. 5, 7–10.
11. A. O. Scott, "'Searchers': How the West Was Begun," *New York Times*, June 11, 2006; Jaime J. Weinman, "Most Flattered Movie of All Time," *Maclean's*, June 5, 2006.
12. Eckstein, "Introduction: Main Critical Issues in *The Searchers*," pp. 33–35, 45, n. 112; Brian Henderson, "*The Searchers*: An American Dilemma," *The Searchers: Essays and Reflections on John Ford's Classic Western*, pp. 47–48; Weinman, "Most Flattered Movie of All Time"; Redman, *A Turning of the Earth*.

13. Hacker, *Cynthia Ann Parker*, pp. 31–33, 35, 47, n. 21; Exley, *Frontier Blood*, pp. 173, 176, 179; Margaret Schmidt Hacker, "Cynthia Ann Parker," *Handbook of Texas*, http://www.tsha.utexas.edu/handbook/online/articles/PP/fpa18.html.

14. Le May, *The Searchers*, pp. 271–72; *The Searchers*, dir. John Ford, 1956.

15. Hacker, *Cynthia Ann Parker*, pp. 36, 38–39.

16. Mary Rowlandson, *A Narrative of the Captivity and Restoration of Mrs. Mary Rowlandson, Women's Indian Captivity Narratives*, ed. Kathryn Zabelle Derounian-Stodola (New York: Penguin, 1998), p. 12.

17. Nancy Woloch, *Women and the American Experience* (New York: Knopf, 1984), p. 2.

18. Ibid., pp. 1, 12; Jill Lepore, *The Name of War* (New York: Knopf, 1998), p. xii; Richard Slotkin and James K. Folsom, eds., *So Dreadfull a Judgment: Puritan Responses to King Philip's War, 1676–1677* (Middletown, Conn.: Wesleyan University Press, 1979), pp. 3–4.

19. Slotkin and Folsom, *So Dreadfull a Judgment*, p. 4.

20. Lepore, *Name of War*, pp. xii, xvii, 166–67, 177; Richard Francis, *Judge Sewall's Apology* (New York: Fourth Estate, 2005), p. 25; Slotkin and Folsom, *So Dreadfull a Judgment*, pp. 28–29, 30–33.

21. Richard Slotkin, *Regeneration through Violence: The Mythology of the American Frontier, 1600–1860* (Middletown, Conn.: Wesleyan University Press, 1973), pp. 144, 158; Lepore, *Name of War*, p. 174.

22. Records are fragmentary, but the two significant studies on the demographics of captivity in New England's colonial era find more men than women were seized. Both draw largely from data collected by two antiquarians who spent decades in the late nineteenth and early twentieth centuries gathering information on 1,606 New England captives taken to Canada. The first study, which looked at 270 of these captives whose sex was known, found slightly more men (142) than women (128). (Narrowing the pool to captives older than twenty-one years, the study found 60 men and 52 women.) The second study, which looked at 535 captives who could be identified by sex and who were taken by Indians alone (in other words, not by the French or in collaboration with the French), found that 349 were men and 186 were women. (This second study didn't look at the sex ratio among adults but identified about half of this group of captives as being sixteen years or older.) Even so, early captivity narratives were overwhelmingly told as a woman's story, most often a woman whose children were also seized, which has led many scholars to this day to contend that, as one noted scholar of the "White Indian" phenomenon expressed it, "'women and children'—the 'weak and defenceless'—were the prime targets of Indian raids." Alden T. Vaughan and Daniel K. Richter, "Crossing the Cultural Divide: Indians and New Englanders, 1605–1763," *Proceedings of the American Antiquarian Society* 90, pt. 1 (1980): 52–57; James Axtell, "White Indians of Colonial America," *William and Mary Quarterly*, 3rd ser., 32 (Jan. 1975): 59–60; Laurel Thatcher Ulrich, *Good Wives: Image and Reality in the Lives of Women in Northern New England, 1650–1750* (New York: Vintage, 1991), p. 203. See also, for the original data, Emma Coleman, *New England Captives Carried to Canada*, vols. 1 and 2 (Portland, Maine: Southworth Press, 1925).

23. Ulrich, *Good Wives*, p. 203.

24. Hector St. John de Crevecoeur remarked in *Letters from an American Farmer* that, while "thousands of Europeans" had gone native, "we have no examples of even one of those Aborigines having from choice become Europeans!" Cadwallader Colden, surveyor-general and member of the king's council, likewise noted the disparity: "No Arguments, no Intreaties, nor Tears of their Friends and Relations, could persuade many of [the English captives] to leave their new *Indian* Friends and Acquaintance[s]," he observed, yet he knew of "not one Instance" where an Indian wanted to stay with the English. Axtell, "White Indians of Colonial America," pp. 57–58; Ulrich, *Good Wives*, p. 203; Vaughan and Richter, "Crossing the Cultural Divide," p. 62; James Axtell, *The Invasion Within* (New York: Oxford University Press, 1985), pp. 303, 305–7.

25. Slotkin, *Regeneration through Violence*, p. 554.

26. June Namias, *White Captives: Gender and Ethnicity on the American Frontier* (Chapel Hill: University of North Carolina Press, 1993), p. 268.

27. The full title of Rowlandson's account is *The Sovereignty and Goodness of God, Together with the Faithfulness of His Promises Displayed, Being a Narrative of the Captivity and Restoration of Mrs. Mary Rowlandson.* Derounian-Stodola, *Women's Indian Captivity Narratives*, p. 3; Woloch, *Women and the American Experience*, p. 13; Gary L. Ebersole, *Captured by Texts: Puritan to Post-Modern Images of Indian Captivity* (Charlottesville: University Press of Virginia, 1995), pp. 9–10; Roy Harvey Pearce, "The Significances of the Captivity Narrative," *American Literature* 19 (1947): 16.

28. Melani McAlister, "Saving Private Lynch," *New York Times*, April 6, 2003.

29. Henry Nash Smith, *Virgin Land: The American West as Symbol and Myth*, rev. ed. (New York: Vintage, 1970), p. 91.

9: HEED THE MOTHERS

1. Mary Rowlandson, *A Narrative of the Captivity and Restoration of Mrs. Mary Rowlandson*, in *Women's Indian Captivity Narratives*, pp. 21, 24–25, 26, 26–27, 38, 42–43; Ulrich, *Good Wives*, p. 228; Woloch, *Women and the American Experience*, pp. 9–10.

2. Rowlandson, *Narrative of the Captivity and Restoration*, pp. 50–51.

3. Jay Fliegelman, *Prodigals and Pilgrims: The American Revolution against Patriarchal Authority, 1750–1800* (New York: Cambridge University Press, 1982), p. 144.

4. Ulrich, *Good Wives*, pp. 55, 215–16; Lyle Koehler, *A Search for Power* (Urbana: University of Illinois Press, 1980), pp. 46–50; Mary Beth Norton, "The Evolution of White Women's Experience in Early America," *American Historical Review* 89 (June 1984): 594, 596, 598, 600–601; Marylynn Salmon, *Women and the Law of Property in Early America* (Chapel Hill: University of North Carolina Press, 1986), pp. 6–9; Slotkin and Folsom, *So Dreadfull a Judgment*, p. 301.

5. Kathryn Zabelle Derounian, "The Publication, Promotion, and Distribution of Mary Rowlandson's Indian Captivity Narrative in the Seventeenth Century," *Early American Literature* 23 (1988): 240, 243, 254; Rebecca Blevins Faery, *Cartographies of Desire: Captivity, Race, and Sex in the Shaping of an American Nation* (Norman: University of Oklahoma Press, 1999), pp. 45–46.

6. Derounian, "The Publication, Promotion, and Distribution of Mary Rowlandson's Indian Captivity Narrative," p. 240; "The Preface to the Reader," *Narrative of the Captivity and Restoration of Mrs. Mary Rowlandson*, p. 9.

7. Annette Kolodny, *The Land before Her: Fantasy and Experience of the American Frontiers, 1630–1860* (Chapel Hill: University of North Carolina Press, 1984), pp. 21–22, 27; Kathryn Zabelle Derounian, "Puritan Orthodoxy and the 'Survivor Syndrome,' in Mary Rowlandson's Indian Captivity Narrative," *Early American Literature* 22 (1987): 86. See also Carroll Smith-Rosenberg, "Subject Female: Authorizing American Identity," *American Literary History* 5 (Autumn 1990): 486.

8. John Demos, *The Unredeemed Captive: A Family Story from Early America* (New York: Vintage, 1995), pp. 8, 13–14; Rowlandson, *Narrative of the Captivity and Restoration*, pp. 16, 34, 43.

9. Slotkin, *Regeneration through Violence*, p. 101; Richard VanDerBeets, ed., *Held Captive by Indians: Selected Narratives, 1642–1836* (Knoxville: University of Tennessee Press, 1973), p. xi; David L. Greene, "New Light on Mary Rowlandson," *Early American Literature* 20 (1985): 25.

10. Margaret W. Masson, "The Typology of the Female as a Model for the Regenerate: Puritan Preaching, 1690–1730," *Signs* 2 (Winter 1976): 305; Elizabeth Reis, "The Devil, the Body, and the Feminine Soul," *Journal of American History* 82 (June 1995): 20; Rowlandson, *Narrative of the Captivity and Restoration*, pp. 21, 24–25, 26–27, 38; Ulrich, *Good Wives*, p. 228; Ann Douglas, *The Feminization of American Culture* (New York: Anchor, 1977), p. 135.

11. Russell Bourne, *The Red King's Rebellion: Racial Politics in New England, 1675–1678* (New York: Atheneum, 1990), pp. 167–68; Woloch, *Women and the American Experience*, p. 3; Rowlandson, *Narrative of the Captivity and Restoration*, p. 22.

12. Rowlandson, *Narrative of the Captivity and Restoration*, p. 44.

13. Demos, *Unredeemed Captive*, pp. 11, 13, 14–15, 17–19, 22, 24, 29.

14. Ibid., pp. 42, 98–99, 105–9; Dawn Lander Gherman, "From Parlour to Tepee: The White Squaw on the American Frontier," Ph.D dissertation, University of Massachusetts, 1975, pp. 70–91.

15. Slotkin, *Regeneration through Violence*, p. 113.

16. Cotton Mather, "A Notable Exploit; wherein, *Dux Faemina Facti*," from *Magnalia Christi Americana*, in *Women's Indian Captivity Narratives*, p. 58; Derounian-Stodola, *Women's Indian Captivity Narratives*, p. 55; "Hannah Duston," *The Devil May Care*, ed. Tony Horwitz (New York: Oxford University Press, 2003), pp. 25–27; Frances Roe Kestler, *The Indian Captivity Narrative: A Woman's View* (New York: Garland Publishing, 1990), pp. 81–82.

17. Mather, "A Notable Exploit," pp. 59–60; Derounian-Stodola, *Women's Indian Captivity Narratives*, p. 55; Kathryn Whitford, "Hannah Dustin: The Judgement of History," *Essex Institute Historical Collections* 108 (Oct. 1972): 310, http://www.hawthorneinsalem.org/page/11903/; "Hannah Duston," p. 26; "Deposition of Hannah Bradley of Haverhill, June 1735," *Massachusetts Archives*, vol. 31, p. 260, http://www.hawthorneinsalem.org/page/12187/; Axtell, "White Indians of Colonial America," pp. 70–71.

18. Whitford, "Hannah Dustin: The Judgement of History," pp. 308–9; Sybil Smith, "Judging Hannah," *Yankee*, Jan. 1995, p. 50.

19. Ulrich, *Good Wives*, pp. 167–68, 200–201; Francis, *Judge Sewall's Apology*, p. 190; Whitford, "Hannah Dustin: The Judgement of History," p. 304; Mather, "A Notable Exploit," p. 60; Smith, "Judging Hannah."

20. Ulrich, *Good Wives*, pp. 169–70; Mather, "A Notable Exploit," pp. 59–60; Tara Fitzpatrick, "The Figure of Captivity: The Cultural Work of the Puritan Captivity Narrative," *American Literary History* 3 (Spring 1991): 15; Kolodny, *The Land before Her*, p. 24; Derounian-Stodola, *Women's Indian Captivity Narratives*, p. 56.

21. *Holy Bible: The New Scofield Reference Bible*, King James Version, Judges 4:8–9 (New York: Oxford University Press, 1969), p. 293.

22. Increase Mather, "An Earnest Exhortation to the Inhabitants of New-England," *So Dreadfull a Judgment*, p. 171.

23. Ibid., p. 172.

24. Ibid., pp. 177, 179, 190; Increase Mather, "A Brief History of the Warr with the Indians in New-England," *So Dreadfull a Judgment*, pp. 113–14.

25. Samuel Nowell, "Abraham in Arms," *So Dreadfull a Judgment*, pp. 288, 290; Slotkin and Folsom, "Samuel Nowell: Prophet of Preparedness," *So Dreadfull a Judgment*, pp. 258–59, 263.

26. Mather, "An Earnest Exhortation," pp. 176–77.

27. Mary Beth Norton, *In the Devil's Snare* (New York: Knopf, 2002), p. 297.

28. Ibid., pp. 11–12; Carol F. Karlsen, *The Devil in the Shape of a Woman: Witchcraft in Colonial New England* (New York: Vintage, 1987), p. 51.

29. Norton, *In the Devil's Snare*, p. 298; Slotkin and Folsom, *So Dreadfull a Judgment*, pp. 75–76.

30. Norton, *In the Devil's Snare*, pp. 20–21, 58–59, 132, 103–5, 140–43, 159–60, 180, 239–40, 299–300.

31. Karlsen, *Devil in the Shape of a Woman*, pp. 3, 40, 51; Paul S. Boyer and Stephen Nissenbaum, *Salem Possessed: The Social Origins of Witchcraft* (Cambridge: Harvard University Press, 1974), pp. 107–9; Norton, *In the Devil's Snare*, pp. 4, 327–28, nn. 3, 4; Anne C. Zeller, "Arctic Hysteria in Salem?" *Anthropologica* 32 (1990): pp. 239–64.

32. Reis, "The Devil, the Body, and the Feminine Soul," p. 25.

33. Karlsen, *Devil in the Shape of a Woman*, pp. 101–17, 149, 150.

34. Ibid., p. 149.

35. Norton, "The Evolution of White Women's Experience in Early America," pp. 609–10; Frances Hill, *A Delusion of Satan* (New York: Da Capo Press, 1995), p. 195; Koehler, *Search for Power*, pp. 430–36, 440.

36. Karlsen, *Devil in the Shape of a Woman*, p. 226.

37. Norton, *In the Devil's Snare*, pp. 102–3, 178; Cotton Mather, "Decennium Luctuosum," *Narratives of the Indian Wars, 1675–1699*, ed. Charles H. Lincoln (New York: Charles Scribner's Sons, 1913), p. 207.

38. Norton, *In the Devil's Snare*, pp. 176–79, 181.

39. Cotton Mather, "A Brand Pluck'd Out of the Burning," *Narratives of the Witchcraft Cases 1648–1706*, ed. George Lincoln Burr (New York: Charles Scribner's Sons, 1914), pp. 260, 264–65, 271–72.

40. Ibid., pp. 251, 261, 266, 267, 261, 282. See also Slotkin, *Regeneration through Violence*, pp. 131–41.

41. Mather, "A Brand Pluck'd Out of the Burning," p. 270.

42. E. W. B. Taylor, "Hannah Duston Memorials: History of Memorial Organizations and Other Matters of Interest," undated, http://www.hannahdustin.com/association_history.htm; "Images Related to 'The Duston Family,'" http://www.hawthorneinsalem.org/Literature/NativeAmericans&Blacks/Hannah Duston/Images.html; "Hannah Duston, Boscawen 1697" (1973), booklet reproduced in "The Story of Hannah Dustin/Duston of Haverhill, Massachusetts," http://www.hannahdustin.com/hannah_files.html.

43. "Hannah Dustin Memorial," *Rail-Trails of New Hampshire*, http://members.fortunecity.com/railtrails/NH/CW/Duston.htm; Leland Meitzler, "Hannah Dustin Memorial Vandalized," *Concord Monitor*, Oct. 18, 2005; personal interview with Brenna Langenau, director of the Haverhill Historical Society, March 1, 2007; "Images Related to 'The Duston Family'"; Derounian-Stodola, *Women's Indian Captivity Narratives*, p. 57; Smith, "Judging Hannah"; Leon W. Anderson, "*Hannah Duston: Heroine of 1697 Massacre of Indian Captors on River Islet at Boscawen, N.H.* (Concord, N.H.: Evans Printing, 1973), unpaginated.

10: HERE IS OUR FATHER! NOW WE ARE SAFE!

1. Slotkin, *Regeneration through Violence*, pp. 153–54, 180–81, 183, 184, 187; James Smith, "Prisoner of the Caughnawagas," and Thomas Brown, "Death in the Snow," *Captured by the Indians: 15 Firsthand Accounts, 1750–1870*, ed. Frederick Drimmer (New York: Dover Publications, 1961), pp. 25–60, 61–72.

2. "God's Mercy Surmounting Man's Cruelty, Exemplified in the Captivity and Redemption of Elizabeth Hanson," in *Women's Indian Captivity Narratives*, pp. 66–79; Pearce, "The Significances of the Captivity Narrative," pp. 4–7; Derounian-Stodola, *Women's Indian Captivity Narratives*, pp. 63–64.

3. Greg Sieminski, "The Puritan Captivity Narrative and the Politics of the American Revolution," *American Quarterly* 42 (March 1990): 39.

4. Namias, *White Captives*, pp. 34–35; Sieminski, "The Puritan Captivity Narrative," pp. 37, 39–42.

5. Namias, *White Captives*, p. 31; Alexander Scott Withers, *Chronicles of Border Warfare* (Cincinnati: R. Clarke, 1895; Parsons, W.Va.: McClain Printing, 1975), pp. 405–6.

6. Castiglia, *Bound and Determined*, pp. 30–31; Namias, *White Captives*, p. 31.

7. Castiglia, *Bound and Determined*, pp. 110–11, 112.

8. Linda K. Kerber, *Women of the Republic: Intellect and Ideology in Revolutionary America* (Chapel Hill: University of North Carolina Press, 1980), pp. 139–55, 283, 288; Elaine F. Crane, "Dependence in the Era of Independence," *The American Revolution: Its Character and Limits*, ed. Jack P. Greene (New York: New York University Press, 1987), pp. 262–68, 271–72; Salmon, *Women and the Law of Property in Early America*, pp. xv–xvii; Rosemarie Zagarri, "The Rights of Man and Woman in Post-Revolutionary America," *William and Mary Quarterly* 55 (April 1998): 203–30; Rosemarie Zagarri, *Revolutionary Backlash: Women and*

Politics in the Early American Republic (Philadelphia: University of Pennsylvania Press, 2007).

9. Paul Baepler, *White Slaves, African Masters: An Anthology of American Barbary Captivity Narratives* (Chicago: University of Chicago Press, 1999), pp. 1–2, 8–9, 25; James R. Lewis, "Savages of the Seas: Barbary Captivity Tales and Images of Muslims in the Early Republic," *Journal of American Culture* 13 (1990): 76, 77; Anne G. Myles, "Slaves in Algiers, Captives in Iraq," *Common-Place* 5 (Oct. 2004), in http://www.common-place.org; Cotton Mather, "The Glory of Goodness," *White Slaves, African Masters*, pp. 61, 69; Richard Zacks, *The Pirate Coast: Thomas Jefferson, the First Marines and the Secret Mission of 1805* (New York: Hyperion, 2005), pp. 18–25, 27–30, 279.

10. Baepler, *White Slaves, African Masters*, pp. 10–11, 12, 147; Lewis, "Savages of the Seas," p. 78; *History of the Captivity and Sufferings of Mrs. Maria Martin*, in *White Slaves, African Masters*, pp. 147–57.

11. Timothy Dwight, *Travels in New England and New York*, vol. 1, letter 39 (New Haven: S. Converse, 1821), rpt. in http://www.hawthorneinsalem.org/Literature/NativeAmericans&Blacks/HannahDuston/Literature.html.

12. B. Bernard Cohen, "The Composition of Hawthorne's 'The Duston Family,'" *New England Quarterly* 21 (1948): 239–40; Whitford, "Hannah Dustin: The Judgement of History," pp. 316, 320.

13. John Greenleaf Whittier, "The Mother's Revenge," *Legends of New England* (1831) (Ann Arbor: University of Michigan Humanities Text Initiative, 1998), pp. 127, 130, in http://www.hti.umich.edu/cgi/t/text/text-idx?c=amverse;idno=BAH8738.0001.001.

14. Nathaniel Hawthorne, "The Duston Family," *Indian Captivity Narrative: A Woman's View*, pp. 88, 89, 93; Robert D. Arner, "The Story of Hannah Duston: Cotton Mather to Thoreau," *American Transcendental Quarterly* 18 (1973): 19–23.

15. Shawn Regan, "Hannah Duston: Heroine or Villianess? Festival Posters Rekindle Age-Old Debate," *Eagle-Tribune*, Aug. 18, 2006; Jay Lindsay, "Hannah Dustin: A Hero or a Murderer," *Union Leader*, Oct. 1, 2006; Tom Long, "Heroism Is in the Eye of the Beholder," *Boston Globe*, Sept. 3, 2006; "Colonial Heroine at Center of Modern Downtown Controversy," *PR News*, http://www.prnewsnow.com/PR%20News%20Releases/Lifestyle/Colonial%20Heroine%20at%20Center%20of%20Modern%20Downtown%20Controversy; "Now They Want a HOLIDAY . . . but I Finally Get It," Haverhill Community Forum, http://www.boardzero.com/haverhillforum/haverhillforum-about159.html; Barney Gallagher, "In Hannah Duston Saga, There Is Blame on All Sides," *Eagle-Tribune*, Sept. 10, 2006; Douglas Lloyd Buchholz, "Heroic? Hannah Duston Was a Murderer," *Concord Monitor*, Sept. 1, 2006; S. J. Reidhead, "Hannah Dustin Now a Murderer," The Pink Flamingo, Sept. 11, 2006, http://thepinkflamingo.blogharbor.com/blog/_archives/2006/9/11/2317448.html.

16. Annette Kolodny, "Turning the Lens on 'The Panther Captivity': A Feminist Exercise in Practical Criticism," *Critical Inquiry* 8 (Winter 1981): 344; Fliegelman, *Prodigals and Pilgrims*, 140.

17. "A surprising account of the Discovery of a Lady who was taken by the Indians in the Year 1777, and after making her escape, she retired to a lonely

Cave, where she lived nine years," *Women's Indian Captivity Narratives*, pp. 86–90.

18. Fliegelman, *Prodigals and Pilgrims*, pp. 137–41. The painting is John Vanderlyn's 1804 *Death of Jane McCrea*. For discussions of "The Panther Capitvity," see also Kolodny, *The Land before Her*, pp. 57–62, and Slotkin, *Regeneration through Violence*, pp. 256–59.

19. Vivien Green Fryd, "Two Sculptures for the Capitol: Horatio Greenough's 'Rescue' and Luigi Persico's 'Discovery of America,'" *American Art Journal* 19 (1987): 17, 19, 20, 34, 38; Slotkin, *Regeneration through Violence*, pp. 440–41.

20. Fryd, "Two Sculptures for the Capitol," pp. 40–41.

21. John Mack Faragher, *Daniel Boone: The Life and Legend of an American Pioneer* (New York: Owl Books, 1993), p. 302.

22. Faragher, *Daniel Boone*, pp. 17–19, 39, 167, 175, 199–200, 228, 229,230–31; Daniel J. Herman, "The Other Daniel Boone: The Nascence of a Middle-Class Hunter Hero, 1784–1860," *Journal of the Early Republic* 18 (Autumn 1998): 434–35.

23. Faragher, *Daniel Boone*, pp. 50, 60, 93, 97, 131–38, 214, 221–23, 238–39, 245–48, 265, 273; Slotkin, *Regeneration through Violence*, p. 300; Herman, "The Other Daniel Boone," pp. 434–35; John Bakeless, *Daniel Boone* (Harrisburg, Pa.: Stackpole, 1965), p. 38.

24. Faragher, *Daniel Boone*, pp. 2–3, 323; Herman, "The Other Daniel Boone," p. 438; Slotkin, *Regeneration through Violence*, pp. 270–71, 274, 278–94; Smith, *Virgin Land*, p. 54; John Filson, *The Discovery, Settlement and Present State of Kentucke* (New York: Corinth Books, 1962), pp. 49–82.

25. Slotkin, *Regeneration through Violence*, p. 312; Timothy Flint, *The First White Man of the West: Life and Exploits of Col. Dan'l. Boone, the First Settler of Kentucky; Interspersed with Incidents in the Early Annals of the Country* (Cincinnati: Applegate, 1856), p. 87.

26. Slotkin, *Regeneration through Violence*, pp. 323–24, 348–49; Faragher, *Daniel Boone*, pp. 323, 324; Herman, "The Other Daniel Boone," p. 436; Filson, *Discovery, Settlement and Present State of Kentucke*, pp. 54, 55, 81.

27. Herman, "The Other Daniel Boone," p. 441; Slotkin, *Regeneration through Violence*, p. 350.

28. Daniel Bryan, *The Mountain Muse: Comprising the Adventures of Daniel Boone and the Power of Virtuous and Refined Beauty* (Harrisonburg: Davidson and Bourne, 1813).

29. Herman, "The Other Daniel Boone," p. 449.

30. Flint, *First White Man of the West*, p. 247; Slotkin, *Regeneration through Violence*, p. 300; Faragher, *Daniel Boone*, pp. 109–10, 131, 134–36, 139–40, 193, 204; Bakeless, *Daniel Boone*, 127–29; Filson, *Discovery, Settlement and Present State of Kentucke*, p. 72; Neal O. Hammon, ed., *My Father, Daniel Boone: The Draper Interviews with Nathan Boone* (Lexington: University Press of Kentucky, 1999), pp. 49, 50.

31. Faragher, *Daniel Boone*, pp. 154–58, 170–72, 174; Slotkin, *Regeneration through Violence*, p. 284; Bakeless, *Daniel Boone*, pp. 160, 177, 181; John S. C. Abbott, *Daniel Boone: The Pioneer of Kentucky* (New York: Dodd, Mead, 1898), p. 203.

32. Faragher, *Daniel Boone*, pp. 320, 323, 336–37; Flint, *First White Man*, pp. 12–13, 21, 107, 108, 123, 247.

33. Slotkin, *Regeneration through Violence*, p. 286; Flint, *First White Man*, pp. 86–96; Filson, *Discovery, Settlement and Present State of Kentucke*, p. 60; Edward S. Ellis, *The Life and Times of Col. Daniel Boone: Hunter, Soldier, and Pioneer* (Philadelphia: Porter and Coates, 1884), pp. 70, 77.

11: TOUCH ME NOT

1. James Fenimore Cooper, *The Last of the Mohicans* (New York: Penguin, 1986), p. 109.

2. Faragher, *Daniel Boone*, p. 331.

3. Cooper, *Last of the Mohicans*, pp. 80, 337, 345–46; Cooper, *The Sea Lions, or the Lost Sealers* (New York: G. P. Putnam, 1886), p. 223; David T. Haberly, "Women and Indians: *The Last of the Mohicans* and the Captivity Tradition," *American Quarterly* 28 (Autumn 1976): 440–41.

4. Gherman, "From Parlour to Tepee," p. 3.

5. Castiglia, *Bound and Determined*, pp. 32–33; Pearce, "The Significances of the Captivity Narrative," pp. 11–12.

6. Douglas, *Feminization of American Culture*, pp. 51–52.

7. Rachel Plummer, "Narrative of the Capture and Subsequent Sufferings of Mrs. Rachel Plummer, Written by Herself," in *Held Captive by Indians*, pp. 349, 353–55.

8. *Narrative of the Captivity and Extreme Sufferings of Mrs. Clarissa Plummer* (New York: Perry and Cooke, 1838), in Edward E. Ayer Collection, Newberry Library, pp. 8, 11–15, 20, 22; Pearce, "The Significances of the Captivity Narrative," pp. 16–17.

9. John Mack Faragher, *Women and Men on the Overland Trail* (New Haven: Yale University Press, 1979), pp. 4, 11; VanDerBeets, *Held Captive by Indians*, p. xxi; Glenda Riley, *Women and Indians on the Frontier, 1825–1915* (Albuquerque: University of New Mexico Press, 1984), pp. xiv, 18, 98, 105.

10. Riley, *Women and Indians on the Frontier*, pp. 91–95, 106, 155, 294, n. 160; Lillian Schlissel, *Women's Diaries of the Westward Journey* (New York: Schocken, 1992), p. 154; John D. Unruh Jr., *The Plains Across: The Overland Emigrants and the Trans-Mississippi West, 1840–60* (Urbana: University of Illinois Press, 1979), pp. 175–76, 184, 185.

11. Riley, *Women and Indians on the Frontier*, pp. 202, 311, n. 199; Castiglia, *Bound and Determined*, pp. 112, 172; Derounian-Stodola, *Women's Indian Captivity Narratives*, p. 121; Namias, *White Captives*, pp. 148, 152; "A Narrative of the Life of Mrs. Mary Jemison," in *Women's Indian Captivity Narratives*, pp. 129, 147, 149, 156–58, 160, 177–78, 184–85, 209.

12. Rowlandson, *Narrative of the Captivity and Restoration of Mrs. Mary Rowlandson*, p. 46; Axtell, *Invasion Within*, pp. 310–11; Susan H. Armitage, "Women's Literature and the American Frontier: A New Perspective on the Frontier Myth," *Women, Women Writers, and the West*, ed. L. L. Lee and Merrill Lewis (Troy: Whitston Publishing, 1980), p. 7; Riley, *Women and Indians*, pp. 209–10; James Axtell, *The European and the Indian: Essays in the Ethnohistory of Colonial North America* (New York: Oxford University Press, 1981), pp. 194–95.

13. Namias, *White Captives*, pp. 97, 109; Richard Irving Dodge, *The Plains of the Great West and Their Inhabitants* (New York: Archer House, 1959), p. 395; Glenda Riley, "The Specter of a Savage: Rumors and Alarmism on the Overland Trail," *Western Historical Quarterly* 15 (Oct. 1984): 435.

14. "Erastus Dow Palmer: *The White Captive*," *Timeline of Art History* (New York: Metropolitan Museum of Art, 2000); Joy S. Kasson, *Marble Queens and Captives: Women in Nineteenth-Century American Sculpture* (New Haven: Yale University Press, 1990), pp. 74, 79–80; James R. Lewis, "Images of Captive Rape in the Nineteenth Century," *Journal of American Culture* 15 (1992): 70; Fryd, "Two Sculptures for the Capitol," p. 39, n. 45.

15. Derounian-Stodola, *Women's Indian Captivity Narratives*, p. 238; Namias, *White Captives*, pp. 216, 221; Carol Chomsky, "The United States–Dakota War Trials: A Study in Military Injustice," *Stanford Law Review* 43 (Nov. 1990): 27, 28, 47–48, 53; Marouf Hasian Jr., "Cultural Amnesia and Legal Rhetoric: Remembering the 1862 United States–Dakota War and the Need for Military Commissions," *American Indian Culture and Research Journal* 27 (Jan. 1, 2003–March 3, 2003): 91–92.

16. Sarah F. Wakefield, "Six Weeks in the Sioux Tepees: A Narrative of Indian Captivity," in *Women's Indian Captivity Narratives*, pp. 298, 300, 301, 304, 305, 310; Namias, *White Captives*, pp. 226–27. For an excellent study of Wakefield's experience, see *White Captives*, pp. 204–61.

17. Namias, *White Captives*, pp. 231, 356, n. 56.

18. Wakefield, "Six Weeks in the Sioux Tepees," pp. 303, 308; Namias, *White Captives*, pp. 224, 236–37, 298, 300, 301, 304, 310; Chomsky, "The United States–Dakota War Trials," pp. 32, 89–90.

19. *Miss Annie Coleson's Own Narrative of Her Captivity among the Sioux* (Philadelphia: Barclay & Co., 1875), pp. 45, 55, in Wright American Fiction Project, 1851–1875, Indiana University Digital Library Program, http://www.letrs.indiana.edu/cgi/t/text/textidx?c=wright2;idno=Wright2-1716.

20. D. H. Lawrence, *Studies in Classic American Literature* (New York: Viking, 1969), p. 54; Smith, *Virgin Land*, p. 120; Albert Johannsen, *The House of Adam and Beadle and Its Dime and Nickel Novels*, Northern Illinois University Libraries, Dekalb, http://www.niulib.niu.edu/badndp/bibindex.html.

21. Richard Slotkin, *Gunfighter Nation: The Myth of the Frontier in Twentieth-Century America* (New York: Atheneum 1992), pp. 183–84, 188; Jacquelyn Dowd Hall, *Revolt Against Chivalry: Jessie Daniel Ames and the Women's Campaign Against Lynching* (New York: Columbia University Press, 1979), p. 145; Jacquelyn Dowd Hall, "'The Mind That Burns in Each Body': Women, Rape, and Racial Violence," in *Powers of Desire: The Politics of Sexuality*, ed. Ann Snitow, Christine Stansell, and Sharon Thompson (New York: Monthly Review Press, 1983), p. 347, n. 14.

22. Hall, "'The Mind That Burns in Each Body,'" pp. 329, 334, 341; Hall, *Revolt Against Chivalry*, pp. 134–35, 145, 149; Ida Wells-Barnett, *On Lynchings* (New York: Arno Press, 1969), pp. 7–11; Herbert Shapiro, *White Violence and Black Response: From Reconstruction to Montgomery* (Amherst: University of Massachusetts Press, 1988), p. 32; Nancy MacLean, *Behind the Mask of Chivalry: The Making of the Second Ku Klux Klan* (New York: Oxford University Press, 1994), pp. 142, 144.

23. MacLean, *Behind the Mask of Chivalry*, p. 142; Hall, *Revolt Against Chivalry*, pp. 146–147, 150, 151; Forrest G. Wood, *Black Scare: The Racist Response to Emancipation and Reconstruction* (Berkeley: University of California Press, 1968), pp. 145–46.

24. Michael Rogin, "'The Sword Became a Flashing Vision': D. W. Griffith's *The Birth of a Nation*," *The Birth of a Nation*, ed. Robert Lang (Brunswick, N.J.: Rutgers University Press, 1994), pp. 250, 291; Stanley F. Horn, *Invisible Empire: The Story of the Ku Klux Klan, 1866–1871* (Boston: Houghton Mifflin, 1939), p. 397; MacLean, *Behind the Mask of Chivalry*, pp. 10, 114–15.

25. Rogin, "'The Sword Became a Flashing Vision,'" p. 250; *The Birth of a Nation*, dir. D. W. Griffith, 1915; Slotkin, *Gunfighter Nation*, p. 241.

26. Paul S. Boyer, *By the Bomb's Early Light: American Thought and Culture at the Dawn of the Atomic Age* (New York: Pantheon, 1985), pp. 7, 8, 14, 21.

27. Ibid., pp. 335, 336, 352.

28. Peter Beinart, "A Fighting Faith," *New Republic*, Dec. 13, 2004, p. 17; Beinart, *The Good Fight: Why Liberals—and Only Liberals—Can Win the War on Terror and Make America Great Again* (New York: HarperCollins, 2006), p. 171; George Packer, "Can Liberals Take Foreign Policy Back from the Republicans?" *New Yorker*, Feb. 16, 2004, p. 100; Will Marshall, ed., *With All Our Might: A Progressive Strategy for Defeating Jihadism and Defending Liberty* (Lanham, Md.: Rowman and Littefield, 2006); Anatol Lieven and Will Marshall, "On Might, Ethics, and Realism," *National Interest*, Nov. 2006–Dec. 2006, p. 84; Arthur M. Schlesinger Jr., *The Vital Center: The Politics of Freedom* (Boston: Houghton Mifflin, 1949), pp. 36–37, 40, 41, 46, 49; Schlesinger, "The Crisis of American Masculinity," *Esquire*, Nov. 1958, rpt. in *The Politics of Hope* (Boston: Houghton Mifflin, 1963), pp. 237, 238, 239. See also K. A. Cuordileone, "'Politics in an Age of Anxiety': Cold War Political Culture and the Crisis of American Masculinity," *Journal of American History* 87 (Sept. 2000): 515–45.

29. Betty Friedan, *The Feminine Mystique* (New York: Laurel Book/Dell, 1984), pp. 190–92; Barbara Ehrenreich and Deirdre English, *For Her Own Good* (New York: Anchor, 1979), pp. 236, 241; Elaine Tyler May, *Homeward Bound: American Families in the Cold War Era* (New York: Basic, 1988), pp. 94, 96–98; Michael Paul Rogin, *Ronald Reagan, the Movie: And Other Episodes of Political Demonology* (Berkeley: University of California Press, 1987), pp. 243–45, 249–53, 257.

30. May, *Homeward Bound*, pp. 108–9; Ruth Rosen, *The World Split Open: How the Modern Women's Movement Changed America* (New York: Viking, 2000), p. 13.

31. Kristina Zarlengo, "Civilian Threat, the Suburban Citadel, and Atomic Age American Women," *Signs* 24 (Summer 1999): 939, 940, 941–42, 943; JoAnne Brown, "'A is for Atom, B is for Bomb': Civil Defense in American Public Education, 1948–1963," *Journal of American History* 75 (June 1988): 84; Boyer, *By the Bomb's Early Light*, p. 311; May, *Homeward Bound*, pp. 103–6; *The Atomic Cafe*, dir. Jayne Loader and Kevin Rafferty, 1982.

32. Stephanie Coontz, *The Way We Never Were: American Families and the Nostalgia Trap* (New York: Basic Books, 2000), pp. 39–40; May, *Homeward Bound*, p. 101;

Molly Haskell, *From Reverence to Rape: The Treatment of Women in the Movies* (Chicago: University of Chicago Preess, 1987), p. 265; Peter Biskind, *Seeing Is Believing: How Hollywood Taught Us to Stop Worrying and Love the Fifties* (New York: Pantheon, 1983), pp. 271–73.

33. Estelle B. Freedman, "'Uncontrolled Desires': The Response to the Sexual Psychopath, 1920–1960," *Journal of American History* 74 (June 1987): 83, 92–94, 97, 98–99, 101–2; John D'Emilio and Estelle B. Freedman, *Intimate Matters: A History of Sexuality in America* (Chicago: University of Chicago Press, 1997), pp. 293–94.

34. David B. Davis, "Ten-Gallon Hero," *The Western: A Collection of Critical Essays*, ed. James K. Folsom (Englewood Cliffs, N.J.: Prentice-Hall, 1979), pp. 15–16; *Them!*, dir. Gordon Douglas, 1954; *War of the Worlds*, dir. Byron Haskin, 1953.

35. Will Wright, *Sixguns and Society: A Structural Study of the Western* (Berkeley: University of California Press, 1975), p. 5.

36. *Dirty Harry*, dir. Don Siegel, 1971.

EPILOGUE: WHAT IF?

1. Personal interview with Ruth Sergel, Oct. 21, 2006.
2. "Here Is New York: Voices of 9.11," http://hereisnewyork.org/gallery/voices.asp.
3. Ibid; interview with Sergel.
4. Jim Dwyer and Michelle O'Donnell, "9/11 Firefighters Told of Isolation amid Disaster," *New York Times*, Sept. 9, 2005; "Eleventh Public Hearing," National Commission on Terrorist Attacks on the United States, May 19, 2004, http://www.9-11commission.gov/archive/hearing11/9-11Commission_Hearing_2004 05-19.htm.
5. Jonathan Alter, "Grits, Guts, and Rudy Giuliani," *Newsweek*, Sept. 24, 2001, p. 53; Evan Thomas, "The Day That Changed America," *Newsweek*, Dec. 31, 2001, p. 40; Jim Dwyer, Kevin Flynn, and Ford Fessenden, "Fatal Confusion: A Troubled Emergency Response; 9/11 Exposed Deadly Flaws in Rescue Plan," *New York Times*, July 7, 2002; John Joyce and Bill Bowen, *Radio Silence F.D.N.Y.: The Betrayal of New York's Bravest* (Burbank: Chesapeak Books, 2004). A Nexis database search turned up one short article on the revelations in Joyce's book in *Newsday* and one capsule book review in *Small Press Bookwatch*. William Murphy, "New Book on 9/11: Making Radio Waves," *Newsday*, July 20, 2004; "*Radio Silence F.D.N.Y.*," *Small Press Bookwatch*, March 1, 2005.
6. Siobhan Gorman, "U.S. Is Called Still Not Ready for a Disaster," *Baltimore Sun*, Sept. 11, 2005; Carolyn Duffy Marsan, "9/11 Disconnect: 5 Years Later, Many 1st Responders Stuck with Second-Rate Wireless Gear," *Network World*, Aug. 31, 2006; Jonathan LeMire, "FDNY Finally Fine-Tunes Its Radios," *Daily News*, Jan. 4, 2007; Melanie Lefkowitz, "Firefighters, Union Reach Deal," *Newsday*, Dec. 30, 2005; Chris Smith, "Smoldering Fires of 9/11," *New York*, March 18, 2002, http://nymag.com/nymetro/news/sept11/features/5789/index .html; Chris Smith, "Braving the Heat," *New York*, Oct. 1, 2001, http://nymag .com/nymetro/news/sept11/features/5199/index.html; Fontana, *Widow's Walk*, pp. 203–4; Joe Klein, "How Security Moms Became Soccer Moms," *Time*, Feb. 17, 2003, p. 23.

7. Rudyard Kipling, "The Last of the Light Brigade," *Rudyard Kipling's Verse* (London: Rodder and Stoughton, 1973), pp. 200–202.
8. "Evaluation Report on General Situation of Women in Afghanistan," Afghanistan Independent Human Rights Commission, 2006, http://www.aihrc. org.af/rep_eng_wom_situation_8_march.htm; "Taking Cover: Women in Post-Taliban Afghanistan," Human Rights Watch, May 2002, http://hrw.org/back grounder/wrd/afghan-women-2k2.pdf; Karen Baldwin, "Death Threats on 32 Pounds a Month," *Times Educational Supplement*, Dec. 23, 2006, p. 17; Pamela Constable, "Afghan Girls, Back in the Shadows," *Washington Post*, Sept. 23, 2006.
9. "Iraq: Decades of Suffering, Now Women Deserve Better," Amnesty International, Feb. 22, 2005, http://web.amnesty.org/library/index/engmde140012005; "Promising Democracy, Imposing Theocracy: Gender-Based Violence and the U.S. War on Iraq," Madre, March 6, 2007, http://www.madre.org/articles/ me/iraqreport.pdf; Katha Pollitt, "Theocracy Lite," *Nation*, Sept. 19, 2005, p. 10.
10. Hassan M. Fattah and Eric Lipton, "Gaps in Security Stretch All Along the Way from Model Port in Dubai to U.S.," *New York Times*, Feb. 26, 2006; Gwyneth K. Shaw, "Testimony, GAO Probe Reveal 'Blind Spot' in Cargo Security," *Baltimore Sun*, March 29, 2006; "Status of Key Recommendations GAO Has Made to DHS and Its Legacy Agencies," July 2, 2004, http://www.gao.gov/htext/ d04865r.html; "Final Report on 9/11 Commission Recommendations," 9/11 Public Discourse Project, Dec. 5, 2005, http://www.9-11pdp.org/press/2005-12-05_ report.pdf; Thomas H. Kean and Lee H. Hamilton, "A Formula for Disaster," *New York Times*, Dec. 5, 2005; Breitweiser, *Wake-Up Call*, pp. 270, 271.

Acknowledgments

The first glimmerings of *The Terror Dream* emerged from a handful of talks I was scheduled to give right after 9/11 — in that terrible period when it seemed pointless to talk about anything else but so hard to know what to say. I'm grateful to those audiences for their tolerance and encouragement as I stumbled toward clarity, in particular the group of students who approached me after one such event and said, "Would you please *write* about this?" On a later visit to Stockholm (which coincided with the 7/7 terrorist attack of 2005 in London), some important conversations with my beloved friend, Swedish writer Maria-Pia Boëthius, planted the seeds that grew into this book.

Pursuing the idea for *The Terror Dream* took me down some odd and certainly unexpected byroads, most especially into the early traumas of early American history and the cultural mythologies those traumas ultimately bred. In that pursuit, I am indebted to many remarkable scholars of American history and literature whose work illuminated the way. I would like especially to single out the profound difference that feminist-informed studies in the last quarter century have made in opening up new vistas for understanding our history and culture. For my understanding of captivity narratives, I owe much to the works of Richard Slotkin, June Namias, Kathryn Zabelle Derounian-Stodola, Annette Kolodny, and Christopher Castiglia, to name just a few. I'm especially grateful to the generosity of scholars Richard Slotkin and Andrew Delbanco for taking the time to read the manuscript and for their extremely thoughtful and helpful comments. My appreciation to the able librarians at the Mechanics Institute; the San Francisco Public Library; the University of California, Berkeley, Library; the Newberry Library; and Haverhill Historical Society for their aid in tracking down elusive works. And to Mark Singer, research librarian at the Mechanics Institute, whose guidance on navigating the more elusive realms of the Web was extremely useful to my research.

My agent, Melanie Jackson, has seen me through some difficult turnabouts on the road to doing this book and I appreciate her boundless patience and unfailing good sense. The staff at Metropolitan Books has been a joy to work with—an island of accomplished professionalism in a besieged industry. I was the lucky beneficiary of Riva Hocherman's careful read and keen insights at every stage of the process. My heartfelt thanks, as well, to Roslyn Schloss for her meticulous copyediting, to Sally McCartin, Maggie Richards, and Megan Quirk for all their hard work and dedication, and to John Sterling, who graciously supported my sometimes wavering path to publication. Most of all, I'm deeply grateful to my editor, Sara Bershtel, for her inexhaustible ministrations to both the book and her author. Her vision for seeing a book's larger possibilities and her unerring ability to detect and untangle the gnarled parts of an argument make her the editor every writer hopes for and rarely is privileged to find.

My thanks, as well, to Judy Sloan for her help, to Jane Palecek—whose idyllic retreat was a scene of critical writing breakthroughs—and to so many other friends and family who have provided cheer and encouragement along the way. And, as ever, to Russ Rymer, in-house editor-seer, sustainer, and soulmate.

Index